MONTAGING PUSHKIN
PUSHKIN AND VISIONS OF MODERNITY IN RUSSIAN TWENTIETH-CENTURY POETRY

Studies in Slavic Literature and Poetics

Volume XLVI

Edited by

J.J. van Baak
R. Grübel
A.G.F. van Holk
W.G. Weststeijn

MONTAGING PUSHKIN
PUSHKIN AND VISIONS OF MODERNITY IN RUSSIAN TWENTIETH-CENTURY POETRY

Alexandra Smith

Amsterdam - New York, NY 2006

Cover design: Aart Jan Bergshoeff

The paper on which this book is printed meets the requirements of "ISO 9706:1994, Information and documentation - Paper for documents - Requirements for permanence".

ISBN-10: 90-420-2012-1
ISBN-13: 978-90-420-2012-2
©Editions Rodopi B.V., Amsterdam - New York, NY 2006
Printed in the Netherlands

CONTENTS

Acknowledgements	7
Introduction	11
1. From Pushkin's poetics of exile to the concept of writing as dwelling	**39**
Preamble	39
Pushkin's lyric "To the Sea" and the formation of the poetic self	54
Tsvetaeva's dialogic poetic self and the Pushkin canon	74
2. Pushkin's Petersburg as comic apocalypse	**103**
Preamble	103
Pushkin's Petersburg: dandy, aesthetic rag-picker and madman	108
3. 20th-century Pushkinian poetic responses to modernity & urban spectatorship	**163**
Preamble	163
Annenskii's Pushkin as spectacle, Eisenstein's concept of imagery	167
Pushkin's Petersburg as a living experience in new contexts	180
Urban spectacles and Eisenstein's montage of attractions	213
Narrating the city: from modern object to postmodern sign	227
4. Modernity as writing: Pushkin readers & the Pushkin Myth	**255**
Preamble	255
Russian émigré poets as readers of Pushkin's texts	269
Pushkinian readings of the city in pain & dynamics of subjectivity in Russian contemporary poetry	304
5. Conclusion	**327**
Bibliography	**333**
Additional Reading	**351**
Index	**353**

ACKNOWLEDGEMENTS

The concept of a book that would identify the influence of Pushkin's poetry on Russian twentieth-century poetry has occupied my thoughts since 1979, when I suggested it as my MA thesis topic to Svetlana Timina, my supervisor at Herzen State Pedagogical University, Leningrad. She responded that it would take me at least twenty years, if not my entire life, to complete such a study, so I settled for the less demanding task of investigating aspects of the artistic psychology of Pushkin and Tsvetaeva, focusing on their views on creativity and investigating the relationship between the rational and emotional aspects of their creative psychology. In 1980 I defended my thesis, and I was enriched by the many helpful comments provided by my examiner, Vladimir Alfonsov. My interest in literary theory, semiotics and European literature was sustained and strengthened during my years at Herzen by B. Egorov, Ia. Bilinkis, V. Kotelnikov, Iu. Lotman (who had been invited from Tartu in 1980 to deliver several lectures), V. Markovich (who was a visiting professor from Leningrad State University), A. Romm, V. Marantsman, and G. Stadnikov (whose lectures on Rabelais introduced me to Bakhtin's theoretical writings). I am very happy to be able to express here my gratitude to them, and to all the other people and institutions I mention below.

My late school teacher of Russian literature, the late Alexandra Lobkova, a former PhD student of Boris Eikhenbaum, gave lectures on Russian futurism that for me brought to life the performative aspects embedded in the poetry of the 1910s. My close friend, the late Iraida Gracheva, legendary Leningrad teacher of Russian literature in the 1970-80s, spent many hours with me discussing Russian literature and literary theory and provided me with samizdat reading for several years. My late mother Evgeniia Nefedova, also a graduate of Herzen Pedagogical University and a teacher of Russian literature, thought to introduce me to Pushkin's poetry when I was three years old. I still remember by heart many poems I learnt at this early age!...

After moving to England in 1983 I continued my studies at SSEES, University of London, defending a thesis on Pushkin and Tsvetaeva in 1993. During my life in England I befriended many wonderful specialists on Russian literature with whom I had numerous discussions of Russian poetry and literary theory, including Angela Livingstone, Neil Cornwell, Julian Graffy, Pamela Davidson, Joe Andrew, Robert Reid, Gerald Smith, Valentina Polukhina, Robin Aizlewood and Barbara Heldt (who was then dividing her time between England and Canada). I also had several opportunities to talk to Olga Sedakova when she visited England, and in Paris in March 2005. Over the last eleven years, while researching this book, I received the most generous support and encouragement of many colleagues and friends in Europe, the United States and Russia.

Caryl Emerson read my PhD thesis on Tsvetaeva and Pushkin in 1994 and encouraged me to publish it. Since then I have had many opportunities to discuss at great length with her Pushkin's works, Bakhtin, the Russian Formalists, Pushkin biographies, and films. Caryl Emerson's own numerous publications, including books and articles, as well as her outstanding lectures delivered at the University of Canterbury in June 2003, inspired and enriched me, sharpening my vision of many theoretical points. Caryl Emerson and the Slavic Studies department at Princeton allowed me use of the remarkable collection of books and periodicals at Princeton University's library when I visited in March 2004. I discovered in their library valuable Russian émigré periodicals that helped me with my research. Caryl Emerson's profound comments on several chapters of this book and on some of my published and unpublished articles were extremely helpful and stimulating. Caryl Emerson is for me an exemplary scholar and her presence is very much felt in this book.

I have had many expressions of support and encouragement from, and conversations on Russian poetry and Pushkin, with David Bethea, Olga Hasty, Carol Ueland, Catherine Ciepiela, Stephanie Sandler, Nina Gourianova, Jane Taubman, Svetlana Boym, Anna Lisa Crone, Irina Reyfman, Vera Zubareva and Andrew Reynolds. Several engaging discussions with Bernice Rosenthal on Russian and the European history of ideas helping me formulate some of the concepts expressed in this book. I have had warm support and advice from Véronique Lossky over the last thirteen years. The 1992 Tsvetaeva anniversary conference at the Sorbonne in was one of the most memorable experiences for me, not only because I developed long standing friendships with many wonderful poetry specialists, including the late Efim Etkind, Elena Korkina and Liudmila Zubova, but also because I also had the chance to hear Andrei Voznesenskii's analysis of Tsvetaeva's poetry which in itself was an act of creative reading and performance.

    Willem Weststeijn and Joost van Baak furnished support and stimulating discussions on Russian poetry on many occasions over the years. The University of Canterbury provided me with a research grant for this study in 1996, and its School of Languages and Cultures was forthcoming with numerous travel grants enabling me to participate in several conferences and consult libraries abroad. My colleagues in the University of Canterbury's Russian programme, Henrietta Mondry, Evgeny Pavlov and Natalia Grineva, gave me important support and advice. My husband's patience and help made possible the realisation of this project.

Alexandra Smith

Christchurch, New Zealand

INTRODUCTION

Grigorii Chernetsov's painting "Parade on Tsaritsyn Field" («Парад на Царицином лугу»), undertaken between 1831 and 1837, shows a large St Petersburg crowd, numbering more than two hundred, enjoying the spectacle of a military parade.[1] The gathering is glamorous, including many outstanding people of the period. In the crowd is the Russian poet Alexander Pushkin. Chernetsov places the poet in such a way that he is the main spectator at the event, yet his figure is depicted as almost pushed back, against the edge of the canvas frame. Chernetsov's painting creates an impression that Pushkin is wanting to withdraw, if not to exclude himself altogether, from participating in the celebration, a massive event to glorify the Russian empire's growing might and sanction its violence.

Pushkin's intent, inscribed in Chernetsov's painting, to stand back from the marching soldiers and keep hold of his hat, is a metaphorical depiction of the pain and horror arising from his recognition that the parade ground is a hierarchically-organised open space – a space designed for the circulation of air and light, but primarily soldiers, and therefore a space embodying that society's totalising order. Chernetsov's work communicates an empowered social order that tolerates no deviations. Pain has no place in that regularised landscape. It is painted to represent a near-perfect geometric abstraction, premised on a normalisation of violence.

The Tsaritsyn Field itself is the main object of Chernetsov's painting. Its space signifies the ideal of the sanitary void, impersonating the totalising desire for clean, open spaces and linear structures. The painted space aspires to represent the textual sublime in the text of the city, with its distinctive, hierarchical definitions of worker and bourgeois, public and private, family and anomie. It is an exemplary embodiment of a sublime commodity, both massive in its grand appeal and mass produced. It is an emblem of the imperial regime, of the form and force of the capital of Russia's empire, of an empire eager to expand.

This depiction of Tsaritsyn Field anticipates the vision of Andrei Belyi's fictional character Apollon Apollonovich in the novel *Petersburg* (*Петербург*). Apollon sees Petersburg as the embodiment of the Western Enlightenment's legacy and metaphysical flights of thought: "There is an infinity of speeding avenues with an infinity of speeding intersecting phantoms. All of Petersburg is the infinity of an avenue raised to the nth power. Beyond Petersburg there is nothing" (Belyi 1979: 34). Regularisation is the password to the architectonics of the Petersburg of Pushkin's times.

Given the linear structures of social paternalism prevalent in that period, pain represented a disturbance to clear delineation. Pain was therefore inadmissible. To make pain readable, as Pushkin's poetry succeeded in doing, was to subvert an officially-sanctioned lineage descending from the means of production to the labour of the producer. And so Chernetsov's remarkable achievement was to uncover in his painting the pain behind the glamorous façade of the Russian empire. We are prompted to feel the other's pain as our own, and to desire its suspension. We cannot but sympathise with the figure of the distraught poet holding onto his hat.

The scene inscribes both resistance to the conceptualisation of absolute power within pain, and the poet's articulation of it. The painting pushes the figure of Russia's first poet to the edge of the crowd, towards a group of superfluous and marginalised women. Pushkin's place near the edge of the painting is ironic, as if the power of Pushkin's gaze is shared with the artist himself. Also Chernetsov's irony inscribes a sense of intellectual superiority, and foregrounds the interdependence of ironising and ironised voices. In sum, Chernetsov's portrayal of the military parade is a gesture converting power into pain, into an ontological feeling of the human body's fragility.

To help assess how Pushkin's followers were influenced by his strategies of resistance to the totalising order of the absolute power manifested in Petersburg's growing splendour, we can view Pushkin as a forerunner of Charles Baudelaire. At this point we can indicate a connection between Chernetsov's depiction of Pushkin with Vaheed

Ramazani's interpretation of the origin of Baudelaire's irony: "The shock defence meets violence with counter-violence of consciousness is both similar to and different from the violence it opposes; similar because consciousness combats violence — like a weapon, it moves outward to make contact with the threatening other; similar, too, because consciousness absorbs and so, in yet another manner, duplicates the violence of the other like a wound, it records the impact of the shocks; different, however, because, like weapon and wound together, yet like neither weapon nor wound altogether, consciousness simultaneously includes and excludes, repeats and repels — in short, *parries* the shock" (Ramazani 1996: 205-206).

This book will argue that the consciousness of counter-violence, embedded in Pushkin's narrative poems and lyrics, are reproduced and reinforced by several visions of modernity in Russian twentieth-century poetry. Marina Tsvetaeva's 1931 cycle "Poems to Pushkin" («Стихи к Пушкину») is very representative of this trend. Tsvetaeva has a powerful formula: "Do not attack me with your allusions to Pushkin! Because I myself attack you in this way!" («Пушкиным не бейте/ Ибо бью вас — им!») (Tsvetaeva 1988, volume 1: 278). Not coincidentally, Dmitrii Shostakovich uses a poem from this Tsvetaeva cycle in his 1973 vocal cycle Opus 143. Shostakovich makes this an empowering gesture, in defiance of Soviet attempts to censor its artists and musicians and to violate their individual private space and creativity. Bella Akhmadulina's poem "The Duel" («Дуэль») also contextualises the perpetual struggle between a mass conformity, based on commodity aesthetics, with the cult of extreme individualism that strives to preserve authenticity and personal style. Later in this book we will see how twentieth-century poets mimicked, and largely improved on, Pushkin's irony and parodic gesturing, by translating their own painful experiences of urban life into subversive laughter.

The legendary and eccentric Soviet pianist Maria Iudina often combined her performances with a recital of Boris Pasternak's poetry lyrics. She would place a picture of Étienne-Maurice Falconet's monument to Pushkin's Bronze Horseman on her piano. This illustrates how Pushkin captured the imagination of Russian readers, even in the Stalinist 1930s-1950s: Pushkin's imaginary dialogue with ruthless advocates of modernity, with rationalisers of space and masses, had huge appeal. Pushkin displayed such dialogue at its best in "The Bronze Horseman" («Медный всадник»). Iudina translated the performative qualities of this Pushkin text into the language of music, communicating Pushkin's personal thoughts to the imagination of a Soviet audience, and recreating the sense of profound terror evoked by the galloping Bronze Horseman. This caused the audience to find themselves situated in two time periods at once: the period of Peter the Great, which has never stopped haunting Russians; and the period of Stalin, which evokes the image of another powerful ghost and visionary advocate of modernity.

A composer in the audience at one of Iudina's performances mentioned to her that her performance of a Mozart sonata had been unjustifiably emotional and fast. She responded that she had felt completely under the sway of the monument and had wanted Mozart's music to convey the gallops, chase and fear evoked by this monument (quoted in Ospovat and Timenchik: 326). This anecdote suggests that Pushkin's text displays certain performative qualities that help contemporary readers re-enact the urban drama Pushkin so skillfully presented in the "The Bronze Horseman". I also suggest that the example provided by Iudina illustrates how interrelation between private body, public body and urban geography is readable as a negative version of Pushkin's dialectic of the self's vaporisation and centralisation.

The historical pain communicated through Pushkin's "The Bronze Horseman" text comes from the pure physical experience of negation. The text projects its disruptive effects through the framing signifier of the city. Iudina's act of performance helps restore a sense of wholeness, and to dissolve dichotomies between self and other, weapon and wound, empowerment and disempowerment. So, Iudina's re-enactment of fear and excitement at Peter the Great's galloping monument testifies to the power of Pushkin's text: like Pushkin, Iudina is both overwhelmed and horrified at the living legacy of Peter the Great's grand vision of modernity, a vision that continues to affect Russia even into the twenty-first century. Later I will show how "The Bronze Horseman" stands close to the poem about Cleopatra in Pushkin's story "Egyptian Nights" («Египетские ночи»). This story was also of paramount significance for Russian twentieth-century poets and artists. Valerii Briusov's attempt to finish this fragment testifies to the strength of Pushkin's creative impulse to merge performance and poetry, an impulse which became contextualised in the twentieth-century and resulted, very innovatively, in a deepening of the aesthetics of everyday life.

Russian twentieth-century poets sometimes equated modernity with the topography of public space. Pushkin's poetry provided these poets with an opportunity to withdraw into small arenas of private space. We can see that many followers of Pushkin began to perceive modernity as associated with a self-enclosure that is psychological and spatial. Modernity supplied a refuge from the banalities of mass society, and led them to desire alternative imaginary spaces shaped by a sense of intellectual superiority. Rita Felski's description of several modernist texts sums up well the chief qualities of a similar trend exhibited in European modernism, a trend that might be defined as the solitary cultivation of the arcane and the exotic: "The exterior explorations of the flâneur give way to the interior explorations of the collector, who ranges mentally across space and time in the contemplation of his heterogeneous accumulation of artefacts and objets *d'art* — described by Walter Benjamin as the phantasmagorias of the interior. Yet temporal and spatial difference are curiously neutralised and decontextualised through the synchrony of the nonsynchronous, as the texts and objects of past cultures and exotic traditions are appropriated by the aesthete to serve as markers of stylistic differentiation through which he signals his own uniqueness" (Felski 1995: 98-99).

Alexander Blok in his poem 1921 "To Pushkin House" («Пушкинскому дому») associated Pushkin with inner secret freedom: "Pushkin! We sang you a song of secret freedom" («Пушкин! Тайную свободу пели мы вослед тебе») (Blok, volume 1 1955: 458) This is an example of the concern of modernists with the semiotics of style, and of aesthetes' anxiety at continuing dependency on the commodity culture, against which they sought to establish a position of intellectual superiority.

Vladimir Nabokov's reproduction in English of Onegin's stanza in *Eugene Onegin* mimics the old-fashioned idiosyncratic expressions of Pushkin's poems. Nabokov reveals an elitist consumer endlessly searching for the unique object that secures his desired self image and status. As Malcolm Bradbury reminds us, "Modernism is less a style than a search, for a style in the highly individualistic sense; and indeed the style of one work is no guarantee for the next" because every modernist "is perpetually engaged in a profound and ceaseless journey through the means and integrity of art" (Bradbury 1976: 29).

Alexander Kushner's poetry might be interpreted in the same vein: as a reflection on the solitary cultivation of exotic and highly refined artefacts. Yet, Felski compellingly argues that "the aesthete's attempt to create a uniquely individual style reveals his inevitable reliance upon the very categories of evaluation against which he ostensibly puts himself". Felski goes on to explain: "Similarly, while he affects a disdain for modern industrial and technological processes, these same processes form the taken-for-granted preconditions of his own pursuit of distinctions and refined pleasures" (Felski 1995: 99).

A recent book by Stephanie Sandler explores the ways in which Russia has commemorated Pushkin. In conclusion Sandler suggests that Andrei Siniavskii's vision of art in his *Strolls with Pushkin* (*Прогулки с Пушкиным*, 1975) is a free play of imagination in truly Pushkinian spirit. Sandler believes that Pushkin, in Siniavskii's playful style set within a theatrical spectacle, would continue to inspire contemporary artists concerned with style and performance, yet also serve the needs of new commercial culture. Siniavskii says that "to have had a national poet [...] was to have had an inspiring example in the past of how to be a writer in public and in private" (Sandler 2004: 310).

In the minds of many interpreters of Pushkin's works, the private/public boundaries remain blurry. This is especially true for Russian readers and poets seeking to appropriate Pushkin's images and stylistic masks. I will argue that, more often than not, readers/poets define for themselves the private/public boundaries, because Pushkin in his own poetry expressed his private space very subjectively and tentatively. The most obvious reason for the inability to distinguish between private/public stems from the peculiar failure of Russian culture to adopt important tenets of the Western Enlightenment and sentimentalist thinking. I believe that, by focussing on the manifestations of urban experiences in Pushkin's poetry, we can see the private and public worlds interacting within Pushkin's artistic imagination and how his poetic world was permeated with counter-violence gestures. We can also see how Russian twentieth-century poets further developed his desire to challenge the Russian patriarchy's harsh and benevolent authoritarianism, which legitimised corporal punishment. Pushkin's purpose can be seen in his essay "On National Education" («О народном воспитании»), written on 15 November 1828 at the request of Tsar Nicholas I, but which had to wait until 1884 for publication in Russia. The essay boldly states that physical punishment in Russian schools should be abandoned, and that students should be educated to respect honour, be compassionate, and love others: "Extreme cruel education turns young people into executioners, not managers" («Слишком жестокое воспитание делает из них палачей, а не начальников») (Pushkin 1958, volume 7: 47).

Mark Raeff explains how the individual and corporate property rights of the Russian nobility in the eighteenth and nineteenth centuries were poorly defined. Russia's absolute monarchy opposed attempts to rationalise public life and to establish appropriate legal frameworks (Raeff 1984: 41-87). I believe that, given this context of legal rights, Pushkin's poetic concern with violence touched a nerve that resonated within the poetry of his followers. I will draw on several insightful findings by Irina Reyfman, presented in her outstanding study of ritualised violence in Russia, to explain how Pushkin contributed to the treatment of ritualised violence, and I will review its consequences in modernist and postmodernist poetry. According to Reyfman, "paradoxically, the raw physical violence of Russian duelling behaviour is not inconsistent with the fact that duelling emerged in Russia as a means of countering violence against the individual — violence both by other individuals and by the state" (Reyfman 1999: 10). The fascination of Russian twentieth-century poets with Pushkin's own duel, and with the poetics of terror which his poetry communicated, testifies to Russian readers' continued preoccupation with individual physical inviolability and the definition of private space. Reyfman pertinently points out: "Duelling in Russia was primarily about protecting the personal space of a gentleman in the most direct sense: it was about the individual's right to physical inviolability, his right to be beaten by peers and superiors, not to be subjected to corporal punishment by institutions of law enforcement" (ibid.). In the light of Reyfman's study, it becomes clear why the powerful opposition to violence, evident in Pushkin's poetry, inspired followers to continue imaginary duels with abusers of power and vigilant censors by employing Pushkinian images and poetic devices.

The growing anarchist movement at the beginning of the twentieth century was destined to become the first Russian intellectual trend to have significant international impact. The movement also informed a strong interest in Pushkin's life and writings. Steven Marks sums up the main thrust of the anarchist movement thus: "Given the overbearing power of the tsarist state and the sudden encroachments of capitalism, Russia's intellectuals were naturally receptive to European ideas like anarchism, and in fact Russians became the acknowledged leaders of the international anarchist movement as it developed after the 1860s. These radicals transformed anarchist thought from a philosophy dreamed up by a few eccentric western Europeans into a strategy of revolutionary action. Their anarchism was a form of underground political warfare that battled to destroy the existing political-economic system and prepare the ground for a new egalitarian era in human existence" (Marks 2003: 7). In fact, Russian poetry of the 1910s-1930s is full of references to ritualised violence, revolt and revolutionaries, anarchists and soldiers. The most vivid examples include Blok's narrative poem "The Twelve" («Двенадцать»); Vladimir Maiakovskii's narrative poem "Lenin" («Ленин»); Pasternak's narrative poem "1905" («1905 год») and "Lieutenant Schmidt" ("Лейтенант Шмидт"); Sergei Esenin's long poem "Pugachev" («Пугачев»); Tsvetaeva's cycle "The Swan Encampment" («Лебединый стан») and her poems commemorating the suicides of Esenin and Maiakovskii; Alexander Tvardovskii's *Vassilii Terkin* (*Василий Теркин*); Anna Akhmatova's "Requiem" («Реквием»); Leonid Gubanov's narrative poems "Pugachev" («Пугачев»), "Ivan the Terrible" («Иван Грозный») and "Peter the Great" («Петр Первый»); and Alexei Parshchikov's long poem "I Lived on the Battlefield of Poltava" («Я жил на поле Полтавской битвы») — to name just a few. In this book I will demonstrate just how significant was Pushkin's presence in some of these most influential and characteristic Russian poetic texts of the twentieth century, as they came to depict responses to ritualised violence and traumatised language.

Not all of Pushkin's poetic texts dealing with traumatised language and body are linked to urban experiences. But I would argue that the negative depiction of the imperial order, manifested in the rationalised spaces of Petersburg, informs Pushkin's striking responses to the modernity that lies at the heart of his artistic imagination. The inter-relation between Pushkin, the image of Petersburg, and the Petersburg myth is often noted by scholars of various backgrounds.[2] Contemporary Petersburg critics A.M. Gordin and M.A. Gordin have described the first three decades of the nineteenth century as Pushkin's epoch. More importantly the Russian empire's capital, with its half-million population, court, officialdom, merchants and servants in the period 1810-30, is labelled Pushkin's Petersburg by the Gordins: "In our minds, historical Petersburg has the same place as the mythical Jerusalem of the New Testament used to occupy the minds of our predecessors. It is a place where old Russian history has finished and the new historical chapter was opened. It is a place where many legendary figures lived and many important events took place. [...] Having become part of Pushkin's artistic world, Petersburg continued its existence thanks to him and through him" (Gordin 1999: 5). Chernetsov's painting, together with the Gordins' belief in the objectifications of the body that comprise the constructed world of physical and verbal artefacts, reinforce the point made by Peter Stallybrass and Allon White that "the body cannot be thought separately from the social formation, symbolic topography and the constitution of the subject" because it is "neither a purely natural given, nor is it a textual metaphor" (Stallybrass 1986: 192).

In a seminal study of Baudelaire, Benjamin proposes that urban space in Baudelaire's poetry should be viewed in terms of the presence of the metropolitan crowd as a hidden figure. The inference of such a figure is of paramount importance to the text's meaning (Benjamin 1973: 167). In this book I will suggest viewing Pushkin as a forerunner of Baudelaire, the poet of modernity whose poetry invokes experience of great cities as the very condition of possibility of an aesthetics of the poetic text. I will show that Pushkin's vision of a modernity closely linked to urban experiences hugely impacted the Russian twentieth-century poetry that went on further to explore interaction between private and public spaces. I will demonstrate, in examining Russian twentieth-century poetry's numerous allusions and references to Pushkin and his writings, that intertextuality is not merely an optional feature of reading, but is of the essence. And, when we look at twentieth-century poems which portray Pushkin, allude to his texts, or reproduce formal features or poetic devices found in his works, we should from now on keep in mind that any depiction of a real person or object is actually a cultural construct.

That leads me to repeat the question asked by Karol Berger, in his illuminating and provocative article on poetic modes and the matter of artistic presentation. In analysing the absent personage in pictorial and literary works, Berger asks: "But is it truly absent, or — like the setting at times — only attenuated and implicit? The admittedly speculative claim I would like to make is that those presented worlds from which a personage is absent present, precisely though paradoxically, an absent personage. The claim cannot be tested and is unfalsifiable and hence unprovable. It can be understood only as interpretative postulate or wish designed to ensure that even the presented worlds from which personages are absent can serve the art's aim of human self-presentation, -imagining, and -knowledge. We want the presented world to be not just any world, but *Lebenswelt*, the world of man" (Berger 1994: 432). Furthermore, Berger ascribes the same cultural significance to non-representational arts, including architecture. In Berger's view, architecture "invites us to imagine ourselves as pursuing certain ways of life, to put on masks and rehearse imaginary roles" more directly than do the representational arts. He continues: "For a dizzying moment afforded by aesthetic experience, the work of architecture, the most real of all artistic objects, invites us to shed our own reality and to transform ourselves into imaginary beings. But the difference with the representational arts is one of degree only, and a small degree at that. The imaginary worlds presented by poets, painters, and composers also invite us to enter them, they are only somewhat less insistent, or make it less easy for us to accept the invitation" (Berger 1994: 433).

If we combine Berger's observation with the Gordins' eagerness to entwine Pushkin with the image of Petersburg of the first half of the nineteenth century as shaped by the poet, then we see that Pushkin was eminently successful in accomplishing the strategy he embedded into his texts: to present the poet as spectator of urban experiences. Further, his merger of poetry with architecture makes for one of the most splendid spectacles of all. Pushkin's 1836 poem "Monument" («Памятник») persuasively inscribes the poet's body into the imaginary space of the city that he is observing, and with which he interacts. Pushkin achieves this very expressively by abandoning representational art, and thereby revealing his belief in himself as another artefact, shaped by the ever-evolving metropolis.

We have already mentioned Nabokov's translation of Pushkin's *Eugene Onegin* (*Евгений Онегин*). The translation has, more often than not, been criticised for its obscure old-fashioned language, elaborate comments and whimsicality.³ In fact Nabokov, a great master of style, and a writer not unsympathetic to the dandyism and aestheticisation of everyday life, produced an incredible translation of Pushkin's work. In his Introduction, Nabokov defines Pushkin's novel in verse as "first of all and above all a phenomenon of style" (Pushkin, 1975: 7). Nabokov appears to welcome Pushkin into the age of modernity as a dandy who approached texts of nineteenth-century predecessors from the perspective of performance, stylistic masks, masquerade and reinvention of self. Such an approach had already been advocated by Nikolai Evreinov, who linked the questioning of the authentic self to the reinvention of private/public spaces in the age of modernity, and who defined the outcome as "theatre for oneself" (Evreinov 1915-17).

Nabokov's aesthetics are deeply rooted in fin-de-siècle preoccupation with style and appearance, manifested in the expanding aestheticisation of everyday life and in mediation of experience through consumption of images and commodities. As Felski informs us, "The aesthete's recognition of the artificiality of identity [...] derives from a context in which mass-produced signs, objects, and commodities constitute increasingly significant yet unstable markers of subjectivity and social status" (Felski 1995: 99). Felski explains that the growing self-differentiation of the aesthetic sphere in the late nineteenth century does not necessarily represent an ultimate rupture with a rationalised and ritualised social environment. Felski proposes early modernism as a continuum of a more general textualisation of the social and the natural. In the context of modernist authors' belief that being natural is just a pose, Pushkin's own desire to embrace the vibrant world of Petersburg's pre-modern development as a European metropolis places him and other Russian writers of the first half of the nineteenth century in the avant-garde of mass spectacle and rapid expansion of the aestheticisation of everyday life.

Nikolai Karamzin foregrounded the concept of the theatricality of modern urban life that was central to the concerns of Russian modernists and postmodernists. It is as if he was already anticipating early modernist developments, including Evreinov's theory, which present theatrical instinct as biological and common to both animals and humans. Thus in Karamzin's *My Confession* (*Моя исповедь*) we come across a young nobleman's remarkable statement linking urban life and performance: "This century may be called the century of openness in the physical and moral sense: look at our beauties! [...] Before, people used to hide in dark homes behind the cover of high fences. Nowadays, there are bright homes everywhere with large windows facing the street: please look in! We want to live, act, and think behind transparent glass" («Нынешний век можно назвать веком *откровенности* в физическом и нравственном смысле: взгляните на наших красавиц! [...] Некогда люди прятались в темных домах и под щитом высоких заборов. Теперь везде светлые домы и большие окна на улицу: просим смотреть. Мы хотим жить, действовать и мыслить в прозрачном стекле» (Karamzin 1964, volume 1: 729). Pushkin went further than Karamzin, and discerned the performative qualities of Russian authors as distinctive traits of the Russian national character, as if Italy's tradition of commedia dell'arte permeated everyday Russian life with its creative impulses to parody everyone and everything. It is worth pointing out here that Pushkin saw satire and burlesque forms of literature as a manifestation of the native Russian genius for cunning and fun-poking at its best. For example Pushkin comments: "Someone has justly remarked that simplicity (naiveté, bonhomie) is the innate virtue of the French people; in contrast, the distinctive traits of our temperament are a certain gay craftiness, a spirit of mockery, and a vivid way of expressing ourselves" (quoted in Clayton 2000: 1). I will argue that Pushkin's interest in parody and the burlesque does not derive from his profound interest in the Russian national character, but is triggered by the poet's desire to embrace the age of modernity and all that brings in terms of the urban pleasures of spectacle and social interaction.

We now take an initial look at Pushkin's impact on the creation of a special theatrical space of perpetual public/private interaction, by examining Pushkin's early poem "The Little Town" («Городок», 1815). The poem is largely informed by the theatricality of modern urban life which instigates parody, spectacle, double-consciousness and playful creativity. Dmitrii Blagoi, a famous Soviet interpreter of Pushkin's writings, says in his analysis of the poem: "In general, both from the choice of the names included in 'The Little Town' list, and from the characterisations which are given, it follows without a doubt that from all our past Russian literature, and partly from European as well, he chooses [...] the 'light', and particularly the comical-satirical-joyful strain" (Blagoi 1941: 106). Clayton has suggested that Pushkin's resurrection of the burlesque tradition signifies his return to eighteenth-century values (Clayton 2000: 12). I take a different approach and suggest that Pushkin, in order to express the theatrical and fragmented world of modernity that evokes dialogisation of speech and double-consciousness, had to look elsewhere to employ laughter and parody, to create a new space, and to let its truly carnivalesque features show through.

Pushkin's interest in England as the homeland of parody will be of particular relevance in this book. Pushkin's essay "England is a Homeland of Caricature and Parody" («Англия есть отечество карикатуры и пародии») (Pushkin 1958, volume 7: 144-45) is suggestive of his dissatisfaction with the Russian tradition of subversive laughter — as best expressed in Tsvetaeva's formula "to laugh when it is forbidden" («смеяться, когда нельзя») — and of his wish to create a new imaginary space enabling laughter and parody in his own native land.[4] I will argue that twentieth-century poets well understood Pushkin's desire to create an imaginary playful space with a readership culture allowing a free exchange of ideas and jokes. The self-designated heirs of Pushkin, from Blok to Andrei Bitov and Timur Kibirov, all seized upon the performative opportunities provided by this space.

For Nabokov, the very process of translating Pushkin's *Eugene Onegin* offered the opportunity to impersonate Pushkin and to experience the imaginary textual space of Pushkin's novel in verse as playful cultural space and another Petersburg artefact. Nabokov established his own criteria for the perfect translator: criteria that are informed both by performance theories and by Pushkin's own representation of the theatricality of metropolitan life in nineteenth-century Petersburg. Nabokov declares the ideal translator should, in addition to having considerable talent, be a knowledgeable scholar who "must thoroughly know the two nations and the two languages involved and be perfectly acquainted with all details relating to his author's manners and methods, with the social background of words, their fashions, history and period associations". Nabokov expects the translator to be an outstanding performer who "must possess the gift of mimicry and be able to act, as it were, the real author's part by impersonating his tricks of demeanor and speech, his ways and his mind, with the utmost degree of verisimilitude". In his 1955 poem "On Translating *Eugene Onegin*", Nabokov playfully conveys his experience of performing Pushkin in the capacity of translator:

> What is translation? On a platter
> A poet's pale and glaring head,
> A parrot's screech, a monkey's chatter,
> And profanation of the dead. [...]
> O, Pushkin, for my stratagem:
> I travelled down your secret stem,
> And reached the root, and fed upon it;
> Then, in a language newly learned,
> I grew another stalk and turned
> Your stanza patterned on a sonnet,
> Into my honest roadside prose —
> All thorn, but cousin to your rose. [...]
> Elusive Pushkin! Persevering,
> I still pick up Tatiana's earring,
> Still travel with your sullen rake.
> I find another man's mistake [...].
> This is my task – a poet's patience
> And scholiastic passion blent:
> Dove-droppings on your monument.
> (Nabokov 1970: 175)

The poem gushes in admiration for Pushkin's genius in authoring a Petersburg text that presents the Russian capital as a palimpsest. Nabokov especially praises the inventiveness and elegance of the all-encompassing Onegin stanza which inspired numerous attempts at imitation.[5] Nabokov also light-heartedly fashions himself as an ideal playmate of Pushkin, one who could make his text exciting for a modern English speaking readership. Pushkin himself would not take an aesthetic stand on dove-droppings, the way Nabokov does: the latter's remark is tongue-in-cheek, marking the boundary between the aesthetics of modernity and postmodernity. Here Nabokov extends the sphere of art and invites Pushkin to treat dove-droppings as artefacts, thereby welcoming his nineteenth-century predecessor into the age of modernity and intertextuality.[6] As Neil Cornwell's study reminds us, Nabokov regarded Pushkin as the greatest poet of his time, perhaps of all time (second only to Shakespeare). The language of Nabokov's poem includes a reference to the organic world; it presents Pushkin's work as a living organism, with its own stem and roots. It places Pushkin in the world of nature, in contrast to the artificial world of modernity to which Nabokov himself belongs, and highlights the tension between the somatic and the semantic.

Nabokov's "On Translating *Eugene Onegin*" presents the notion that the process of language renewal is somewhat similar to nature's evolutionary processes. Nabokov seems to be addressing not Pushkin the monument but Pushkin the creative impulse himself, who through the legacy of his work continues to communicate with his readers and to inspire creative interaction. Nabokov reveals a tangible bond with the Russian poets and artists who displayed neo-primitivist tendencies – Olga Rozanova, Natalia Goncharova, Mikhail Larionov, Elena Guro, Tsvetaeva and Aleksei Kruchenykh. These modernists had a strong interest in Slavic archaic and folk rituals, and wanted to touch the living roots of art, to transcend into the realm of the inherent logic of primal intuition.[7] They wanted to combine intellect with intuitive reasoning. Nabokov expressed abundant ideas on creativity, aiming for a renewal of thought and attacking fixed habits of mind and speech. Nabokov's ideas echoed many concepts that revolved around the existence of organic poetics in Russian art, fiction and poetry of the 1900s-1930s. I will show how Pushkin acted as a precursor for this trend by highlighting the tension between somatic and semantic in his own poetry.

Nabokov makes Pushkin the person almost interchangeable with Pushkin's imaginary Petersburg space. The juxtaposition of Pushkin, the forerunner of modernity, with the cityscapes of a Petersburg that in the first half of the nineteenth century was emerging as a true European metropolis, is not unique in the context of Russian avant-garde poetry. Many modernist poets, including Akhmatova,

Pasternak, Benedikt Lifshits and Georgii Adamovich, to name just a few, used the imaginary cityscapes constructed in Pushkin's writings either to expand the space of their own texts, or to create a simultaneity effect and present their interaction with Pushkin's narratives as a spectacle. Two Pushkin texts in particular contributed to the creation of the spectacle of Petersburg: "The Bronze Horseman" and *Eugene Onegin*. Russian modernist, neo-modernist and post-modernist poetry all make numerous allusions to these two texts, as will be discussed later.

To Preserve a Sad Tale... («Печальну повесть сохранить...») is an informative study by Alexander Ospovat and Roman Timenchik of the impact of "The Bronze Horseman" on Russian twentieth-century culture. The study shows how phrases, intonations, various poetic fragments and even the plot of this text of Pushkin "were dissolved in the elements of Russian speech" (Ospovat and Timenchik 1987: 324). I will challenge this notion, and question the possibility that any text of Pushkin can be dissolved in any contextual setting. I will argue that the statement by Ospovat and Timenchik suggests Pushkin's art only *appears* to contemporary readers to be assimilated in twentieth-century cultural tradition; that in fact we should be clear that the image of Pushkin created in the imagination of twentieth-century artists and poets is merely a cleverly constructed cultural artefact, an object of consumption shaped by their own aesthetic needs and subjective worldviews.

Harold Bloom, in his encompassing study of twenty-six internationally renowned writers *The Western Canon: The Books and School of the Ages*, compellingly argues that *to be strange* is important precondition for an author and his works to become canonical. Bloom's concept of strangeness derives from his studies on English Romanticism. But in an over-arching manner Bloom advocates strangeness, merged with the sublime, as an important quality for any writer. Bloom explains: "I have tried to confront greatness directly: to ask what makes the author and the works canonical. The answer, more often than not, has turned out to be strangeness, a mode of originality that either cannot be assimilated, or that so assimilates us that we cease to see it as strange. [...] Read freshly, all that *The Divine Comedy, Paradise Lost, Faust Part Two, Hadji Murad, Peer Gynt, Ulysses* and *Canto General* have in common is their uncanniness, their ability to make you feel strange at home. [...] Shakespeare, the largest writer we ever will know, frequently gives the opposite impression: of making us at home out of doors, foreign, abroad. His powers of assimilation and of contamination are unique and constitute a perpetual challenge to universal performance and criticism" (Bloom 1994: 3). A glance at twentieth-century poetic allusions and references to Pushkin's life and poetry would indicate that Bloom's concept of anxiety of influence is only partly applicable to Russian experience, because the whole status of Russian cultural tradition maintains its value even in the age of postmodernism. Yet, as I will argue, Pushkin presents a considerable challenge to poets, critics and performers even in the context of Russian twentieth-century poetic tradition. The cultural models based on the idea of language renewal and estrangement, discussed in the works of Henri Bergson, Iurii Tynianov and Viktor Shklovskii, better explain the dynamics of Russian poets' everlasting dialogue with Pushkin.

According to Michel Foucault, "the great obsession of the nineteenth century was history: themes of development and arrest, themes of crises and cycles, themes of accumulation over the past, a great overload of dead people, the threat of global cooling. [...] The present age may be the age of space instead. We are in an era of the simultaneous, of juxtaposition, of the near and far, of the side-by-side, of the scattered" (Foucault 2000: 175). Russian twentieth-century poetry is a good illustration of Foucault's concerns, because many avant-garde and neo-avant-garde poets, including Pasternak, Tsvetaeva, Joseph Brodsky, Olga Sedakova, and Viktor Krivulin, turned modern concepts of simultaneity and space into their chief devices for constructing performance-oriented narratives. Thus Tsvetaeva in her 1932 essay "Epic and Lyric of Contemporary Russia" («Эпос и лирика современной России») describes Pasternak – in terms similar to common definitions of a modern metropolis – as being in a state of flux, self-renewal and constant evolution. This helps Tsvetaeva present Pasternak as a true modernist poet in search of a new style and novel experiences. In conspicuously Baudelairian manner, Tsvetaeva describes Pasternak himself as an invitation to travel: "Pasternak is solely an *invitation au voyage* of self-discovery and world-discovery, solely a point of departure; a place from which. Our unmooring. Just enough space for weighing anchor. [...] Something leads beyond. You might say that the reader himself writes Pasternak" (Tsvetaeva 1992: 119). Tsvetaeva's words expose the mind of the modernist poet at its best: her formula, that the reader himself writes the text he reads, demonstrates the act of reading Pushkin in the twentieth century as simultaneous construction and deconstruction, as an invitation to an imaginary journey, a point of departure to imaginary dwellings. The experience of reading Pushkin's texts for Russian poets is entwined with the notion of dwelling as poetic category, to use terms suggested by Martin Heidegger, a notion that binds together building, dwelling, thinking and speaking through a cognitive connection.

Akhmatova's poetic persona, described in her 1911 poem "A swarthy youth walked in these alleys…" («Смуглый отрок бродил по аллее…»), makes the imaginary space of Tsarskoe Selo a place for playful interaction where two poets can dwell simultaneously and enjoy reading together the love poems of Evariste de Parny. In other words, the meeting of the young female modernist poet with the young Pushkin takes place in the imaginary space of Tsarskoe Selo made known to her through Pushkin's poetry. We can also look at Heidegger, for whom dwelling is a poetic category and a fundamental feature of the human condition that internalises the sense of dwelling. Heidegger in his analysis of Friedrich Hölderlin's poem "In lovely blueness…" explains that the Poet constructs the dwelling of himself, and presents Being as man and even dwelling through poetry (Heidegger 1971: 215). Viewed in the light of Heidegger's notion of dwelling, many Russian twentieth-century poems that allude to Pushkin's texts help uncover a new mode of communication that can loosely be defined as polyphonic lyric. I will be using this term in the sense suggested in Berger's study of diegesis and mimesis in various forms of artistic presentation, including literature, arts and music. Berger notes: "Thus our two modal dichotomies are operative not only in the narrative text-type or form, but also in the lyric. A polyphonic lyric is conceivable, though a monophonic one is far more usual. And the lyrical voice may belong either to a personage (whether implied or explicit), making no difference to his own 'now' and the 'now' of the world of which he speaks, or it may belong to a narrator whose 'now' is not that of the world of which he speaks (as happens when he uses the preterite)" (Berger 1994: 413). Such lyrics that use Pushkin's voice and may be read as polyphonic provide us with examples of images and devices of Pushkin's poetry that remain unassimilated in twentieth-century poetic speech - and hence stand out as strange. The strangest poems to trigger the imagination of many Russian poets, and which are often misread, include Pushkin's poems of the 1820s-1830s, which today are seen as canonical. They include "Monument" («Памятник»), "Incantation" («Заклинание»), "Prophet" («Пророк») and "Devils" («Бесы»). It can be easily argued that Parshchikov's cycle *Figures of Intuition* («Фигуры интуиции», 1989) is the most daring attempt so far to present Pushkin's text as a space of its own, infused with the postmodern condition. In his work Parshchikov defines his newly-invented poetic persona as a figure of intuition who exists separately from the poet. In the poem "Money" («Деньги») in his cycle, Parshchikov writes:

> Фигуры интуиции! В пустыне
> они живут, проткнув зрачки
> колючками. Святые
> коммуны их в верховиях реки
> времен. У нас есть кругозор и почта,
> объятья и земля, и молния в брикете...
> У них нет ничего, того, что
> Становится приобретеньем смерти.
> Они есть моцарты трехлетние.
> Ночь. Высь взыскательна.招бориста тоска.
> Тогда фигура интуиции заметнее:
> Она идет одна, но с двух концов моста.
> (Parshchikov 1989)

> (Figures of intuition! They live
> In the desert, their pupils pierced
> By spikes. Their holy
> Communes sit high toward the source
> Of time's river. We have vistas and e-mail,
> Embraces and earth, and lightning in a bottle.
> Death can't afford
> What they have to sell.
> They are three-year-old Mozarts.
> It's night, the heights exacting, the yearning brute.
> Now the figure of intuition grows more visible.
> It walks alone from both ends of the bridge.)

Parshchikov aspires to canonise the impersonal gaze as the most sacred mode of writing. If history is a sack, with an abyss of money inside, the subject who could "carry the powerful centuries on a stick," as Parshchikov's poem suggests, dissolved himself. In provocative manner the poet admits his historical amnesia: "And who was a figure of intuition to whom?" («И кто был для кого фигурой интуиции?»). He is happy to part with his pain and historical consciousness, for the sake of experiencing transrational inspiration and prime logic, the somatic experience that came to replace semantic order and some metaphorical patriarchal dwelling, usually known as the Logos.

Henri Lefebvre explains that Heidegger described a search for dwelling as a double movement, which makes readers "think through the deeper existence of the human being by taking dwelling and the dwelling as our starting point — thinking of the essence of Poetry as a form of 'building', a way of 'making dwell' [*faire habiter*] *par excellence*" (Lefebvre 2003: 122). Lefebvre points out that the traditional house filled with symbols and mysterious attics uniting dreams and memories and keeping human beings safe has been vanishing from the modern world. It has been replaced with lodgings built for technological demands, lacking the body and poetic soul of a patriarchal dwelling. Pushkin's elegiac sublime is a term used by Harsha Ram in a recent study of the imperial sublime in Russian poetry (Ram 2003: 160-211). The elegiac sublime received a new twist in the context of Russian émigré, Soviet and post-Soviet poetry infused with nostalgia. Yet themes of remembering in Russian twentieth-century poetry go back to Pushkin's own desire, expressed in some of his poems, to perform rites of mourning and burial for his friends executed for organising the 1825 Decembrist revolt, as a mark of nostalgia for the organically-evolved national community.

In dealing with the legacy of Pushkin's poetry to the Russian twentieth-century poetic universe, we must take into account important correctives to the reader-response criticism undertaken in recent years by prominent feminist scholars. Patrocinio Schweickart refers to the established reader-response theories of such scholars as Jonathan Culler, Riffatere, Wolfgang Iser and Stanley Fish as largely utopian. Schweickart expresses the view that reader-response criticism needs to include feminist-theoretical approaches in order to account for the significance of gender in the act of reading (Schweickart 1986: 36-37). Schweickart shares Culler's opinion that a dualistic theory crediting the contributions of both text and reader is needed, and argues that even Iser's theory does not sustain this balance: it tends to collapse either into a monism of the text or a monism of the reader. I find compelling Schweickart's argument that "androcentric literature structures the reading experience differently depending on the gender of the reader" (Schweickart 1986: 41). This approach subverts the expectation of the relative tranquillity of the reader-author relationship and brings to the fore a possibility of conflicts, sufferings, and passions that might be unravelled in accounts of the reading experience. In the words of Judith Fetterley, "as readers and teachers and scholars, women are taught to think as men, to identify with a male point of view, and to accept as normal and legitimate a male system of values, one of whose central principles is misogyny" (Fetterley 1978: xx). Fetterley's view is that the female reader is co-opted into participating in the experience of reading the canon, in order to identify herself as male against herself, since she is explicitly excluded in the formation of this canon. If we accept this, then even a brief examination of the poetry of the most outstanding Russian female twentieth-century poets — such as Tsvetaeva, Akhmatova, Olga Berggolts, Akhmadulina and Elena Shvarts — uncovers a version of anxiety of influence in relation to Pushkin's works that translates itself into a dialectical model of reading. Their example provides us with some interesting answers to questions such as "How does woman write as woman?" and "What does it mean for a woman to read a canonical author without condemning herself to the position of other?"

Important implications for reading creative responses to Pushkin's poetry stem from Schweickart's suggestion that Fish's belief — that the production of the meaning of a text is mediated by the interpretative community and depends upon the interpretative strategy one applies to it — is applicable to the feminist readership community. One can easily interpret, for example, numerous references to the image of androgynous youth (отрок) in the poetry of Akhmatova and Tsvetaeva as attempts to find common ground with Pushkin's own subjective fluid self, a self not yet transformed into the identity closely linked to patriarchal canonical constructs. Both Akhmatova and Tsvetaeva seem to relate well to the image of a

Pushkin in early youth, opening up thereby the interesting possibility of reading Pushkin's texts from an androgynous viewpoint. In some ways, long narratives such as Tsvetaeva's 1926 poems — "Poem of the Hill" («Поэма горы») and "Poem of the End" («Поэма конца») — and Akhmatova's "Poem without a Hero" («Поэма без героя») are attempts to depart from the androcentricity of Pushkin's *Eugene Onegin* imposed upon them as participants in the literary and critical enterprise of Russian cultural history through the act of reading. Although neither Akhmatova nor Tsvetaeva identified themselves with feminist readers as such, I will argue that their creative responses to Pushkin's poetry contribute largely to the recovery, articulation and elaboration of positive expressions of the female viewpoint.

Schweickart establishes three important aspects of the dialectics of reading by feminist readers. To summarise them: firstly, "reading induces a doubling of the reader's subjectivity, so that can be placed at the disposal of the text while the other remains with the reader"; the second moment of the dialectic involves "the recognition that reading is necessarily subjective"; and finally "the need to keep it from being *totally* subjective ushers in the third moment of the dialectic". As Schweickart aptly points out, within the above-outlined framework of the dialectic of reading, "reading becomes a mediation between author and reader, between the context of writings and the context of reading" (Schweickart 1986: 53-54). In the light of this useful observation, it is not far fetched to suggest that modernist readers' reception of Pushkin's texts was largely shaped by Dostoevskii's pre-Symbolist reading of Pushkin as expressed in his 1880 speech. Dostoevskii's speech can be seen as the boldest attempt to canonise Pushkin as a strange author whose writings are ascribed with esoteric meanings and secret language. Dostoevskii concluded his speech in an open-ended manner, pointing the way to new interpretative strategies applicable to reading Pushkin's texts: "Had Pushkin lived longer, there would perhaps, amongst ourselves, have been fewer misunderstandings and arguments than exist at present. But God ordained otherwise. Pushkin died at the height of his powers and indisputably carried off some great secret with him to the grave. And now that he is no longer among us, we are seeking to divine this secret" (Richards and Cockrell 1976: 88).

By calling upon readers of Pushkin works to seek out the secrets interjected in his works, Dostoevskii prefigures concerns expressed in Iser's reader-response theory. Dostoevskii foregrounds Iser's understanding of the capacity of the text to open up an inner world in the reader, of which the reader is unconscious. Dostoevskii's gesture to remove the image of the historical Pushkin from the process of reading is conspicuously close to Iser's idea that the result of the reading process is therapeutic to the reader, enabling the reader to formulate himself, since "a layer of the reader's personality is brought to light which had hitherto remained hidden in the shadows" (Iser 1978: 155). I will argue that both modernist and postmodernist poets recognise that there are two selves involved in the process of reading Pushkin: the other self which text elicits, and the reader's predefined self which cannot be completely absorbed by the other.

Some recent correctives and additions to reader-response theories include a method of polar reading that permits the participation of any reader in the text and offers a wide range of literary experience, including the affirmation of the reader's value through the polarising aspects of one's real self. I am particularly indebted to Jean Kennard's research that translates Joseph Zinker's ideas about the role of the creative process in gestalt therapy into a methodology of reading (Kennard 1986: 66-73). Although Kennard herself limited her application of this method to lesbian reading of text, she suggests that this method is particularly appropriate to those whose experience is not frequently reflected in literature because "it is based in readers' individual differences" (Kennard 1986: 77). Zinker has a concept of the individual as a composite of opposing characteristics (polarities) in accordance with which a person's self encompasses both the characteristics of kindness and softness as well as their polarities such as cruelty and hardness (Zinker 1977: 197). Zinker highlights the importance of experiment for gestalt psychology, equating it with playful acting out of new imaginary behaviour, that does not necessarily constitute real behaviour, and this experiment helps people to get in touch with their hidden selves. As Kennard explains, "What we become, for a time during the experiment is an extreme form of an aspect of ourselves, often a denied one; the experiment is basically a means of differentiation for the purposes of self-awareness" (Kennard 1986: 69). Zinker explains his methodology thus: "My theory of polarities dictates that if I do not allow myself to be unkind, I will never be genuinely kind. If I am in touch with my own unkindness and stretch that part of myself, when my kindness emerges it will be richer, fuller, more complete. I call this an 'around the world' phenomenon: If you keep flying north long enough, you will eventually be heading south" (Zinker 1977: 202).

The implications of this method for the understanding of readers' responses to Pushkin is straightforward. The main conclusion to emerge from analysis of twentieth-century poetic responses to Pushkin is the sense that Russian twentieth-century poets, in performing a creative act of reading Pushkin, tend to recover their suppressed intuitive selves and to link their poetic language with sensuous experiences of reality. The list of these selves, or playful masks, include various definitions and archetypes such as Orpheus (Adamovich, Tsvetaeva, Sedakova); craftsman (Briusov); dandy and master of style (Nabokov); poet-aristocrat, holder of the sacred lyre (Blok, Vladislav Khodasevich); fun-poker and rebel (Tsvetaeva, Tvardovskii, Parshchikov); man of passion (Vladimir Solov'ev); soul-mate (Dmitrii Merezhkovskii, Tsvetaeva, Akhmatova); Muse of Lament (Akhmatova); playmate (Nabokov, Kibirov); mystic (Irina Odoevtseva, Shvarts) — these are just the most important.

This study has a focus on montaging Pushkin in order to highlight the striking analogies between poetry and cinema already articulated by scholars such as Tynianov, Chris Eagle and Monika Greenleaf. I link this method of reading to the lenses of modernity, so to speak, since ironic, modern and fragmentary modes of writings seem the most important marks of the Romantic and Modernist worldviews. As Greenleaf observes, "The intriguing kinship between the fragmentary modes of the 1820s and the 1920s may be more than a coincidence. It is possible [...] to trace the use of fragment and fragmentariness to an age's conscious perception of itself as 'post-revolutionary', irrevocably severed from Antiquity and cultural wholeness, and qualitatively modern and ironic [...] There is no question that twentieth-century Modernism, perhaps with the help of cinematography, has sharpened our awareness of the fragment as genre or mode" (Greenleaf 1992: 287). Some studies on modernism suggest that we can see this movement as a historical paradigm somehow caught between the breakdown of modern rational discourse and attempts of this discourse critically to evaluate its own ideologies and functions. For example Astradur Eysteinsson says: "The various individual devices of modernist disruption or interruption are elements of a paradigmatic effort to interrupt the 'progress' of rationality, and perhaps to initiate a 'new' discourse which we can […] not really know, since it is (still) the negativity of the discourse in which we are immersed" (Eysteinsson 1990: 240).

Today, when modernism has become a tradition in its own way, we have a blurry understanding of differences between modernist, avant-garde, neo-avant-garde, neo-modernist and postmodernist poets. I find helpful Eysteinsson's suggestion to view both terms 'modernism' and 'avant-garde' in conjunction with each other, providing we bear in mind their functional differences. Eysteinsson's point that the term 'avant-garde' implies "a general sense of exploration and experimentation that, unlike 'modernism', is non-specific in historical terms" (Eysteinsson 1990: 177) is very valid for the purpose of this study, which will attempt to differentiate between metatextual, parodical and norm-breaking responses to Pushkin. Many scholars see the avant-garde movement at the cutting edge of modernism: in their eyes, the term 'avant-garde' signifies more radical aspects of modernism. It is beyond the scope of my inquiry to contribute significantly to these debates, but I would point to recent studies that refer to alternative modes of Russian musical and literary expression as neo-avant-garde or avant-garde (Savitskii 2002; Cherednichenko 2002). I prefer to apply here the method of reading suggested in Eysteinsson's study, which allows us to see the same works as both modernist and avant-garde if we want to focus on their non-traditional structures and radicalised correlations of form and content. We need to bear in mind, however, that "while the avant-garde movements are historical phenomena in their own right, they are also salient motors of modernism" (Eysteinsson 1990: 178).

As a valuable starting point for Russian twentieth-century poetic responses to Pushkin, I use Richard Murphy's assumption that "postmodernism's unproblematic acceptance of art's status" leads either to the acceptance of aesthetic autonomous as a fact of artistic life or to realisation that the realms of art and life are irreversibly intertwined "in the era characterised by simulation and aestheticisation of politics" (Murphy 1998: 284).

By highlighting forms of montage in this book's title, I emphasise the dynamics of readership akin to performance, bringing forward the notion of classical realist text as a theoretical model against which subversive text constitutes itself. As Marc Schreurs notes, "The cinematic term 'montage' has frequently been used by literary critics when describing specific structural features of Russian literature in the modernist period. These features are among others: erratic juxtapositions of contrasting elements (styles, narrative positions, themes/motifs); exchanges of dislocated, disconnected text fragments; illogical transitions time and space, etc. The effects of fragmentation created by such elements are characteristic of novels and stories by Modernist writers like Evgenii Zamaitin, Boris Pil'niak and Isaak Babel" (Schreus 1989: 1). Given the fact that Sergei Eisenstein, the most influential advocate of montage principles, defined the modernist period as the age of montage and thought that montage principles were widely represented in all forms of art (Eisenstein 1964: volume 2: 188), it would be useful to investigate this phenomenon in Russian twentieth-century poetry. Several scholars, including Iurii Tynianov and Monika Greenleaf, identified some manifestations of montage thinking in Pushkin's works; I develop this approach further and present Pushkin as a precursor of Russian modernist aesthetics. The ultimate aim of my book is to show the main readings and appropriations of Pushkin undertaken by Russian twentieth-century poets as a multifarious montage of discourses and viewpoints inseparable from the poets' own responses to modernity.

NOTES

1 G.G. Chernetsov's painting is on the website of The State Russian Museum in Moscow www.rusmuseum.ru/eng/exhibitions/?id=168&i=1&year=2003&pic=3 (accessed October 2005).
2 Pushkin's Petersburg has become a popular subject of discussion in Russian scholarship. A list of themes related to this topic would include: discussion of the representation of sculptural and architectural monuments in Pushkin's writings; Pushkin's personal mythology that pivots around certain landscapes; Pushkin's depiction of Peter the Great; the employment of Petersburg urban folklore in Pushkin's poetry (Tomashevsky 1949; Jakobson 1975; Lotman 1984; Mintz 1984; Ospovat and Timenchik 1987; Virolainen 1999; Gordin 1999; Smith 2003).
3 I examine aspects of Nabokov's translations of the poetry of Pushkin and Tiutchev in my article "Vladimir Nabokov as Translator of Russian Poetry"

Introduction 37

(Smith 2003).
4   Sergei Averintsev says that the concept of laughter in Russian culture is associated with the Devil and subversive behaviour: "In Russia people laugh a great deal, but to laugh is always more or less 'impermissible' — not only because it is forbidden by state or ecclesiastical authorities, but because this is how people feel about it themselves. Any permissiveness on this point in Russia is rather shallow. It is impermissible to laugh, but impossible not to laugh. From this complicated and uneasy experience comes the longing glance towards that place where laughter *is* permissible, towards the West" (Averintsev 1993: 13).
5   According to Michael Wachtel's analysis of the Onegin stanza, for his *Eugene Onegin* Pushkin "devised a stanza unprecedented in literary history" and its uniqueness "produced an extraordinary firm formal and semantic constellation for Russian readers" (Wachtel 1998: 121). I talk at some length about Nabokov's own imitations of the Onegin stanza, especially in his novel *The Gift* (Dar, 1935-37), in my article "Vladimir Nabokov as Translator" (Smith 2003: 142-146).
6   As Cornwell's study reminds us, Nabokov regarded Pushkin as the greatest poet of his time, and perhaps of all time (second only to Shakespeare) (Cornwell 1999: 24).
7   The Petersburg linguist Liudmila Zubova, in her superb study of linguistic experiments and poetic devices embedded in Tsvetaeva's poetry, indicates a tendency towards abstraction and the transrational in Tsvetaeva's works, though without offering a comparison with the poetry of the Russian Futurists and Cubo-Futurists.

ONE

FROM PUSHKIN'S POETICS OF EXILE TO THE CONCEPT OF WRITING AS DWELLING

Preamble

Pushkin's portrayal of St Petersburg has attracted considerable attention among Pushkin scholars, and could be said to overshadow other areas in the study of Pushkin's texts. The numerous examinations of this topic have included attempts to examine Pushkin's images of Petersburg among the body of texts which Russian literary scholarship has defined within these contexts: the "Petersburg text" (Iurii Lotman; Zara Mintz); the descriptive approach (Boris Tomashevskii); the topographical approach (L. Mederskii); the intertextual approach (Shmuel Schwarzband; Andrei Kodjak; Vaclav Lednitskii); and the mytho-poetical approach (Roman Jakobson, John Bailey). Analysis of the various statements and poetic responses made by Russian twentieth-century poets to Pushkin indicate that the image of Petersburg is of paramount importance to their vision of Pushkin's poetic self. The poets define this image of Petersburg in terms that are more spatial than temporal. I would say that Russian twentieth-century readers became obsessed with Pushkin's Petersburg texts because of their vision of Pushkin as a precursor of modernity.

Before proceeding to analyse twentieth-century poetic responses to such works as "The Bronze Horseman", *Eugene Onegin* and "Monument" («Памятник»), I will outline an important exilic discourse in Pushkin's oeuvre which Pushkin's readers often underestimate. I will reveal the emergence in Pushkin's lyrics of his autonomous poetic space, which acts as a hinge between northern and southern identities. This poetic space appears akin to the notion of potential space which has been scrutinised by some recent psychoanalytical studies on child psychology.

In this chapter I will borrow Otto Boele's concept of literary representations of the North in Russian literature, which he discusses in his outstanding book *The North in Russian Romantic Literature*. Boele views the North "as a symbol of national particularity", "as a spatial-ideological point of reference upon which Russia's cultural and national identity is projected" (Boele 1996: 1). Boele's study provides us with important tools for assessing Pushkin's own sense of displacement and construction of identity, within the broader context of Russian nineteenth-century culture. To help describe the worldview of Pushkin which influenced Russian twentieth-century poets, let us keep in mind Boele's observation that, in Russian romantic literature, the North replaced the East as the symbol of national identity. According to Boele, the North was turned into a spatial symbol of nationhood, providing the key to the Russian national character (Boele 1996: 43). Boele suggests a paradigm that puts the North in opposition to the South and presents them as two polarities revolving around the inner and outer worlds. I would argue, though, that Pushkin's poetry partially overcame the binary opposition between the South and the North thanks to the emergence of an exilic discourse based on the concept of a bridge that links the two cultural traditions. In this chapter I will focus on Pushkin's 1824 poem "To the Sea" («К морю») to demonstrate that Pushkin's undervalued achievement is the creation of a special poetic space — which, as the poem expresses, is a space that hinges on the transitional space placed between the borders of different worlds. Furthermore I will illustrate that this poem was of great interest to the many twentieth-century poets who experienced a sense of cultural and political displacement because of the poem's construction of a modern subject. The poem also contains hidden allusions to Dante's *Divine Comedy*, significant because Dante's presence is strongly felt in Russian modernist and postmodernist poetry, especially in the works of Blok, Belyi, Osip Mandelshtam, Tsvetaeva, Akhmatova, Joseph Brodsky and Olga Sedakova.

According to modernisation theory, some significant features of modernisation include the shift from a network of predominately rural communities reliant on agrarian self-subsistence to an increasingly urbanised, market-oriented society driven by mechanised industry. Simon Dixon's analysis of Russian modernisation in 1676-1825 gives us a clear view of all the complexities of Russian modernisation. Dixon stresses, for example, that "nowhere in Europe was popular participation in politics so severely discouraged" (Dixon 1999: 256). Dixon establishes a solid theoretical framework for analysis of cultural and social transformation in Russia during this time.

For the purpose of the present study, it is worth mentioning here the two main mechanisms employed in the process of shaping a modern society in Russia, namely nationalism and literacy. Dixon suggests: "Whereas traditional communities were stable hierarchies dominated by kinship networks, modern social mobility creates a more impersonal society in which national loyalties outweigh social ones. In this sense, nationalism generates nations, and not the other way around" (Dixon 1999: 1). Dixon proposes that modernity brings greater freedom of choice to individuals. Freedom of choice empowers, not only by enabling an increase in affluence, but also through the spread of literacy.

We might thus summarise Dixon's observations of the consequences of modernisation: the written word replaces face-to-face contact as the principal mode of communication; with the help of technology, scientific discoveries become popularised; high culture becomes more accessible and increases opportunities for talented people to have careers; education demystifies the world and gives modern man time to contemplate his past and future; society becomes politicised (Dixon 1999: 2). However Dixon points out that there is a price to pay for this change, because of the increasing sway over individuals that was held by bureaucratic institutions established by law. As a result, "autonomous individuals may become alienated from their fellows and are likely to be beset by doubt in a secular modern world" (Dixon 1999: 2). Pushkin's poetry after the 1825 Decembrist revolt displays a growing sense of such alienation and disillusion with the Russian pace of modernisation.

The overpowering presence of the monarchy continued to affect Russia's path towards a modern state in the 1810s-1830s. Nevertheless Vissarion Belinskii believed Russian literature of the first half of the nineteenth century retained independence from foreign models and displayed a full complement of artistry and elements of vitality. Belinskii wrote in 1842: "In spite of the poor state of our literature, it has vital impulses and organic development, therefore it has history" («Несмотря на бедность нашей литературы, в ней есть жизненное движение и органическое развитие, следственно, у нее есть история») (Belinskii 1988: 415). In a recent analysis of various manifestations of the imperial sublime in Russian poetry, Ram observes that "in its attitudes to empire, Russian romanticism wavered characteristically between 'odic' triumphalism and 'elegiac' mourning". In Ram's view, Pushkin's narrative poem "Prisoner of the Caucasus" («Кавказский пленник», 1822), "with its elegiac plotline and belligerently odic epilogue", perfectly exemplifies Russian romanticism's oscillating worldview (Ram 2003: 11). Alongside Ram's comment we should highlight the significant role of foreign literature in the formation of the Russian national consciousness. Dixon, for example, identifies a strong bond between English and Russian literatures in the first half of the nineteenth century: "It was the literary example of Sir Walter Scott and Lord Byron that encouraged Russian writers in the 1820s to emulate Pushkin's 'Prisoner of the Caucasus' […] and create a new poetic image of the periphery as sublime wilderness. Later their work helped to generate a potentially subversive Romantic regionalism in the Russian empire. Before 1825, however, Russia remained almost as centralised in cultural terms as it was politically" (Dixon 1999: 174). I would go further and say that in Pushkin's 1824 poem "To the Sea" (which I will be discussing in detail) we can already sense a change in the societal and artistic values that were linked to various manifestations of subversive regionalism.

Ram sees Pushkin as a poet caught between two worldviews, and whose poetic output contains responses to different paradigms oscillating between odic and elegiac modes of expression; whereas Belinskii sees Pushkin as a captive of his time. In his articles Belinskii perceives Pushkin's worldview as having been shaped by the poet's immediate social and cultural environment, which was rapidly transitioning from Alexander I's epoch into Nicholas I's. After the death of Alexander I, the Decembrist rebellion broke out on 14 December 1825. As Dixon puts it, the consequences of their actions were momentous: "Dissent in Russia could never be the same again;

the newly enthroned Nicholas determined in vain to suppress it altogether" (Dixon 1999: 23). Dixon characterises the stage of modernity in Russia in December 1825 thus: "By then, a century of sustained Westernisation had introduced into Russia a hierarchy of rationally ordered government institutions, detailed social regulation and cultural influences ranging from Italian opera to the political economy of Adam Smith. Yet it had also been responsible for freemasonry, fortune-telling, and Swedenborg's mystical Christianity" (ibid).

An understanding of this political environment is important for interpreting Pushkin's poetry. Shortly after the death of Pushkin in 1837, Belinskii acutely felt that the intrinsic bond between Pushkin and the environment had effectively shaped Pushkin's artistic psychology. In his articles, Belinskii speaks on behalf of readers in the 1840s to claim that many of the concerns expressed in Pushkin's poetry had lost their relevance for subsequent generations. Yet he pinpoints the sublime character and vitality of Pushkin's poetry infused with rich references to real life. Belinskii wrote: "The more sublime the cultural phenomenon is, the more vital it is; this means that our comprehension of it depends even more upon our understanding of the reality that shaped it" («Чем выше явление, тем оно жизненнее, а чем жизненнее явление, тем более его сознание зависит от движения и развития самой жизни») (Belinskii 1988: 410).

Belinskii's statement helps us contextualise Pushkin's works and uncover the dynamics of Pushkin's relationship with his own epoch. In the light of Belinskii's observation, it is appropriate to use a psychoanalytic relational model in order to discuss the self-representations and ideas expressed in Pushkin's poetry, and to understand twentieth-century approaches to Pushkin's legacy. It is evident that scholars and poets have viewed Pushkin not as a separate entity but in conjunction with others. Pushkin's poetic self has been discussed as a dynamic self with a double vision, one that incorporates a constant awareness of the objective reality and other subjective worldviews. Thus such terms as "Pushkin's Petersburg", "Pushkin's pleiad", "Pushkin's epoch", and "the Pushkin century" permeate Russian modernist and postmodernist writing. In fact, Pushkin's self-representations have striking similarities with contemporary theories of the mind, especially the current relational model in psychoanalytic theory. Pushkin's poetry undercuts binary oppositions such as imagination and nature, subjective mind and external world, which often have been applied to his texts by scholars who viewed his artistic imagination in the light of a Cartesian dualism. The oppositions that we find in Pushkin's verse are vitally interconnected and interdependent, allowing for symbolic thinking and imaginative growth.

From the relational perspective, the mind is essentially social, being dependent upon relational configurations. As Stephen Mitchell stresses, "Mind has been redefined from a set of predetermined structures emerging from inside an individual organism to transactional patterns and internal structures derived from an interactive, interpersonal field" (Mitchell 1988: 17). Many of Pushkin's poetic works, in fact, anticipate such understanding of the world order. Pushkin's story "Egyptian Nights" («Египетские ночи» 1835) includes poems and features performance, and specifically one that implies a playful space of interaction with fragments and transactional objects used for symbolisation. As I will demonstrate below, "Egyptian Nights" resonates well with the contemporary theories of self that emerged as part of modern developments and paradigms. "Egyptian Nights" effectively shows how intricate relational patterns and interactive dynamics constitute Pushkin's poetic and moral consciousness, and how his creative imagination derives from socially negotiated states.

In accordance with relational-model theories, mind is viewed not as combination of physically-based urges, but as shaped by a matrix of relationships with other people. A holistic conception of the self emphasises not the individual as separate entity, but the interactive space within which an individual articulates himself. Mitchell describes this model of self: "The person is comprehensible only within the tapestry of relationships, past and present [...] the figure is always *in* the tapestry, and the threads of the tapestry (via identifications and introjections) are always in the figure" (Mitchell 1988: 3). Boris Gasparov's thesis, that Russian modernists replaced the image of Pushkin as historical figure with the more abstract concept of Pushkin as an absolute and eternal creative principle, corresponds to Mitchell's vision of self as something that forms an integral part of the tapestry of relationships. Gasparov in his article on the analogies between the Golden and Silver Ages of Russian poetry appears to view Pushkin as a historical figure, alongside the phenomenon he labels the Pushkin myth. The concept of the Pushkin myth implies the notion of a certain cultural construct that impacted the formation of the artistic psychology of Russian modernist poets and thinkers (Gasparov 1992).

Gasparov identifies various stages in the modernists' rediscovery of Pushkin. He asserts that the Pushkin myth played an important role in the Russian modernists' "tapestry of relationships, past, and present", to use Mitchell's phrase. As Gasparov puts it, "The constant, mythological incarnation of Pushkin's age in early twentieth-century Russian culture operated as a sublime synthesis, an ideal unity that combined the real and the transcendental [...]. At different stages in Modernism's development, various modernist tendencies would thrust into the foreground various dimensions of this synthesis: the sacral-liturgical, the metaphysical, the aesthetic or the cultural-historical" (Gasparov 1992: 6-7). Gasparov's very valuable approach seems to provide an overarching answer to the complex question of the interaction between the canon and experimental modes of artistic expression. However it does not empower us with an understanding of the more specific nature of the poetic dialogue between twentieth-century poets and Pushkin. One must not understate, though, how useful is the concept of the Pushkin myth for creating a framework to examine more closely the specific references and indebtedness to Pushkin. Gasparov's study forms an important stepping stone for further investigations into this topic.

Mitchell's model of the mind offers a useful methodological framework to complement the intertextual approach to modernist texts. His model introduces the concept of the transitional realm between outside and inside. This concept derives from Donald Winnicott's notions of potential space and transitional object, which have been employed in child development studies. Winnicott's notion of potential space explains why infants use dolls, teddy bears and blankets as transitional objects to master their anxiety of individuation and separation from the mother. Winnicott's essay "Playing" emphasises that transitional objects do not form a part of the infant's body, yet at the same time they are not fully recognised by infants as part of the external world. Winnicott describes this space in terms of an intermediate area of experience, arguing that both inner reality and external life contribute to this space of interaction; it is also a resting place in that the individual keeps his interrelated inner and outer realities separated. This view of the world replaces the Cartesian principle of dividedness, whose vision of a transitional space now becomes redefined as inner relatedness. Winnicott explains: "This area of playing is not inner psychic reality. It is outside the individual, but it is not the external world. [...] Without hallucinating, the child puts out a sample of dream potential and lives with this sample in a chosen setting of fragments from external reality [...]. In playing, the child manipulates external phenomena in the service of the dream and invests chosen external phenomena with dream meaning and feeling" (Winnicott 1971: 51). I will return to the psychoanalytical theoretical approaches of Mitchell and Winnicott when I examine the creative dialogue between Pushkin and several important twentieth-century poets.

To view Pushkin's texts in conjunction with their psychoanalytical theories — those which centre on the concept of the interacting sense of self — is to highlight the validity of Pushkin's self-representations for the construction of poetic self in modernist and postmodernist contexts. Pushkin's vision of the creative self gained greater currency in the twentieth century than in the second half of the nineteenth century, because it coincided with many important developments in psychology and science that affected the formation of subjectivity and creativity in the periods of modernity and postmodernity. Pushkin's "To the Sea" embodies the intermediate space that is comparable to the infant's imaginary potential space constructed with the help of transitional objects: both spaces have a somewhat blurred boundary between the emerging self and the m/other.

In a famous 1921 speech known as "The Poet's Role" («О назначении поэта»), Blok notes Pushkin's preoccupation with inner concerns rather than with ideological or state affairs. Blok underlines the child-like innocence embedded in Pushkin's writings, saying that all Russians' memories from early childhood preserve "a happy name — Pushkin". Blok's speech provides evidence for Pushkin's impact upon Russian twentieth-century poetry: "From early childhood our memories preserve a happy name — Pushkin. This name, its very sound, fills many days of our lives. The names of emperors, generals, inventors of weapons of slaughter, torturers and martyrs are forbidding. But next to them stands this light and elegant name — Pushkin" (Blok, in Richards and Cockrell 1976: 127). It is significant that Blok locates Pushkin's identity within a tapestry of related greats. Moreover, Blok introduces the notion of poetic essence and creative force, a notion strikingly similar to Bergson's concept of *élan vital*.

Blok puts forward the idea that multi-levelled manifestations of the creative spirit are embedded in Pushkin's works: "We know Pushkin the man, we know Pushkin the friend of the monarchy, and we know Pushkin the friend of the Decembrists, but all this pales before Pushkin the poet" (Blok, in Richards and Cockrell 1976: 128). In his speech Blok stresses on several occasions the indestructibility of the essence of poetry, and that any great poet is a child of harmony, cosmos and Logos. Like Bergson, Blok highly values the creative mind's intuitive faculties, proposing this vision of creative evolution: "The life of the world comprises the continuous creation of new breeds and new species. They are cradled in anarchic Chaos, but tended and selected by culture; harmony gives them shapes and forms, which again dissolve in the anarchic fog. The meaning of this process we do not understand, and its essence is unclear; we console ourselves with the thought that the new species are better than the old, but the wind soon extinguishes this little candle with which we attempt to illuminate the darkness of the world [...]. In the world we observe perpetual change, and we ourselves participate in the evolution of species. Our part is largely inactive: we degenerate, we grow old and we die. Sometimes it is active: we may occupy a position in the culture of the world and promote the formation of new species" (Blok 1976: 128-9).

Blok formulated his idea of the role of poet at a time when many Russian poets were discovering the huge performative potential of poetry and were seeking ways to merge theatre, dance and poetry. For example, Irina Odoevtseva's memoirs talk of the rather avant-garde attempts to bring together dance and versification that had been attempted by the Philological Institute of the Living Word (Институт живого слова) at which she matriculated in 1918. Her lecturers included many famous critics, translators and poets including Kornei

Chukovskii, Mikhail Lozinskii and Nikolai Gumilev. The students at the Institute took courses in literary studies and rhythmical gymnastics based on the system of Swiss theoretician Emile Jacques-Dalcroze.

There was active interest at the beginning of the twentieth century in such concepts as creative evolution and 'living' art in Russian culture. The interest was fermented, to a large extent, by Bergson's ideas: most of his writings were published in Russia before 1917, and Pasternak names Bergson as one of the most fashionable philosophers of his generation (Pasternak 1970: 20). We might say that Blok's Pushkin above all appears to be an excellent performer, who transformed his life into a brilliant spectacle. At the same time Blok redefined, in the style of Bergson, Belinskii's notion of the vitality of Pushkin's language.

Several of Russia's symbolist and post-symbolist authors attended Bergson's lectures in Paris and befriended him. Among them were Zinaida Gippius, Maximilian Voloshin and Nikolai Otsup. Bergson had a strong impact on Russian culture, extending even into the Russian émigré memoir literature that accentuated the notion of living as a manifestation of creative impulse: examples of this include Gippius's memoirs, known as *Living Persons* (*Живые лица*, 1925), and Tsvetaeva's essay on Maximilian Voloshin (with a title not easy to render in English) "Living about the Living" («Живое о живом», 1931).

Recent studies have convincingly argued that Bergson's metaphysics was of paramount importance to the aesthetic development of both the avant-garde and postmodernist cultures. David Wedaman says it is possible today to talk about phenomena that can be loosely defined as Applied Bergsonism. As well as Bergson himself, Guillaume Apollinaire and Maiakovskii contributed to this distinct mode of the avant-garde that foreshadows aspects of postmodernism, such as the theoretical tenets of Gilles Deleuze (Wedaman 2003: iv). Wedaman maintains that Deleuze's thinking proves the vitality of Bergson's ideas: "It hints that these core ideas seem to belong together as a package, and that they are in no danger of disappearing. That particular sort of faith in indeterminacy; the idea that positive, cyclical change is necessary to evolution; the desire to shatter static systems with novelty; the refusal to accept intellectual construction as given; the assumption that art can play a role in social evolution; the dogged attention to the preconceptual and pre-linguistic concrete; the belief that this concrete is fluid, real and valuable; and the delight that comes from a view of the world as a creation in progress that permits, or even demands, the individual's participation — all these assumptions seem to inhere in a particular approach to life and art that is as relevant now as it was in the early years of the last century" (Wedaman 2003: 205). Hilary Fink goes not quite so far as does Wedaman in her analysis of the influence of Bergson's ideas on Russian modernist culture (Fink 1999). Fink suggests we should take the main tenets of Bergson's metaphysics as a package. This develops an approach that helps analyse the radical and innovative tendencies of cultural developments.

We can now begin to sense, in the many twentieth-century writings that concerned themselves with Pushkin, a Bergsonian preoccupation with active involvement in creative evolution. The list of such writings includes: Blok's 1921 speech on Pushkin; Maiakovskii's poem on Pushkin, with its famous declaration that he loves not his monument but the living Pushkin; and Tsvetaeva's 1931 cycle "Poems to Pushkin" («Стихи к Пушкину»), in which Pushkin appears to censors and critics in the shape of a living weapon.

We could stop here and say that many twentieth-century poets viewed Pushkin through the eyes of Bergson, so to speak. But closer examination of Pushkin's own aesthetic principles, as seen in his writings, reveals aspects of Pushkin's artistic psychology which enabled Russian modernists to look at his creative output and equate Pushkin the poet with a creative principle. Bergson emphasised the creative action that was heavily dependent on both intellectual effort and intuitive simultaneous perception of the past/present/future. This allows the reader to reflect on creation itself, from the viewpoint of his own psychic experience. Such a standpoint helps creative individuals overcome the binary opposition between the past and future that often is subjugated to a deterministic worldview. Bergson's metaphysics therefore helped Russian modernists to combine a sense of continuity with the search for novelty: Pushkin's language became a stepping stone for subsequent expression of modern experiences. The artistic outlook of Russian modernist and post-modernist poets does not just hinge on a Nietzschean concept of eternal return. It also reveals that the living, creative impulse of Pushkin's text goes on to interact with the poetic selves of Pushkin's disciples in a new context.

Bergson offered contemporary readers a vision of the true democracy to follow Middle Ages Christianity. This presents important ethical challenges which call for closer examination of the dynamic worldview expressed in Bergson's metaphysics. Leonard Lawlor, for example, analyses in great detail Bergson's concepts of pure memory (emotion) and memory-image (symbolic vision), as expressed in *Matter and Memory* and *The Two Sources of Morality and Religion*. Lawlor concludes that Bergson views ethics as fundamentally mnemonic. Lawlor also points to Bergson's concept of memory as being not just psychological but ontological (Lawlor 2003: 110). "Bergson's mystical ascetic, his 'Zoro-aster', his star-gazer, re-ascends, turns his eyes to the heavens <...>, using his 'telescope' of memory. More than an archaeology, more than a genealogy, Bergson's anti-Platonism is an astronomy that looks for other forms of life" (Lawlor 2003: 211).

Utopian overtones are suffused in Bergson's idea of justice, which stretches the Christian concept of brotherhood toward the idea "that everyone, insofar as being human, were of equal worth and that the community of essence conferred on them the same fundamental rights" (Bergson 1977: 77). And we should look to Bergson's understanding of creativity as an attempt to represent mystical all-encompassing love as irreproducible, since it includes not only all humanity, past and present, but also animals, plants — all nature, in fact. Bergson's concepts of the detour and the reciprocal implication stand close to reader-reception theoretical approaches. They reveal the interactive process of reading based on dialogic consciousness. Bergson states: "A personality brought up from the depths of the soul into the light of consciousness, stirring into life within us, which we felt might completely pervade us later, and to which we wished to attach ourselves for the time being, as the disciple does to the master. As a matter of fact, this personality is outlined from the day we have adopted a model; the desire to resemble, which is ideally the generator of a form to be taken, is already resemblance; the word, which we shall make our own, is the word whose echo we have heard within ourselves" (Bergson 1977: 35). In other words, Bergson suggests that the mystic resurrects memory and so creates new living species. The analogy between the creator and the mystic is not new, and was employed widely in Europe's romantic and symbolist periods, but acquires a different meaning in Bergson's works, insofar as the word "memory" is explained in Bergson's teaching in a new vein: his cogito implies the original synthesis of the past and the present with the view to the future. It foresees the concepts of estrangement and displacement that gained currency in avant-garde practices and theories.

Moments of estrangement, mystical experiences as part of creative moments, are abundant in Pushkin's lyrics, as in such poems as "Prophet" («Пророк») and "To the Sea". We also come across the mystic-poet, who simultaneously perceives several temporal and spatial dimensions, in his 1827 poem "Near the places where golden Venice rules..." («Близ мест, где царствует Венеция златая»), believed to be a translation of an André Chenier poem, which conveys the dream of a peaceful and idyllic gondola passage along Venetian canals, suggesting the notion of secret and sacred poems inspired by the poet's deep contemplation. This important key to Pushkin's creative psychology and imagery is provided in the last stanza of "Near the places where golden Venice rules...". It is a key found in several of Pushkin's lyrics:

> На море жизненном, где бури так жестоко
> Преследуют во мгле мой парус одинокий,
> Как он, без отзыва утешно я пою
> И тайные стихи обдумывать люблю.
> (Pushkin 1957, vol.3: 23)

> In the sea of life, where storms with such cruelty
> Chase my lonely boat in the darkness,
> I sing my songs of solace with no response,
> Like the boat, enjoying dreams of secret poems.

The juxtaposition of the sea of life, the sea storm, the lonely boat and the poet's creativity is also found in "To the Sea". It would be far-fetched to suggest that Pushkin's fluid poetic self conveyed in the above poem has strong Bergsonian overtones, yet in its intensity it certainly comes close to Bergson's understanding of creative evolution, since the idea of secret poems hints at active realisation of poetic utterances with a politically subversive slant. Therefore the stanza quoted above is suggesting a redefinition of static forms of life in accordance with endless flow and creative change. The allusion to secret poems indicates inner psychic activity receptive to change, involving both contemplation and creation. Bergson explained that the thousands of incidents in our psychic life appear disconnected only because we tend to analyse them as separate acts: "Our attention fixes on them because they interest it more, but each is borne by the fluid mass of our whole physical existence. Each is only the best illuminated point of a moving zone which comprises all that we feel or think or will – all, in short, that we are at any given moment. […] Now, states thus defined cannot be regarded as distinct elements. They continue each other in an endless flow" (Bergson 2002: 172).

Pushkin's active engagement with the psychic life and with the intuitively comprehensible flow of existence (to use Bergsonian terms again) was of particular interest to Russian modernists, whose cult of the man-artist was core to their thinking and was oriented towards surpassing any forms of the deterministic outlook. It is not a coincidence that Khodasevich aptly identified the juxtaposition of numerous manifestations of Pushkin's concern for individual freedom with imagery linked to the impersonal forces of history and fate: "He compares everything external that lies beyond individual control with bad weather, storms, hurricanes. Evil government, mass revolt, plague, war, state necessity, mass violence against individual; everything that restrains individual freedom; everything that exists outside the boundaries of a private house, — all this is bad weather. It is fate. It is possible to protect oneself from it; hide into one's inner world; switch on lights and fill glasses with wine; lock one's doors for a while in fear of plague; but to overcome it and escape it completely impossible, Pushkin himself thought of a flight into the distant realm of labour and pure aesthetics but he did not do it in time and did not lock the doors — and he perished as a result" («С дурной погодой, с бурею, с ураганом сравнивает он все, что лежит вне поля воздействий отдельной личности. Злое правительство, народный мятеж, мор, война, государственная необходимость, насилие массы над личностью, все, что сковывает индивидуальную свободу, все, что за стенами дома, — все это дурная погода. Она судьба. От нее можно отгородиться, уйти в себя, «зажечь огни, налить бокалы», запереться на время, как от чумы, — но побороть ее и вовсе уйти от нее — нельзя. […] Сам Пушкин только 'замыслил' побег от 'черни' 'в обитель дальную трудов и чистых нег', но не успел бежать, не 'запер дверей' — и погиб») (Khodasevich 1999: 166). Khodasevich makes a most valuable observation, one that brings Pushkin closer to a Bergsonian understanding of duration, in his discussion of the representations of farewells, departures, disappearances and flights which were portrayed in Pushkin's poetry. Khodasevich was examining the dynamic juxtaposition of the usage of the past and present tenses in Pushkin's poetic expressions of the flow of time, and the occasional usage of direct speech in between the descriptions of past and present moments (Khodasevich 1999: 236-40). Khodasevich's discussion of some important dialogic tenets within Pushkin's poetry is a useful insight into the mind of a Russian modernist artist eager to see himself in the stream of the eternal creative flow of life, searching for a style and a method to represent life's ephemerality.

A feature that was strikingly common to both the 1810-1830s and 1910-1930s was their tendency to aestheticise everyday life. Both periods favoured the concept of the man-artist and various kinds of spectacles in private and public spaces. Such an orientation makes artists more visible, and ascribes them with a double-consciousness that takes into account a continuous interaction between spectator and performer. RoseLee Goldberg maintains that "Whether tribal, ritual, medieval passion play, renaissance spectacle or the 'soirées' arranged by artists in the 1920s in their Paris studio, performance has provided a presence for the artist in society" (RoseLee Goldberg 1993: 8). The artist's presence in society depends upon the nature of the performance, and could include provocative, esoteric or entertaining modes of expression. Goldberg associates the twentieth century's strong orientation towards performance with the age of modernity seeking perpetually to reinvent itself.

The whole development of theatrical modes of expression in the twentieth century is summed up by Goldberg thus: "The history of performance art in the twentieth-century is the history of a permissive, open-ended medium with endless variables, executed by artists impatient with the limitations of more established art forms, and determined to take their art directly to the public. For this reason its base has always been anarchic" (RoseLee Goldberg 1993: 9). Goldberg also sees the history of modernist and postmodernist performance as an expression of artists' desire to create art forms which function outside the confines of museums and galleries. Goldberg's explanation implies a crisis of representation, one that made performance important for the age of modernity, because the nature of performance escapes rigid definition (except for the basic notion of live art performed by artists). However, since performance draws freely on other disciplines and media for material — including literature, music, dance and architecture — it helps reinvent other forms of expression and create novel experiences.

Below I will discuss some of the theatrical gestures and playful qualities of Pushkin's lyric "To the Sea" that shaped the construction of the poetic self in twentieth-century poetry. I will attempt to demonstrate that Pushkin's vision of poetry as autonomous space and imaginary dwelling, a vision which was exemplified in his lyrics, including "To the Sea", set a strong precedent for his modernist and postmodernist followers to look at Pushkin as a playmate and interlocutor, more often that not.

Pushkin's lyric "To the Sea" and the formation of the poetic self

Sandler, in her informative study of Pushkin's exilic poetry "Distant Pleasures: Alexander Pushkin and the Writing of Exile", firmly locates Pushkin's 1824 lyric poem "To the Sea" («К морю»), together with such poems as "The Countryside" («Деревня») and "To Ovid" («Овидию»), within the tradition of exilic writing. In Sandler's view, "To the Sea" is a poem "about the passion of ending" that provides "a sharper image of Pushkin's early growth as a poet of exile" (Sandler 1989: 57). With the help of Winnicott's concept of imaginary potential space as an allegorical depiction of reality construction, Sandler's analysis of "To the Sea" presents an opportunity for a richer reading of the poem.

For my own analysis of the poem I will use Sandler's reference to the process of lingering as the main physical activity described in "To the Sea", in order to show how Pushkin's poem creates a playful imaginary space that is neither subjective nor objective, but rather intermediate and dialogic. Sandler notes: "The entire physical activity of 'To the Sea' is one of lingering, and it could also be said that its cognitive and emotional activity is equally an attempt to pause, to muse over an otherwise fleeting moment of change and try to fix in memory what the change involves" (Sandler 1989: 58). In fact, Sandler's insightful observation on the use of pause in the poem resonates well with Winnicott's concepts of potential space and transitional objects that "are not part of the infant's body yet are not fully recognised as belonging to external reality" (Winnicott 1971: 2).

Psychologists at the Stone Centre have developed Winnicott's theories further. They have recognised that the infant's process of increasing differentiation from the m/other and the use of illusion could be seen as occurring in the larger context of relationships. So we can regard artistic activity more as reality construction, rather than as the product of sublimation and defence that the Freudian approach suggests (see Shapiro 1998: 21). In fact, "To the Sea" evokes the idea of a child playing at the seaside, and suggests strong analogy between shared playing and cultural experience. For example Pushkin writes with affection about the sea as a playmate who responds to various mental games and instigates flights of poetic fantasy:

> Как я любил твои отзывы,
> Глухие звуки, бездны глас,
> И тишину в вечерний час,
> И своенравные порывы!
>
> Смиренный парус рыбарей,
> Твоею прихотью хранимый,
> Скользит отважно средь зыбей:
> Но ты взыграл неодолимый, —
> И стая тонет кораблей.
>
> Не удалось навек оставить
> Мне скучный неподвижный брег,
> Тебя восторгами поздравить
> И по хребтам твоим направить
> Мой поэтический побег.
> («K moriu», Pushkin 1956, vol.2: 198-99)
>
> How I loved your responses,
> Soft sounds, the call of abyss,

And evening silence,
And impulsive gusts!

The fishermen's submissive sail,
Protected by your will,
Slides daringly across the waves:
But you, as ever invincible, grew rough
Sinking the whole fleet of ships.

I could not manage to leave behind
For ever this dull immobile shore
And greet you with rapturous sounds,
And set out on my poetic flight of fantasy
Across your crests.

The above extract from "To the Sea" represents three of the poem's fifteen stanzas: stanzas 4, 5 and 6 (which, together with stanza 13, are the most inventive). Stanzas 6, 7 and 13 contain five lines and have the same rhyming pattern: ababb. It significantly differs from the rest of the poem that features four-line stanzas with the rhyming pattern abab. It seems that it was Pushkin's intention for stanzas 5 and 6 to match stanza 13 semantically and structurally, as they have striking imagery and intonation. Stanza 13 reads as follows:

Мир опустел... Теперь куда же
Меня б ты вынес, океан?
Судьба земли повсюду та же:
Где капля блага, там на страже
Уж просвещенье иль тиран.
(«K moriu», Pushkin 1956, vol.2: 200)

The world emptied... Ocean,
Where would you have placed me now?
The fate of earth is the same everywhere:
For every drop of virtue there is a vigilant
Eye either of the enlightenment or of the tyrant.

Pushkin evidently connects the images of displacement with the creative activity that binds together poetry and dwelling. In the line "the world emptied..." Pushkin alludes to the death of Byron, whom he saw as the last Romantic poet. It seems that the uneven structural organisation of Pushkin's poem is due to the void created by Byron's death: thus, stanzas 5, 6 and 13 break the linear perception of the poem, so to speak, thereby indicating some sense of discontinuity.

Pushkin appears anxious to recover the mystery of writing that Byron took with him to the grave. Pushkin was undoubtedly shocked by the death of Byron, to whom he felt especially close. Pushkin's sense of shock is comparable to the sense of anxiety over the disappeared word, expressed as a distinctive way of thinking, in Maurice Blanchot's seminal essay "Death of the Last Writer". Blanchot muses on the death of the last writer thus: "We can dream about the last writer, with whom would disappear, without anyone noticing, the little mystery of writing. To give a touch of the fantastic to the situation, we can imagine that Rimbaud, even more mythical than the real one, hears that speech fall silent in him, and it dies with him. Finally we can suppose that, throughout the world circle of civilizations, the final end would be noted. What would be the result? Apparently a great silence. That is what is polite to say when some writer disappears: a voice has fallen silent, a way of thinking has disappeared. […] Such eras have existed, will exist, such fictions are reality at certain times in each of our lives" (Blanchot 2003: 218). Pushkin's reference to Byron as "spiritual leader" («властитель дум») resonates well with Blanchot's definition that a great writer is capable of imposing silence upon speech.

Blanchot considers that a literary work can be a rich resting place consisting of the silence caused by void and shock — at least for those who know how to penetrate the density of such silence (ibid: 219). We can also see that the space created by "To the Sea" is both as a space to mourn a deceased spiritual leader, and a space allowing for recovery from the anxiety of individuation from the m/other. And thus we come to understand that Pushkin's imaginary sea is akin to an area of play, one described by Winnicott as a ground for creativity and "a resting-place for the individual engaged in the perpetual human task of keeping inner and outer reality separate yet inter-related" (Winnicott 1971: 2). In "To the Sea" Pushkin portrays the process of negotiating the formation of this creative symbol in terms of outer and inner movement: the poetic persona aspires to reach out to the object of desire and remains still and spellbound, enchanted by an incredible passion («могучей страстью очарован»). This particular poetic persona reminds us of Blanchot's mythical Rimbaud figure, who hears speech fall silent within himself. The poetic persona in "To the Sea" intends to take with him, wherever he goes next, the sounds of the sea — including "sad sound", "inviting call", "echoes", "soft sounds", "call of the abyss", and even "silence" heard during the night. These sounds are analogous to the above-discussed notions of Winnicott concerning transitional objects, such as the dolls or teddy bears required by infants to enable them to create their imaginary intermediate spaces. For Pushkin these transitional objects are the sounds of the sea that spoke to him in the language of Byron and Dante, his spiritual teachers. In this sense, Pushkin identifies the sea with his m/other, referring to it in the first stanza as "element" («стихия»), notably using a feminine noun.

The poetic persona portrayed in "To the Sea", in response to the polyphony of sounds offered him by the sea (which symbolically represents the m/other), wishes to translate them all into his own exultant language. The poem's lyric hero dreams of greeting his imaginary interlocutor "with rapturous sounds", setting off on his "poetic flight of fantasy" across the wave crests. In other words, the poetic persona constructs his own reality and hybrid identity, to which contribute both psychic reality and the external world.

In any discussion of reading and aesthetic experience of reception, relational-model concepts are particularly useful, because they uncover dynamics of interaction between various worldviews. According to the relational model used in linguistics (which differs significantly from the Lacanian system with its understanding of language as an alienating force), the role of language in society is binding and unifying: it unites different mentalities in a common symbolic system and a common culture base (Stern 1985: 172). Of particular relevance to this examination of "To the Sea" is Gilbert Rose's comment that "the function of myth, religion, art, and science is not, for example, escape through wishful distortion of the world, but orientation towards it — a system of ideas to envisage one's relationship to society, the world, life and death — all in the service of the reality principle" (Rose 1987: 349). And Christopher Bollas sees aesthetic experience in terms of re-enactment of the infant's experiencing of relating with the mother (Bollas 2000: 32).

In addition to these psychoanalytical models, Rose's notion of creative artists' extreme sensitivity to any loss is also highly valuable to the present study. In his *Trauma and Mastery* we read: "One might say that the unconscious reminiscence of lost unity before the birth of self and otherness is probably universal, but the creative artist is loss-sensitive and separation-prone. Therefore, his wound may be deeper; the split in the ego is such that is set on an endless course of repeating the loss in order to repair it [...]. The novelist, then, would be one who redefines his lost world by creating one of his own, peopled with products of self" (Rose 1987: 127). The very need for reenactment of the situation of loss is highlighted at the end of "To the Sea":

> В леса, в пустыни молчаливы
> Перенесу, тобою полн,
> Твои скалы, твои заливы,
> И блеск, и тень, и говор волн.
> (Pushkin 1956, vol. 2 : 200)

> Into the forests, into the silent deserts
> I, full of your noises, will carry with me
> Your rocks, your coves,
> And glitter, and shadow, and waves' murmur.

"To the Sea" is telling us that, in order to reconstruct wherever he goes the space of interaction with the m/other (personified in the poem as the sea), the poet needs the help of transitional objects to redefine his lost world in any new contextual setting. In this regard my reading of "To the Sea" departs from Sandler's view that it "values escape" and presents "the sea as potential and much desired avenue of escape" (Sandler 1989: 61). I would suggest the poem embodies a ritualistic-like action that creates an imaginary space for interaction, not of escape.

Sandler discusses similarities between Alphonse Lamartine's poem "Farewell to the Sea" ("Adieu à la mer", 1822) and Pushkin's "To the Sea". She also mentions briefly Byron's self-representation as a child of the sea as stemming from the Romantic association between the sea and spiritual freedom (Sandler 1989: 61, 63). Byron's vision of himself as a child seeing the sea as his mother reinforces the point that Pushkin's "To the Sea" allegorically depicts aesthetic experience as a repetition of the infant's primal experience of fitting with the m/other.

Pushkin's numerous allusions in the poem to the sea's sounds indicate that he views searching for pristine language as necessary to help repair traumatised language. Pushkin's description of the objects and sounds that are necessary luggage can remind us of religious experience, because transitional objects can act as the magical tools required in the performing of sacred rituals. This is a good illustration of Langer's statement that "only through the act of symbolising do we give meaning to ourselves and our experience" (Shapiro 1998: 21).

Before we can proceed to create the genealogy that derives from the vision of modernity expressed by Pushkin in "To the Sea", some points need further clarification in the light of earlier observations. As mentioned above, stanzas 5 and 6 structurally match stanza 13. It is not far fetched to suggest that these stanzas have special significance in the poem: they outline the modern condition in which Pushkin finds himself, and for which he must discover a new language of representation. Thus stanza 5 indicates that the idyllic condition of peaceful existence has been disrupted: the old ways of life, symbolically represented by the image of the fishermen's submissive sail being violently destroyed. Pushkin alludes to a sudden storm sinking several ships. The abrupt change in weather links to the next stanza's description of poetic freedom: the free flight of fantasy has been seized and restrictive conditions imposed upon the poet, rendering futile his dream of escape. Furthermore, stanza 13's description of the tragic loss of an important poetic voice alludes to the irreplaceable void left in the world by Byron's death. To use Blanchot's terms, the poetic persona in "To the Sea" experiences loss of poetic speech. The traumatic experience conveyed in Pushkin's poem stems from perception of what Blanchot calls the recoil of silence: "To the surprise of common sense, the day this light goes out, the era without language will not arrive not because of silence but because of the recoil of silence, the rending of the silent density and, through this rending, the approach of a new sound. Nothing serious, nothing loud; scarcely a murmur, which will add nothing to the great tumult of cities from which we think to suffer" (Blanchot 2003: 218). Pushkin's poem well illustrates the state of awaiting the emergence of a new sound. His lyric persona uses the sea as interlocutor, whose responses are important for the creation of a new symbolic language. Stanza 13 implies that Byron's death threatens the world, since the voice of liberty and of powerful criticism of injustice has been silenced. It is clear from reading "To the Sea" that in Pushkin's eyes Byron stands out as a poet of liberty who turned the virtues of exile into creative impulses.

Pushkin is telling us that virtue and justice are threatened by the vigilant eyes of tyranny and the Enlightenment's legacy. In fact the publication of Stanza 13 of "To the Sea" was delayed for its explicit criticism of Russia's autocracy and censorship, and of the form of modernity mercilessly imposed upon the Russian people. According to Tsiavlovskaia's informative account of the publication history of "To the Sea" (and of other lyrics published with omissions during Pushkin's life) stanza 13 was first published in Evgenii Iakushkin's 1858 article "On the Publication of the Last Collected Works of A.S. Pushkin" (Tsiavlovskaia 1956: 193-98). The rest of "To the Sea" had first appeared in 1824 in the fourth issue of the literary almanach *Mnemosine* (*Мнемозина*) edited by Vladimir Odoevskii and Wil´gel´m Kiukhel´becker, who were close friends of Pushkin. The editors cut stanza 13's first four lines down to just the first line's fragment "The world became an empty place", and they used blank spaces in place of the remaining three and a half lines. The poem was published with an editorial explanation that the poet had left three and a half lines of dots in this space. Tsiavlovskaia believes that the editors wanted to protect their close friend, who was in exile in Odessa, and avoid him getting more deeply into trouble. Yet their act might be also seen as a political gesture, the inscribing of powerful symbolic meaning into the lines omitted from a Pushkin poem.

The editors may have partly intended to play with the reader by such an allusion to subversive comments of great significance the exiled Russian poet may have authored. The employment of such device - significant lines implied by dots — was not uncommon during the first half of the century. It was widely used either out of playfulness — a cat and mouse game with readers — or for political reasons. Thus Tsiavlovskaia talks of Pushkin's friend Iakushkin, who in 1858 in the journal *Bibliographical Notes* (*Bibliograficheskie zapiski*) had been the first to publish Pushkin's politically-charged lyrics, including stanza 13 of "To the Sea". Tsiavlovskaia comments that Iakushkin wanted to reveal Pushkin's real political views to Russian readers. Although Iakushkin's articles did bring to light much previously unpublishable material, Iakushkin still in places resorted to

Aesopian allegorical allusions, abrupt comments and suggestive blank spaces (Tsiavlovskaia 1956: 197).

Tsiavlovskaia also refers to Nikolai Lerner's survey of several publications of "To the Sea" which have distorted stanza 13. Lerner explained Pushkin's equation of tyranny with the Enlightenment like this: "Several editors of Pushkin's poem wanted to further revolutionise this stanza. In the meantime, Pushkin's purpose remains very clear: it is an expression of the old belief of Romanticism that 'Enlightenment' embodies superficial culture and amounts to a tissue of lies and pretence. Pushkin thinks the Enlightenment is just as hostile as tyranny to the benefits of true and essential freedom" (Lerner 1909: 514; quoted in Tsiavlovskaia 1956: 198).

Tsiavlovskaia's analysis of all the available drafts of "To the Sea" includes her summary of the compositional and semantic structures of the poem's final version. Tsiavlovskaia's analysis may be summarised as follows: stanzas 1-5 convey the theme of farewell to the sea; stanzas 6-7 talk of the lyric hero's unsuccessful attempt to escape his country and his strong passion for an unnamed person who restrained him; stanzas 8-9 weave into the narration a historical theme focusing on Napoleon and Byron, the two important cult figures of Pushkin's generation; stanza 13 reveals the chief idea of the whole poem, providing readers with the poet's outline of the totalitarian framework for his poetry's operation, and reflects in romantic vein on Pushkin's disillusionment with life; the last two stanzas contain the farewell scenes again.

Throughout her analysis of all draft and final versions of "To the Sea", Tsiavlovskaia stresses that stanza 13 is the most significant of all. She praises especially highly Pushkin's contrast in the stanza between "a drop of virtue" and the tyrant image. Tsiavlovskaia considers the stanza to be the most illuminating and insightful, in that it reveals Pushkin's worldview in 1824. Furthermore, she labels it the perfect poetic expression of a tragic idea (Tsiavlovskaia 1956: 207). Given that Tsiavlovskaia wrote her article immediately following Stalin's death, it is not surprising that she paid so much attention to Pushkin's philosophical meditation on the cost of Russia's modernisation that was associated with totalitarianism.

Tsiavlovskaia's statement on the importance of the theme of tyranny and the Enlightenment for Pushkin's worldview in 1824 is supported by Iurii Lotman's 1979 article on the gender of the word 'sea' («море») in "To the Sea". Lotman compellingly argues that Pushkin's occasional addresses to the sea which use the masculine gender (for example in such lines as «ты ждал, ты звал» and «ты взыграл, неодолимый») can be fully understood when read in conjunction with Pushkin's 1826 poem "To Viazemskii" («К Вяземскому»). "To Viazemskii" has the sea image in its opening line: "Thus the sea, the ancient tyrant..." («Так море, древний душегубец...»), and allegorically associates the sea with the god Neptune, who is characterised as simultaneously genius and tyrant. Pushkin sent his poem to Petr Viazemskii on 14 August 1826 as a response to Viazemskii's own poem "The Sea" («Море»). "To Viazemskii" has political overtones in that Pushkin is thought to have heard rumours (which proved false) that Nikolai Turgenev had been arrested in London and brought by boat to Russia on charges relating to his involvement in the Decembrist plot. It is worth looking at the complete text of "To Viazemskii" so that we may assess its links with Pushkin's "To the Sea":

> Так море, древний душегубец,
> Воспламеняет гений твой?
> Ты славишь лирой золотой
> Нептуна грозного трезубец.
> Не славь его. В наш гнусный век
> Седой Нептун земли союзник.
> На всех стихиях человек —
> Тиран, предатель или узник.
> (Pushkin, vol.2: 331)

> So the sea, ancient torturer of souls,
> Inspires your genius?
> You use your golden lyre
> To praise Neptune's fierce trident.
> Praise him not. In our disgusting century
> Grey Neptune is ally of Earth.
> At all elements there is man:
> Either tyrant, traitor or prisoner.

We next review Lotman's interpretation that "To Viazemskii" contains at least two key images of paramount importance for comprehending Pushkin's symbolic language and artistic psychology.

First, Lotman points to the strong mythopoetic tradition in European art for Neptune to personify the sea, which Pushkin used as subtext in "To the Sea". Since Neptune is a male god, Lotman thinks the neuter 'sea' ('море') and the masculine Neptune are interchangeable in Pushkin's lyrics. So Lotman argues compellingly that in "To the Sea" when Pushkin refers to the sea as a human being and uses the masculine gender, he is indicating Neptune. Pushkin's definition of the sea as 'torturer of souls' ('душегубец') in "To Viazemskii" also creates the image of an interlocutor of masculine gender. Notwithstanding Lotman's observation, "To the Sea" expresses the image of the sea in words of all three genders masculine, neuter and feminine ('ты звал', 'море', 'стихия'). The image of the sea appears to be transgressive, free of fixed gender characteristics. According to several linguistic studies (Peshkovskii 1938; Vinogradov 1972; Zubova 1999) the concept of gender is underdeveloped in Russian language; neuter nouns are especially favoured for various playful purposes by Russian poets wanting to create tension between the abstract and personified qualities of the Russian language. Aleksandr Vinogradov points out that neuter nouns often represent abstract images, such as deities: "We associate with the neuter gender some of the most abstract notions about objects that are not persons (such as 'being' and 'deity', for instance) [...]. The neuter gender functions in the language as an abstract form which represents impersonal objects" («Со средним родом сочетается самое отвлеченное представление о категории не-лица [сравни: *существо, божество*]. [...] Средний род выступает как отвлеченная форма обезличенной предметности») (Vinogradov 1972: 75). In the light of Vinogradov's observation, we can see how Pushkin used the grammatical notion of gender effectively to convey the transgressive qualities of the neuter gender.

Second, Lotman provides an interesting explanation regarding Pushkin's association of the sea with tyranny in both "To the Sea" and "To Viazemskii". Lotman demonstrates convincingly that Pushkin's vision of Neptune as an ally of the Earth alludes to the 1618 painting "The Union of Earth and Water" by Peter-Paul Rubens[1]. For this painting Rubens took several figures from classical mythology. Resting on his trident is the god of the sea, Neptune, representing Water, whilst Cybele (Mother of the Gods), with the horn of plenty in her hand, is Earth. The prosperous union of Earth and Water, bringing mankind wealth and plenty, is blessed by the goddess of Victory, heralded on a conch by Triton. The painting displays political overtones as an allegorical representation of the union between Antwerp and the River Scheldt, the mouth of which was at the time blocked by the Dutch in order to deprive Flanders of its important river passage to the sea. In the painting Rubens brings together myth and reality, nature and man, Antiquity and national history. Lotman's observations mean that "To the Sea" presents the union of earth and sea from the viewpoint of a man bitter and disillusioned about the lack of civil rights in his country. He is mourning the death of the great men Napoleon and Byron (Lotman 2000), because he sees them as icons of modernity. Lotman's explanation helps us to understand Pushkin's disenchantment with Russia's modernising reforms and his eagerness to use the power of the poetic voice to influence further progress towards a liberal state.

Pushkin's attitude in 1825 to Russia's political climate illustrates well Dixon's assessment that Russia's modernisation resulted in a paradox: "The more Russian rulers tried to modernise their state, the more backward their empire became" (Dixon 1999: 256). Dixon believes that by 1825 Russia had achieved much, such as the creation of the highly cultured and resourceful imperial elite and the successful use of serf labour in many areas of life. Yet, in Dixon's view, Russian state-led modernisation could not keep up with the pace of reforms elsewhere in Europe. Dixon writes: "The problem came when, elsewhere, new technology and the rise of the nation-state made Russia's dynastic empire look increasingly anachronistic and inflexible. Everywhere in Europe, the revolutionary occupation helped to stimulate nationalism; only in Russia did French troops serve to discredit the cause of rational reform. [...] In Russia, rationalism after 1825 was tarred with the brush of Decembrist subversion. Nikolaevan Russia was not a stagnant pool. Beneath its placid surface, reformist ideas circulated in the chancelleries of St Petersburg and the theological academies of the Orthodox church, just as much as in the underground circles of the radical intelligentsia. But the tsar himself had set his face against change" (Dixon 1999: 256-57). In "To the

Sea" Pushkin moulds himself into the image of a representative of the radical intelligentsia eager to circulate subversive ideas of liberty akin to western concepts of modernisation and civil society. Given that Pushkin was exiled to Odessa for his politically charged and revolutionary poetry, it comes as no surprise that Pushkin used that opportunity to mourn Byron's death from the standpoint of a political outcast inspired by Byron's liberal ideas and politically charged literary output.

Returning to Tsiavlovskaia's article, it quotes letters by several of Pushkin's friends responding to "To the Sea", from which it was evident to many of Pushkin's contemporaries that stanza 13 could not be published in Russia in 1824, because of its subversive message of bitter criticism of the Russian monarchy. Thus on 6 November 1824 Alexander Turgenev wrote to his brother Nikolai, who was abroad, as follows: "I will try to send you Pushkin's poetic address to the sea. It's wonderful; but it will remain hidden in his briefcase for a long, long time" (quoted in Tsiavlovskaia 1956: 192). Stanza 13 of "To the Sea" was memorised by Pushkin's friends and circulated among members of the radical intelligentsia opposed to Russia's absolutist monarchy. As Tsiavlovskaia puts it, stanza 13 acquired a life of its own: "It was circulated in hand-written copies and for many years it lived its underground life independently from the whole poem" (ibid).

Tsiavlovskaia, Lotman and Sandler have not provided us with an explanation of the word «добродетель» ('virtue') used in stanza 13 juxtaposed with the word 'tyrant'. This juxtaposition adds to our understanding of "To the Sea". It seems this line holds Pushkin's direct accusation of the Tsar who had exiled him to Odessa. The Odessa of Pushkin's time was very cosmopolitan, and so one stage removed from the concerns of the bulk of the Russian state. Dixon describes Odessa at the beginning of the nineteenth century as a city with a strong Italian community: "In Odessa (f.1794), where Italian — the *lingua franca* of the Mediterranean business community — was used on street signs, relative ease of access allowed an Italian opera company to begin in 1811 a series of annual visits broken by the war of 1812-14" (Dixon 1999: 174). In his letter to Viazemskii of 4 November 1823, Pushkin complained that in Odessa he had no access to Russian journals or books because it was too European: "Imagine, I have not yet read your article which outwitted our censors! This is how it feels to live like an Asian, without reading any journals. Odessa is a European city: that is why there are no Russian books here" («Вообрази, что я еще не читал твоей статьи, победившей цензуру! Вот каково жить по-азиатски, не читая журналов. Одесса город европейский – вот почему русских книг здесь и не водится») (Pushkin 1958, volume 10: 70). Pushkin's letter illuminates the extent of the poet's isolation from the centre of Russia's cultural and political life which he strived to influence by his verse. Thus it appears that stanza 13 of "To the Sea" was ascribed with the particular significance of political comment uttered by an exiled poet. It is evident that Pushkin wanted to draw attention to his poem and was eager to alert his friends to this empowering, politically significant gesture.

It is important to contextualise Pushkin's usage of the word «добродетель» ('virtue'). In juxtaposing the words 'virtue' and 'tyrant', Pushkin is alluding to the tragedies of Aleksandr Sumarokov that contain a vision of a civilised Russian monarch displaying virtue and compassion. Dixon explains the significance of the word 'virtue' to the Russian concept of civil society: "In the absence of constitutional restraints, Russians concentrated instead on the need for monarchical self-discipline. Believing that only virtue limited a monarch, Sumarokov set out to show in his tragedies that it was by behaving justly, with humility and virtue, that the sovereign identified himself as the representative of divine power on earth. As this example implies, virtue in the Russian context not only carried the secular associations of republican patriotism, but also acquired the Christian overtones of German Pietism, still prominent in the education of many Russian nobles" (Dixon 1999: 202-203). Furthermore, Dixon highlights the concept of virtue as a political principle of paramount importance to Russian intellectuals, including the two Decembrist groups. The Introduction to the Decembrists' Union Constitution of 1818 identified virtue as a desirable attribute of the populace and as an important pillar of the state: in the Decembrists' eyes, in the absence of virtue both the government and the legal framework would cease to exist (Dixon 1999: 203).

The concept of virtue had also greatly exercised Dante, who undoubtedly was on Pushkin's mind in Odessan exile, not least because of the strong admixture of Italian culture in everyday Odessan life. We know that Pushkin found Odessa very foreign and was amazed by its Italian atmosphere. Given this, it is impossible to imagine that Pushkin did not compare his situation to Dante's exile. Pushkin's declared his reverence for Dante's genius in several works. For example in "Mozart and Salieri" («Моцарт и Сальери», 1833) Pushkin writes:

> Мне не смешно, когда маляр негодный
> Мне пачкает Мадонну Рафаэля,
> Мне не смешно, когда фигляр презренный
> Пародией бесчестит Алигьери.
> (Pushkin 1957, volume 5: 360)

> I'm not amused when a bad painter
> Soils Rafael's Madonna before me,
> I'm not amused when a spiteful performer
> Dishonours Alighieri by parodying him.

But the most important of Pushkin's works to feature Dante, the one enabling us to recover a Dante subtext in "To the Sea", is the 1829 poem "Drums signal sunrise…" («Зорю бьют…»). It remains outside the Pushkin canon, but nevertheless caught the attention of both Tynianov[2] and Lotman. Here is the text of "Drums signal sunrise…":

> Зорю бьют… из рук моих
> Ветхий Данте выпадает,
> На устах начатый стих
> Недочитанный затих.
> Дух далече улетает.
> Звук привычный, звук живой,
> Сколь ты часто раздавался
> Там, где тихо развивался
> Я давнишнею порой.
> (Pushkin 1957, volume 3: 149)

> Drums signal sunrise…
> A fragile volume of Dante's poems
> Slips from my hands, the poem
> Half-uttered and half-read frozen on my lips.
> My spirit flies far away.

> The familiar sound, the living sound,
> How often you were heard
> Over there, where I grew
> Quietly a very long time ago.

Lotman thinks this poem resists conventional interpretation because it gives the impression of a raw flow of narration, akin to the narratives found in fiction (Lotman 1996: 155). For his own analysis Lotman borrows the tools of film criticism and uses two definitions of montage given by Tynianov and Boris Eikhenbaum. Tynianov explains: "The visible world is presented in film not as the real world as such but in accordance with some semantic links. Montage does not amount to the sequence of shots: it is a differentiated change of shots; but this is precisely why only those shots can replace each other that have something in common" (quoted in Lotman 1996: 155).

Lotman refers to "Drums signal sunrise…" as 'one single narrative-monologue' («единое повествование-монолог») that contains two parts: stanza 1 has five lines; stanza 2 has only four (Lotman 1999: 156). As was mentioned earlier, "To the Sea" also contains three five-line stanzas which impart dramatic overtones to the whole narrative and break the flow of narration, adding a sense of animation to the monologue. According to Lotman, while the first part of "Drums signal sunrise…" conveys transition into another state of being, the second part presents an enclosed segment of continuous duration (Lotman 1996: 159). Lotman's reading of this poem suggests that its main semantic focus is expressed in the line that mentions the living sound. It is subjugated to the main theme of the poem, which pivots around the idea that its life is manifested in the unity of the moving and sounding world (Lotman 1996: 159). Furthermore, Lotman considers this poem representative of Pushkin's late poetry which is often open-ended and suggestive, and enables a multiplicity of interpretations. Readers can thereby experience for themselves the situation described in the poem, and in their imagination perform a reading of Dante's poems for a whole night and then hear the sound of drums early in the morning. Lotman also points to the poem's mnemonic qualities, which allow readers to recall similar reading experiences of their own and to hear the interrupting sounds of early morning.

Most importantly, Lotman interprets Pushkin's use of discontinuous speech in "Drums signal sunrise…", which gives the impression of something unspoken and unfinished, as a sign of the realist mode of expression. Lotman maintains that such freedom of narration with respect to extra-textual links makes realist modes of narration more encompassing than romantic texts would have allowed: "Romantic disjunction of the text is created against the backdrop of the one-dimensional fixed system of meanings; realist disjunction creates a coherent continuous text that accommodates nevertheless various contextual readings. Contrary to popular belief, realist text is always more suggestive" (Lotman 1996: 162). Lotman emphasises two organising ideas in the poems, namely time and memory, that are related to Pushkin's growing understanding of the importance of cultural memory towards the end of the 1820s.

We can also say that "Drums signal sunrise…" portrays the process of reading Dante's poetry as an act of mystical experience and spiritual awakening. The reference to a wandering spirit and to the awakening sounds of the drums infuse the poem with awareness of the spiritual unity of the world and of the perpetual flow of creative opportunities. In fact, "Drums signal sunrise…" stands close to Bergson's metaphysical concepts of duration and creative evolution, mentioned above. The poem also prefigures the French Surrealists' attempts to produce a form of automatic writing which registers subconscious states of mind such as dreams and hallucinations. André Bréton in his "Manifesto of Surrealism" talks of spontaneous and free speech, and investigates the elements of shadow dialogue. In Bréton's opinion, automatic listening requires one to listen intensely to silences that make for the possibility of a shadow dialogue: "The forms of Surrealist language adapt themselves best to dialogue. Here two thoughts confront each other; while one is being delivered, the other is busy with it; but how is one busy with it?" (Bréton 1972: 34). It seems that the displacement of spirit described in "Drums signal sunrise…" signals a failure of symbolisation, because the sound of drums breaks the moment of silence. Pushkin understands silence as a precondition for articulation and as a form of unfolding of meanings; the lyric hero of the poem is portrayed as a reader caught in flux and parallel meanings.

The unravelling of the mystery of life in "Drums signal sunrise..." is easily comparable to Bréton's description of brief intervals that lead from experience to discourse as part of the human communication process. In his famous narrative *Nadya*, Bréton prompts readers to decipher life as a cryptogram. He suggests imagining a man in a museum at night examining the portrait of a woman: "Secret staircases, frames from which the paintings quickly slip aside and vanish (giving way to an archangel bearing a sword or to those who must forever advance) [...] we may imagine the mind's great adventure as a journey of this sort to the paradise of pitfalls" (Bréton: 133). Pushkin's reading of Dante is also entwined with the mind's journey triggered by the inspiring images of Dante's poetry. In "To the Sea" Pushkin formulates his responses to Byron in a more elaborate manner, inscribing his own traumatic experiences into the poem by the construction of a silence juxtaposed to noises of the sea. And Pushkin's responses to Byron's death seem to be more engaging and specific than his responses to Dante's poetry.

Close examination of "To the Sea" suggests multiple readings are possible, and I give two here. First, as in "Drums signal sunrise...", the surrounding world in "To the Sea" is portrayed as in flux, filled with changes and sounds needing translation into the language of poetry. The poem might be read as a manifestation of the theme of cultural memory. Thus its very title "To the Sea" might be seen as a challenge to the external forces of history that bring sudden changes to the world order and its system of cultural values. Second, "To the Sea" can be read as a poem containing the archetypal model of exilic writing. It evokes not only the names of Napoleon and Byron, but also establishes a direct analogy between Pushkin and Dante, the two poets in exile whose political and artistic views converged on so many occasions. The flight of the spirit described in the poem "Drums signal sunrise..." is associated with displacement, triggered by the desire to articulate evanescent moments of intensive engagement with Byron and his image of the sea. Indeed, "To the Sea" infiltrates into some intimate imaginary conversations with exiled spiritual leaders and poets in exile, and establishes a poetic genealogy of exilic writing.

Clearly, both Byron and Pushkin mastered exilic discourse through engagement with their favourite poet Dante. Oscar Kuhns, for example, maintains in his 1899 article that Byron spoke very highly of Dante in his works and correspondence, translated his *Divine Comedy* into English, and generally "often compared his life to Dante" (Kuhns 1899: 176-186). Byron talks of Dante with much reverence, for example as in these remarks: "Why there is gentleness in Dante beyond all gentleness when he is tender?", "Dante's heaven is all love and glory and majesty", and "I don't wonder at the enthusiasm of the Italians about Dante. He is the poet of liberty. Persecution, exile, the dread of a foreign grave, could not shake his principles" (quoted in Kuhns 1899: 179). In Byron's *Childe Harold* we find a passage (Canto LVII) in which Byron apostrophises Dante's native city as follows:

> Ungrateful Florence! Dante sleeps afar,
> Like Scipio, buried by the upbraiding shore;
> Thy factions, in their worse than civil war,
> Prescribed the bard whose name for evermore
> Their children's children would in vain adore
> With the remorse of ages; and the crown
> Which Petrarch's laureate brow supremely wore,
> Upon a far and foreign soil had grown,
> His life, his fame, his grave, though rifled – not thine own.
> (Byron 1987: 234-35)

Pushkin's expressions of missionary aspiration in "To the Sea" invite comparison with the poetic voice found in Dante's *Divine Comedy*. It is possible that Pushkin may have borrowed some views from Dante's masterpiece. In highlighting a pilgrim's experiences and spiritual journey, Dante aptly demonstrated that man can become eternal and transcend temporal and spatial boundaries. "To the Sea" expresses a similar theology of exile when it points to the Enlightenment and tyranny as oppressors of virtue: the concerns of Pushkin's lyric persona are intensified by the implied feeling of irrevocable self-exile from the humanity which he so harshly judges. Giuseppe Mazzotta writing on Boccacio's vision of Dante is relevant here: "The view of allegory as a common mode of signification for both poetry and theology elides the sharp distinction that Dante himself draws between the two in the *Convivio* and the *Epistle to Cangrande*, where he explicitly claims that the *Divine Comedy* is patterned on the paradigm of Exodus, the account of the Jews' exile and return from Egypt to the Promised Land. The relationship Boccacio perceives between theology and poetry stops short of Dante's insight to link joining theology and poetry of exile" (Mazzotta 1984: 648). Mazzotta maintains that the *Divine Comedy* offers numerous specific references to various experiences of exile. These include: political exile; exile as a spiritual condition; etymological meanings of exile; and the language of exile. Mazzotta concludes that "in the *Divine Comedy* the writing of poetry is tied in no ambiguous terms to the experience of exile" (Mazzotta 1984: 649) and links Dante's exilic discourse to the theological tradition that favours prophets. Mazzotta convincingly argues that Dante's notion of displacement does not amount to complete withdrawal from reality: "Exile is the condition in which his voice rises, but the displacement does not entail a complacent isolation within a world largely indifferent to the private truth the poet witnesses. Actually, the references to his own words as palpable and edible substance place the poem within the tradition of public utterances of the Biblical prophets. Like the prophets, Dante makes of exile a virtue and a necessary perspective from which to speak to the world and from which he can challenge the expectations and assumptions of the world; like the prophets, he also acknowledges that the truth he communicates, paradoxically, is that which alienates him further from the world he has already lost" (Mazzotta 1984: 650).

So Mazzotta's summary of Dante's exilic references in the *Divine Comedy* bring us to a closer understanding Pushkin's final stanza: like Dante, Pushkin speaks of an alienation from the world reinforced by his condition of exile, but at the same time the lyric persona of "To the Sea" turns this condition into a valuable experience and perspective that would allow him to contemplate secret thoughts and inner freedom. This position of independence seems expressed in terms strongly reminiscent of Dante's vision of exile and paradise: Pushkin dreams of maintaining his sense of contemplation, his private space of creative interaction in silent deserts and forests. References in "To the Sea" to blue waves suggest that Pushkin's own imaginary seascape in "To the Sea" overlaps with references to the natural features of the Black Sea on which Odessa stands and which was renowned for its navy-blue water. In the narrative flow of the poem he can only partly achieve his farewell to the sea itself, because the sea is a necessary contributor to the maintenance of his potential space emerging from dialogue with his interlocutor, comparable to the image of the m/other discussed earlier. His dialogue with predecessor exiles, such as Dante and Byron, merge with the sea image — and produces memorable sounds. We may imagine Pushkin's image of Dante's blue Adriatic Sea merges with the image of the Black Sea, since the reference to blue waves does bring the Adriatic to mind. But more importantly, the moment of farewell to the sea becomes a valuable experience helping view exile as a virtue contributing to the emergence of a private poetic space based on interacting discourses.

Tsvetaeva's dialogic poetic self and the Pushkin canon

Tsvetaeva's narrative poem "From the Seaside" («С моря», 1926) stands conspicuously close to the relational model of the mind discussed earlier: it features precisely the same interactive imaginary space described by Winnicott. The poem is conceived as a dream, featuring a seaside as a suitable playful space that enables Tsvetaeva to engage in a creative dialogue with Boris Pasternak: she compares them both to two children. This model of self touches upon the essential nerve of modernist art, especially the latter's avant-garde manifestation that needs to define itself as novel and experimental against a background of the established order.

Tsvetaeva's narrative poem might be seen as a re-fashioned version of the elegiac sublime, as found in Pushkin's "To the Sea" addressed to Byron as the romantic poet of exile. Tsvetaeva's long poem "New Year Greetings" («Новогоднее», 1927) also presents an attempt to develop the dialogic poetic self, which had been embryonically manifested in "To the Sea". For Simon Karlinsky this poem comprises "a combination of personal letter, epitaph and elegy" (Karlinsky 1985: 168). Karlinsky links it to other long poems by Tsvetaeva of the same period, such as the "Essay of a Room" («Попытка комнаты») and "Poem of the Air" («Поэма воздуха»), and he considers it "also a metaphysical meditation on the nature of life, death and time" (ibid.).

In addition to Karlinsky's observations, we can add that all these poems of Tsvetaeva are saturated with a strong dialogicity. They concern themselves with the Bakhtinian notion of surplus vision related to such concepts as hybrid construction of identity, and sidelong-gazing word; these concepts imply a search for open-endedness, and unpredictability of being. The poems reinforce the fundamental Bakhtinian presupposition of two consciousnesses as the basic condition for an aesthetic act. It appears that in "New Year Greetings" Tsvetaeva uses Pushkin's apostrophe and a dialogue with the living poetic spirit of the deceased Byron, in order to construct her own dialogue with the deceased Rainer-Maria Rilke.

In fact, a large corpus of Tsvetaeva's oeuvre is occupied by encounters with spirits of dead poets; several encounters feature imaginary meetings of Tsvetaeva's spirit with her future readers and followers. Examples are found in the poems "You, so similar to me, are passing by…" («Идешь на меня похожий…») and "To you after a hundred years" («Тебе — через сто лет»). As Catherine Ciepiela compellingly argues, "Tsvetaeva's writing is openly, almost programmatically apostrophic" (Ciepiela 1996: 422). In another comment Ciepiela maintains that "Tsvetaeva's poetry is strongly inclined toward the discursive present" (ibid). Given that the apostrophic poem "is not narrating anything, but is to be the happening" (Culler 1977: 67), such a poem may be viewed in terms of Bakhtin's notion of outsidedness and of Winnicott's concept of potential space enabling an interaction of several identities.

With the apostrophic nature of Tsvetaeva's poetry, it is not surprising to see that in her autobiographical essay "My Pushkin" («Мой Пушкин», 1936) she singles out Pushkin's "To the Sea" as her favourite text for its influence upon her poetic self. Tsvetaeva's description of her childhood experiences which were linked to her reading "To the Sea" is saturated with allusions to Pushkin's exile and to the rich multiplicity of lyrical voices woven into the poem. She animates Pushkin's text and turns it into a space where several voices are engaged. However, in Tsvetaeva's essay the engagement of two poets — the teacher and his disciple — does not constitute an act of sympathetic understanding to produce a fusion of "I" and "Thy". The engagement presents, rather, an excess of vision, in terms akin to the dialogic mentality described in Bakhtin's article "Author and Hero in Aesthetic Activity" («Автор и герой в эстетической деятельности»). Bakhtin here sees the self as something situated in time and space in a unique and unrepeatable manner, resulting in a surplus of seeing. By this he means that our uniqueness in time and space creates an inimitable way of looking at the world. Bakhtin writes, "This always present *excess* of my seeing, knowing, and possessing in relation to any other person is founded in the uniqueness and irreplaceable nature of my place in the world: since only I — the one-and-only I — occupy in a given set of circumstances this particular place at this particular time having all other persons outside me" («Это всегда наличный по отношению ко всякому другому человеку *избыток* моего видения, знания, обладания обусловлен единственностью и незаместимостью моего места в мире: ведь на этом месте в это время в данной совокупности обстоятельств я единственный нахожусь — все другие люди вне меня») (Bakhtin 1979: 23). This excess of seeing depends on our incarnation in time and space, the one manifested in relation to the other. Bakhtin thinks that if we do not use our surplus relationally, all that would remain would be our own limited perspective on the world.

The Tsvetaeva passages describing her engagement with Pushkin's "To the Sea" perfectly illuminate how to use Bakhtin's surplus of seeing for artistic purposes. Tsvetaeva based expression of her poetic self on the dialogic consciousness that ascribes Pushkin's text with magic power: "*To the Sea*. The whole of the past summer of 1902 I transcribed it from my textbook into my self-made notebook. Why was it necessary to have another copy of it in my notebook when I already had this poem in the textbook? In order to carry it with me always in my pocket, in order to walk with the Sea at Pachevo and take it with me to the tree stumps to read, so it would be *mi-ine*, so it would feel as if I wrote it myself" («*К Морю*. Все предшествовавшее лето 1902 года я переписывала его из хрестоматии в самосшивную книжку. Зачем в книжку, раз есть в хрестоматии? Чтобы всегда носить с собой в кармане, чтобы с Морем гулять в Пачево и на пеньки, чтобы *моее* было, чтобы сама я сама написала») (Tsvetaeva 1984: 331). In fact, Tsvetaeva re-enacts here the desire Pushkin inscribed in "To the Sea" to take with him everywhere the poetic spirit of Byron's poetry with its distinctive images of sea voyages and apostrophic poetic pronouncements.

Tsvetaeva replaces Pushkin's images of silent deserts and forests with tree-stumps and Pachevo, a village named specifically. Her personal mythology reveals the dialogic consciousness common to any creative act which strives to be unique, but is nevertheless dependent upon a dialogue with predecessors. Tsvetaeva's reading of Pushkin's "To the Sea" reveals her profound and intimate bond with the poem which gave her scope for a personal mythology and which shaped her poetic voice. The poem now appears for Tsvetaeva as a place for dwelling and an invitation to an imaginary voyage. Repeated encounters with the sea and imaginary conversations with Byron, which Pushkin conveyed in "To the Sea", are mimicked in Tsvetaeva's essay. Tsvetaeva features an implied conversation with Pushkin the person and Pushkin the poet. Tsvetaeva's "My Pushkin" is proof that "To the Sea" provides readers with a rich experience of active engagement with the several poetic voices inscribed in the poem. One can doubt the story of Tsvetaeva being actively engaged in reading this particular Pushkin at a very early age, because we know that she wrote "My Pushkin" in emigration in 1937, as a 45 year-old poet of significance. Her motive for writing such an account of reading "To the Sea" gives a useful insight into her own artistic mind: she favoured apostrophic and open-ended poetic speech. It is also possible to see in this essay Tsvetaeva's desire to present herself in the image of 'child of the sea', an image very dear to Byron's heart. By engaging in 1937 with Pushkin's "To the Sea", Tsvetaeva creates her own poetic genealogy of the poet in exile which stems from the exilic experiences of Dante and runs through Byron and Pushkin.

In fact, in "New Year Greetings" («Новогоднее») Tsvetaeva brings Pushkin and Dante together: in apostrophic writing mode she questions the desire to secretly escape, which Pushkin expressed in "To the Sea". She understands it not as a literal desire to leave Russia, but as an expression of the poet's desire to escape the imperfections of a mundane life that interrupt the free flow of creativity. This type of escape was also expressed in Pushkin's 1834 poem "It's time, my friend, it's time!" («Пора, мой друг, пора!») which can be seen as Pushkin's definition of paradise as the desire to escape into pure aesthetics:

> Пора, мой друг, пора! Покоя сердце просит —
> Летят за днями дни, и каждый час уносит
> Частичку бытия, а мы с тобой вдвоем
> Предполагали жить... И глядь — как раз — умрем.
> На свете счастья нет, но есть покой и воля.
> Давно завидная мечтается мне доля —

Давно, усталый раб, замыслил я побег
В обитель дальную трудов и чистых нег.
(Pushkin 1957: 278)

It's time, my friend, it's time! My heart requires peace.
Day after day flies past, and every hour takes away
A small part of life; and I and you
Hoped to live... And look - just now - we will die.
This world holds not happiness, but peace and will.
Long I have been dreaming of another lot:
Long ago I, a tired slave, thought to take flight
Into a far dwelling of labour and pure joyful moments.

Pushkin's manuscript of "It's time, my friend, it's time!" contains an outline of the poem in which he clearly explains his vision of a home, and of a happiness encompassing friends and family. The poem does not express the idea of escape into pure aesthetics, but rather the idea of longing for an idyllic traditional form of life, with pastoral pleasures and an autonomous creative existence, free of political pressures and urban theatricality.

Pushkin's vision of 'poetic dwelling' substitutes for the idea of 'traditional dwelling' that was becoming displaced within modern urban landscapes. In 1834 when "It's time, my friend, it's time!" was written, Pushkin dreamed of resigning from the civil service in order to settle in the country; but the Tsar did not grant his wish. In the 1830s the poet was trapped in the torment of a junior civil servant working in the archives in Petersburg. Pushkin writes: "Youth does not need to have a sense of 'being at home'; mature age is horrified by the prospect of loneliness. Blessed is the person who finds a female friend — then he can go *home*. Oh, will it be possible for this to happen soon? So that I could take my dwelling into the country — family, love, etc. — religion, death" («Юность не имеет нужды в at home, зрелый возраст ужасается *своего* уединения. Блажен, кто находит подругу — тогда удались он *домой*. О, скоро ли перенесу я мои пенаты в деревню — поля, сад, крестьяне, книги; труды поэтические — семья, любовь etc. — религия, смерть») (Pushkin 1957, volume 3: 521). The patriarchal dwelling of which Pushkin writes in the manuscript of "It's time, my friend, it's time!" may already have been perceived by Pushkin and his contemporaries as an unattainable ideal. One might therefore suggest that it was Pushkin's dream of a quiet life in the 1830s that further alienated him from Petersburg's social and cultural environment. This alienation is comparable to the exilic condition, since the poet felt distanced from the organic life and natural environment for which he had developed a strong affinity, prior to his starting family life. So, poetry and dwelling merged in Pushkin's imagination once again, as they had during his exile in Odessa in 1824.

Poetry and dwelling are brought together in some of the ideas of Heidegger developed by Lefebvre in his study of the country and the city. Such an approach perceives poetry-writing in terms analogous to the building of a dwelling, and nicely illuminates Pushkin's image of escape into the higher realm of contemplation and creativity. The approach also brings together Pushkin and Russian modernist poetry, inasmuch as Pushkin's poetry might itself be seen as an object woven into the poetic self and into the poetic dwelling constructed in their poetry. Yet the most important point of convergence of Pushkin's worldview with the views of Russian modernists, especially those of avant-garde views, lies in the understanding of self in a Bakhtinian sense, namely in relation to others. Pushkin's merger of ethics and aesthetics comes close to Bakhtinian dialogic consciousness.

We shall here take a small digression to consider Lotman's assertion that Pushkin departs from the vision of 'natural man' found in the writings of Jean-Jacques Rousseau. According to Rousseau, natural man lives by himself, having need of others only in relation to agricultural production and property; he does not possess a developed sense of justice or ethics; and he is free of passions. Lotman maintains that Pushkin's long narrative poem "Gypsies" («Цыгане») is strongly influenced by the ethical thinking of the French materialist philosophers. As Lotman explains, Pushkin's perceives happiness and dwelling in terms similar to the relational psychological model discussed above. Lotman sums up Pushkin's views as follows: "Man is born for collective existence. Collective cohabitation is a natural type of existence. People enter society on their own will and for their own benefit. Relationships between parents and children, on the one hand, and between married people, on the other hand, are founded not on duty but on love and realisation of mutual benefit" («Человек рожден для общежития. Общественное существование и есть 'естественное'. Люди вступают в общество добровольно и для собственной пользы. Отношения между родителями и детьми, с одной стороны, и супругами, с другой, основаны не на долге, а на любви и собственной выгоде каждого» (Lotman 1996: 604). In the light of Lotman's explanation, it becomes understandable that the type of ideal dwelling suggested by Pushkin's "It's time, my friend, it's time!..." is based on the relational model of mind. For Pushkin, creativity is entwined with interaction with others, allowing the poet to see himself through the eyes of the other.

The apostrophic mode of expression used in "It's time, my friend, it's time!" does imply a direct dependence upon the other for a realisation of the complete self. Bakhtin, in "Author and Hero", says that if two persons look at each other, the one can see aspects of the other, and of the space occupied by the other, that the other does not and cannot see. Thus this dynamic is relational: since I can see things about the other that he cannot see, so he can see things about me that I cannot. Michael Holquist aptly sums up Bakhtin's thesis: "The dialogical paradox of this formulation is that *every* human being occupies such a determinate place in existence: we are all unique, but we are never alone. Bakhtin's enterprise is founded on the situatedness of perception and thus the uniqueness of the person, but it abhors all claims to oneness. It is not only the case that from my unique situation in space and time I am able to see things you do not: it is also — and simultaneously — the case that from the vantage of *your* uniqueness you can see things that *I* cannot" (Holquist: xxvi). Pushkin's statement, that happiness is replaced in this world by will and peace, does imply a unique vantage point of the contemplation needed for creativity and realisation of the poetic self through work and leisure.

More importantly for the present discussion, Pushkin situates the space of contemplation outside the boundaries of everyday urban life, suggesting thereby that poetry is displaced by modern, rationally organised spaces. Lefebvre explains that the poet constructs the dwelling of the human in such a way as to equate the dwelling to the being in man: "It could be, says Heidegger, that our dwellings that lack poetry, our inability to take the measure of man and his heart, spring from a strange kind of excess: a rage for measurement and calculation" (Lefebvre 2003: 122). Lefebvre refers both to Gastón Bachellard and Heidegger in order to highlight the modern condition that replaces the concept of the traditional house and patriarchal dwelling with the technologically advanced and rationally organised spaces that push away what is required for continuity and contemplation. Lefebvre continues: "The strange, oneiric, unique house Bachellard tells us about, this house that brings together in its unity of the dream the dispersed fragments of the Ego, is a traditional house, a patriarchal dwelling [*demeure*], packed with symbols and full of attics and mysterious concerns! The philosopher could say of this house: 'It is one of the strongest forces for integrating man's thought, his memories and dreams... It keeps man safe through earthly and heavenly storms... It is body and soul.' This house is disappearing. We no longer have the skills or capacity to build houses like it. [...] Heidegger now shows us a world ravaged by technology, that through its ravages leads towards another dream, another (as yet unperceived) world. He warns us: a lodging built on the basis of economic and technological dictates is as far removed from dwelling as the language of machines from poetry" (ibid.).

These observations of poetry's displacement into isolated rural places of contemplation gives us insight into Tsvetaeva's autobiographical essay "My Pushkin". The essay contains an account of her copying Pushkin's "To the Sea" on numerous occasions in her countryside house. She interprets Pushkin's expression "free element" as a reference to poetry, emphasising that her favourite part of the poem is the line "In vain my soul strived to reach there" («Вотще рвалась душа моя»). Tsvetaeva correctly senses that this line omits the name of the space towards which the lyric hero of the poem reaches, since the verb 'to strive' («рваться») is used with the preposition 'to' and requires the noun's dative case. She creates her own mythology and ascribes a double meaning to 'alas' («вотще»), presenting it as a symbolic allusion to a sacred space functioning as poetic dwelling. This opens possibilities of symbolisation triggered by reading the text anew, so to speak, from a child's viewpoint. Tsvetaeva writes: "Alas means over there. Where to? Where I want to be. On the other bank of the river Oka, which I cannot ever reach, because the river Oka is between us; and in La Chaux de Fonds, in my aunt's childhood where a guard walks at night with a piece of wood; [...] and where everyone switches off the lights; and if they don't switch the lights off, a doctor comes or children are put into prison; *alas* means getting another life with another family, without Asya, so I could be the favourite daughter; perhaps, I could be called Katya or Rogneda, or perhaps, a boy named Alexander" («Вотще — это туда. Куда? Туда, куда и я. На тот берег Оки, куда я никак не могу попасть, потому что между нами Ока, еще в La Chaux de Fonds, в тетино детство, где по ночам ходит сторож с доской [...] — и все тушат огни, а если не тушат, то приходит доктор или сажают в тюрьму; *вотще* — это в чужую семью, где я буду одна без Аси и самая любимая дочь, с другой матерью и с другим именем — может быть, Катя, а может быть, Рогнеда, а может быть, сын Александр») (Tsvetaeva 1984, vol.2: 332). Tsvetaeva associates this space with pristine existence and pre-symbolic language. She talks of a child-like state of androgynous identity, suggesting that definitions imposed upon readers by language and the social order create unnecessary obstacles for one's true development. She says, "My God! How much a person loses when he/she obtains gender qualities; when such words as *alas, over there, that, there* obtain names; when all the blueness of longing and of the river turns into specific forms of a face, nose, eyes [...]. And how severely we are mistaken when we name this as *that*, and how were we *not* mistaken then!" («Боже мой! Как человек теряет с обретением пола, когда *вотще, туда, то, там* начинает называться именем, из всей синевы тоски и реки становится лицом, с носом, с глазами [...]. И как мы люто ошибаемся, называя это — *тем*, и как *не* ошибались тогда!») (Tsvetaeva 1984, vol.2: 332). Tsvetaeva's model of symbolic construction of the world illustrates well the relational psychoanalytical theories discussed above. More importantly, it is difficult not to notice that Tsvetaeva introduces into her rendering of Pushkin's "To the Sea" the concept of the obstacle that hinders the organic world's natural evolution. She gives a very modernist twist to Pushkin's idea of the negative effects of the Enlightenment and tyranny on virtue.

A true modernist writer in search of a style, Tsvetaeva in "My Pushkin" depicts herself as a disciple of Pushkin wanting to grasp the essence of his writing through copying. She makes a point of producing several self-made books containing her hand-written copies of "To the Sea". It seems she was trying to relive, many times, the experience portrayed in the poem through her own performance of this experience of farewelling favourite objects.

Most importantly, however, Tsvetaeva presents Pushkin's text as a living word, as a text impregnated with real potential for re-enactment and multiple readings that allow aesthetic experience to be reintroduce into the world. Thus she demonstrates how a child would read such a text: "It was the apogee of my inspiration. As soon I started reading 'Farewell, the sea...', tears were pouring out of my eyes. His promise to the sea 'Farewell, the sea! I will not forget...' is like the promise not to forget I make to that my birch tree, my hazelnut grove, my Christmas tree, whenever I leave Tarusa for Moscow" («Это был апогей вдохновения. С 'Прощай же, море...' начинались слезы. 'Прощай же, море! Не забуду...' — ведь он же это морю — обещает, как я — моей березе, моему орешнику, моей елке, когда уезжаю из Тарусы») (Tsvetaeva 1984, vol.2: 333).

Tsvetaeva's descriptions of her childhood experiences of reading "To the Sea" seem double-edged. On the one hand, they pose an important question of control: does the text control the reader, or vice versa? If we accept the feminist angle that a text differently affects a female reader, since a male reads the text as a meeting ground of the personal and the universal, then Tsvetaeva's "My Pushkin" reveals the dynamics of the woman reader's encounter with androcentric literature at its best. Pushkin's text offers Tsvetaeva the option of adopting the identity of a boy, Alexander, moulded in the image of the canonical poet Pushkin whom she requires as her model. From this we may see that Tsvetaeva is fully aware that the text can control the reader and can lead female readers to think like men. She finds gender-predetermined reading an obstacle. Her thinking anticipates recent feminist critical concerns. For example Fetterley writes that "the cultural reality is not the emasculation of men by women, but the *immasculation* of women by men. As readers and teachers and scholars, women are taught to think as men, to identify with a male point of view, and to accept as normal and legitimate a male system of values, one of whose central principles is misogyny" (Fetterley 1978: xx). At the same time, Tsvetaeva recognises that the power of male text creates a false consciousness into which both women and men have been socialised. In Schweickart's opinion, however, "*certain* (not all) male texts merit a dual hermeneutic: a negative hermeneutic that discloses their complicity with patriarchal ideology, and a positive hermeneutic that recuperates the utopian movement — the authentic kernel — from which they draw a significant portion of their emotional power" (Schweickart 1986: 43-44).

Tsvetaeva employs positive hermeneutics by uncovering an empowering mythos in the image of a flying magic figure that strongly resembles the image of Baba-Iaga, an explosively mobile magic woman who breaks the boundaries of restrictive society. The narrator of "My Pushkin", who is reading the final stanza of "To the Sea", develops a highly whimsical vision of Pushkin as a magic flying creature who carries the whole sea above his head and within his body: "And here is a vision: Pushkin who carries across and transports above my head — the whole sea, which he also carries within himself (filled with you); so everything inside him is blue as if his whole body is placed inside an oval egg that he also carries within himself. Like Pushkin, whose monument on Tverskoy Boulevard holds the whole sky, this one will hold the whole sea and pour it over the desert, so it will turn into a sea" («И вот — видение: Пушкин, переносящий, проносящий над головой — все море, которое еще и внутри него (тобою полн), так что и внутри у него все голубое — точно он весь в огромном до неба хрустальном продольном яйце, которое еще и в нем. Как тот Пушкин на Тверском бульваре, который держит на себе все небо, так этот перенесет на себе все море — в пустыню и там прольет его — и станет море») (Tsvetaeva 1984, vol.2: 334).

We may infer that, if in "My Pushkin" Tsvetaeva identifies the sea with the poetic element and free flow of speech, then her image of Pushkin must be representing the poet as the living word, a creative principle per se, and one that could take any form. At the same time, in "My Pushkin" — written in the year of widespread celebrations in Russia and abroad of the anniversary of Pushkin's death — Tsvetaeva demonstrates her ability to recognise that androcentric texts held her in sway. She is aware of her essential role in the process of reading for the formation of a female readership. This dualistic nature of her narrative creates a powerful dynamic between the two options: either submit to the power of the text, or control the experience of reading it. Certainly, Tsvetaeva's autobiographical essay displays all the features of feminist consciousness and commitment to emancipatory praxis.

The image in "My Pushkin" of Pushkin holding the sea enclosed in an egg links to the Hellenistic tradition of creation. Formally, the tradition includes three myths of creation: as expressed in Homer's *Iliad*; by the divinity Orpheus; and by the epic poet Hesiod. The myths share a common outline. In the beginning was Night (Nyx) in the form of a black-winged bird. Nyx was impregnated by Wind and laid a silver Egg in the gigantic knee of Darkness (Erevos). From Egg sprang Wind's son Eros, a god of cosmic love with golden wings, also known as Protogonos and Phanes. Eros lit up the whole Cosmos, everything previously hidden in the silver Egg. Up above was a void named Sky or Aether or the *primordial radiation* (synehes ousia), known also as Chaos (void) or the *vacuum of space* (meriste ousia). In equating Pushkin to the god Eros, Tsvetaeva accesses her creative role as a woman reader to employ a new strategy for reading the Pushkin canon. She thereby affirms her subjectivity, demonstrating that Pushkin's texts can become actualised only through the activity of the reader.

In fact, by inventing a child narrator for "My Pushkin", Tsvetaeva produces a sort of therapeutic analysis of Pushkin's texts, "To the Sea" included, in the way of a feminist reading. She presents herself as a reader recalling her natural reading of a male text to undermine the androcentric power it imposed on readers. Clearly, Tsvetaeva hopes other women will recognise themselves in her story of reading Pushkin's poems and join her attempt to resist emasculation. Similar aspirations are also expressed in Tsvetaeva's 1928 poem "Naiad" («Наяда») where Tsvetaeva regards gender as an obstacle blocking true love and soul-mate friendship:

> Проходи стороной,
> Тело вольное, рыбье!
> Между мной и волной,
> Между грудью и зыбью —
>
> Третье, злостная грань
> Дружбе гордой и голой:
> Стопудовая дань
> Пустяковине: полу.

Узнаю тебя, клин,
Как тебя ни зови:
В море — ткань, в поле —тын,
Вечный третий в любви.
(Tsvetaeva 1984, vol.1: 287-8)

Stay away from me,
Free body of fish!
Between me and the wave,
Between my chest and the ripple

There is the third one, the wretched
Border that divides proud and naked friendship.
It is a heavy token of respect
To a trivial thing: gender.

I recognise you, stick in between,
Whatever you're called:
In the sea it's fabric, in the field it's fence,
The eternal third person in love.

The lyric persona in "Naiad" talks of her self-consciousness at her birfurcated self. Unlike the lyric hero depicted in Pushkin's "To the Sea", she finds herself swimming in the sea. So Tsvetaeva's poem further developed Pushkin's idea of portable potential space and presented it as a communicative situation that is always dialogic. As a female writer/reader, Tsvetaeva finds herself reading Russian canonical texts both as a man and as a woman, being unable to come back to the natural way of perceiving the poetic speech and symbolic order in which she has to participate. Her longing for the natural self and its uncultured body stands close to the attempts of some of her contemporaries, such as Evreinov, Isadora Duncan and Vassilii Nezhinskii, to search for something beyond the confines of their cultural environment.

Tsvetaeva's "Naiad" draws on Pushkin's references to the elements and the impersonal forces of destruction, in order to articulate violence and soma and the clash between the somatic and the semantic. The paronomasia in stanza 1 that juxtaposes such words as 'free' and 'wave' ('вольное' and 'волной') highlights the clash between the external and internal worlds, recalling the powerful images in Pushkin's "To the Sea" of boats and submissive fishermen as victims of historical change and external forces. Tsvetaeva interweaves into her poem some rawly violent images that refer to White Army battles in the Crimea, reminding her readers that violence and soma interact outside artistic texts through various types of social performance in real life. In fact, the lyric hero in "Naiad" appears to be self-fashioned in the clothes of a performer-poet who acts as a medium for organic art: the act of swimming in the sea and speaking to waves becomes analogous to Isadora Duncan's dancing, which at the time offer a naturalistic approach to artistic endeavours. Tsvetaeva's engagement with the sea appears to be more direct and more intimate than the situations described in Pushkin's "To the Sea". Tsvetaeva seems have an affinity with the maternal image of the sea found in Pushkin's text. This privileged position empowers the speaker of "Naiad" to address issues relating to cultural and natural people, and to the gender-oriented reading of poetry.

In correspondence with Pasternak, Tsvetaeva says her favourite mode of communication is otherworldly, the seeing of another person in a dream and conversing to him through dreams (Tsvetaeva 1972: 271). So it is not surprising to see Tsvetaeva resorting in her long poem "From the Seaside" («С моря», 1926) to a playful mode of poetic communication, which she identifies as dreaming together. Tsvetaeva's interest in the subconscious language of communication stands very close to Bréton's experiments of automatic writing. "From the Seaside" was written in the period when Louis Aragon and other surrealists were engaged in a war against cubism. Thus Aragon in his book *The Peasant of Paris* (*Le Paysan de Paris*) — which was written mostly in 1918-20 and published in 1926 — complained that wherever the marvellous is dispossessed, the abstract moves on. Aragon sought out the lairs where marvels had taken refuge after being expelled from the mechanised and rationalised city. Surrealists dismissed both abstraction and realism, thinking that while realism reduced the world to commodities, the abstract world was desolate and uninhabitable. The main enteprise of the surrealists was constantly to make the ordinary objects of everyday life quite sacred. Soupault, who joined Bréton in various experiments in automatic writing, saw in surrealism a demonstration of freedom and liberation of mind. Soupault's view of mental development differed from Freud; as Peter Conrad notes, "In psychoanalysis, the id surrenders to the ego's tutelage, and the ego in its turn learns to respect the moral imperatives of the superego. Surrealism, subverting reason and flouting morality, licenses the ribald id" (Conrad 1998: 303).

In "From the Seaside" Tsvetaeva portrays her imaginary seaside encounter with Pasternak: she writes to him in Moscow a letter from St Gilles-sur-Vie; toying with the idea they can communicate in a transitory space of dreams. The apostrophic "From the Seaside" is infused with metatextual qualities; but the poetic dialogue with Pasternak is constructed in the form of an imaginary game that strongly resembles Pushkin's imaginary dialogue with Byron portrayed in "To the Sea". To borrow Ciepiela's words aimed at a different Tsvetaeva poem, it is possible to state that "Tsvetaeva's poem dramatizes the act of apostrophe, unfolding its paradoxical logic" (Ciepiela 1996: 423). As Ciepiela aptly points out, "Tsvetaeva finds that her apostrophe ('giving myself through verse') overwhelms any possible response; it is necessarily unanswerable" (Ciepiela 1996: 426). Taking Ciepiela's observation further, I would suggest that the goal expressed in "From the Seaside", to write a three-minute letter to Pasternak, has striking similarities with the experiments of Bréton and Soupault in automatic writing, which amounted to taking dictation from their pooled unconsciousness. In the same manner as Aragon insisted that a single image could playfully annihilate the entire universe, Tsvetaeva subverts the whole tradition of letter writing by pretending to record a hurried stream of thoughts and images that resembles intensive telepathic contact:

Сон три минуты
Длится. Спешу.

С кем – и не гляну! –
Спишь. Три минуты.
Чем с Океана –
Долго – в Москву-то!

Молниеносный
Путь запасной.

Из своего сна
Прыгнула в твой.
Снюсь тебе. Четко?
Глядко? Почище
Чем за решеткой
Штемпельной. Писчей –

Стою? Почтовой –
Стою? – Красно?
Честное слово
Я, не письмо.
[…]
Всех объегоря –
Скоропись сна!
Вот тебе с моря –
Вместо письма!
(Tsvetaeva 1990: 542-43)

The dream lasts
For three minutes. I'm in a hurry.

It's better than sending something
From the Ocean that takes time to reach Moscow!

It's as speedy as lightening
To use this reserved route.
I jumped from my dream
Into yours.

Are you seeing me in your dream? clearly?
Without difficulties? I look cleaner
Than the image behind the bars
Of the post stamp. Have I the value

Of writing paper? Or of letter
Paper? – Do I look beautiful?
Honestly, I'm not
A letter!
[…]

Having fooled everyone –
This is swiftness of automatic writing of dream! –
I could offer it to you –
Instead of a letter!

Tsvetaeva makes a pun on the two meanings of 'письмо' signifying the concepts of 'letter' and 'writing'. It resembles a surrealist-like playful gesture, especially because the poetic message is defined in the poem as "a heap of play" («горстка игры»). Most of the poem's lines are short and have just two stresses. They give the impression of a stream of unconsciousness hurriedly recorded. Most importantly, the lyric heroine in "From the Seaside" presents her interlocutor with an imaginary gift — a starfish. In her eyes, this object brings together the French Atlantic coast at St Gilles-sur-Vie and Moscow, a transgression of all ideological and geographical boundaries, since the image of the red star used in Soviet iconography for ideological purposes is stripped in Tsvetaeva's poem of its political connotations:

Но припасла тебе напоследки
Дар, на котором строй.
Море роднит с Москвой,

Советороссию с Океаном.
[...]
И доложи мужикам в колосьях,
Что на шлыке своем краше носят
Красной – не верь: вражду
Классов! — морей звезду!
(Tsvetaeva 1990: 546)

 I've prepared for you towards the end
 A gift, which holds a space.
 The sea brings me closer to Moscow.
 [...]
 It binds together Soviet Russia with the Ocean.
 [...]
 Do report to the peasants,
 Who wear stars on their hats
 That it is not the red star of class hatred,

Don't believe it is the red star. They have a more
Beautiful star which comes from the sea!

Karlinsky, in his brief analysis of Tsvetaeva's "From the Seaside", maintains that the poem stems from Tsvetaeva's correspondence with Pasternak at the end of May 1926, in which she talked about Pushkin's "To the Sea". Karlinsky writes: "During four days from May 23 to 26, Tsvetaeva wrote Pasternak a long, lyrical letter about her yearning for a dream encounter with him that would take them back to their respective childhoods and about her inability to appreciate the ocean as Pushkin had in his poem 'To the Sea', which she had loved as a child, the ocean which Pasternak has described in his 'The Year 1905', which she had recently read" (Karlinsky 1985: 165). Indeed Tsvetaeva, in her letters from this period, refers several times to the images of the sea found in the poetry of Pasternak and Pushkin. Yet it is clear from these letters that Tsvetaeva was searching for her own image of the sea and for a way to express her creative responses as reader and poet to Pasternak's long narrative poem "1905".

In one of those letters of Tsvetaeva, first published only recently, it is revealed that Tsvetaeva's confession of creating her own poem about the sea can now be seen as creating a poetic dwelling based on her dialogue with Pasternak. This letter is located in the Tsvetaeva archive, along with a draft of "From the Seaside". Tsvetaeva says in the letter: "B. I will fall in love with the sea when I'll start writing it, when I will concern myself with it, when I will grasp its essence. You ascribe to the word 'contemporary' all the meanings that I ascribe to the concept 'outside any temporality'. You are more than anyone else full of conditional acceptance of reality. I have my own image of the sea that belongs to both of us" («Б. Море я полюблю, когда начну его писать, займусь им, вникну в него. Ты в слово современный вкладываешь все, что я во вневременный. Ты более чем кто-либо оговорочен. У меня мое море, наше с тобой.») (Tsvetaeva 2004: 220). Tsvetaeva's comment suggests that she does not treat her description of the sea as purely mimetic: it is clear that her image has dialogic and metatextual overtones. In the words of Karlinsky, "From the Seaside" is a "long, semi-humorous poem [...] about a dream encounter, its mode is realistic and also strongly satirical, the barbs being aimed at Soviet censorship of literature and the journal *On Guard*, which was denouncing both Pasternak and Tsvetaeva" (Karlinsky 1985: 165-66). Thus Tsvetaeva's reference in this poem to censors eager to destroy true creative impulses evokes Pushkin's vision of tyranny and the Enlightenment as oppressors of virtue.

Aragon's narrative *Le Paysan de Paris* presented several Parisian locations as erotic zones inhabited by spirits, with shop windows containing the fauna of human fantasies choked with marine vegetation. Similarly, Tsvetaeva's surreal descriptions of reality prompt her interlocutor Pasternak to discover remnants of recent dreams in Moscow and through his art stir revolutions within the mind of the modern reader. According to Conrad, French surrealists liked bridges for their vantage points and aerial views, for their aspiration to revise space. He writes: "But all they had in mind was a safe optical experiment, demonstrating how the eye telescopes perspective and cancels out distance. Aragon moved much closer to the edge. For him, the only use of such a bridge was that you could throw yourself from it, succumbing to 'the vertigo of the modern'. The secret at the centre of the park is our self-destructiveness, which the surrealists laughingly encouraged" (Conrad 1998: 311). Conrad explains that the surrealists regarded suicide[3] as the one credible reaction to a world filled with the absurd. The concluding lines of Tsvetaeva's "From the Seaside" are consistent with the French surrealist desire to experience the vertigo of the modern and achieve the sensation of walking along a precipice. It sounds like an invitation to the interlocutor to die together and to transgress all physical boundary through a spiritual reunion:

[...] Давай уснем.

Вплоть, а не тесно.
Огнь, а не дымно.
Ведь не совместный
Сон, а взаимный:

В Боге, друг в друге.
Нос, думал? Мыс?
Брови? Нет, дуги,
Выходы из –

Зримости.
(Tsvetaeva 1990: 547)

Let's go to sleep together.

Side by side, not too close.
There is fire, but no smoke.
Since this dream is not a shared one,
But a mutual dreaming:

Through God, one to the other.
Did you think it was nose? It is a spit!
Eyebrows? No, curves,
Passages into the world —

Of the invisibility.

Tsvetaeva attributes to Pasternak her ability to see poetry as imagination reaching to the surreal world. She suggested that Pasternak's seascapes in "1905" enriched her understanding of Pushkin's "To the Sea". She takes her cue from Pasternak who taught how to transform cityscapes into surreal spectacles. Pasternak's snapshots of reality, presented as free flow of images in his poetry of the 1920s, was indeed a novel device for Tsvetaeva which she successfully imitated in "From the Seaside". Tsvetaeva wrote in her letter to Pasternak of 23 May 1926: "What is the result? What I was carrying and what I was hoping to get was YOUR POEM which signifies the transformation of object. It was foolish of me to expect to see *for real your* sea — a distant one, above visibility, beyond visibility. 'Farewell, the free element' (my 10 years) and 'Everything becomes habitualised' (my thirty) — this is my sea" (Tsvetaeva 2004: 213).

The seascapes created by Pasternak and Tsvetaeva in 1926 stem from Pushkin's "To the Sea", but are given a surrealist twist. Their impressions of associations related to the image of the sea are recorded camera-like, as if their writing signifies an entrance into the realm of snapshots and the instantaneous. As Conrad observes, this period's obsession with the camera was linked to surrealist visions of reality: "The camera, like a quick-acting hallucinogen, demonstrated the oddity or derangement of everyday things. It was a machine for surrealizing reality. Man, as Paul Éluard said, 'will need merely to close his eyes for the gates of the marvellous to open'. The camera's shutter was such a gate, flicking open to capture an unregarded marvel and seal it in darkness" (Conrad 1998: 307). It appears that Tsvetaeva merges Pushkin with Pasternak in order to articulate the value of poetic imagination of the modern time. She stands close to the French surrealists who valued savagery more than civilisation. In 1937, for example, Éluard extolled the Marquis de Sade as an exemplary democrat: "To restore to civilised man the power of his primitive instincts" is "to liberate the erotic imagination" since Sade "believed only in this way could true equality be born" (Conrad 1998: 304). Thus, the image of dreams featured in Tsvetaeva's long narratives, including "From the Seaside", might be also examined from the viewpoint of the surrealist mode of automatic writing akin to camera techniques.

The image of Pushkin as a savage, a son of natural elements participating in creative evolution, is already strongly featured in Pasternak's 1918 cycle "Variations" («Вариации»). Pasternak depicts Pushkin at the seaside, and claims his identity is linked to the dialogic interaction between organic and artificial worlds:

Что было наследием кафров?
Что дал царкосельский лицей?
Два бога прощались до завтра,
Два моря менялись в лице:

Стихия свободной стихии
С свободной стихией стиха.
Два дня в двух мирах, два ландшафта,
Две древние драмы с двух сцен.
(Pasternak 1977: 191)

What was the kaffirs' legacy?
What was the local lycée's impact?
Two gods farewelled each other till tomorrow,
Two seas changed their appearances:

The element of free elements

> With the free element of poetry.
> Two days in two worlds, two landscapes,
> Two ancient plays from two scenes.

Pasternak's poem is already infused with a vision of the liberating and transgressive qualities of poetry. It corresponds to the notion of the poetics of impersonality, which came into favour in the modernist period: Pasternak replaces the vision of the historical Pushkin in Odessa addressing the sea with an impersonal speaking subject defined as poetic element. Pasternak's cycle "Variations", which includes the poem quoted above, superimposes the axis of the mimetic and merges the narrational with the figural. As a result, it portrays a communicative situation in which the narrative voice of the poetic element per se becomes almost indistinguishable from the voice of the interlocutor, represented in the poem by sounds of the natural water element.

In the style of cinematic writing, Pasternak throws at readers of "Variations" several events and synecdochic details of the action itself, rather than a view of the subject as a whole. The cinematic mode of writing had become established in German expressionist fiction and poetry as early as 1918, so Pasternak's poetry might be regarded as yet another manifestation of the expressionist poetics of duplicity, which involves the tendency of any act of representation simultaneously and paradoxically to reveal and conceal its object. This poetics is usually equated with the logic of the unconscious and the dream image. Döblin in his 1913 "Berliner Programme" defined the external and non-interpretative mode of writing as 'cinematic style' ('Kinostil'): "Given the enormous mass of already formed material a cinematic style is needed for representation. The fullness of appearances should march past us with the terseness and precision. One must wring out of language the utmost plasticity and liveliness [...] one does not narrate, one builds" (Murphy 1998: 118).

In "From the Seaside" Tsvetaeva insinuated a geophysical comparison of poets to spits of land, entities which stick out into the sea, displaced surpluses. This produces a disjointed perspective, projecting outward movement attributed to the object-world, in the manner of the overloaded condition of perceptive prevalent in modernity. Pasternak's allusion to Pushkin's African ancestry creates the image of the poet in exile whose displaced sense of self is shaped by the inner tension between his cultural and primitive selves. Pasternak's "Variations" illustrates and redefines the situation portrayed in Pushkin's "To the Sea" in avant-garde vein. It is consistent with Winnicott's psychoanalytical theory of potential space, because Pasternak's Pushkin resembles a child whose identity is being shaped and determined by his ongoing dialogue with the m/other.

Tsvetaeva's 1932 essay "The Poet and Time" («Поэт и время») extended Pasternak's and Pushkin's metonymical association between autonomous poetic existence and the elements into her powerful statement that "Every poet is essentially an *émigré*". Here Tsvetaeva perfectly articulates Bergsonian notions of the creative impulse and creative evolution, stripping a poet of any genius of their special aura of superhuman knowledge. In Tsvetaeva's eyes, poets of genius require superhuman effort and intuition to render meaningful their contribution to the continuing creative flow of life. She writes: "Every poet is essentially an *émigré*, even in Russia. *Émigré* from the Kingdom of Heaven and from the earthly paradise of nature. Upon the poet — upon all who belong to art, but most especially upon the poet — there is a particular mark of discomfort, by which you'll know him even in his own home" (Tsvetaeva 1992: 93). Tsvetaeva in "The Poet and Time", in a manner akin to both Blok and Pasternak, refers to the eternal youth of Pushkin, maintaining that in matters of art the philistine "leaves the ranks at around the age of thirty" and starts "rolling uncontrollably backwards — through non-understanding of others' youth — to non-recognition of his own youth, to non-acknowledgement of any youth — till he arrives at Pushkin, whose eternal youth he transforms into eternal oldness, and whose eternal contemporality he transforms into antiqueness from the word go" (Tsvetaeva 1992: 94).

Tsvetaeva goes on in "The Poet and Time" to pose important questions regarding the Enlightenment project in Soviet Russia: like Pushkin in his "To the Sea", she wishes to subvert the notion of modernity that proclaims, somewhat aggressively and superficially, ideas of innovation that oppress the free flow of creativity and deprive art of the autonomy it needs. Reflecting on the literary output of Pasternak and Maiakovskii, Tsvetaeva says that a poet of the revolution and a revolutionary poet are not the same. She distinguishes between the imperative of the communist party to celebrate the revolution and the imperative of time to unleash creative impulses and become revolutionary (Tsvetaeva 1992: 97). Tsvetaeva's statement that "a political command to a poet is not command of the time, which issues its commands without intermediaries" evokes Pushkin's own expressions of freedom of speech in many of his lyrics, including "To the Sea". It appears that this particular poem communicated to Tsvetaeva the need to question the notion of contemporality as understood in terms of the Enlightenment's vision of modernity. Moreover, Tsvetaeva's belief that the sole legitimate command a government could issue to poets, "do not write against us, for you are a force" (Tsvetaeva 1988: 368), also stems from the privileged, distanced and autonomous position of a poet in exile, such as Pushkin defined in "To the Sea".

Brodsky, another prominent poet of exile, whose artistic mind was influenced by both Pushkin and Tsvetaeva, also appears to be keenly aware of the responses to modernity embedded in Pushkin's "To the Sea". In his poem "To Evgenii" («К Евгению») Brodsky fashions himself in the clothes of Byron's Childe Harold, and reports his adventures and tours to his friend and fellow poet, whom he had left behind in Russia. Brodsky talks of the pyramids and deities he saw in Mexico in terms that invite comparison with Peter the Great's Petersburg project: the poet empathises with the slaves who built beautiful pyramids sacrificing their lives for the sake of technological advancement.

Brodsky's implied analogies between dehumanised visions of modernity in Russia and Mexico also evoke Sergei Eisenstein's 1931 uncompleted film *Qué Viva Mexico!* Mexico had a liberating effect upon Eisenstein: it signified the call to the parts of his self-imaginative, sensual, spiritual self which was denied validity in the new revolutionary culture. In the manner of Pushkin's philosophical pronouncement on the world order and the state of civilisation, Brodsky concludes "To Evgenii" with his own response to "To the Sea". He says:

> Скушно, жить, мой Евгений. Куда ни странствуй,
> Всюду жестокость и тупость воскликнут: «Здравствуй,
> Вот и мы!» Лень загонять в стихи их.
> Как сказано у поэта, «на всех стихиях...».

Далеко же видел, сидя в родных болотах!
От себя добавлю: на всех широтах.
(Brodsky 1991: 163)

I'm bored with living, Evgenii. Wherever one travels,
Everywhere cruelty and stupidity exclaim, "Hello,
Here we are!" I'm too lazy to fit them in my poems.
As the poet said, "across all elements...".
He could see so far, from the midst of his native marshes!
I'll just add my own comment: across all latitudes.

It is striking to see in Brodsky's comment an attempt to bring together philology and writing. He seems to be correcting Pushkin's abstract notion of the impersonal forces of fate, destruction and tyranny. At the same time, this comment displays self-conscious qualities, and playfully brings into the poem the optical illusion of a mistake, a technique favoured by many acmeists including Akhmatova. Brodsky's comment about Pushkin's vision of the world, and the direct quote from "To the Sea", give the impression that Pushkin wrote his poem to Byron when in Petersburg, but in fact he wrote it in Odessa. Brodsky's references to Pushkin's entrapment in Petersburg's marshes presents Pushkin as an essentially exilic figure, understood in the metaphysical terms conveyed by Tsvetaeva's seminal essay on modernity and contemporality "The Poet and Time". Brodsky's replacement of Pushkin's allusion to the elements with reference to latitudes recalls Tsvetaeva's image in "From the Seaside" of the letter with the franked postage stamp featuring peasants. Brodsky playfully appropriates Tsvetava's apostrophic mode of writing, and conceals his sharp political statements on the price of modernity within the format of a postcard. Brodsky's visual image of latitudes evokes the idea of censorship and oppression that obstructed free expression of spontaneous speech and creative flow. Brodsky sees art as essentially subversive, thereby continuing Tsvetaeva's surrealist project to explode from inside any discourse that identifies beauty with the utility prevalent in the Soviet Union, and exposing the irrationality of language. The juxtaposition between Pushkin and the lyric hero in Brodsky's "To Evgenii" elevates Brodsky to the position of an intellectual holding independent critical views.

Tsvetaeva's own vision of a poet who uses his displacement to subvert dominant discursive frameworks resonates well with Julia Kristeva. Her article "A New Type of Intellectual: the Dissident" suggests that the fundamental role of the intellectual is constantly to question existing structures and meanings. In Kristeva's view, the intellectual is a permanent dissident who moves away from fixed identities relating to authorship, gender and meaning, and who exhorts the assumption of the language of exile as his truest home, however evasive it might be. Kristeva writes: "How can one avoid sinking into the mire of common sense, if not by becoming a stranger to one's own country, language, sex and identity? Writing is impossible without some kind of exile." (Kristeva 1986: 298). Several scholars who have examined Brodsky's exilic images and themes (Aleksei Losev 1977; George Kline 1990; Maija Könönen 2003) identify Brodsky's indebtedness to Dante. They suggest that Brodsky saw his lost city everywhere he travelled, to the effect that all his poems featuring foreign landscapes inscribe his gaze of an exile, not of a tourist. Könönen sees "in Brodsky's poetry, despite the sense of loss, separation and estrangement, a courageous acceptance of the absurdity of human existence — a kind of being-at-home in homelessness — a condition that he shares with his great predecessors" (Könönen 2003: 133).

The opposition between the civilised North and the exotic South, discussed earlier, is reinforced in Brodsky's poem with the aim of subverting the established discourse of the Enlightenment and modernity. As with Pushkin, who was keen to express his opinion on the modernity project on the shores of the Black Sea in 1824, Tsvetaeva in "From the Seaside" was eager to deconstruct some of the dominant ideological and cultural symbols of the Soviet regime. Brodsky's "To Evgenii", written in the 1970s in the form of a poetic letter to his fellow poet in Russia, touches upon the same poetic tradition that highlights the contradictions between modernity and primitivism, mind and body. One can say that both Tsvetaeva and Brodsky, in their poems of exile, employed Dantean subtexts more vigorously than did Pushkin. Thus the image of a starfish in Tsvetaeva's "From the Seaside" has strong Dantean overtones: in *The Divine Comedy* Dante concludes each section of his three-tiered universe with an allusion to stars, which to him signify the familiar guiding objects at the end of his wanderings in hell and purgatory;

they also symbolise love. Brodsky's 1977 poem "The Fifth Anniversary" («Пятая годовщина»), dedicated to the fifth anniversary of Brodsky's forced emigration to the west, mimics Dante's *Terza rima*, and uses iambic hexameter, the most classical verse of Russian poetry. "The Fifth Anniversary" contains allusions to Dante's numerology and images of stars, and most importantly is written in apostrophic mode forcing the interlocutor to gaze into distant space, thereby transgressing temporal and spatial boundaries: "Look, look over there at where it's better not to gaze" («Взгляни, взгляни туда, куда смотреть не стоит») (Brodsky in: Appendix, Könönen 2003: 328). Like Pushkin who in "To the Sea" turns his poetic language into a form of dwelling, Brodsky uses his displacement from his homeland for the construction of a mnemonic space which contributes to his creative existence in and through language. In ironic vein, Brodsky as a Russian poet of significance separates himself from the grand narrative based on the binary opposition between West and East, and in the concluding stanza of "The Fifth Anniversary" retreats to create the poetics of Pushkinian silence:

> Мне нечего сказать ни греку, ни варягу.
> Зане не знаю я, в какую землю лягу.
> Скрипи, скрипи, перо! Переводи бумагу.
> (Brodsky in: Appendix, Könönen 2003: 328).
>
> I've nothing to say to the Greek or the Varangian.
> Because I don't know where I'll be buried.
> Squeak, squeak, nib! Keep wasting paper.

The imperative to continue writing in any space and any time, conveyed in Brodsky's "To Evgenii", also evokes Pushkin's "It's time, my friend, it's time!". Both poems envisage an autonomous creative existence uninterrupted by political concerns, fashion or the constraints of modernity. Given that the modernist writer is engaged in a perpetual search for perfect style and for ways to express the vital creative impulse, then Brodsky's poem testifies to the validity of modern times' ambitious project to equate art with life, which prefigured Pushkin's poetry in embryo form.

The approaches of both Brodsky and Tsvetaeva to Pushkin's "To the Sea" were shaped by many modernist tenets and preconceptions. The surreal overtones found in the manifestations of their exilic writing that stem from Pushkin's "To the Sea" are entwined with parodic touches. They both understood parody in terms suggested in the works on laughter and parody penned by Bergson and Tynianov. These works proposed the thesis that laughter served the purposes of progress and creative evolution. For Bergson, laughter presents a liberating force that removes the obstacles that block vital élan, and succumbs to the spontaneous flow of life free of mechanical inelasticity and repetition. (Bergson 1999: 14-15).

Both Tsvetaeva and Brodsky discovered in Pushkin a prefigured notion of space that is unique to language, and which was elaborated in the poetry of Russian and European modernists, especially Mallarmé. According to Blanchot, Mallarmé's *Un coup de dés*, for example, "was born from a new understanding of literary space: by new links of movement, new relationships of comprehension can be engendered in it" (Blanchot 2003: 235). Blanchot's insightful comments on the construction of space in Mallarmé's poetry help illuminate the cognition of space found in the poetry of Pasternak, Tsvetaeva and Brodsky; which derives from Pushkin's lyrics featuring exilic experiences and dreams of escape into the realm of creative existence. Blanchot's observations seem applicable to Russian twentieth-century poetry, which also concerned itself with spontaneity in the manner similar to French literary development.

Blanchot explains the new understanding of space thus: "We create nothing and we speak in a creative way only by a preliminary approach to the place of extreme vacancy where, before becoming determined and denotative words, language is the silent movement of relationships, that is to say 'the rhythmic scansion of being' […]. Poetic space, both the source and 'the result' of language, is never the same as a thing; but always, 'it spaces itself out and disseminates itself' […]. Poetic emotion is thus not an inner sentiment, a subjective modification, but a strange outside into which we are thrown in us outside of us" (Blanchot 2003: 235). Such a phenomenological view of being outside and inside at the same time through intensive poetic emotion resembles Bakhtin's dialogic consciousness discussed above. Blanchot considers Mallarmé truly profound because his poetry opens us, breaks away with linear representation and supposes a space with many dimensions. Blanchot says that Mallarmé's spatial profundity must be apprehended simultaneously on different levels. The seascapes and exilic images discussed in this chapter also yield to the creation of a space with many dimensions that must be perceived simultaneously. This space eroticises the tension between the cultured north and exotic south, presenting Russia as a youthful country.

In a metonymic way, the twentieth-century poets whom we have discussed aspired to reinforce this view through the creation of the image of an eternally youthful and child-like Pushkin. The m/other image of the sea is also explored by twentieth-century poets, and juxtaposed with the image of poetry as yet another element: all poets of avant-garde mould appear keen to fashion themselves in the Romantic image of children of the sea as did their poetic forebears, namely Byron and Pushkin. Yet their poems evoking Pushkin's "To the Sea" also boast strong Dantean overtones relating to exilic experience and spiritual quest. Unlike Pasternak, who posed for his father's painting which depicted Pushkin in Odessa in 1824, Tsvetaeva and Brodsky had to visualise their bond with the Pushkin in exile, the author of "To the Sea", in their own imagination and animate it through words. Their writings and lives are permeated by the spirit of self-transformation and theatricality that served the cause of the creative evolution understood here in Bergsonian terms. The utopian outward movement into new lands and into the future was imitated to such effect by the representatives of Russian modernism and postmodernism we have discussed that it turned Pushkin's "To the Sea" into the archetypal text of dialogical consciousness and of becoming.

NOTES

1 Rubens's painting is on the website of the Hermitage museum www.hermitagemuseum.org/html_En/04/2004/hm4_1_73_0.html (accessed October 2005)
2 I discuss Tynianov's usage of this poem in his unfinished novel *Pushkin* in my article "Conformist by Circumstance v. Formalist at Heart: Some Observations on Tynianov's Novel *Pushkin*" (Smith 1998).
3 Tsvetaeva's suicide is a complex matter that was related to psychological, moral, financial and political pressures and anxieties. Yet I think one certainly might compare something of the suicidal tendency in her poetic personality to the surrealists' preoccupation with death.

TWO

PUSHKIN'S PETERSBURG AS COMIC APOCALYPSE

Preamble

In the words of Deborah Parsons, "The urban writer is not only a figure within a city; he/she is also the producer of a city, one that is related to but distinct from the city of asphalt, brick, mind and space, and stone, one that reveals the interplay of self/city identity. The writer adds other maps to the city atlas; those of social interaction but also of myth, memory, fantasy, and desire. That the city has been habitually conceived as a male space, in which women are either repressed or disobedient marginal presences, has resulted in an emphasis in theoretical analysis on gendered maps that reflect such conditions" (Parsons 2000: 1-2).

In this chapter I will examine Pushkin's role in constructing a powerful myth of Petersburg as a European metropolis. We will look at his striking images of the flâneur and other urban spectators, which influenced Russian twentieth-century descriptions of poets as flâneurs. I will argue that the flâneur, as the intended agent of demystification, has himself become one of the mysteries of the modernist city.

Pushkin's surrealist mode of aesthetic sociology, as manifested in his poetry on Petersburg, led to the creation of various modernist urban nomads such as the dandy, the rag-picker, the beggar and the picaro. It is not coincidental that Belyi in his 1906 article "The Laurel Wreath" («Венец лавровый») called Valerii Briusov the most distinguished modernist author of Russian urban poetry, Pushkin's double. Belyi recognised the fragmentation of Pushkin's self caused by the unfolding of modernity and by the contradictions of urban life. Belyi in effect acknowledged Pushkin's contribution to the intellectual debate on the city and modernity by regarding the identities of Pushkin and Briusov as somewhat interchangeable. Belyi wrote:

> Изучение поэзии Брюсова открывает нам верную тропу к лучезарным высотам пушкинской цельности. И в то же время тайна Пушкина, о которой говорил нам Достоевский, разгадана Брюсовым. Тайна пушкинской цельности оказывается глубочайшим расщепом души, дробящим, как меч, всякую цельность жизни. Цельность жизни оказывается противопоставленной цельности творчества. […]. Пушкин оказывается не только поэтом, но и священным трагическим героем, укрывшим священство свое под ризой поэзии. Все это узнаем мы о Пушкине потому, что видим в поэзии Брюсова несомненную цельность […]. То, что укрыл Пушкин, выдал Брюсов. Брюсов и Пушкин дополняют друг друга. И если в Брюсове мы подчас угадываем Пушкина, то в Пушкине с равным правом мы начинаем видеть ряд новых брюсовских черт.
> (Belyi 1910: 453)

> The examination of Briusov's poetry reveals to us the right path leading to the heights of Pushkin's wholeness. At the same time Pushkin's mystery — which Dostoevskii told us about — was uncovered by Briusov. The mystery of Pushkin's wholeness turns out to be the deepest crack in the soul which breaks any wholeness of life into small pieces. The wholeness of life turns out to be in direct opposition to artistic wholeness. […] Pushkin turns out to be not just a poet but also a tragic hero who covered his holiness with the gown of poetry. We learn such things about Pushkin because we see in Briusov's poetry some distinctive wholeness. Things which Pushkin kept hidden were revealed by Briusov. Briusov and Pushkin complement each other. And while we sometimes recognise Pushkin coming through Briusov's poetry, by the same token we also begin to see some new Briusovean features in Pushkin's verse.

Briusov in fact encouraged the view of himself as Pushkin's heir: his self-representation revolved around the image of himself as the poet of modernity and the urban mode of writing. He also saw Pushkin as a teacher of generations. His role in the canonisation of Pushkin's work in the 1910s-1920s was immense.[1] For example Briusov wrote in 1904: "We will always have a common awe and reverence for the divine poetry of Pushkin, for its pure colours and sounds. My poetry was born from Pushkin's poetry to the same extent as we are all orginated from Paradise" («У нас всегда останется общим восторг и преклонение пред божественной поэзией Пушкина, пред ее чистыми красками и чистыми звуками. Моя поэзия родилась от пушкинской в той же мере, как мы родились в раю») (Briusov 1987, vol.2: 536).

Belyi's analogy between Pushkin and Briusov derives from the long standing tradition that speaks of modernity in the male gender. Felski, in responding to Marshall Berman's book *All That Is Solid Melts Into Air*, makes the valuable point that Berman's book is not unique in its overarching assertion that all heroes and symbols of modernity are male. She writes: "All the exemplary heroes of his text — Faust, Marx, Baudelaire — are of course symbols not just of modernity, but also of masculinity, historical markers of the emergence of new forms of bourgeois and working-class male subjectivity. Both in Berman's account of Faust and in his later evocation of Baudelaire's flâneur, the stroller who goes botanizing on the asphalt of the streets of Paris, the modern individual is assumed to be an autonomous male free of familial and communal ties. Here Berman's book fits comfortably into a long-standing tradition of writing that reads modernity as an Oedipal revolt against the tyranny of authority, drawing on metaphors of contestation and struggle grounded in an ideal of competitive masculinity" (Felski 1995: 2).

As Felski points out, Berman's position derives from an established view of modernity understood in terms of a polarised opposition between the individual and society. This view of modernity is also conveyed in Briusov's poetry and essays, including his 1909 essay "The Bronze Horseman" («Медный всадник»). Briusov portrays Pushkin as an advocate of the Oedipal revolt against the tyranny of authority and proposes to view Pushkin's image of Peter the Great as symbol of autocracy. Briusov explains the main idea of

"The Bronze Horseman" thus: "The revolt of individual against autocracy inevitably turns into revolt against historical determinism and the cult of personality [...]. According to the poet's vision as expressed in his poem, Peter the Great embodies the might of autocracy manifested in its extremes; poor Evgenii is meant to symbolise the extreme powerlessness of the isolated and insignificant individual" («Мятеж личности против самодержавия невольно становится мятежом против *исторической необходимости* и против *обожествления личности* [...]. *Великий Петр*, по замыслу поэта, должен был стать олицетворением мощи самодержавия в ее крайнем проявлении; *бедный Евгений* — воплощением крайнего бессилия обособленной, незначительной личности») (Briusov 1987, vol.2: 169-70).

However, it was Blok, not Briusov, whom Russian modernists widely saw as Pushkin's double. To a large extent, in a Pushkinian manner Blok became not just a figure in the city but a producer of the city. His surreal images of Petersburg mesmerised his contemporaries. In 1908, for example, Blok's theatrical and commedia dell'arte image of Petersburg inspired Vsevolod Meyerhold to stage Blok's lyrical drama *The Puppet Booth (Балаганчик)*. Blok's 'mysticism in everyday life' forms the essence of his surrealist sociological and artistic exploration of Petersburg. It stands close to Pushkin's visionary-like and profound depictions of Petersburg as a newly emerged European metropolis. For Blok, Petersburg stands out as the Venice of the North permeated with the carnival atmosphere that makes the commedia dell'arte mode of artistic expression rather fitting. In a passage in his notebook for 18 January 1906 titled "Religion and Mysticism" («Религия и мистицизм»), we come across Blok's thoughts on the nature of his artistic vision: "Mysticism is the bohemian element of the soul, religion is standing watch. As to 'religious art': there is *no* such thing except as a transitional form. True art does not coincide in its aims with religion. Art has its own Rule, it is a monastery of historical formation, i.e. a monastery that has no room for religion. Religion is (or is about) that which is to be, mysticism is that which was and is. *Mysticism in everyday life* is a fine theme and a rich one [...]. The cornerstone of religion is God; of mysticism — mystery... Mysticism requires ecstasy. Ecstasy is solitude. Ecstasy is not religious. Mystics love to be poets, artists.

Religious people do not, they divide themselves from their craft (art)" (Blok, quoted in: Pyman 1979, volume 1: 231).

The Petersburg actress Natal′ia Nikolaevna Volokhova, with whom Blok was infatuated in 1908, recalls in her memoirs her numerous walks along the streets of Petersburg. Volokhova says that she and other friends from Blok's milieu not only loved and constantly recited verse, but also lived through poetry, stressing that at the beginning of the twentieth century the aesthetisation of everyday life was widespread. Many close associates of Blok saw Volokhova as the poet's Muse, a true Snow Maiden, or even a sectarian Madonna who inspired Blok to create his magical wintery image of Petersburg in his cycle of poems "The Snow Mask" («Снежная маска»). It is worth quoting one of Volokhova's recollections here, to see how Blok's engagement with Petersburg was just as intensive as Pushkin's active interaction with Petersburg life in the 1820s-1830s. Volokhova presents Blok as the creator of an imaginary Petersburg:

> Once, after the theatre, we went for long walks and Aleksandr Aleksandrovich introduced me to 'his town', as he called it. Passing the deserted Marsovo Pole, we would take the Troitsky Bridge and gaze enthralled into the endless chains of street lamps, set like burning fires along the river [...]. We would walk further and stroll about the outskirts of the town, along the embankments, along the canals, crossing bridges. Aleksandr Aleksandrovich showed me all the places connected with his play, *The Stranger*: the bridge where the Astrologer had stood and met the Poet, the place where the Stranger had first appeared and the alley of street lamps into which she had vanished. [...]. Reality was so intermingled with the invention, the dreams of the poet, that I involuntarily lost the boundaries of the real and entered with awe and enchantment into this world of poetry that I had never known before. I had the feeling that I was receiving this extraordinary, legendary city as a gift at the hands of the poet.
> (Pyman 1979: 273)

By the same token, the Petersburg myth, of which Pushkin was the main author, should be somehow viewed as a prototype narrative of modernity revolving around urban dwelling and city writing. After all, it appears that the texts most influencing the artistic mind of Russian modernist poets were penned by Pushkin, including *Eugene Onegin*, "The Bronze Horseman", and the unfinished tale "Egyptian Nights" («Египетские ночи») which includes several poems. In other words, Russian twentieth-century poets who embarked on the mode of urban writing borrowed heavily from Pushkin's poetry. Their own images of modernity and urban dwelling are often juxtaposed to Pushkin's poetic self and space. The discussion below will touch upon the essential features of Pushkin's urban writing. It will investigate the development of Pushkin's ideas and imagery insofar as they relate to Petersburg in the modernist and postmodernist periods.

Pushkin's Petersburg: dandy, aesthetic rag-picker and madman

Pushkin's 'kinetic' poetic model of Petersburg as a young European city anticipates Bergson's metaphysical concept of 'duration' ('durée'). Such a postulate supplies cohesion for Pushkin's imagery of Petersburg. To the extent that Pushkin's poetry moves to touch the living roots of art and transcends it into the realms of inherent logic of primal intuition, Pushkin's surreal mode of writing Petersburg can be seen as part of the inner consciousness, or 'Intuition' in Bergson's terminology. Bergson's concepts enable us to see the dynamic nature of Pushkin's works. They open the way to the discovery in Pushkin's writings of intertextual dialogism and the reproduction of various cultural artefacts, such as architectural landmarks and sculptures.

Renate Lachmann has tested this approach in her analysis of Pushkin's poem "Monument" («Памятник») which links intertextuality to cultural memory in general (Lachmann 1997: 194-221). According to Lachmann, Acmeist poetics exemplify Bergson's theory at its best, stressing the coexistence of all cultures (production of a synchronic paradigm). In such a worldview, "the past is grasped as becoming, as meaning that neither was nor is but that is, rather, always being projected into the future as deferred meaning. [...] Deferral prevents the death of culture, and mnemonic writing guarantees deferral" (ibid: 234). The concept of cultural memory can be applied not only to the beliefs and imagery of contemporary popular urban culture, but equally to discussion of Pushkin's Petersburg, including his non-verbal images. What appears paramount to the discussion of Pushkin's Petersburg is Bergson's idea of the inner unity of matter and spirit, achieved through the spatialisation of time.

The role of Pushkin as a creator of Petersburg as the centre of Russian culture has often been compared to the role of Peter the Great in creating the capital of the modern Russian empire. As Caryl Emerson maintains, "Pushkin's genius appeared at precisely the right time for this fledgling secular-aristocratic culture. In the pre- and post-Napoleonic era, from the venerated intellectual centres of France, England, and the German and Italian states, the literati of Russia's two capitals were exposed to a steadily influx of styles and genres: neoclassical odes, sentimental ballads, society tales, gothic narratives, Byronic verse epics, romantic dramas, Waverley historical novels. With great virtuosity, Pushkin absorbed these models, transfigured them, integrated them, parodied them, and then readied himself — and the Russian language — for the next wave" (Emerson 1998: 653). In this sense, Pushkin's *Eugene Onegin*, the first Russian novel in verse, might be seen as the best manifestation of the 'fledgling secular-aristocratic culture', to use Emerson's phrase.

William Todd III makes the insightful observation that life and the novel form a unity in *Eugene Onegin* because they both manifest the same creative process (Todd 1999: 180). It can be argued that Pushkin 'reads' Petersburg as a book, as an evolving and open-ended text which can be used both for inscribing the poet's self and as a source of inspiration, as an artefact that helps Pushkin, the poet, to develop his own creative potential. This is especially true if we bear in mind that the Petersburg of Pushkin's times was developing rapidly, changing its appearance in order to conform to the new imperial image, with many features of the Petrine baroque being replaced with classical elements. Pushkin's vision of Petersburg as expressed in *Eugene Onegin*, "The Bronze Horseman" and "The Queen of Spades" («Пиковая дама») "reflects on the dynamic image of the city's cultural space where different memories and cultural imprints co-existed, with the classical 'solemn' image still very much evolving". Pushkin's Petersburg text "transgresses its own boundaries and opens up into the greater text of culture, macrotext" articulating the "flowing movement that runs through texts and that constitutes them" (Lachmann 1997: 234).

Two distinct periods in Pushkin's representation of Petersburg in his texts are usually given special attention in Pushkin scholarship. The first period comprises Pushkin's early years in Petersburg (1817-20). This may be characterised as the period of active intellectual and cultural life, when the young poet became increasingly involved in the social and cultural activities of the Russian capital. The second period runs from 1827 to 1837. This is marked by Pushkin's growing pessimism and a somewhat split poetic persona. In spite of the rapid growth of the city after the end of the war with Napoleon (1812-15), which Pushkin witnessed, the poet expressed some strong anxieties about the capital's urban life. Pushkin caught the new appearance of the city in a number of poems, especially in the opening stanzas of "The Bronze Horseman", in which he inscribes into the text the glorious look of the renovated Admiralty building, which was the most striking innovation of the Petersburg cityscape in the period 1806-27. The image of the renovated and improved city must have held enormous appeal to Pushkin in 1827, when he returned to Petersburg after several years of exile. Several grand projects, though, were still in progress: St Isaac's cathedral, for example, was completed only after Pushkin's death. By the early 1830s, the forty-eight supporting columns of the cathedral's portico attracted many admirers. One newspaper wrote, "This work is the highest example of human stamina, might and knowledge. The most courageous projects of the Middle Ages cannot be compared to it, and are much inferior. As a good comparison, one might refer to Ancient Egypt, which represents the youthful stage of our Universe" (Tomashevskii 1949: 304). Curiously, there are no references to this or to several other city developments in Pushkin's poetry. It appears that after 1827 the several aspects comprising Pushkin's personal poetic mythology developed into a coherent mythopoetic model.

It has become something of a cliché to say that Pushkin contrasts Petersburg to Moscow, in the manner of the Biblical distinction between Jerusalem as the city of God and Babylon as a scarlet woman and city of exile. In the words of Weitzman, the binary opposition 'Jerusalem — Babylon' can be presented as follows:

"Jerusalem is the true home of the chosen, God's site for the Temple and the throne. Yet it is subject to corruption and wavering allegiance and thus condemned by the prophets, particularly Hosea and Jeremiah. Babylon in contrast is the fallen city of sensuality, greed, and disobedience to God's will; there men worship idols and false values" (Weitzman 1975: 471). A similar attitude can be sensed in Pushkin's reference to Petersburg as the cursed city. Thus, upon receiving news of the flood of November 1824, Pushkin in exile wrote to his brother: "The very thing for cursed Petersburg" (Pushkin 1991: xii). Indeed, Pushkin's image of the old Moscow and the new capital invites such an opposition. This might be explained by the Romantic fashion of the 1830s to promote the male genius as a Romantic hero. Young Petersburg fitted their image. This view was reflected in Pushkin's differentiation of the two cities on the basis of gender principles. Thus in *Eugene Onegin* Pushkin labels Moscow as grandmother. Furthermore, Pushkin does not see the two cities as equal any more, comparing the two capitals to two hearts that cannot co-exist in the same body. Pushkin summarises his view in the essay "Journey from Moscow to Petersburg" («Путешествие из Москвы в Петербург») (1833-34):

> Петр 1 не любил Москвы, где на каждом шагу встречал воспоминания мятежей и казней, закоренелую старину и упрямое сопротивление суеверия и предрассудков [...]. Упадок Москвы есть неминуемое следствие возвышения Петербурга. Две столицы не могут в равной степени процветать в одном и том же государстве, как два сердца не существуют в теле человеческом. Но обеднение Москвы доказывает и другое: обеднение русского дворянства, происшедшее *частию* от раздробления имений, исчезающих с ужасной быстротой.
> (Pushkin 1957-58, vol.7: 275).

> Peter the Great did not like Moscow, where every corner evoked in his mind the memories of revolts and executions, the unchangeable ancient world and the stubborn resistance of superstition and prejudices [...]. The decline of Moscow is the inevitable consequence of the rise of Petersburg. Two capitals cannot flourish at the

same time in the same state, just as two hearts cannot co-exist in the human body. Yet Moscow's impoverishment proves another point: the Russian aristocracy's impoverishment that was *partly* due to the fragmentation of estates vanishing at horrifying speed.

Pushkin's 1827 poem "What a night! The crispy frost..." («Какая ночь! Мороз трескучий...») alludes to the execution of the rebellious strel´tsy by Peter the Great in Moscow's Red Square. It features a rider galloping across a Red Square covered with the corpses of executed rebels. This image foreshadows the portrayal of the Bronze Horseman chasing Evgenii along the night streets of Petersburg. The chaos and violence in post-flood Petersburg as presented in "The Bronze Horseman" challenged the grand utopian plans of modernisation meant to harness the natural flow of life and organic developments. Its imagery stands close to Adam Mickiewicz's impressions of the 1824 Petersburg flood conveyed in "The Monument of Peter the Great" ("Pomnik Petra Velikogo") and "Oleshkevich" ("Oleszkiewiez"). In the latter poem the Polish painter and freemason Oleszkiewicz stands out as a prophet, comparing Petersburg to a new Babylon and predicting its demise.

M.N. Virolainen believes that Pushkin's "The Bronze Horseman" does contain polemical allusions to Mickiewicz's poems (Virolainen 1999: 208). Schwarzband suggests that "perhaps, [...] Mickiewicz's 'Peter the Great's Monument' [...] inspired Pushkin to use the horse as an allegory of Russia, and the rider as an allegory of the autocracy" (Schwarzband 1988: 76). Bailey emphasises that Pushkin knew Mickiewicz's poem "Forefathers' Eve" which describes Petersburg, but "Everything about the poem must have outraged his aesthetic sense, but like the grit in the oyster it worked in him until the final casting of the pearl at Boldino in 1833. 'The Bronze Horseman' is not a reply to Mickiewicz's poem, but it might not have been written without it" (Bailey 1971: 131). Briusov in his article "The Bronze Horseman" («Медный всадник») makes the valuable observation that Pushkin could not leave unnoticed his portrayal by Mickiewicz in "The Monument of Peter the Great" as a poet of Russian people. Mickiewicz's Pushkin verbally attacks the monument to Peter the Great, calling it "a cascade of tyranny". Furthermore, Briusov shares the view of Jósef Tretiak, the author of the book

Mickiewicz and Pushkin (published in Warsaw 1906), who thinks Pushkin might have found it offensive to read in Mickiewicz's poems some strong accusations implicating Pushkin of slavish approval of the Tsar and betrayal of the ideals of liberty (Briusov 1987, vol.2: 168).

In Briusov's opinion, Pushkin in the mid-1820s became disillusioned in his revolutionary beliefs and developed a philosophical view of the concept of freedom. Briusov thinks Pushkin grew to favour an evolutionary model of modernisation over revolutionary changes, and came close to formulating the concept of a civilised society. Briusov maintains: "He started assessing the concept of freedom more from the philosophical point of view rather than from the political standpoint. He eventually started to realise that it would not be possible to achieve *freedom* through the revolutionary and violent change of the political regime for it should come as result of spiritual development of the human race" («На вопрос о *свободе* он начал смотреть не столько с политической, сколько с философской точки зрения. Он постепенно пришел к убеждению, что *свобода* не может быть достигнута насильственным изменением политического строя, но будет следствием духовного воспитания человечества») (Briusov 1987, vol.2: 184). In his analysis of "The Bronze Horseman" Briusov presents Evgenii as a courageous individual who feels free to speak his mind and advocate freedom. Briusov sees his empowering gesture as a sign of revolt which makes the monument chase him for the whole night, because Peter the Great would not tolerate the revolt of the individual soul.

Gary Rosenshield locates in "The Bronze Horseman" an important theme of violence and madness in a suggestion that Peter the Great's project of creating an ideal city was declaredly based only on reason and a rationalised vision of progress, whereas in reality it contained the idea of contagious madness comparable metaphorically to the chaotic forces of nature personified in the narrative by the mad Neva. Rosenshield writes: "When Evgenii challenges the Bronze Horseman, Peter engages the world of Evgenii and chases him through the streets of Petersburg. The words the narrator applies to the mad Evgenii become attached to Peter. The association not only brings Evgenii and Peter together, it brings them together in madness; it suggests that the madness does not belong to Evgenii alone; it is a shared disease. The association of the river and Peter also brings Peter and the Neva closer together in terms of rebellion and madness. Peter and the Neva share the fire and power. Peter's fire and power, the engine of the Petrine legacy, are as potentially destructive as the mad fury of the Neva. On the one hand, Peter symbolises order, stability, and reason; on the other, like the river, he embodies the principle of rebellion, revolt and revolution" (Rosenshield 2003: 136). Thus, Rosenshield wryly identifies allegories of madness and violence in Pushkin's Petersburg which reveal the city's dark side; a diseased body hides behind the façade of a European city. Pushkin's "The Bronze Horseman" also foregrounds Baudelaire's collection of poems *Le Spleen de Paris*; this also conveys the violence and trauma that form essential aspects of the dominant motif of a distinctly urban genre. According to Ramazani, "it is above all the experience of physical aversiveness that is 'spoken' through the symbolic topography of the city in *Le Spleen de Paris*. As the title's medical metaphor (*Spleen*) implies, the hidden figure of the city (*de Paris*) mediates the symptoms of a social body afflicted by alienated relations of class, gender, and race, it can be said that the city is in pain" (Ramazani 1996: 201).

Pushkin's description of the 1824 flood gives an impression of Petersburg as a city in pain and as a city embodying pain. Here are some examples which indicate the signs of madness as a sort of contagious disease:

> Над омраченным Петроградом
> Дышал ноябрь осенним хладом.
> Плеская шумною волной
> В края своей ограды стройной
> Нева металась, как больной
> В своей постели беспокойной.
> (Pushkin 1957, vol. 4: 384)

> Above a Petrograd become gloomy
> November breathed out its cold air.
> Throwing its waves noisily
> At the elegant fence
> The river Neva rushed from side to side,
> Like an sick person in his bed.

In another passage the river appears to resemble a mad animal attacking the city: "And suddenly, like outraged an animal, it set upon the city" («И вдруг, как зверь остервенясь, на город кинулась») (Ibid: 386). Both Evgeny and Peter the Great are portrayed as madmen, who mimic the pain of the city affected by the violent flood.

It would stretch comparison too far to equate Pushkin's Petersburg with Baudelaire's Paris. Yet it is useful to point out that Pushkin anticipated the Baudelairian mode of writing the city from a kaledoscope-like viewpoint that reflects on the experience of shock and fragmentation. Benjamin, in his articles on Baudelaire, assessed the importance for the artistic mind of urban writers and poets of increased traffic flow and of technological interference in the private life of urban dwellers in nineteenth-century Paris. Benjamin's observations provide us with understanding of the new form of cognition of urban life that emerged in response to the advance of modernity. In Benjamin's opinion, Baudelaire coined a new type of modern writer, a man who acts like a kaleidoscope equipped with consciousness. This type of artistic mind is already present in its embryo form in Pushkin's poetry of the 1820-1830s, as we will discuss below.

First let us consider Benjamin's understanding of the modern stroller who gathers impressions of urban life, and the effect of Benjamin's vision on a new mode of writing which can be broadly defined as impressionistic. Benjamin writes in his article "On Some Motifs in Baudelaire": "The invention of the match around the middle of the nineteenth century brought forth a number of innovations which have one thing in common: one abrupt movement of the hand triggers a process of many steps [...]. Moving through this traffic involves the individual in a series of shocks and collisions. At dangerous intersections, nervous impulses flow through him in rapid succession, like the energy from the battery. Baudelaire speaks of a man who plunges into the crowd as into a reservoir of electric energy. Circumscribing the experience of the shock, he calls the man 'a *kaleidoscope* equipped with consciousness' [...]. Thus technology has subjected the human sensorium to a complex kind of training. There came a day when a new and urgent need for stimuli was met by film. In a film, perception in the form of shocks was established as a formal principle. That which determines the rhythm of production on a conveyor belt is the basis of the rhythm of reception in film" (Benjamin 1999: 170-71). However, Iurii Tynianov's articles on Russian verse language and Pushkin allow us to have a more coherent view of the peculiarities of the new 'cinematic' mode of writing which stem from Romanticism's preoccupation with miniatures and fragments.

According to Greenleaf's penetrating article "Tynianov, Pushkin and the Fragment", Tynianov's theory of perceptible montage — which implies a textual discontinuity to the effect that the spectator is empowered with an active interpretative role — is largely informed by Tynianov's scholarship on Pushkin's fragments, partial omissions, and the role of interlocutor in Pushkin's poetry. Greenleaf maintains: "Analogies from the Pushkin period spring readily to Tynianov's mind as he ponders aesthetic 'universals'. In his article on the foundations of cinema he even appears to come full circle: a discussion of the semantics of montage leads him back to the question of digression or discontinuity in Pushkin's first Romantic *poema*. As the reader works to synthesize the scattered 'far-off' material of the *otryvki*, he generates a 'big form' out of proportion to its number of pages, its *miniatiurnost*'" (Greenleaf in Gasparov et al 1992: 278). There are several passages in Pushkin's "The Bronze Horseman" which resemble the camera-like cognition of urban landscapes. As Tynianov points out, "The 'jumping' nature of cinema, the role in it of frame coherency, the semantic transformation of everyday objects (words in verse, things in cinema) — all of these bring cinema and verse together" (quoted in Gasparov 1992: 280). Tynianov's term of the jumping nature in cinema corresponds well to Benjamin's concept of perception in the form of shocks, which was discussed above. Such passages that are akin to the jumping nature of cinema and to the cognition of reality as a sequence of jolts are especially evident in the second part of Pushkin's "The Bronze Horseman" in which Evgenii observes the consequences of the flood. The passage below recalls an organised cinematic take which even attempts to inscribe into the narrative the sense of shock and experience of a void:

> Несчастный
> Знакомой улицей бежит
> В места знакомые. Глядит,
> Узнать не может. Вид ужасный!

Все перед ним завалено;
Что сброшено, что снесено,
Скривились домики. Другие
Совсем обрушились, иные
Волнами сдвинуты; кругом,
Как будто в поле боевом,
Тела валяются. Евгений
Стремглав, не помня ничего,
Изнемогая от мучений,
Бежит туда, где ждет его
Судьба с неведомым известьем,
Как с запечатанным письмом.
И вот бежит уж он предместьем,
И вот залив, и близок дом...
Что ж это?... Он остановился.
Пошел назад и воротился.
Глядит... идет... еще глядит.
(Pushkin 1957, vol.4: 391-92)

The miserable one.
He runs across the familiar street
To familiar places. He looks,
He cannot recognise. Such a horrible sight!
Everything is rubble in front of him;
Things are scattered; some destroyed.
Houses are bent; some
Have collapsed completely; some are shifted
By waves; everywhere,
Just like on a battlefield,
Bodies are scattered around. Evgeny
Rushes further — hastily,
Having forgotten everything,
Tormented by his suffering —
Runs to where his fate
Awaits him with an unknown message,
Like a letter sealed in an envelope.
And already he is running through a suburb,
And here is the Finnish gulf; and the house is nearby...
What is that?... He stopped.

He went back and returned to the same spot.
He is looking... walking... looking again.

The comparison in the second part of "The Bronze Horseman" of the river Neva to the exhausted steed returned from battle («И тяжело Нева дышала,/ Как с битвы прибежавший конь») allows us to see that Pushkin presents both the Bronze Horseman and the Neva as part of the same elemental destructive forces that lie beyond the control of any individual. In Pushkin's "To the Sea", discussed in chapter one, analogies between the adverse aspects of modernity and sea storms were advanced. In "The Bronze Horseman" the impersonal forces of history are equated once again with the uncontrollable forces of nature. Khodasevich's words about the role of images of bad weather in Pushkin's poetry — discussed in chapter one — are also applicable to "The Bronze Horseman". As Khodasevich aptly puts it, in Pushkin's oeuvre "everything that exists outside the boundaries of a private house, — all this is bad weather" (Khodasevich 1999: 166). Khodasevich's discussion of Pushkin's poetic images of bad weather may be seen as complementing Tynianov's observations on the role of fragments and suggestiveness in Pushkin's poetry. Undoubtedly, Pushkin's description of the shock that Evgeny experiences in "The Bronze Horseman" alludes to the traumatic experiences of many Russians and Finns, whose wooden houses were vanishing rapidly in the Petersburg suburbs in the face of the advance of modernising building programme aimed at the creation of stone buildings and rationalised spaces.

To a great extent "The Bronze Horseman" also speaks of the collapse of the boundary between inside and outside that stems from the experience of pain. In the above passage, a tacit inversion of inside and outside, a translation of inside into outside, and an externalised sensation of pain are portrayed with the help of parallel structures and ellipses. The final line, which frames the episode of Evgenii absorbing pain before he is pronounced mad, is presented as an act of mirroring: "He is looking... walking... looking again." It seems obvious that Pushkin is trying here to construct a language of pain and shock which lies outside speech: it is a visual language of gestures that match psychological and physiological movements, in the style of the cinematic utterance found in silent movies. It is not coincidental that Tynianov identified in Pushkin's poetry several forms of utterance which are analogous to cinematographic narration and montage. And Julia Kristeva maintains, "From its beginnings, cinema has considered itself as a language and has looked for its syntax. One could even say that the search for the laws of cinematic enunciation was more marked during the period when cinema was being constructed outside speech: silent cinema was looking for a language with a different structure from that of speech" (Kristeva 1989: 316).

Keeping in mind Pushkin's keenness to represent movement and time in cinematographic-like manner we recall the comments about the Soviet pianist Iudina in the Introduction above. While playing classical nineteenth-century pieces at extra-fast tempo she was looking at a photo of the Bronze Horseman; she was transposing Pushkin's language into music. She would tell her audience that she had been under the influence of "The Bronze Horseman" and possessed by Pushkin's dynamic verse. Iudina's transposition of Pushkin's text into the music of Mozart (for example), in order to inscribe a new syntax to represent the jolting movements of shock — "the beating movements of the horse's hooves, and the chase, and the fear" (Ospovat and Timenchik 1987: 326) — suggests that, as Tynianov had done, Iudina discovered in Pushkin's poetry forms of modernist expression which lead to the cognition of reality as pure illusory fiction. It seems that Iudina had used the terms of displacement and estrangement to understand the modern subject, who appears to her as a little man chased to the margins of existence by modernisation's giant wave.

The modern subject's experience of shock and fragmentation and his shattered and neurotic self are reflected in Pushkin's search for the new language of simultaneity; this anticipates Bergson's theoretic models and modernist narratives. Such a language stands closer to cinema than to photography. Indeed, while photography is a document of the "reality from which we are sheltered" (Barthes 1977: 44), "cinema calls for the subject to project himself into what it sees; it is not presented as an evoking of a past reality, but as a fiction that the subject is in the process of living" (Kristeva 1989: 315). Kristeva compellingly argues that "the reason for the impression of imaginary reality that cinema elicits has been seen in the possibility of representing movement, time, the narrative, etc." (Kristeva 1989: ibid.). Kristeva suggests that Sergei Eisenstein demonstrates the importance of montage not only in cinematographic production, but also in every signifying production: "Cinema does not copy the reality proposed to it in an 'objective', naturalistic, or continuous fashion. It cuts up sequence, isolate shots, and recombines them by means of further montage. Cinema does not reproduce things, it manipulates, organises, and structures them. And it is only in the new structure obtained by editing these elements that they take meaning. The principle of montage, or better, that of joining isolated, similar, or contradictory elements, whose collision provokes a signification they don't have by themselves, was found by Eisenstein in hieroglyphic writing [...]. According to him, a film must be a hieroglyphic text in which each isolated element has meaning only in the contextual combination and according to its place in the structure" (Kristeva 1989: 315-16).

Looking closely at the passage from "The Bronze Horseman" below, which describes Evgenii's immediate response to the tragic death of his fiancée, we can see that his mad behaviour and convulsive laughter are framed so as not to be seen as extraordinary, or at least out of the ordinary. Evgenii's inability to mourn his beloved, to express his trauma in words, is juxtaposed with the scene of a restless city unable to sleep:

> Глядит... идет... еще глядит.
> Вот место, где их дом стоит;
> Вот ива. Были здесь вороты –
> Снесло их, видно. Где же дом?
> И, полон сумрачной заботы,
> Все ходит, ходит он кругом,
> Толкует громко сам с собою —
> И вдруг, ударя в лоб рукою,
> Захохотал. Ночная мгла
> На город трепетный сошла;
> Но долго жители не спали
> И меж собою толковали
> О дне минувшем.
> (Pushkin 1957, vol. 4: 392)

> He looks... walks... he looks again.
> This is the spot where their house stands;

> Here is the willow. There were gates here —
> They were washed away, seemingly. Where is the house?
> And, full of sad anxiety,
> He is walking, walking around all the time,
> Talking to himself loudly.
> And suddenly, slapping his forehead,
> He burst into laughter.
> The night darkness
> Has fallen on the trembling city.
> But Petersburgers stayed awake for hours
> And talked to each other
> About the day that had gone.

The incongruity between reality and Evgenii's subjective cognition of the objects he sees is expressed in the passage above with the help of the collision of the past tense 'they were washed away' («снесло их») with the present tense 'their house stands' («их дом стоит»). The phrase 'here is the spot where their house stands' («вот место, где их дом стоит») reveals Evgenii's confused and disorderly thoughts: a moment later he registers that the gates have evidently been washed away. Only after observing the gates' absence does he comes to realise that the house must also have gone. The question 'Where is the house?' clearly comes from Evgenii, not the narrator of the events.

The willow tree in the passage above is the landmark that triggers Evgenii's memory and evokes the memory flashback to the house standing intact besides the tree. The laughter that bursts out after the scene of confused walking stems from awareness of the absent dwelling. Pushkin's Evgenii is estranged from reality and muses incoherently. His walk around where Parasha's house had once stood emulate the sense of imaginary space that Evgenii created for himself. Once again, Pushkin has linked language, trauma and space, thereby presenting a speaking subject as spatially bound. This example illustrates well Kristeva's concept of the dependence of different ways of speaking upon spatial variations: "Any spatial representation provided from within a universal language is necessarily subject to teleological reason, contrary to what 'romantic minds' might maintain, attracted as they are to the 'mythico-magical' […]. The history of the speaking being (spatially bound precisely because he speaks) is only spatial variation [...]. It is henceforth clear that meaning's closure can never be challenged by another *space*, but only by a different way of *speaking*: another enunciation, another literature" (Kristeva 1980: 281). Evgenii's laughter can be viewed in terms of the mother-child relationship studied by Kristeva in relation to language development: "During the period of indistinction between '*same*' and '*other*', infant and mother, as well as between 'subject' and 'object', while no space has yet been delineated (this will happen with and after the mirror stage-birth of the sign), the semiotic *chora* that arrests and absorbs the motility of the anaclictic facilitations relieves and produces laughter" (Kristeva 1980: 284). Furthermore, Kristeva points out that while a child lacks a sense of humour, he laughs easily "when motor tension is linked to vision (a caricature is a visualization of bodily distortion, of an extreme, exaggerated movement, or of an unmastered movement"; when a child's body is too rapidly set in motion by the adult [...]; when a sudden stop follows a movement" (ibid.).

Given this semiotic and psychoanalytical explanation of the origin of laughter, we can suggest that Pushkin's caricaturised images of Petersburg, together with Evgenii's behaviour in the post-flood capital, reflect on the advanced course of modernity in Russia which spotlights the collision between the old and the new forms of life. Pushkin's Evgenii represents the modern speaking subject who is learning to speak a new symbolic language, in the meantime filling the void with laughter. Pushkin's skillful dramatisation of trauma and its many signifying processes in "The Bronze Horseman" brings to mind Shakespeare's tragedies. The French feminist and dramatist Hélène Cixous has said that every Shakespeare character embodies his own little theatre, for he gets up on his own stage and has his own little micro-kingdom. Cixous writes that each inhabitant of Shakespeare "is rich, he effects us, he fascinates us, he is not a person without a kingdom whom we may cross in the street" (Cixous 1997: 34-35). It is curious that Pushkin's image of the willow next to Parasha's house, which remains intact after her death, does evoke the image of the willow associated with Shakespeare's Ophelia. In *Hamlet* we find the Queen's story about the last moments of Ophelia's life:

> There is a willow grows aslant a brook,
> That shows his hoar leaves in the glassy stream;
> There with fantastic garlands did she come
> Of crow flowers, nettles, daisies, and long purples [...].
> There, on the pendant boughs her coronet weeds
> Clambering to hang, an envious sliver broke,
> When down her weedy trophies and herself,
> Fell in the weeping brook.
> (Shakespeare 1982: 826)

It appears that Pushkin alludes to Shakespeare's *Hamlet* in order to draw readers' attention to the different definitions of madness of the Middle Ages and of modern times. Evgenii's madness also has distinctive parallels with Hamlet's disturbed state of mind and melancholy: both characters might be seen as political thinkers and voices of moral conscience. Rosenshield, in his study of the genres of madness in Pushkin's works, draws a comparison between Shakespeare and Pushkin and concludes, "In Shakespearean tragedy and after, madness is largely psychological or psychologised. The times may aggravate the propensity to madness, if not cause it; but it is not an external force that is to blame but the individuals themselves [...]. However, Evgenii's insight, his elevation through madness, and his threats against Peter are all presented as objective realities. The only event affecting Evgenii's madness that may be interpreted as being purely his imagination is the Bronze Horseman's descent from its pedestal and its pursuit of Evgenii, and only on the condition that we completely dismiss the possibility of the supernatural" (Rosenshield 2003: 122). In addition to Rosenshield's observation, it is possible to point out that Evgenii's drama derives from the realisation that the modern world of artefacts blurs the boundaries between the imaginary and the real. As a dweller in man-made Petersburg, he becomes a puppet of the narrative designed by Peter the Great.

Evgenii perceives Petersburg as a theatrical space which revolves around the monument to Peter the Great. The external body of the city internalised within Evgenii's imagination, and his own inner shock, became exteriorised. It is as if his piercing, intense look crossed the boundary between the inside and outside, like a camera. At the end of the first chapter of Pushkin's "The Bronze Horseman",

Evgenii is depicted motionless, as if his terror at the uncontrollable flood had turned him into a monument too. The exchange between Evgenii's sentient body and the Peter the Great monument as a non-sentient weapon, is palpable:

> И он, как будто околдован,
> Как будто к мрамору прикован,
> Сойти не может! Вкруг него
> Вода и больше ничего!
> И, обращен к нему спиною,
> В неколебимой вышине,
> Над возмущенною Невою
> Стоит с простертою рукою
> Кумир на бронзовом коне.
> (Pushkin 1957, volume 4: 389)

> And he cannot move, as if
> He is bewildered, as if he
> Is fixed to the marble. There is
> Only water around him! Nothing else!
> And the idol with stretched arm
> On the bronze horse stands
> In the undisturbed heights
> Above the anguished Neva.

In the passage above the images of the immobile Evgenii and the Peter the Great statue are presented in the form of a montage and semantic collision: seemingly Evgenii is emulating the statue. Taking into account that Benjamin's discussion of Baudelaire's urban writing suggests that the reflective consciousness can protect itself from shock only by reproducing shock, in effect by responding to violence with violence; so Evgenii's madness can be interpreted as an imitation of Peter the Great's madness. Benjamin defines Baudelaire as a traumatophile type "who made it his business to parry the shocks, no matter where they might come from, with his spiritual and his physical self" (Benjamin 1999: 160). The passages quoted above reproduce Evgenii's immediate shock at the horrible condition of the post-flood suburb where his fiancée had lived. The question 'What is that?...' engages readers to visualise the scene witnessed by Evgenii and to experience the sense of terror triggered by the sight of corpses and ruined houses.

Pushkin omits a graphic description of Evgenii's tormented soul, but at the end of the passage describing the place of the missing house he mentions that Evgenii was unable to speak, but broke into laughter having realised that his fiancée and her mother were killed by the flood. The loss of the traditional dwelling, symbolised in "The Bronze Horseman" by the wooden house of Evgenii's fiancée, is entwined with the theme of laughter. The act of laughing can be understood as Pushkin's attempt to inscribe into the narrative the void experienced by Evgenii after the realisation of his loss. At the same time, Evgenii's laughter can be seen as a sign of trauma and discontinuity related to the collapse of the temporal and spatial frameworks of the past. If we can accept life in any European metropolis, including Petersburg, is akin to a theatrical experience, then to assess the surreal overtones of Pushkin's Petersburg we should remember Foucault's point that theatricality displays something less of character but rather more of incorporeal reality, such that Pushkin's Petersburg is highlighting a philosophy of phantasm and simulacra. In Foucault's words, theatricality articulates "the expanding domain of intangible objects that must be integrated into our thought". As a consequence of our exposure to it, "we must articulate a philosophy of phantasm that cannot be reduced to a primordial fact through the intermediary of perception or an image, but that arises between surfaces […] in the temporal oscillation that always makes it precede and follow itself" (Foucault 1997: 218). In a theatrical manner, Pushkin portrays crowds of Petersburg dwellers very quickly forgetting all their traumatic experience of the flood, continuing the next morning to live as normal. They are described as emotionless marionettes:

> Утра луч
> Из-за усталых, бледных туч
> Блеснул над тихою столицей
> И не нашел уже следов
> Беды вчерашней; багряницей
> Уже прикрыто было зло.
> В порядок прежний все вошло.
> Уже по улицам свободным

С своим бесчувствием холодным
Ходил народ. Чиновний люд,
Покинув свой ночной приют
На службу шел. Торгаш отважный,
Не унывая, открывал
Невой ограбленный подвал.
(Pushkin 1957, vol.4: 392)

The ray
Of the morning sun shone
Out of the tired, pale clouds
Above the quiet capital;
And found no trace
Of yesterday's misfortune; all the evil
Was covered in crimson.
All returned to normal.
Already crowds, indifferent and cold,
Walked along cleared streets. Officialdom,
Having left its shelter for the night,
Walked to work. The valiant shop-keeper
Cheerfully opened up
His cellar the Neva had robbed.

Pushkin's description of the city's routine lets us know that, just as with Baudelaire, shock was a paramountly important experience for Pushkin's personality. From the passage above it seems that Pushkin denounces those indifferent, mediocre and robot-like dwellers who were quick to forget the tragedies associated with some adverse aspects of modernisation. Their conformity and lack of moral consciousness are portrayed in "The Bronze Horseman" with bitter irony. Pushkin's image of the amorphous crowd of passers-by, the people in the street, prefigures similar depictions of urban life found in the poetry of Baudelaire, Blok and Pasternak. It appears that Evgenii in "The Bronze Horseman" stands out as the voice of moral consciousness and a painful reminder of the price paid for the creation of civilisation's numerous wonders, including Petersburg. Evgenii's madness is contrasted to the indifference of the crowd forgetful of the pain inflicted on the inhabitants by the autocratic authors of Russian modernisation. Evgenii challenges Peter the Great, the builder of the new modern space that fragmented life, disrupted the established order favouring liquid modernity (Bauman 2000), and displaced subversive laughter and critical thinking.

Evgenii also protects the private space of individuals which pivots around the concept of the little man's happiness. As Joost van Baak convincingly demonstrates, "The Bronze Horseman" advocates the importance of two metaphors related to the idea of private space: 'house as body' and 'house as personality' (van Baak 1994: 31). Van Baak's penetrating analysis of the myth of house in Russian literature — as conveyed in his article "Myth of House in Russian Literature" («Миф дома в русской литературе») — identifies two major trends in the representation of private space and dwelling in Russian literature which competed with each other for almost three hundred years. Van Baak broadly renders them as 'open house' based on the assimilation of other cultures and outside influences, and 'closed house' associated with an understanding of the world as a hermetic space focussed on the patriarchal order requiring artificial preservation and protection: "If we were to search for manifestations of the House Myth in Russian cultural history, having in mind the broadest global framework possible, we come across at least two ambiguous images. They might be viewed as two versions of the same mythopoetic motif which can be defined as Building House. Both versions of this mythopoetic model include historically specific contextual imagery, as well as an archetypal, collectively meaningful paradigm which determines the mythopoetic potential and semantic productivity of the image of House. I have in mind these two images *House Building* and *Window upon Europe*" («В поисках функций МД в русской культурной истории на самом глобальном модальном уровне мы встречаем по крайней мере два амбивалентных образа. Их также можно рассматривать как два варианта одного основного мифического мотива: Строительство Дома. Они оба соединяют в себе конкретно-историческую образность, и тот архетипический, коллективно-значимый масштаб, который ответствен за мифопоэтическую емкость и семантическую продуктивность образа Дома. Я имею ввиду следующие образы *Домострой и Окно в Европу*») (van Baak 1994: 28). Van Baak points out that Pushkin's rendering in "The Bronze Horseman" of Peter the Great's thoughts such as "It was determined by natural cause that we should create a window upon Europe in this place" («Природой здесь нам суждено в Европу прорубить окно») reflect upon Peter the Great's expansive behaviour which resulted in the destruction of the pre-Petrine model of state and social system. In van Baak's view, Evgenii's dreams of a peaceful family life with Parasha in a cosy house («приют смиренный и простой») imply a self-centred philistine existence in the style of German's concept of *Biedermeier* (van Baak 1994: 31). Also, as van Baak rightly pinpoints, Evgenii's dream of a quiet peaceful existence amounts to the dream of every little man, and reflects on the fragile and vulnerable modes of life of Petersburg dwellers whose life was always at the mercy of the elements. In Petersburg both natural and historical catastrophes make houses and cemeteries (the dwelling of the dead) vanish:

Обломки хижин, бревна, кровли,
Товар запасливой торговли,
Пожитки бедной нищеты,
Грозой снесенные мосты,
Гроба с размытого кладбища
Плывут по улицам! Народ
Зрит божий гнев и казни ждет.
(Pushkin 1957, vol.4: 387)

The remains of huts, trunks, roofs;
Merchants' stores;
The baggage of the miserable poor;
Bridges destroyed by the storm;
Coffins from the flooded cemetery
Float along the streets! The crowd
Gazes upon God's anger and awaits execution.

The gazing, submissive crowd described by Pushkin is akin to a spectatorship drawn to violence as a form of mass entertainment. Evgenii's madness, however, illustrates the extreme effect of a shock that could affect any urban dweller, especially in a Petersburg — an open space that is more more prone to natural disasters and 'the bad weather', to use Khodasevich's expression. As Ramazani observes in his discussion of Benjamin's essays on Baudelaire, "if the experience of shock is a complex of training it is because its transformative effects reach deep into (sentient) personhood" (Ramazani 1996: 204). In his discussion of Baudelaire's poems, Ramazani suggests that "modern alienation is at bottom physical, then we might reasonably expect that Baudelaire's prose poems will tell us something about the interior structure of that alienation and, ultimately, about the relation between the somatogenic features of modern consciousness and the broader system of social and political representations in which they are necessarily enmeshed" (Ramazani 1996: 205). Evgenii's madness seems conspicuously similar to the locus of counterviolence of consciousness described in Benjamin's works on Baudelaire: it is like a weapon and a wound together, it includes and excludes the shock, repeats and repels it, but at the end of the day it parries the shock (Ramazani 1996: 206). Thus the psychological landscape of Evgenii's consciousness incorporates shock and violence, and results in madness which displaces him as a homeless man. The loss of his dream of peaceful living and a traditional home renders Evgenii a vagabond; he becomes a spectacle for urban louts who abuse him physically and verbally.

In his seminal study *Madness and Civilisation: A History of Insanity in the Age of Reason* Foucault points out that in classical experience the work of art and madness were unified: "For there existed a region where madness challenged the work of art, reduced it ironically, made of its iconographic landscape a pathological world of hallucinations; that language was delirium, not a work of art" (Foucault 1988: 285-86). In his study on the concept of madness Foucault makes the important observation that the apocalyptic dreams which emerged during the Renaissance differed considerably from the fantastic iconography of the Middle Ages, in that the early modern time gave way to a vision of the world where all wisdom was annihilated. The end became perceived as "the advent of a night in which the world's old reason is engulfed" (Foucault 1988: 23). Pushkin's images of post-flood Petersburg are also entwined with the advent of the night, into which the old way of life dissolved. Pushkin's "The Bronze Horseman" can also strongly evoke Dürer's "Horsemen of the Apocalypse" about which Foucault writes: "It is enough to look at Dürer's Horsemen of the Apocalypse, sent by God Himself: these are no angels of triumph and reconciliation; these are no heralds of serene justice, only the dishevelled warriors of a mad vengeance. The world sinks into universal Fury. Victory is neither God's nor the Devil's: it belongs to madness" (Foucault 1988: 23). Pushkin's treatment in "The Bronze Horseman" of issues of modernity and madness which became associated with traumatic

Russian historical experiences in the pre-Soviet and Soviet periods had a great impact on Russian twentieth-century poetry, as I will show below.

Pushkin's Petersburg can also be seen as a playful theatrical space constructed with the aid of urban folklore. Thus, in "The Bronze Horseman" the moving statue joke has received extensive treatment in Pushkin scholarship. Virolainen argues there were many legends about the moving statue, including the dream of Count A.N. Golitsyn, but probably all of them were inspired by Pushkin's imagination as expressed in "The Bronze Horseman" (Virolainen 1999: 217). According to the legend, in 1812 Alexander I intended to relocate the monument, but Golitsyn saw a 'good omen' in his dream and warned him against it. Golitsyn says he saw himself walking to Elagin Island to deliver a report to the Tsar, but the Bronze Horseman chased him on his way to the palace, and in front of the palace told the Tsar and Golitsyn not to relocate it, because of its usefulness as the city's protector. It is known that Golitsyn recounted the dream to Alexander I who then changed his mind about the relocation of the monument (Ibid.).

The monument's sculptor, Falconet, was partly responsible for the impression it made. The statue can be seen as a parody of Italian equestrian statues. It adds a carnivalesque overtone to the city's landscape. According to the critic George Levitine, Falconet decided on a straightforward concept and avoided overt symbolic detail: "In this conception, Falconet departed from the main tradition of equestrian monuments, whose source was the Roman statue of Marcus Aurelius, in the Capitoline square. This tradition was based on the image of a triumphant horseman mounted on a powerful steed, majestically advancing at walking pace on the flat surface of a geometrically shaped pedestal. Exemplified during the Italian Renaissance by Donatello's 'Gattamelata' (Padua) and Verrocchio's 'Colleoni' (Venice), this type of equestrian representation culminated in France in Girardon's famous statue of Louis XIV, which stands in the Place Vendôme, in Paris" (Levitine 1972: 54). There is an inner symbolic meaning in Falconet's statue, detectable to spectators, arising from Falconet's unusual placing of the monument on the edge of a rocky elevation. This added a definite twist to the old theme, producing an unprecedented dramatic context. Falconet explains in some of his letters that he portrayed "Peter the Great not as a conqueror, but as a benevolent reformer and legislator; the monarch of the 'philosophers' and the benefactor of the new Russia" (Levitine 1972: 55). In his extensive study of Falconet's career Levitine points out: "In his writings, Falconet repeatedly explained the meaning of various aspects of his statue. Instead of the traditional pseudo-Roman martial attire, the tsar is given a 'heroic' but nondescript garb which, according to the sculptor, belongs to 'men of all times'. The sculptor acknowledges the fact that this garb recalls the shirt worn by Volga boatmen, and one can note an additional, distinctly Russian, touch in the wolf skin used in the monarch's saddle [...]. He has reached the summit of the rocky elevation that symbolises the difficulties he has overcome" (ibid. 55-56). These distinctly 'barbaric' features of Falconet's horseman reflect Peter the Great liking for playing the jester, and enjoyment of the guise of 'the people's Tsar'.

From the very start of Falconet's project several factors conspired to create some local legends. The monument itself is a living memory of the saga of its creation. A striking example is the stone forming the statue's base, made from part of what Russians called the "Thunderstone", weighing over 3 million pounds; this gigantic monolith was brought from the Karelian marshes where, according to Karelian legend, Peter the Great had used it many times as an observation point. The monument itself entered urban folklore, with numerous accounts by witnesses of some movement by the statue; contributing to this 'kinetic' effect were the vast space surrounding the monument and some important features of the monument itself. In Levitine's view, "It is not a mere question of size. The arresting effect of this silhouette is also the result of the powerful ascending diagonal movement that abruptly releases its energy after having reached its apogee. Animated by a different rhythm, the theme of upward élan, culmination and break is repeated twice: in the bronze horseman, with the horse rearing over emptiness, and its mountain-like base, with the jutting shape of the cliff. Naturally this theme is the energising force of the great triangle that gives the group its monumental character" (Levitine 1972: 59-60).

The sculptor's chief achievement lies in the theatrically conceived staging. Contemporaries including Didérot referred to

Falconet's monument as 'epic drama', or even 'Falconet's epic poem' (ibid.: 60). Theatricality formed an essential part of the Petrine period, and is essentially part of the living legacy of Peter the Great in Petersburg. As Levitine puts it, "Benevolent or ominous, *Peter the Great* came to be popular as the jealous guardian of the destiny of the city, a kind of awesome palladium" (ibid.: 59). It is known that Countess Anna Tolstaya, Pushkin's friend, visited Falconet's monument on 7 November 1824 after the flood; she expressed disgust at the monument's failure to protect the city, sticking her tongue out at the statue (Ospovat and Timenchik 1987: 24).

Clearly, the mixed responses to the 1824 flood included both the tragic and the comic. Pushkin's take on this event can be seen as an extension of the comic apocalypses constructed in the popular imaginations of Petersburg dwellers. (The term "comic apocalypse" was coined by Mark Seiden. It is included in the title of his PhD thesis *Dickens's London: The City as Comic Apocalypse* (1967). Seiden lists Pushkin among pre-modern writers who engaged in writing modern metropolis.)

Some reflected with humour on the event (see the satirical poem by Aleksandr Izmailov in the style of Berange, written on the day after the event: "God decided to punish all the sinful here..."), others in an apocalyptic vein. The number of texts bearing the marks of the unravelling Apocalypse, especially prose tales, outweighs the number of more humorous or satirical texts. Such works include the historical tale "The Black Box" by K. P. Massalskii, the novella "The Joke of a Dead Man" by V. F. Odoevskii (published in 1833), and the Petersburg tale "The Feast of Death" by Vladmir Pecherin (1833), to name a few. Pushkin seems to have incorporated both tendencies in his Petersburg tales, also embedding some parodies on existing texts. Virolainen interprets "The Bronze Horseman" in several ways as an example of polyphony in the Bakhtinian sense; in Virolainen's view, historical truth emerges as a collection of voices (Virolainen 1999: 219).

Close examination of Pushkin's Petersburg texts reveals that Falconet's statue was not the only focus for the city's popular mythology. The monument to Alexander I, a new city landmark unveiled to the public by Nicholas I on 30 August 1834, also affected people's imagination and triggered many anxieties. Pushkin avoided the ceremony, finding it humiliating to appear there as a minor civil servant. Commenting on the enormous weight and height of the column, Countess Anna Tolstaya predicted that it would fall down; she avoided going near it in her carriage. Alexander I's column became the butt of many rumours, jokes and parodies (Ospovat and Timenchik 1987: 47). With so many jokes and literary responses to the creation of a monument to the Tsar in front of the Winter Palace, one that would soar above all neighbouring buildings, it is striking that Pushkin chose Alexander's column for comparison with his own art, the non-verbal monument, in his poem "Monument" (1836). By juxtaposing himself to the column, Pushkin creates a poetic montage in order to point to the interdependence of poet and tsar, seen metaphorically as wound and weapon in the context of urban developments. Pushkin's desire, articulated in his poetry, to be regarded as the poet of liberty can be seen in "Monument" in the image of yet another artefact to express shock as a defensive reaction, and a consciousness to combat violence and parry the shock. Pushkin depicts himself in the form of a displaced person who nevertheless will be always associated with the tsar's monument and who will challenge existing power structures through poetry and collective memory: the fantasy about a monument becomes a powerful gesture of articulating the void and displacement. It is important that Pushkin envisages his own immortalised self as being located in the space of Petersburg, because the position of his poetic self, between the imperial sublime and the elegiac sublime, requires a completely new symbolic language. Furthermore, Pushkin's self-characterisation in "Monument" as a person who 'told the Tsars the truth with a smile on his face' resembles Evgenii's role as the Holy Fool in "The Bronze Horseman". If we consider Pushkin's narrative of the city in terms of the comic apocalypse, both prophetic and humorous traits merge in his art.

The image of Petersburg in Pushkin's *Eugene Onegin* is closely linked to the impressionistic view of urban life's richness, dynamism and excitement rendered by the view of Baudelairian kaleidoscopic consciousness. Several scenes are presented in a kinetic manner: as if busy city life is seen through the eyes of a person riding through Moscow and Petersburg streets. The lively kaleidoscopic representation of the description of Moscow's busy Tverskaya Street, as perceived by Tatiana in *Eugene Onegin* (chapter 7, part XXXVIII), strongly resembles Petersburg's busy streets seen by Onegin in the early hours of the morning (chapter 1, part XXXV):

> Что ж мой Онегин? Полусонный
> В постелю с бала едет он:
> А Петербург неугомонный
> Уж барабаном пробужден.
> Встает купец, идет разносчик,
> На биржу тянется извозчик,
> С кувшином охтенка спешит,
> Под ней снег утренний хрустит.
> Проснулся утра шум приятный,
> Открыты ставни; трубный дым
> Столбом восходит голубым,
> И хлебник, немец аккуратный,
> В бумажном колпаке не раз
> Уж отворял свой *васисдас*.
> (Pushkin 1957, vol.5: 25).

> What about my Onegin? Half asleep,
> He drives from the ball to his bed,
> While hyperactive Petersburg
> Has been woken by the drum.
> The merchant is up; the messenger is on his way;
> The Okhta suburb girl hastens with a jug;
> Morning snow creaks under her feet.
> Morning's pleasant noise is awake;
> Window shutters are open; chimney smoke
> Rises into the sky in a blue column;
> And the baker, a punctual German,
> In his cotton cap has more than once
> Opened his *vasisdas* window.

The passage above resembles a cinematographic presentation of the flow of life. From his carriage Onegin observes the Petersburg cityscape, as might a moving camera. Furthermore, Pushkin's describes Onegin as half asleep, which adds a surreal overtone to Onegin's presentation of a dream-like reality. In discussing the relationship between word and visual image we should keep in mind Boris Eikhenbaum's perceptive observation that literature and film are different forms of expression, with cinematographic language having its own peculiarities. This language is not moving photography, notes Eikhenbaum, but a special form of photogenic expression comparable to the visual images in dreams. Eikhenbaum maintains that, despite some mimetic qualities, film language is akin to dreaming when asleep: "The effect is such as if you see dreams while you are asleep: the face comes closer to you, then you see only eyes, then only arms; then everything disappears, and you see another face, a window, a street, etc. It is as if you see a novel you've read earlier in your sleep" (Eikhenbaum 1969: 297). Eikhenbaum suggests that the cognitive processes of film viewers differ significantly from readers' perception of the printed word: to view a film is the opposite of reading since perception moves "from object, from linking of various shots towards their cognition, naming, and towards the organisation of an inner speech" (ibid.). As Eikhenbaum aptly sums up, the language used in film is a somewhat trans-rational language that allows viewers to play with objects with the help of montage and editing (Eikhenbaum 1969: 298).

Pushkin's urban mode of visual observation as expressed in his poetry in general, and in *Eugene Onegin* in particular, prefigures several modes of visual engagement with the urban environment. Edgar Allen Poe's 1845 short story "The Man of the Crowd" conveyed such modes; the story has been a model for major theoretical studies of the representation of the modern city. Dana Brand examines three modes of urban spectatorship in Poe's story: detached observation; desperate search for sensation; and shadowy pursuit. She finds that they correspond to three urban types discussed in Walter Benjamin's work on Baudelaire: the *flâneur*, the *badaud* (gaper) and the *detective* (Brand 1991). In the passage above, Onegin's gaze seems to penetrate behind the façade of busy street life: he is not only a gaper but also a visionary. The smoke image can be seen as an allusion to Dante's *Divine Comedy* (*Commedia*): in "Purgatory" ("Purgatorio") the word 'modern' ('moderno') is associated with the description of anger triggered by the dense and acrid smoke. In this chapter Dante presents himself outside modernity: he tells the angry soul of Marco Lombardo that he is privileged to see God's court "in a mode wholly outside modern use" ("in modo tutto fuor del moderno uso") (Purgatory, canto 16). The image of Onegin observing Petersburg from his carriage infers a gaper's vision entwined with creative cognition. His melancholy seems to imitate the melancholy of the modern subject portrayed in Dante's *Divine Comedy*. According to Jean-François Lyotard, modernity is not a historically specific term, since regardless of the epoch in which it appears it "cannot exist without a shattering of belief and without the discovery of the 'lack of reality', together with the invention of other realities" (Lyotard 1984: 77). The fact is that Onegin's rhythm of life is different: he is about to go to bed while the city embarked on its busy routine. His dreams and melancholic vision of life makes him a stranger both to the city he observes and to himself. Here, Onegin's perception of a strikingly different flow of time, beyond modernity, is akin to Pushkin's self-representation of himself as dreamer and reader of Dante's poetry as found in Pushkin's lyric "Drums signal sunrise..." reviewed in chapter one. In both texts we encounter the image of modern male youths whose melancholy displaces from their immediate environment.

Commenting on the vivacious and dynamic portrayal of urban life employed in *Eugene Onegin*, Nikolai Nadezhdin, one of the most important Russian critics of the first half of the nineteenth century, compared Pushkin's image to the paintings and engravings of the English artist William Hogarth (1697-1764). Hogarth's satirical realism and lively rendering of urban life captured the imagination of Pushkin and his contemporaries. Nadezhdin writes in his review on *Eugene Onegin* with great enthusiasm that Pushkin's "portrayal of Moscow is truly Hogarthian!" and that "Pushkin's talent here is at its best" (quoted in Mashinskii 1974: 350). Hogarth's prints and engravings were well known in Russia in the first half of the nineteenth century. Viazemskii, for example, includes his name among the artists who were most influential on Russian cultural development in the first half of the nineteenth century (quoted in Smirnova-Rosset 1989: 589). It appears that Nadezhdin wanted to map some new directions in Russian literature (which would include some Hogarthian qualities) and to link Pushkin's impressionistic mode of urban writing to the various verbal portraits and interiors imitative of Hogarth's art found in eighteenth-century English literature. Nadezhdin's comments on the englishness of Pushkin's work echo Pushkin's own belief that England was a motherland of parody, and he identifies in Pushkin's poetics a strong subversive trait: "Pushkin's muse is a mischievous young girl, who does not care tuppence for the world. Her element is to mock at everything, good and bad [...] not out of spite or scorn, but simply out of desire to poke fun. It is this which shapes in a particular way Pushkin's poetic process and clearly distinguishes it from *Byronic* misanthropy or the humour of Jean-Paul Richter [...]. There is nothing that can be done about it [...] what is true, is true [...]. A master can mock and ridicule [...] provided, of course, he has a sense of honour and proportion. And if one can be great in small matters, then it is perfectly possible to call Pushkin a genius — *at caricature!*" (quoted in Richards and Cockrell 1976: 246). Indeed as Nadezhdin points out, Pushkin's mode of writing is full of playfulness and an impressionistic rendering of reality.

I identify this mode of expression as theatrical: it revolves around the relationship between the modern metropolis and the practice of urban spectatorship. Both Pushkin and Hogarth shared a great love for the theatre. They mocked the theatrical in the routine of the middle class and aristocracy. Hogarth's innovative techniques revived the baroque and introduced new themes and a vast new world of descriptive realism that occasionally blended irrational elements of fantasy derived from popular art and mannerism (Antal 1962: 25). Pushkin's city writing is similarly enriched by popular art and urban folklore linking the irrational aspects of life with the mythology of Petersburg everyday life. Even Tatiana Larina's vision of Moscow found in *Eugene Onegin* chapter seven (XXXVII) is constructed in the same surreal manner as Onegin's impressionistic cognitive map of Petersburg; it offers this list of city attractions:

> Прощай, свидетель падшей славы,
> Петровский замок. Ну! Не стой.
> Пошел! Уже столпы заставы
> Белеют; вот уж по Тверской
> Возок несется чрез ухабы.
> Мелькают мимо будки, бабы,
> Мальчишки, лавки, фонари,
> Дворцы, сады, монастыри,
> Бухарцы, сани, огороды,
> Купцы, лачужки, мужики,
> Бульвары, башни, казаки,
> Аптеки, магазины моды,

Балконы, львы на воротах
И стая галок на крестах.
(Pushkin 1957, vol.5: 156)

Farewell, witness of fallen glory.
Peter's castle. Well! Don't wait here,
Move on! The border posts
Are turning white; already on Tverskaya Street
The sleigh-coach sweeps across bumps.
The sentry boxes, peasant women flicker past,
Urchins, grocers, street lamps,
Palaces, gardens, monasteries,
Bukharans, sleds, allotments,
Merchants, hovels, peasant men,
Boulevards, towers, Cossacks,
Pharmacies, fashion shops,
Balconies, lions on the gates,
And a flight of jackdaws on the crosses.

Although that kaledoiscope-like view of Moscow does not offer such an exciting spectacle as Petersburg, and seems more oriental than European, the mode of spectatorship ascribed to Tatiana does not differ from the way Onegin observes Petersburg. Both Onegin and Tatiana are presented in *Eugene Onegin* as creators of visual montage, as badaud figures. Certainly, Tatiana's rendering of urban spectacles is infused with humorous overtones and direct responses to the contrasts of Moscow life: she sees expensive fashion shops and old huts, merchants and peasants, street lamps and allotments. But the image of Peter the Great's castle is an awkward reminder of Moscow's former glory, now superseded by Petersburg's modern look and the historical events linked to the emergence of a new imperial identity. Tynianov's seminal article "On the Composition of *Evgenii Onegin*" («О композиции *Евгения Онегина*») defines as comic the verse novel's urban scenes in Moscow and Petersburg which we have discussed. Tynianov thinks that both passages, with the impressionistic and kaleidoscope-like view of city life through the eyes of Tatiana (Moscow) and Onegin (Petersburg), use a device of listing objects («прием пересчета»). For Tynianov the device of listing objects in poetic speech creates the effect that the semantic meaning of all the randomly-linked words becomes significantly different from the meaning of the same words used in fiction. As Tynianov elaborates, "Undoubtedly, there is a peculiar comic effect in this passage which stems from listing of *different* objects (it occurs in fiction, too) as well as from their metrical equality and poetic monotony of intonation" («Несомненно, здесь особый комизм перечисляемых *разных* предметов (что есть и в прозе), но и в их метрической равности, в стиховой монотонии») (Tynianov 1977: 75). Tynianov also explains that the description of Onegin observing the German shop owner makes the Petersburg scene more comic than the Moscow scene.

At this point Tynianov stops short of referring to the concepts of the comic developed in Henri Bergson's book *Laughter: An Essay on the Meaning of the Comic* (published widely in Europe in 1911). To Bergson, the comic element consists of a certain 'mechanical inelasticity' (Bergson 1999: 15). Bergson's discussion of caricature emphasises the role of exaggeration: "For exaggeration to be comic, it must not appear as an aim, but rather as a means that the artist is using in order to make manifest to our eyes the distortion that is of moment and interest" (Bergson 1999: 29). In the Moscow scene, the most comic element in Tatiana's eyes must be the jackdaws sitting comfortably atop the church crosses. As for Onegin's mosaic of impressions, the punctual German shop-keeper's repeated opening of his shop window (a reminder of a cuckoo clock, or actors choreographed through doors in a French farce scene), is particularly amusing. The rhyme 'not once — vasisdas' («не раз — васисдас») highlights the comic potential of the rigid movement. Onegin is amused by the artificiality and rigidity of Petersburg life that turns people into automatons. In the case of Tatiana's experience the images of peasants and idle lads exemplify the badaud-type — the man of the crowd, the curious observer, the rubberneck. In his analysis of the popular imagination in nineteenth-century France, Gregory Shaya makes the point that mass culture in France was made "not through *flânerie* 'for and by the masses' but through the image of the *badaud*" (Shaya 2004: 46). In *Eugene Onegin* Pushkin also identifies the badaud as a spectator, who could play a role in the making of a mass public.

As mentioned above, the three modes of urban spectatorship appearing in Poe's "The Man of the Crowd" correspond well to

Benjamin's concept of the three urban types of flâneur, badaud and detective. Tom Gunning notes: "These three ideal types may shade into each other within the course of a narrative [...] but they can also be morphologically distinguished" (Gunning 1997: 26). In Pushkin's *Eugene Onegin*, while Onegin views the city as a locale to be endlessly crisscrossed in search of excitement, the narrator attempts to decode city types and is constantly impelled into a detective-like act of shadowing. Tatiana in chapter eight is also presented as an experienced spectator and detective who easily recognises the various masks and social acts of Petersburg dwellers. She is depicted as sitting next to men and women who seem to be within a living painting (Pushkin 1957, vol.5: 168). She is thinking about Onegin, whom she has just spotted in the crowd at a social gathering. The narrator's voice imitates colloquial speech, containing fragments of conversations, kaleidoscope-like. Onegin himself appears as a spectacle, a man of many social roles and a true dandy concerned with style:

> Все тот же ль он иль усмирился?
> Иль корчит также чудака?
> Скажите: чем он возвратился?
> Что нам представит он пока?
> Чем нынче явится? Мельмотом,
> Космополитом, патриотом,
> Гарольдом, квакером, ханжой,
> Иль маской щегольнет иной.
> (Pushkin 1957, volume 5: 168)

> Is he the same, or grown more content?
> Or does he still play the eccentric?
> Tell me, in what guise did he return?
> What will he stage for us meanwhile?
> What will he appear as now? As a Melmoth?
> A cosmopolitan? A patriot?
> A Harold? A Quaker? A hypocrite?
> Or will he show off some other mask?

In the passage above it appears that Onegin is regarded by Petersburg high society as a novel spectacle because he had been absent awhile. The narrator seems to act as a detective, voicing Tatiana's perspective of Onegin that might have crossed her mind, and her thoughts of how he might have been regarded in high society in recent gossip. The passage presents various stylistic masks for the narrator's speech. It contains parodic touches and an ironic mimicry of the language of others. The responses to Onegin's artificial behaviour and masks are presented in the above lines as an object of representation, "the novelistic image of another's style", to use Mikhail Bakhtin's term (Bakhtin 1981: 44).

In the same chapter eight of *Eugene Onegin*, the narrator reflects on the psychology of the Petersburg crowd from the viewpoint of an observer estranged from the crowd yet compelled to participate in its ritualistic activity. Although he finds the lack of creativity and the search for sensational gossip distasteful, he is nevertheless is drawn to participate in the representation of reality as spectacle. The analysis by Vanessa Schwartz in *Spectacular Realities: Early Mass Culture in Fin-de-Siècle France* suggests that the early mass culture of late nineteenth-century Paris was built on the visual representation of reality as spectacle (Schwartz 1998: 6). For Schwartz, the crowd assembled in front of spectacular and sensational urban life is not a body of passive spectators manipulated by the mass media, as suggested by Jürgen Habermas (Habermas 1989). Rather it is a new crowd composed of all classes, of men and women, a new crowd formed by a democratising commercial culture, sharing a common interest crossing lines of class and gender.

In *Eugene Onegin* Pushkin displays incredible sensitivity to all manner of spectators, thereby prefiguring the concerns of modernist writers and critics of the Silver Age. For example, Bakhtin's concept of novelistic images (images of another's language) found in abundance in *Eugene Onegin* can also be understood in terms of mass spectatorship. According to Bakhtin, while Pushkin's verse novel "does contain poetic imagery in the narrow sense", "it is of secondary importance for the novel"; it acquires in the novel "quite special functions that are not direct" (Bakhtin 1981: 43). Bakhtin talks of several passages in the novel which contain the representation of Onegin's style and worldview and should not be read as a direct poetic utterance of the author. In Bakhtin's view, "the hero is located in a zone of potential conversation with the author, in a zone of *dialogical contact*"; most importantly, however, "the author sees the limitations and insufficiency of the Oneginesque language and worldview that was still fashionable in his (the author's) time; he sees its absurd, atomised and artificial face" (Bakhtin 1981: 45). Bakhtin's analysis of various passages of *Eugene Onegin* implies that Pushkin represents Onegin's language as an image that speaks and "to a certain extent he even polemicises with this language, argues with it, agrees with it and eavesdrops on it, ridicules it". According to Bakhtin, Pushkin had a dialogical relationship with Onegin's language which Pushkin aptly defines as "a Muscovite in the cloak of a Childe Harold" whose lexicon is full of fashionable words (ibid.). Among the dialogised images of the novel's whole languages, Bakhtin also lists the language of Lenskii, and the complex and profound language-image associated with Tatiana. He identifies at the heart of this image a dialogised combination of the language of a dreamy provincial girl who reads sentimental literature in the folk language of fairy tales told by her nanny, folk songs and fortune-telling. Bakhtin maintains that "what is limited, almost comical, old-fashioned in Tatiana's language is combined with the boundless, serious and direct truth of the language of the folk. The author not only represents this language but also in fact is speaking in it. Considerable sections of the novel are presented in Tatiana's voice-zone" (Bakhtin 1981: 46).

As a mode of urban spectatorship, this language combines the visions of badaud and of detective. In this sense both the narrator and Tatiana possess a penetrating gaze which unmasks the masquerade of urban life. Pushkin as the author of the novel shares with Tatiana not only a desire to cherish in his heart the image of his beloved nanny, but also a desire to escape into the space where peaceful contemplation, reading and creativity would be entwined with the transitional world of childhood. In other words, just as in the poem "To the Sea", we come across again in the concluding chapters of *Eugene Onegin* the theme of displacement associated with love and trauma. This is how Tatiana voices her profound disillusionment with busy urban life and high society's theatrical existence:

«А мне, Онегин, пышность эта,
Постылой жизни мишура,
Мои успехи в вихре света,
Мой модный дом и вечера,
Что в них? Сейчас отдать я рада
Всю эту ветошь маскарада,

Весь этот блеск, и шум, и чад
За полку книг, за дикий сад,
За наше бедное жилище,
За те места, где в первый раз,
Онегин, видела я вас,
Да за смиренное кладбище,
Где нынче крест и тень ветвей
Над бедной нянею моей...
(Pushkin 1957, vol.5: 189)

"Yet as to me, Onegin, this pompous existence,
The tinsel of this anaemic life,
My triumphs in the whirlwind of high society,
My fashionable house and evening gatherings,
What do I care for them? ... Now I would be happy
To give up all this pretence,
All this glamour, and noise, and smoke,
For a shelf with books, for a wild garden,
For our poor dwelling,
For those places, where I saw you
For the first time, Onegin.
And for the humble churchyard too,
Where there is a cross now hidden
In the shade of branches over my poor nanny...

Again we come across, in the passage above, the device of listing (as Tynianov puts it). Yet the kaleidoscope-like description of high society's life of pretence and glamour is produced this time by Tatiana, the novel's protagonist, not its narrator. Tatiana's speech mimics perfectly the speech of the narrator himself: it renders his fragmented and impressionistic worldview, giving thereby the impression that Tatiana had learned to be a full member of Petersburg society, to control her emotions and develop a keen awareness of spectatorship and performance. We encounter here two images of language that form a dialogue. However, in Tatiana's speech the juxtaposition of the masquerade with the quiet cemetery in the scene of her final conversation with Onegin appears to be a spectacle in its own right, infused with a melancholy which displaces the subject. The passage above presents high society living as a monotonous routine where the sense of novelty is wearing out. In the phrase 'my fashionable house' («мой модный дом») we come across the mirror-like repetition of the word 'house', since the phrase 'fashionable house' contains a palindrome («модный дом»). Thus Tatiana speaks here in the imitative manner of the artefacts she wishes to mock and reproduce, presenting herself as a capable actress and detective. Taking into account that Bakhtin's comments emphasise the theatrical and metatextual qualities of *Eugene Onegin*, as did Nabokov's vision of the novel (as we discussed earlier), we can suggest that this verse novel does lend itself to a modernist reading. The artefact quality of Pushkin's narrative is also seen in its structural design: it is neither novel, nor verse, but altogether a new genre: a novel in verse.

Tynianov rightly identifies the deformities and artificial nature of *Eugene Onegin*. He concludes: "This novel is metatextual through and through; its female and male characters appear in front of us as parodic shadows seen against the novels that are envisioned as backstage; *Onegin* is like a novel that constructs imaginary reality: Onegin imagined himself to be Childe Harold; Tatiana imitates the whole gallery of female literary characters; her mother does the same. Beyond them are cliches (Olga, for example) which also boast an exaggerated literature-oriented artificiality" («Роман этот сплошь литературен; герои и героини являются на фоне старых романов как бы пародическими тенями; «Онегин» как бы воображаемый роман: Онегин вообразил себя Гарольдом, Татьяна — целой галереей героинь, мать — также. Вне их — штампы (Ольга), тоже с подчеркнутой литературностью») (Tynianov 1977: 66). Bakhtin also maintains that "Pushkin's novel is a self-critique of the literary language of the era, a product of this language's various strata (generic, everyday, currently fashionable), mutually illuminating one another. But this inter-illumination is not of course accomplished at the level of linguistic abstraction: images of language are inseparable from images of various worldviews and from the living beings who are their agents — people who think, talk, and act in a setting that is social and historically concrete" (Bakhtin 1981: 49).

Olga Hasty in her highly original study *Pushkin's Tatiana* points out that Evgenii's "swift passage through St. Petersburg, his unimpeded progress through the house, and his easy attainment of Tatiana's private chambers", and especially "his entry into Tatiana's boudoir and the state of undress and heightened emotions in which he surprises her" suggest to readers that "the stage is set for the consummation of their love" (Hasty 1999: 198). This observation on the theatricality of the scene describing Evgenii's final meeting with Tatiana can be easily extended to the discussion of the various modes of spectatorship embedded in *Eugene Onegin*. Onegin's intrusive behaviour, indeed, adds a touch of sensationalism to the whole episode: Tatiana's private world is exposed and threatened by the detective-like behaviour of the representatives of Petersburg society eager to contribute to the growing body of sensational stories and gossip columns in newspapers. In this meeting with Onegin, Tatiana exposes his dandyism and strategies for attention- and novelty-seeking to secure an opportunity for him to present himself to Petersburg society as a spectacle:

> Тогда — не правда ли? — в пустыне,
> Вдали от суетной молвы,
> Я вам не нравилась... Что ж ныне
> Меня преследуете вы?
> Зачем у вас я на примете?
> Не потому ль, что в высшем свете
> Теперь являться я должна;
> Что я богата и знатна,
> Что муж в сраженьях изувечен,
> Что нас за то ласкает двор?
> Не потому ль, что мой позор
> Теперь бы всеми был замечен
> И мог бы в обществе принесть
> Вам соблазительную честь?
> (Pushkin 1957, vol. 5: 188)

> Then — is it not so? — in the wilderness
> Far from the futile gossiping,
> I was not to your liking... Why then
> Do you chase me now?
> Why did you mark me as worthy of your attention?
> Could it be because in high society
> I am obliged to appear now;
> Because I am wealthy and of noble rank?
> Because my husband has been wounded in battles;
> Because the Court favours us for that?

> Could it be because my shame
> Would be noticed by everyone now
> And would have brought you
> Sensational prestige?

In the passage above Tatiana vehemently attacks the values and keeping-up-appearances behaviour of the Petersburg society to which she belongs. This politically charged speech highlights her estrangement from society, as well as her analytical and creative powers. The very last phrase — 'sensational prestige' («соблазительная честь») — is a powerful metaphor which underpins the fact that the word 'honour' («честь») in Russian society had devalued: Pushkin finished writing this chapter in Boldino in 1830, so he is likely to be referring here to the period after the Decembrist revolt. In the final scenes of the novel, Tatiana shows the potential to author society tales, a genre that began to gain currency in Russia at the end of the 1820s, when many writers denounced the marionette-like world constructed in popular novels, thereby indicating the need to shift attention to psychological realism.[2] However, in light of the interpretative strategy which Bakhtin and Tynianov applied to *Eugene Onegin*, it is possible to view Tatiana's assessment of Onegin's behaviour, and of high society, in the novel's concluding scenes as an attempt to imitate the voice of Evgenii Baratynskii. Baratynskii also felt estranged from high society: he attacked the lack of moral imperatives and the pretentious masquerade of Petersburg life in his long poems "The Ball" («Бал») and "The Mistress" («Наложница»). Baratynskii exposed the superficial and theatrical existence of Petersburg high society: "Although we take part in social gatherings of high society, we are not part of it. Our brain is trained differently, we have different habits. High society talk appears to us as scholarly conversation, a theatrical performance, since we are estranged from the real life, the real passions of high society" («Хотя мы заглядываем в свет, мы не светские люди. Наш ум иначе образован, привычки его иные. Светский разговор для нас ученый труд, драматическое создание, ибо мы чужды настоящей жизни, настоящих страстей светского общества») (Baratynskii 1951: 505-6).

Tatiana in her boudoir reading her letter to Onegin, and her sincere conversation with Onegin described in chapter eight, are actions representative of the new aesthetic trend of a developing interest in mass psychology. According to Lotman, psychological realism rapidly spread in Russian writing in the 1830s-1840s. One concern of the representatives of this trend was to understand what went on behind the mask of the typical high society person and to map their subject's psychological landscape. Lotman identified not only Baratynskii but also Lermontov as the trend's leading figures. Lotman suggests that Lermontov found the world of high society a locus of crime and tragic existence masked by a façade of pretence. Lotman defines Lermontov as a detective operating undercover in high society, as it were: he wears the mask of pretence to pass as a member of high society so as to observe and expose the vices and real emotions of society members who turn out to be actors (Lotman 1996: 535). I would say that Pushkin's Onegin is another representative-detective operating in high society: Onegin succeeds in catching Tatiana, a popular Petersburg countess, off-guard; he finds her crying over the letter she had written to Onegin back in her youth; she reveals her true feelings about him, declaring their union is a tragic impossibility. Pushkin humorously portrays Onegin in a state of shock, immobile for an instant as if struck by lightening: he froze because Tatiana's acting in front of him differed from what he expected, exposed by the power of Tatiana's outburst of sincerity and emotion. Pushkin uncovers life behind the façades of Petersburg's houses as more spontaneous and irrational than their occupants wanted to be revealed.

  Tatiana's speech in the concluding scene of chapter eight can be seen as a representation of the style of speech found in books she would have read as a woman of her time. It is the novelistic image of another's style. Her mode of expression, apparently sincere and using insightful remarks, probes high society's psychology and Evgenii's personality: "I know that you have pride in your heart and noble intentions" («Я знаю, в Вашем сердце есть и гордость, и прямая честь»). Her mode evokes strongly the poetic voice of Baratynskii, whose poetry Pushkin valued highly and whom he saw as Russia's Hamlet. Pushkin's semi-humorous poem "A Message to Del'vig" («Послание Дельвигу», 1827) playfully alludes to Baratynskii's poem "Skull" («Череп») to creating a strong analogy between the two poets:

Прими ж сей череп, Дельвиг: он
Принадлежит тебе по праву.
Обделай ты его, барон,
В благопристойную оправу.
Изделье гроба преврати
В увеселительную чашу [...].
Или как Гамлет-Баратынский
Над ним задумчиво мечтай:
О жизни мертвый проповедник,
Вином ли полный иль пустой,
Для мудреца, как собеседник,
Он стоит головы живой.
(Pushkin 1957, volume 3: 31)

Accept this skull as my gift to you, Del´vig.
It rightly belongs to you.
Baron, do place this skull
Within a tasteful frame.
Do turn this product of the coffin
Into an entertaining cup.
Or dream melancholically over it,
Just like Hamlet-Baratynskii.
It is like a dead preacher who talks of life,
No matter if it is full or empty;
To a wise man it is an interlocutor,
Not less than a head of a man alive.

In an unfinished poem Pushkin characterised Baratynskii as having deep feelings, a precise mind, and good taste and style free of sentimental mannerism (Stelliferovskii 1988: 130). These qualities are equally applicable to Tatiana, who presents herself to Onegin as a mature person and a philosopher of deep emotions and moral imperatives — in chapter eight, her final speech's allusion to her nanny's grave indicates her preference for elegiac discourse. As discussed earlier, Russian Romanticism's attitudes to empire oscillated between odic triumphalism and elegiac mourning: Tatiana comments that the cemetery of her nanny's grave, representing a place of dwelling, is dearer and more alive to her than her Petersburg home. In continuing to mourn beloved nanny, and hankering for the imaginary space of her ongoing conversations with nanny, her favourite interlocutor, Tatiana parallels the lyric hero in Pushkin's "To the Sea" who is in dialogue with Byron.

Hasty has suggested that *Eugene Onegin* superficially aligns the private world of Tatiana "with the countryside and the public persona with urban society" (Hasty 1999: 223). But I believe her private self is located in the space where the two worlds interact and fuse with each other. It is an imaginary world imbued with mnemonic overtones. Towards the end of the novel Tatiana appears to have a hybrid identity, and be engaged in elegiac mourning. Like Hamlet-Baratynskii, Tatiana is well versed in observing and analysing the high society to which she belongs, and from which she feels estranged. However, it may be Tatiana feels displaced into her imaginary world. If Tatiana's attacks on high society, and presumably Russian autocracy, are moulded in the language of Hamlet-Baratynskii, to use Pushkin's expression, then Tatiana's montage of the image of a Petersburg masquerade with the image of nanny's grave appears politically charged. Pushkin also ascribes Tatiana's dialogised voice-zone, as Bakhtin puts it, with autobiographical overtones. Akhmatova's essay on Pushkin and the Decembrists convincingly demonstrates that Pushkin was tormented at not finding the grave of his close friends executed after the 1825 Decembrist revolt. He searched for it on many occasions (Akhmatova 1976: 521-22). Hence Pushkin, through Tatiana in chapter eight of *Eugene Onegin*, is attacking modern Russian rulers for depriving citizens of proper burial. Pushkin's text is creating a metaphorical dwelling for those deprived of this basic human dignity. The whole concept of building Petersburg as a Russian centre of modernity rests on the idea of sacrifice and its immoral negligence of the value of life.

Brodsky too refers to the dark side of the construction of Petersburg, testifying that the wound inflicted upon people was not healed, leading to dystopian representations of the city. Brodsky maintains: "During Peter's reign, a subject of the Russian crown had the somewhat limited choice of being either drafted into the army or sent to build St Petersburg, and it's hard to say which was deadlier. Tens of thousands found their anonymous end in the swamps of the Neva delta, whose islands enjoyed a reputation similar to that of today's Gulag. Except that in the eighteenth century you knew what you were building and also had a chance in the end to receive the last rites and a wooden cross on the top of your grave" (Brodsky 1987: 73). To Tatiana, the reference to the last rite and the cross above nanny's grave conveys the patriarchal way of dwelling, based on a moral order certain of its rightness. The Petersburg space to which she belongs remains alien, precisely because of its idea of a new home which revolves around the image of the Window upon Europe (as discussed above). Tatiana, who is proud of her husband's heroism in the Napoleonic war, finds Onegin lacking moral imperatives for killing his friend in a reckless duel. Tatiana's vehement attack on Onegin in the concluding scenes of *Eugene Onegin* is a denunciation of ritualised violence. But by sympathising with Onegin and referring to his noble heart, Tatiana also acknowledges Onegin's duel as an act of counter-violence. Reyfman compellingly suggests in her brilliant analysis of duels in Russia that their increased occurrence in nineteenth-century Russia "reflected the nobility's deep anxieties concerning the state's power over bodies". In this respect "the duel served as a strong — although largely symbolic — gesture to counter the state's violence against the individual" (Reyfman 1999: 11).

Tatiana's estrangement from her milieu and from herself stems also from realisation of her entrapment in a loveless marriage. Tatiana's fate has an interesting analogy with that of the protagonist of Baratynskii's "The Ball" («Бал» 1825-28). Nina, protagonist in this poem, commits suicide after a ball where she had met her old flame; Nina is trapped in a loveless marriage but her love for her beloved remains unrequited; the concluding part suggests that news of Nina's death became the centre of attention in Moscow high society, an initial period of silence was followed by her suicide becoming a hot story in many newspapers and the subject of mediocre poetry published in a journal for women: "And one appropriate section published these poems in the journal for women" («И их законная страница в журнале дамском приняла») (Baratynskii 1979: 218). It seems Pushkin's Tatiana was aware of the consequences for a married woman in an affair, and preferred to control her own fate and her own story. Tatiana stands out in the eyes of Onegin, and of *Eugene Onegin* readers, as having the last word. Her support for her husband, the wounded war hero, signals her deep concern for ethics and compassion. A voice of moral conscience, displaced by high society's behaviour, Tatiana writes her own dwelling, her own private space of honour and dignity. Unlike Onegin, in laying out her charge against the hierarchical order and Russian-style modernity, she does not resort to counter-violence, but verbally attacks the lifestyle of contemporary Petersburg as a perpetual crime scene with individuals as victims.

Tatiana expresses herself in the style of Baratynskii's poetic language, which was precise and to the point. Tatiana's speech to Onegin accords with Baratynskii's aesthetic principles, admired and advocated by Pushkin, that every poet should know the mystery of suffering and learn to express himself clearly through the vibrations of the heart. Baratynskii in responding to *Eugene Onegin* compared Pushkin to Raphael, describing his mode of writing as excellent, precise and free (Stelliferovskii 1988: 112). This comment leads us to compare the modes of spectatorship used by Pushkin and Baratynskii. In this passage in *Eugene Onegin* Tatiana is portrayed as a spectator of living canvases:

> Вот села тихо и глядит,
> Любуясь шумной теснотою,
> Мельканьем платьев и речей,
> Явленьем медленным гостей
> Перед хозяйкой молодою,
> И темной рамою мужчин
> Вкруг дам как около картин.
> (Pushkin 1957, vol. 5: 168)

> Here she sat down quietly. She looks around,
> Admiring the busy crowded space;
> The glimpses of dresses and conversations;
> The steady arrival of guests
> In front of the young hostess;
> And the dark frame of men
> Around ladies, as if they are paintings.

Tatiana's mode of spectatorship is again similar to the penetrating gaze of a moving camera which impressionistically registers reality. She is both detective and artist, aestheticising everything she observes: the crowds appear to her as animated framed pictures. Her mode of spectatorship differs strikingly from that of the badaud figure in Baratynskii's "The Ball" witnessing a similar Moscow social gathering:

В роскошных перьях и цветах,
С улыбкой мертвой на устах,
Обыкновенной рамой бала,
Старушки светские сидят
И на блестящий вихорь зала
С тупым вниманием глядят.
(Baratynskii 1979: 198)

Wearing splendid feathers and flowers;
Having frozen smiles on their faces;
In a shape of a frame around people,
High society's old ladies are sitting
And looking at the whirlwind of the hall
With a dull gaze

In contrast to that 'dull gaze', Tatiana's gaze penetrates like a razor to create a synthesised and true image of reality. In her book *Pushkin's Tatiana* Hasty makes the very insightful observation on the impact of Tatiana's creative energy on Russian women poets, especially Tsvetaeva, who looked to *Eugene Onegin* as a model for imitation. Hasty points out that Tsvetaeva "ascribes her own being and coming into being as a poet" to Pushkin's Tatiana. "Even as she creates herself in Tatiana's image, Tsvetaeva establishes a lineage of her own making. *Her* Tatiana — the Tatiana she reads and (re)creates — engenders not a child, but a woman poet" (Hasty 1999: 234). Commenting on Tatiana's final speech in chapter eight, Hasty highlights the role of memory in Tatiana's worldview as expressed in her final conversation with Onegin: "The ascendancy Tatiana accords her rural experience in her speech to Eugene manifests not her preference for the Russian countryside over the European capital, but rather her longing for a past in which her future appeared more open than the one she contemplates from her vantage" (Hasty 1999: 203).

Let us further elaborate how Tatiana remembers her past life, attempts to reconstruct the experiences of her youth as a lasting presence, thereby simultaneously to recreate past events and create her own mythologised version of them. Given Pasternak's words that "man himself is mute, and it is the image that speaks" (quoted in Bachellard 1994: 104), we can establish an analogy between the bonds established with their respective nannies by both Tatiana and Pushkin:

Pushkin's nanny Arina Rodionovna featured in his lyrics. The grave of Tatiana's nanny shaded by a tree is a place of dwelling and intimacy that allows contemplation. This is a description of a location of exile and creativity which enables an urban writer to develop a vantage point. Tatiana's reference to the shadow of the branches over the grave evokes the concept of the old home as nest, in the context in which Bachellard wrote: "If we return to the old home as to a nest, it is because memories are dreams, because the home of other has become a great image of lost intimacy" (Bachellard 1994: 100). Bachellard's axiom comes near to identification of the nest with the world, as found in a text by Pasternak published in the autumn 1954 issue of *Cahiers G.L.M.* In a passage on creativity Pasternak talks of "the instinct with the help of which, like the swallow, we construct the world — an enormous nest, an agglomerate of earth and sky, of death and life, and of two sorts of time, one we can dispose of and one that is lacking" (quoted in Bachellard 1994: 104).

Tatiana's speech to Onegin contains a powerful juxtaposition of life and death, the open and the closed spaces, the theatrical and the sincere. With her words and images she builds an imaginary house for herself. Bachellard indicates the precarious structure of nests, which paradoxically does not interfere with daydreaming about security. He explains this paradox: "When we dream, we are phenomenologists without realising it. In a sort of naïve way, we relive the instinct of the bird, taking pleasure in accentuating the mimetic features of the green nest in green leaves. We definitely saw it, but we say that it was well hidden. This centre of animal life is concealed by the immense volume of vegetable life. The nest is a lyrical bouquet of leaves. It participates in the peace of the vegetable world. It is a point in the atmosphere of happiness that always surrounds large trees" (Bachellard 1994: 103). Pushkin's 1835 lyric "I visited again..." («Вновь я посетил...») is permeated with elegiac overtones which describe the house in Mikhailovskoe, where he lived with his nanny in autumn 1835, and the trees growing nearby to which he often talks. The poem has the lyric hero dreaming that these trees will communicate memories of him to his grandchildren, with whom a special bond had developed. Pushkin thus binds nature and creativity together, so it is no surprise that Pushkin's Tatiana is depicted as a creative person. In the words of Sandler, "*Eugene Onegin* has taught its readers that it values Tatiana's spontaneity, her closeness to nature, her imagination (as seen in her dreams and her reading habits). This very creativity is what permits Tatiana, as a salon hostess in Petersburg's high society, to use the conventions of her culture with such satisfaction" (Sandler 1989: 199). Since *Eugene Onegin* has analogies with Baratynskii's "The Ball", which describes the suicide of a married woman, one can say that Pushkin contrasts Petersburg's image as a comic apocalypse with Moscow precisely because of its enormous creative potential as a theatrical space: unlike Baratynskii's protagonist Nina, Tatiana is versed in the idiom of Petersburg artificiality and uses it for her own reading and writing as dwelling.

In her insightful 1963 article "Pushkin and the Baltic Coast" ("Пушкин и невское взморье») Akhmatova links Tatiana's references to her nanny's grave to the motif of the unknown grave and mourning. Akhmatova identifies in the poetry of Pushkin after 1825 this motif of mourning as relating to the unspecified grave of Pushkin's friends executed after the Decembrist revolt. In Akhmatova's view, Tatiana in the final scenes of *Eugene Onegin* acts as a mouthpiece for Pushkin, who wishes to lament his friends, and possibly also his nanny, whom he saw as his companion and soul mate. According to Akhmatova, "Pushkin shares with the poets of antiquity a high belief in the concept that the grave of a righteous person is a country's treasure and a blessing of the gods" («Пушкин полностью разделяет высокое верование античности [...] о том, что могила праведника — сокровище страны и благословение богов») (Akhmatova 1976: 520). Akhmatova is suggesting that in the final passages of *Eugene Onegin* Pushkin is expressing his secret desire to commemorate his executed friends and ascribe the final part of *Eugene Onegin* as a symbolic burial space, a space of memory and intimate interaction with the souls of his beloved deceased friends.

In support of Akhmatova's observation is the fact that the final meeting between Evgenii and Tatiana takes place in the boudoir in Tatiana's house. The concept of the boudoir originated in the eighteenth century, and more often than not it was seen not as a place for sexual intrigues but as a place for philosophical contemplation. The 1752 edition of the Dictionnaire de Trévoux, for example, specifies its function as follows: "Small closet, very confined cabinet, adjacent to the room one normally occupies, apparently thus named because of the habit of retiring there, to sulk unseen, when one is in a bad mood» («Petit réduit, cabinet for étroit, auprès de la chambre qu'on habite, ainsi apparament, parce qu'on a coûtume de s'y retirer, pour bouder sans témoin, lorsqu'on est de mauvaise humeur») (Lilley 1994: 194). According to Ed Lilley's survey of the image of boudoir in French eighteenth-century literature and culture, at first the boudoir was not intended just for female occupation, although some literary sources linked it to the feminine gender in spite of the fact that it was envisaged initially as a private space of melancholy, "a strait space, useful for hiding one's black mood" (Lilley 1994: 195). Lilley's article on the history of boudoirs in France includes François Franque's 1762 plan of a house for the Marquis de Villefranche in Avignon in which the boudoir "is not a commodious place of enchantment, but a narrow construction that only communicates directly with a corridor, the latter being, of course, a prime enabler of privacy" (ibid.). Lilley argues compellingly that towards the end of the eighteenth century noblewomen in France increasingly became equal partners of their husbands "in a situation where they were accorded (or perhaps demanded) some room specifically for themselves" (ibid.). French encyclopaedias of the period outlined, among specified private female activities, not only dressing and slumbering but also reading as increasingly common activity favoured by educationally oriented noblewomen. As Lilley explains, "The very act of reading, certainly the development of silent, solitary reading was in and of itself an indication of an increased concern for privacy" (ibid.) Lilley links the emergence of the private world of the home to tolerance of the education of aristocratic women: "Reading quietly by oneself developed particularly quickly during the seventeenth century, but with the eighteenth century emergence of the novel, for which there was initially a strong female readership, one may posit a connection between reading and the development of private female space" (ibid.). Bearing in mind Bakhtin's remarks that Tatiana's 'voice-zone' (Bakhtin 1981: 46) includes the voice of Pushkin, as Akhmatova also asserts, it becomes possible to see the boudoir scenes described at the end of *Eugene Onegin* as manifestation of Pushkin's desire to develop and maintain the culture of private spaces which enable readers of books to have quiet moments of contemplation, melancholy and imaginary voyages.

In his article "The Scare of the Self: Sentimentalism, Privacy, and Private Life in Russian Culture, 1780-1820", Andreas Schönle analyses the ethical implications of the ethos of sincerity advocated by Russian sentimalists, including Karamzin. The drive for sincerity "compelled writers and readers to reveal their inmost desires and confess their real and imagined sins" (Schönle 1998: 723). Schönle raises some important questions about the ideological concerns related to Sentimalism's preoccupation with the discourse of intimacy: "How did sentimentalism conceive of privacy? Was it intent on tearing down the walls of intimacy in order to expose the underside of things, perhaps in pursuit of a dream of transparency between people and minds? Did it, on the contrary, seek to privatize public life, as it were, constituting public discourse as a dialogue between private selves rather than as an exchange regulated by social conventions?" (ibid.). Indeed, Tatiana's last conversation with Onegin implies that she might have been infected by the impulse of sincere behaviour that sentimentalist writings instilled in the minds of their readers. On the metonymic level, Pushkin seems also to advocate the need to maintain the right of every individual to have private spaces of contemplation. A room of their own signified the concept of the boudoir, reserved for private expression of melancholy and sadness. The concept of boudoir seems to be welcomed by Pushkin as an urban substitute for the private spaces of the Russian countryside.

Pushkin's "Monument" («Памятник», 1836) is another interesting example of urban writing that touches on the issues of spectatorship and cultural production. It illustrates Pushkin's acute awareness of the importance of memory and dialogic conscience in cultural evolution. His self-created monument is yet another artefact added to the Petersburg space often perceived as a city-museum engaged in a dialogue with European culture. According to Renate Lachmann, "like the Acmeists, Pushkin should be placed in the metonymic paradigm established by intertextuality" (Lachmann 1997: 194). Apart from a strong desire to inscribe his name into the European canon, Pushkin also envisaged his poem as a dialogue with Baratynskii. In Baratynskii's poem "The Last Poet" («Последний поэт», 1835) we find a definition of the 1830s as a utilitarian period concerned with technological advancement and commercial profit. Baratynskii characterises this epoch as the iron century which dismisses poetry as useless dreaming and philosophical contemplation. Baratynskii laments the death of poetry, referring to the 1810s-1820s, a period famous for its poetic achievements, as childish poetic dreaming. Pushkin's Tatiana also seems to be lamenting the period of her youth when Romantic and Sentimentalist literature inspired young people to make their own lives works of art. In "The Last Poet" several goals of modernity and utilitarian concerns, strongly enunciated in the 1830s, pushed Russian lyric poetry to the margins:

> Век шествует путем своим железным,
> В сердцах корысть и общая мечта
> Час от часу насущным и полезным
> Отчетливей, бесстыдней занята.
> Исчезнули при свете просвещенья
> Поэзии ребяческие сны,
> И не о ней хлопочут поколенья,
> Промышленным заботам преданы.
> (Baratynskii 1979: 130-31)

> The century walks along its iron way;
> Hearts are full of selfish gains, and collective dreams
> Are more evidently concerned with immediate benefits
> And pragmatic goals, more shamelessly.
> Poetry's childish dreams
> Vanished in the light of enlightenment,
> And new generations are unconcerned by it,
> Being preoccupied with commercial matters.

The poem above provides a context to understand that Pushkin's "Monument" (written in 1836) is in effect a response to the 'recoil of silence', to use Blanchot's term: the poet's voice becomes recognised not as a creator of imaginary fictions, but as *the* reality "at certain times in each of our lives" (Blanchot 2003: 218) just, perhaps only, when it falls silent. Pushkin is lamenting his anticipation of his own death, which would be the last loss of a poet to be taken seriously by many generations of readers.

Pushkin's voice is broadly that of an archaising innovator. In her discussion of Pushkin's literary output and the role of intertextuality in his poetry, Lachmann says "it would seem that long before Tynianov, Pushkin himself was the first to understand the problematic nature and the inadequacy of a wholesale transfer of the dualism between the Classical and the Romantic to the Russian context" (Lachmann 1997: 191). Lachmann suggests that Russian Romanticism meant to Pushkin the creation of new genres, including the romantic poem and the romantic tragedy: old genres blended together. Lachmann's emphasis on eclectism as Pushkin's trademark is echoed in Tsvetaeva's statement that Pushkin's influence on Russian poets could only be understood in terms of its liberating effect on others (Smith 1994: 35).

Lachmann's identification of Pushkin's achievements is worth quoting in full: "Pushkin revises all the established aesthetic dogmas, both those held by Sentimentalism and those shared by both types of Archaists. He insists on openness and thereby legitimates both his eclecticism and his syncretism. Pushkin becomes an archaising innovator when he steps beyond all literary boundaries between different sects, closely examines all possibilities for creating poetic capital, and experiments with old forms within new ones. In such a manner he arrives at Romanticism after beginning with Sentimentalism, and passing through the archaisms of the younger generation, he thereby crosses the threshold into realism. Thus in a relatively short creative period, Pushkin was able to make his way through all these schools and to perfect their forms. Mastery of form, richness and concision of expression: these are consequently the characteristics of his creative work. Given the fact that all the important lines of thinking from his time converge in his work, the title of classical writer was thoroughly earned by Pushkin" (Lachmann 1997: 191-92). And all the achievements of Pushkin summarised by Lachmann are found in Pushkin's "Monument".

"Monument" is a metaphor of writing as building. The first line of the poem "I erected a monument to myself not built by human hands" («Я памятник воздвиг себе нерукотворный») (Pushkin 1957, vol.3: 373) contrasts with the definition of Peter the Great as "a builder — miracle-worker" («строитель чудотворный») found in "The Bronze Horseman". Heidegger's interpretation of Hölderlin's concept of poetry as dwelling can be easily applicable to Pushkin's own vision of building a place of dwelling through poetry: "Poetry is what really lets us dwell. But through what do we attain to a dwelling place? Through building. Poetic creation, which lets us dwell, is a kind of building" (Heidegger 2001: 213). It is remarkable how Pushkin compares his poetic building to the column commemorating

Alexander I, and suggests his immortal soul will continue to live, in a lyre. He thus inscribes his body into Petersburg's contemporary cityscape, implying that it will attract more attention than the Alexander I monument:

> Я памятник себе воздвиг нерукотворный,
> К нему не зарастет народная тропа,
> Вознесся выше он главою непокорной
>   Александрийского столпа.
>
> Нет, весь я не умру — душа в заветной лире
> Мой прах переживет и тленья убежит —
> И славен буду я, доколь в подлунном мире
>   Жив будет хоть один пиит.
> (Pushkin 1957, vol.3: 373)

> I erected a monument to myself not built by human hands,
> The way for people to reach it will not be overgrown,
> Its rebellious head is raised higher than
>   Alexander's column.
>
> No, I shall not die entirely – in my sacred lyre my soul
> Will outlive my dust and escape decay —
> And my fame shall last so long as even just one poet
>   Stays alive in the sublunar world.

Lachmann's penetrating analysis of this poem pinpoints its links with the tradition of making icons. Russians perceived icons as images not created by the human hand: "The links with iconoclasm are rather clear for this concept. The driving idea behind iconoclasm is that of a utopia of nonrepresentation. The counterposition of the iconodule is rooted in a system that determines the relationships between the original image and its representation. This position initiates a competition between similarity and analogy and explicitly favours the latter while rejecting the former" (Lachmann 1997: 212). Taking this observation further, we could say Pushkin creates the effect of cinematographic writing in this text: although passers-by would see the Alexander column as Petersburg's most prominent landmark, the monument raised by Pushkin would remain in the realm of the invisible and the implied. Pushkin is also mocking the nature of monuments: the poetic word for his monument is a living creative impulse that comes alive in a dialogised context: as long as the future will hold poets, they will ensure that Pushkin's poetry will come alive through the act of reading. Pushkin understands creative evolution in terms that anticipate Bergson's concepts of creative evolution and memory.

Lachmann suggests that Pushkin's "Monument" is imbued with parodic overtones, that it challenges the classical tradition of the *poeta laureatus*: "Pushkin is concerned neither with attaining the classical fame of the *poeta laureatus* nor with taking up the eighteenth-century topos of fame, where abraded myths are reworked in metaphorical form. In a parodic self-portrait that at the same time mocks the style of 'paper icons' [...]. Pushkin draws a picture of himself wearing (only) a laurel wreath and portrays himself as one who would compare himself to Dante, the *poeta laureatus*. Incidently, the words 'Il Gran Padre', the caption at the bottom of the drawing, are a quotation from Lord Byron speaking about Dante. And so, in Pushkin's poem, the idea of 'non omnis moriar' [I shall not die entirely] refers in fact to a different semiotic order, that of a memory that takes in a memory of matter: one of cloth, of stone, of paper" (Lachmann 1997: 213).

Lachmann is articulating the importance of the lyre image in the poem. She suggests it is a metaphor for what is written. As an iconic attribute poetry becomes represented by the instrument as the visual figure of the book: "moreover, it assumes the role of legacy, a testament (and summa) looking back to the past, it is also a promise referring to the future. With this indirect positing of signs, it would appear that Pushkin is repeating his ideologeme of memory" (Lachmann 1997: 215). I would add that, for Pushkin, the lyre image evokes the power of the voice which can soar higher into the sky than can Alexander's column. Pushkin presents himself as a spectacle, as Petersburg's Orpheus, whose verse will become part of the oral tradition of the city he contributed to building through his writings. Bearing in mind that Pushkin equated poetry with geometry and favoured the logic of the fossilised geometry of the animal world, the shape of the lyre might be seen as a perfect example of Pushkin building a house in which he could live. In ancient times a lyre was made from a tortoise shell, another dwelling. Thus Pushkin's lyre in which the poet's soul lives might be also approached from a phenomenological point of view: it is a house of human daydreams, memory and imagination.

So Pushkin's poems gives insight into his home of exile: displaced as a daydreamer from 1830s urban life, Pushkin takes refuge in a house in the form of the shell. In this context the lyre stands out as a fortress city for a man who loves solitude and contemplation, and who can create simple images with which to defend and protect himself.

NOTES

1   A list of works on Pushkin which Briusov published in 1903-24 would include the book *Pushkin in the Crimea (Пушкин в Крыму)* and articles such as "From Pushkin's Life" («Из жизни Пушкина»); "Pushkin and Baratynskii" («Пушкин и Баратынский»); "House in Kolomna" («Домик в Коломне»); "The Bronze Horseman" («Медный всадник»); "Unfinished Tales by Pushkin" («Незаконченные повести Пушкина»); "Egyptian Nights" («Египетские ночи»); "The Sound Structure of Pushkin's Verse" («Звукопись Пушкина»); "Pushkin's Radicalism Manifested in his Rhyme" («Левизна Пушкина в рифмах»); "Pushkin — The Craftsman" («Пушкин — мастер»); "Pushkin's Political Views" («Политические взгляды Пушкина»); "Pushkin's Diversity" («Разносторонность Пушкина»); "Pushkin and Serfdom" («Пушкин и крепостное право»); and "Why is it Necessary to Study Pushkin?" («Почему нужно изучать Пушкина?»). Briusov also edited several publications of Pushkin, including a volume of Pushkin's correspondence with friends and family (1907); a volume of Pushkin's poetry written when at Lycée (1907); a co-edition (with S. A. Vengerov) of Pushkin's collected works (1909-10); prepared Pushkin's long poem "Gavriliada" («Гаврилиада», 1917) for publication; published six volumes of Pushkin's works in 1919; and edited the first volume of the first Soviet edition of Pushkin's collected works in 1920. Briusov's scholarship on Pushkin was highly praised by G. A. Gukovskii, N. V. Izmailov and M. A. Tsiavlovskii. However, the topic of Briusov as critic of Pushkin is still in need of proper evaluation.

2   For example, in the Introduction to his translation of Benjamin Constant's novel *Adolph*, published in 1831, Viazemskii wrote with great enthusiasm that this book does not have all the adventures and marionette-theatre-like comedy of novels because it gives a voice to the human heart and evokes the deepest emotional responses (Viazemskii 1984: 124).

THREE

20TH-CENTURY PUSHKINIAN POETIC RESPONSES TO MODERNITY & URBAN SPECTATORSHIP

Preamble

Akhmatova's insightful comments on Pushkin's urban writing pinpointed some dystopian tenets in the representation of Petersburg in *Eugene Onegin* and "The Bronze Horseman". Akhmatova's reading of Pushkin significantly departs from Blok's image of the happy and merry Pushkin that was known to all Russian poetry readers from their early childhood. Akhmatova writes: "The Petersburg of *Eugene Onegin* and 'The Bronze Horseman'. In the first example we see the charming motherland through the eyes of the young exile; in the second example we see Petersburg presented in Pushkin's letters as a pigsty; it is relentless and gloomy […]. The Introduction (a military capital etc.); the glamorous description in the language of the ode and masking; because of it there are colourful epithets, but they disappear in the long poem without a trace. The diversity and colour of the *Eugene Onegin* scenes vanished in 'The Bronze Horseman'; what is left is impenetrable darkness and whores. Pushkin's weeping over human life. What is felt in the poem is the homelessness of the author" («Петербург Первой главы 'Онегина' и Петербург 'Медного Всадника'. (Первая — милая родина глазами юного изгнанника, второй — свинский Петербург писем, мрачный и беспощадный […]. Вступленье (военная столица итд.), одическое великолепье и маскировка, оттуда и цветные эпитеты, от которых в тексте поэмы нельзя найти и следа. И от всей онегинской пестроты и разнообразия […] остался только непроглядный мрак и шлюхи. Рыданье над человеком. Бездомность автора.») (Akhmatova 1967-1969 , vol.3: 317-18).

Akhmatova's comment corresponds to the binary opposition based on the archetypal model that includes images of a house/settlement and the theme of picaro and spiritual journey.

According to van Baak's study, nomad images were resurrected in Russian culture in the 1910s-1920s and the theme of the loss of a house became especially favoured by Russian avant-garde authors and artists (van Baak 1994: 25). I quote van Baak's outline of the theme of homelessness and its link with the apocalyptic worldview in order to show how various trends which coexisted within the broader framework of Russian modernism came together: "In relation to the avant-garde one can talk about the high interest in the theme of homelessness, which I would like to label as the theme of 'House Loss'. This perspective helps to see both symbolism and the avant-garde as phases in development of the modernist paradigm (in comparison with the previous stage of a realist mode of expression). Some common points between these two phases include the sense of total crisis of the worldview; the loss of modal, emotional and ideological orientation in time and space [...]. The avant-garde artists and writers developed a link between the catastrophic worldview which manifested itself in primitive forms of expression and the occurrence of the mythopoetic outlook" («Применительно к авангарду можно говорить об актуализации темы бездомности, — того, что я бы обозначил как *Потерю Дома*. Тогда с этой точки зрения авангард и символизм рассматриваются как фазы культуры модернизма (в отличие от предыдущей формации реализма). Общие моменты в них — тотальный кризис восприятия мира, разрыв со всеми традициями, потеря мотивации в структуре мира, на всех уровнях, утрата модальной, эмоциональной, идеологической ориентации в пространстве и времени. [...] У авангардистов (как в литературе, так и в изобразительных искусствах) обнаруживается, кроме того, связь между катастрофическим восприятием мира, определенным *примитивизмом* в выражении и возникновением мифопоэтического мышления») (van Baak 1994: 25-26).

Akhmatova's vision of Pushkin's homelessness can be also approached from the point of view of modernist aesthetics, as an attempt to defamiliarise the image of Pushkin and to mould this image into an estranged figure. For Akhmatova, as for Nabokov and Tsvetaeva, Pushkin acts the role of an interlocutor and a playmate, not a canonised poet whose works embody the Russian spirit and the imperial sublime. Pushkin's image had been institutionalised in Soviet times as a very suitable canonical figure in the education of several generations of readers. As Sandler's book *Commemorating Pushkin: Russia's Myth of a National Poet* points out, "A large and complex system of Pushkin shrines [...] emerged in the twentieth century. As significant cultural institutions, these shrines offer visitors historical information and dramatic visualization of Pushkin's world" (Sandler 2004: 47). Sandler mentions 291 monuments to Pushkin, various memorial plaques and numerous museums. They form a significant part of the Russian landscape and are important for keeping alive the myth of the national poet. According to Sandler, "Museums have played an obvious pedagogical role in spreading national myths of Pushkin. They act as elaborate stage sets for encounter with Pushkin, although most museum creators, even in the Soviet period, chose religion, not theatre, as the metaphor to describe their work" (ibid.).

Akhmatova and many other modernist poets whom I will discuss below fought hard against the museum culture and propaganda art that flourished in the Soviet era. They preserved somewhat personal mythologies that revolved around their intimate bond with Pushkin, and created their own landscapes marked by their encounters with their great predecessor. Akhmatova's desire to demystify Pushkin, the canonical figure, stands close to the position of Edward Said who links nineteenth-century realist narrative to the structures of authority that advocate imperialist ideology, bourgeois class hegemony and a male dominated family hierarchy. In Said's view, modernist disruptions to realist narratives have not only an aesthetic implication. They also function to subvert the structures of authority and totality prevalent in nineteenth-century European culture (Said 1975). The poems discussed below engage themselves with Pushkin's texts that touch upon modernity and pre-modernist aesthetics related to urban writing. They all include the principles of simultaneity, intertextuality and dislocated images and motifs which strongly gravitate towards the principles that Eisenstein defines as montage thinking (Eisenstein 1964, volume 2: 188). Schreurs's illuminating study *Procedures of Montage in Isaak Babel's "Red Cavalry"* provides us with a useful outline of the montage principle used in cinema, and discusses its relevance to an analysis of literary texts.

It is useful to refer to some of Schreurs's comments before proceeding to discuss the poems that employ the montage principle and create an illusion of spatial and temporal continuity between objects unrelated in reality. Schreurs explains the cinematic term *montage* thus: "The English-language cinematic terminology, the process of selecting, cutting and connecting shot material is signified by the word 'editing'; the meaning of 'montage', the term used in most other languages to denote this basically technical process, has its origin in the Russian cinema of the nineteen twenties: it refers to creative editing. A montage sequence in today's American cinema is: 'a quick impressionistic sequence of disconnected images, usually linked by dissolves, superimpositions or wipes, and used to convey passages of time, changes of place, or any other sense of transition" (Schreurs 1989: 4). Schreurs examines several approaches to montage found in Eisenstein's work, including the theory of "overtonal montage" («обертонный монтаж») articulated in the article "The Fourth Dimension in Cinema" («Четвертое измерение», 1929) which discusses how the privileged position of one dominant element in montage should be replaced by the device of equality of all stimuli, understood as a complex. Schreurs eloquently examines the effect produced by tonal side-effects in music and visual overtones, and suggests that visual overtones in film shots can be integrated intentionally in the composition of a shot, as in the music of Skriabin, Debussy and other modernist composers.

Within Schreurs's analysis several insightful interpretations of Eisenstein's theoretical approaches to montage are particularly relevant to this chapter. These points include the statement that "overtonal montage of a shot sequence is not based on basic visual vibrations of the separate shots, but on their 'visual overtonal complex' [...], incorporating a special sensation"; this sensation "emerges from collisions and combinations of varied sensory, emotional and intellectual stimuli"; "a step further along the line of a-dominant forms of intellectual montage is the notion of polyphony, a more complex variation of overtonal montage" (Schreurs 1989: 21). In Schreurs view, Eisenstein's understanding of montage changed from "an agitational technique to a much more dynamic and multidifferential system", which includes such concepts of montage as plot construction, "montage as a device to create secondary meaning" and "montage as a device to combine emotional effects and intellectual connotations of extremely diverging and sensuously colliding shots, arranged on a syntactical axis" (Schreurs 1989: 23-24). Schreurs compares Van der Eng's theory of narratology to

Eisenstein's montage teachings and finds that van der Eng's concept of arrangement corresponds in many respects to the devices of montage. Schreurs concludes: "Montage is a synthesis of two opposite tendencies: disintegration and superintegration. A disjoined surface structure is built upon a unifying deep structure. [...] Structural unity depends on thematic lines, in which the intellectual atractions are associated. Using Van der Eng's terms, the 'attractions' are joined in chains of juxtapositions on grounds of similar and dissimilar features of a common thematic level" (Schreurs 1989: 34).

Schreurs analysis revolves around a discussion of narrative constructions and intellectual montage employed in Babel's stories. In this context Berger's concept of polyphonic lyric, discussed earlier in relation to Pushkin's "To the Sea", is useful when we talk about the emotional and intellectual responses to poems of readers when they become obstructed by conflicting narrative elements and by effects of dislocation of the narrative viewpoint. The presence of an implied or openly manifested dialogue with Pushkin in the texts analysed below is felt in two different groups of poems. Some poems stand close to Eisenstein's category of the montage of intellectual attractions; they force the reader to reconstruct the thematic core of a text offering segments that are disjointed, whether compared for contrast or for similarity; this type of texts occurs especially in Futurist poetry which juxtaposes striking intellectual and sensual elements such as metaphors, rhymes and intertextual references. Another group of poems gravitate towards an Acmeist aesthetic project of unity, based on interplay of stylistically complex textual segments and intertextual references.

Annenskii's Pushkin as spectacle, Eisenstein's concept of imagery

The lyrical poems of Innokentii Annenskii are striking early examples of how the image of Pushkin, ascribed with the qualities of the national poet, became destabilised. Annenskii's works had considerable impact on the poetry of Gumilev, Otsup and Akhmatova. Annenskii's poem "Bronze Poet" («Бронзовый поэт») from the short cycle "Trefoil in the Park" («Трилистник в парке»), located in his 1910 collection of poems *The Cypress Chest* (*Кипарисовый ларец*), is linked to the Pushkin statue in Tsarskoe Selo. Nancy Pollak surveys the poems of Annenskii that feature sculptures found in Tsarskoe

Selo, and explains the poem's origin thus: "The second poem, 'Bronze Poet', concerns R.R. Bach's statue of Pushkin on a bench with a book. In his 1899 speech 'Pushkin and Tsarskoe Selo', on the occasion of Pushkin's centennial, Annenskii refers to the raising of the statue, for which he had selected the inscriptions. In his talk Annenskii confirms the park's pervasive Pushkinian presence. He calls Tsarskoe Selo a 'park of *recollections*' [...] and, noting the importance of the poetic form of reminiscence for Pushkin, he refers to Pushkin's verse, in particular the poems inspired by Tsarskoe Selo and related to the theme of memory, as a 'poetry of monuments'. In 'Trefoil in the Park' Annenskii creates his own poetry of monuments" (Pollak 1993: 172). I would add that it seems Annenskii in his poetry featuring parks and sculptures is engaged in polemical dialogue with Alexander Potebnia (1835-1891) who draws analogies between sculptures and words. Pollak notes that Potebnia's studies in cognitive linguistics were of considerable interest to Annensky (Pollak 1993: 171), especially because of Potebnia's comparison of the outer shape of words to sculptures. However, commenting on Annenskii's programme for Pushkin studies in Russian schools (written at the beginning of the 1880s), G. Levinton suggests that Annenskii's views on the concept of the poetic speech were shaped by Potebnia and foregrounded the theories of the Russian Formalists (Levinton, in Stolovich 1992: 361). In his programme Annenskii advocates that the Russian language should be studied through poetry, because poetic speech most fully realises the language's potential and reflects on the nation's spiritual life (Levinton, in Stolovich 1992: 363); and that Pushkin's poetry offers the most vivid expression of Russian speech's potential and abilities (ibid.: 364). In this respect, Potebnia's concept of 'thinking in images' (Steiner 1984: 144) helps view Annenskii's verbal image of the Pushkin monument as a symbol representing the Russian language's poeticity and inner form.

Given that the Pushkin statue comes alive in Annenskii's poem, I would say that Annenskii's vision of creative evolution has distinct Bergsonian overtones. For example, Annenskii's "Bronze Poet" contains a playful allusion to Pushkin's "The Bronze Horseman" in which the monument to Peter the Great comes alive. In the same surreal manner as Pushkin's protagonist Evgenii imagines the statue of Peter the Great coming alive and chasing him, the lyric narrator of Annenskii's poem muses on the possibility of the Pushkin statue becoming animated:

> Не знаю, повесть ли была так коротка,
> Иль я не дочитал последней половины?..
> На бледном куполе погасли облака,
> И ночь уже идет сквозь черные вершины…
>
> И стали — и скамья, и человек на ней
> В недвижном сумраке тяжеле и страшней.
> Не шевелись — сейчас гвоздики засверкают,
> Воздушные кусты сольются и растают,
> И бронзовый поэт, стряхнув дремоты гнет,
> С подставки на траву росистую спрыгнет.
> (Annenskii 1988: 93)
>
> I'm not sure if the tale was so short,
> Or perhaps I did not read the last half of the book?
> The clouds disappeared from the pale cupola,
> And night already descends through the black heights….
>
> And the images of the bench and a man sitting on it
> Became even more frightened and gloomy in the still darkness.
> Don't move: the carnations will start shimmering now,
> The billowy bushes will merge and melt away;
> And the bronze poet, shaking off the burden of his sleep,
> Will jump down from his pedestal onto the damp grass.

Remembering that "Bronze Poet" describes a modernist poet reading a book next to the monument with Pushkin frozen in the same pose, we can say that the text is concerned with the issues of readership and reception of works of art, and the role of poetic speech in the process of communicating and generating new meanings. In mimicking the pose in the Pushkin monument, the lyric hero of Annenskii's poem is entering the role of the national poet reading a book and participating in the process of creative evolution by the act of reading somebody else's book. Annenskii's poem also encapsulates a considerable shift from Aristotelian understanding of mimesis and performance towards the concept of an increasingly diversified and open-ended world, a concept which gained considerable currency in the modernist period.

We can detect in Annenskii's poem an element of playful interaction between various images in the style of the cinematographic communication explained in Tynianov's study *The Poetics of Cinema* (*Поэтика кино*, 1927). In this book Tynianov developed a dynamic theoretical model of art. He pointed out that in cinema the visible world was communicated in its semantic relativity. Thus, the lyric hero of Annenski's poem might be seen as a living Symbolist poet who wishes to impersonate Pushkin, the monument, perceived by him as a static image of a poet reading a book. Yet the image of the moving night walking through the black mountains adds the quality of a film scene to the description of this situation. In this scene the central impulse is the Pushkin monument, but the observation of the image of the descending night acts as a secondary stimulus: it creates the effect of continuous movement, comparable to tonal side-effects that accompany the vibration of the basic sound and form the ultimate sound in modernist music. The concluding lines featuring the statue that came alive, and correspond to Tynianov's differential exchange of shots related to his notion of stylistic montage. Annenskii's poem features three stages of perception: ranging from the segment, that describes the narrator and the sunset, to the close shot that features the monument at which the lyric hero's gaze is directed. Clearly it becomes animated by the change in lighting and the position of the viewer: the poem implies that the street light made the whole setting more striking, as indicated by the allusion to the image of the shimmering white flowers next to the monument that became more visible as the night progressed.

Iser discusses a similar process of perception in relation to paintings and viewers. Iser describes the process of interaction between an artist who wishes to imitate the painting he admires in terms of construction of imaginary reality, rather than mimesis: "Thus an element of play — though in a rather undifferentiated form — inserts itself into the concept of imitation, for only when making and matching, when schema and correction play with or against each other does the illusory object emerge. It appears like an object because the beholder of the picture grasps it as if it were something perceived. The tangibility of the painting derives from these operations, with the schema adapting to conditions of perception in order to allow its reshuffling by correction in such a way that the world envisioned by the painter seems like an object" (Iser 1993: 288). In a very subtle manner, Annenskii's poem suggests that the representation is best understood as a sequence of phases which range from the inherited schemata of the author through to the beholder's stare: in other words, mimesis becomes the representative of performance. Iser makes the interesting observation that the "performative interplay unfolds a graduated process that has to be finalised by the act of reading" and stresses that "the more one analyses mimesis as a process, the more inescapably one is confronted by the performative character of representation" (Iser 1993: 290-91). Thus the act of reading turns into an imaginary encounter with Pushkin that would reduce the lyric hero of Annenskii's poem to a speechless spectator, whose perception of the text he has half read could be completed by an imaginary dialogue with Pushkin.

The act of reading portrayed in "Bronze Poet" is closely related to the creation of a dialogised private space in the style of montage: a new concept of the living word is created, linked to a 'hybrid' voice of authority. The lyric hero of Annenskii's poem is engaged in an ideological form of role playing. Annenskii's purpose in his poem is to imagine himself taking back control of a fragmented and decentred world, by depicting the Pushkin monument as a symbolic figure within bourgeois models of rationalistic and authoritarian language. The reference to the half-read book signifies implied quotes from an abstract set of superior norms of behaviour and attitudes shaped by the dominant social discourse. It is a double-oriented narrative, a hybrid construction, which is explained well by Bakhtin. Bakhtin suggests that a hybrid construction is "an utterance that belongs, by its grammatical (syntactical) and compositional markers, to a single speaker, but that actually contains mixed within it two utterances, two speech manners, two styles, two 'languages', two semantic and belief systems" (Bakhtin 1981: 304). In Annenskii's poem the description of the sky and of the book reproduces key words of Pushkin's poetic speech and imitates some sound patterns featuring the sound "L" , bringing together such words as cupola and cloud. The final stanza, however, is constructed in the style of Symbolist poetic speech, containing some abstract imagery such as billowy bushes and immobile twilight.

Annenskii's poem offers a psycho-narration, a hybrid form of discourse. The poem conflates the boundaries between the diegetic and mimetic, because the description of the Pushkin monument is infused with the character's idiom and outlook. Thus the phrase «Иль я не дочитал последней половины» presents a six-foot iambic meter which evokes Pushkin's usage of six-foot meter in his "To the Poet" («Поэту», 1830). "To the Poet" muses on poetic fame and downplays the need for mass appeal and readership:

Поэт! Не дорожи любовию народной.
Восторженных похвал пройдет минутный шум;
Услышишь суд глупца и смех толпы холодной:
Но ты останься тверд, спокоен и угрюм.

Ты царь: живи один. Дорогою свободной
Иди, куда влечет тебя свободный ум,
Усовершенствуя плоды любимых дум,
Не требуя наград за подвиг благородный.
(Pushkin 1957, vol.3: 174)

Poet! Do not value a nation's love.
The short-lived noise of enthusiastic praise will fade;
You will hear a fool's verdict and indifferent crowd's laugh;
But stand firm, calm and grim.

You are the tsar: live by yourself. Follow the free path
Where your free mind takes you,
Maturing the fruit of your beloved thoughts;
Not asking reward for your noble deed.

Annenskii's "Bronze Poet" also reproduces the structure of Pushkin's "To the Poet": both texts are written in sonnet form. Both advocate creativity, freedom and subjectivity. Curiously, Annenskii's sonnet also employs the rhyming pattern of Pushkin's sonnet "Madonna" («Мадонна», 1830). "Madonna" contains six-foot iambic meter and deals with the theme of spectatorship: the lyric hero claims he would like to spend his whole life admiring Raphael's Madonna. In its subject matter Annenskii's "Bronze Poet", which identifies Pushkin's poetry as a source of inspiration for Annenskii, stands closer to Pushkin's "Madonna" than to Pushkin's lyric "To the Poet".

Annenskii's "Bronze Poet" and Pushkin's "Madonna" have a common rhyming structure in the first two stanzas (rhyming pattern 'abba' followed by 'caca'). There is a slight variation in the last two three-line stanzas: Anneskii's sonnet has 'aabcbc'. The first two stanzas in Annenskii's poem share the same rhyming pattern that alters masculine rhymes with feminine rhymes: облака – вершины – длинны – издалека – коротка – половины – облака – вершины. They mirror Pushkin's rhymes: мастеров – обитель – посетитель – знатоков – трудов – зритель – облаков – спаситель (abbaabab).

Pushkin's "Madonna" displays the model of writing as dwelling. It extends the space of the verbal construction to the visualised image of a private space incorporating Raphael's painting:

> Не множеством картин старинных мастеров
> Украсить я всегда желал свою обитель,
> Чтоб суеверно им дивился посетитель,
> Внимая важному сужденью знатоков.
>
> В простом углу моем, средь медленных трудов,
> Одной картины я желал бы вечно зритель,
> Одной, чтоб на меня с холста, как с облаков,
> Пречистая и наш божественный спаситель
> Она с величием, он с разумом в очах —
> Взирали, кроткие, во славе и лучах […]
> (Pushkin 1957, vol.3: 175)

> I've never wanted to decorate my dwelling
> With a multitude of old masters,
> To invoke a religious reverence in my visitors
> Hanging on the weighty opinions of art experts.
>
> In my simple corner, amid slow labours,
> I would have liked to be an eternal spectator
> Of just one painting, just the one; so that
> The submissive figures of the Virgin and our divine
> Saviour would have gazed at me
> From this canvas, as if from the clouds:
> With dignity in her eyes, with reason in his.

Cloud images appear in both poems as markers of the sublime and poetic imagination. Pushkin required a dwelling which would have Raphael's painting displayed prominently in the house. In Pushkin's poem Raphael's painting is functioning both as icon and the perfect artefact. In Annenskii's "Bronze Poet" the modern poet appears to be pushed into a big city's margins, taking refuge in a suburban park in Tsarskoe Selo, not in a secluded study or boudoir. Annenskii's imaginary dwelling in the park features Pushkin as his interlocutor and muse. While Janet Tucker suggests that Annenskii in "Bronze Poet" advocated the immortality of the visual arts and favoured material forms over ephemeral musical structures (Tucker 1986: 39), Maria Rubins is correct to say that the poem is concerned with the immortality of Pushkin's word and not the abstract notion of the immortality of visual artefacts (Rubins 2003: 189).

More importantly, Annenskii's attitude towards object was similar to the semantic relativity found in cinema. As Schreurs compellingly demonstrates, Eisenstein's application of the term 'imagery' to aesthetic experience is related to the reflexological view on the process of perception, and evokes Thomas Hobbes's sensationalist theory developed in the seventeenth century (Schreurs 1989: 12). Hobbes's description of the relation between memory and imagination has an interesting implication for analysis of Annenskii's poem: "For an after an object is removed, or the eye shut, we still retain an image of the thing seen, though more obscure than when we see it" (quoted in Schreurs, ibid.). Thus, the visual spectacle described in Annenskii's "Bronze Poet" appears triggered by the book on which the lyric hero reflects: the act of reading leads to the creation of an imaginary space in which visual man and visual object are made strange and transformed into signs. The black and white colours featured in the poem recall silent monochrome movies. Bearing in mind that Tynianov considers the absence of colour and sound as the constructive essence of scene composition (Tynianov 1977: 328), it seems important for Annenskii, too, to visualise his dialogue with Pushkin as an act that leads to the creation of new identities and creative possibilities.

In his 1899 speech "Pushkin and Tsarskoe Selo" («Пушкин и Царское село») Annenskii openly attacked Russian institutions for creating an artificial construct from Pushkin's life and works: "But whose celebration is taking place today? Who is coming to the Pushkin anniversaries and who is organising them? People who celebrate them include the warehouses of Russian culture and promoters of Russian culture, everyone from Academy of Sciences members to the most modest secondary school. He did not just create for them the two new forms of creative expression which became world-recognised in the writing of his peers; he gave his followers new forms of creativity: his own language and his own verse" («Но чей же праздник сегодня? Кто идет на пушкинские торжества, кто их устраивает? Празднуют хранилища и рассадники русского просвещения — все от академии Наук до самой скромнейшей школы. [...] он не только отлил для них новые формы творчества, ставшие мировыми под пером его премников, но он дал им два новых орудия небывалой дотоле гибкости: свой язык и свой стих») (Annenskii, in Nepomniashchii 1999: 122).

Most importantly, Annenskii acutely differentiated the Pushkin myth in the popular imagination from Pushkin's writings which testified to the Russian language's vibrant creative impulse and creative potentials. In his anniversary speech Annenskii clearly rejected the commodification of literature reading, which had become a substitute for dwelling, and which undermined the aesthetic purpose of reading poetry. Annenskii points to the necessity of recovering the true voice of Pushkin, through dwelling in his texts and surviving the difficulty of engaging with his texts: "New monuments to Pushkin appear, here, in Odessa, in Petersburg. His monument *not made by hands* — his writings — is not forgotten; and we should hope that our Academy will publish one day the properly edited collection of Pushkin's works and will put a stop once and for all to the naïve mistakes and corrections of editors. It is time to remember Pushkin's agonised efforts — which were evident sometimes even during his schooling — to achieve the precision and musicality of poems. Perhaps, little by little, the real image of Pushkin will replace the construct created through the retelling of him in our mass readership's popular imagination" («Сооружаются новые памятники: у нас, в Одессе, в Петербурге. Не забыт и завещанный им *нерукотворный* — его сочинения, и надо надеяться, что наша Академия, издав их проверенный текст, раз навсегда положит предел наивным ошибкам и дерзким поправкам его издателей. Пора вспомнить, каких часто мучительных усилий, еще с лицейской скамьи, стоили Пушкину точность его выражений и музыкальность стихов. Может быть, и в народных аудиториях подлинный Пушкин мало–помалу заменит рассказанного») (Annenskii in Nepomniashchii 1999: 121).

In his fascinating survey of Petersburg myths and texts, Vladimir Toporov refers to a popular image of Tsarskoe Selo. In this image, the Petersburg suburb in the poetry and memoirs of Silver Age representatives is a place with no sense of history or temporality. According to Toporov, Tsarskoe Selo in the eyes of Russian modernists was untouched by revolutionary upheavals, social conflicts or war. It had the reputation of a dull and sleepy place where dwelling was monotonous, free from worry. It was often, in contrast to Petersburg, an empty place, free from the noise of modern times, as if it was a nineteenth-century suburb frozen in time, suitable for contemplation and creativity (Toporov in Stolovich 1992: 464). Toporov maintains that Tsarskoe Selo, despite being seen by philistines as a place of oblivion and stability far removed from the tumultuous stage of Russian modernity (as represented by Petersburg and Moscow), became an important setting for the staging of personal dramas associated with a subjective perception of history. Toporov lists Annenskii, Vassilii Komarovskii and Akhmatova among the most interesting residents in Tsarskoe Selo who created a new, highly subjectivised mode of historical thinking and writing. Toporov notes: "And Tsarskoe Selo became an exceptionally suitable location for the development of the new historical thinking. In this suburb on the fatal border, the material world became ever thinner, giving the impression that matter was vanishing and everything becoming ephemeral; but this loss of the sense of the physical world was compensated by a sharpening of perception and by a kind of clairvoyant vision" («И вот для возникновения этой новой формы *исторического* Царское Село стало исключительно благоприятной почвой. На роковом пороге материя истончалась здесь до того, что все стало казаться призрачным, но эта потеря *материальности* компенсировалась все большим обострением чувства и своего рода ясновидением духа») (ibid.).

Given Toporov's remarks, we can suggest that the poems in Annenskii's "Trefoil in the Park" appropriated the mode of spectatorship of the detective figure that appears in Pushkin's *Eugene*

Onegin. Annenskii's poems present Tsarskoe Selo as a place of mystery where the story of modern writing unfolds. "Trefoil in the Park" also stands close to Pushkin's poem "Drums signal sunrise...", discussed above, which features a young Pushkin at the lycée reading Dante's poetry. Pollak aptly points out that issues of reception and spectatorship form the core subject matter of this cycle: "In the poems of 'Trefoil in the Park', Annenskii takes a figure that runs the risk of becoming a fixed image — the statue — and shows that its continued life depends on its transformation, its reception and recreation by an observer" (Pollak 1993: 173). In fact, Annenskii's image of the animated statue appearing at the end of "Bronze Poet" suggests that an attentive reader carries the trace of a literary experience long after completing a reading.

Conversely, Annenskii's "Bronze Poet" has a strong cinematic quality in the style of Pushkin's poem "Drums signal sunrise...". "Bronze Poet" gives the impression of an act of continuous recognition, a groping for a continuous present. The speaker in "Bronze Poet" knows exactly what happens every evening to the statue. The last stanza's imperative "Don't move!" ("[...] the carnations will start shimmering now [...] and the bronze poet [...] will jump down from his pedestal") suggests this is a spectacle repeated every night. Use of the future tense in "will jump down" («спрыгнет») adds a comic effect to the description of this gestural slapstick. "Bronze Poet" exemplifies the convergence of modern poetry with the aesthetics of film montage. It prefigures the link between the dislocated, automaton-body of modernity with the subordination of plot to somatic, disjointed rhythms found in avant-garde works. Eisenstein explains in the essay "A Dialectical Approach to Film Form" that poetry reconstructs an event in montage fragments (Leyda 1949: 60-1), and that dramatic tension revolves around the methodology of form rather than plot; this enables us to see how Annenskii invokes Potebnia's poetic polysemy by juxtaposing animated clouds moving across the sky and the unfinished book: Pushkin's name is never mentioned in the poem. The phrase 'bronze poet' involves a mental construct linking the outer form of the word with its figurative meaning.

As I suggested above, Annenskii's "Bronze Poet" presupposes an existing link between the twentieth and nineteenth centuries through the allusion to the bronze horseman figure, an animated statue from Pushkin's "The Bronze Horseman", which helps us see both Pushkin and Peter the Great as authors of modernity. Annenskii's poem poses the question of the problematic notion of memory and the representation of temporal categories. It articulates two important questions of remembrance also formulated in his articles on Pushkin: "What is remembered of the real historical figure and for whom?". It asserts that memory is not to be linked to the past, and gestures towards a present remembrance. The mnemonic qualities of certain spaces that trigger memories and creativity are strongly articulated in Pushkin's poetry as has been demonstrated earlier. Thus, in "The Bronze Horseman" we find Evgenii's illusion triggered by the willow tree: he sees the house of his fiancée Parasha as soon as he sees the tree. Thus an imaginary space was created in his imagination for a short period of time, experienced by him as continuous present, a trick of memory that made his vision blurry and highly subjective. In the same vein, the landscape of Tsarskoe Selo with the Pushkin monument in its park holds special mnemonic significance for Annenskii. It triggers the memory of a poet jumping down from his pedestal, as if from a stage. Clearly, the object-subject relationship in this poem becomes distorted by some personal memories associated with the place that brings together the lifestyle of the poets of the Golden and Silver ages.

Kevin Lynch, the very influential theoretician of urban design, formulated a new criterion — *imageability* — having potential as a guide for building and rebuilding cities. Lynch talks of the importance of the personal experience of an illusory image "long after its inadequacy is conceptually realised" (Lynch 2000: 12). Lynch details the process of constructing a cognitive map: "We stare into the jungle and see only the sunlight on the green leaves, but a warning noise tells us that an animal is hidden there. The observer then learns to interpret the scene by singling out 'give away' clues by reweighting previous signals. The camouflaged animal may now be picked up by the reflection of his eyes. Finally by repeated experience the entire pattern of perception is changed, and the observer need no longer consciously search for give-aways, or add new data to old framework. He has achieved an image which will operate succcesfully in the new situation, seeming natural and right. Quite suddenly the hidden animal appears among the leaves, 'as plain as day'" (Lynch 2000: 12). Lynch suggests that our ability to develop an image of the environment by taking into account both the physical shape and our internal learning process is a new phenomenon that derives from the fragmentation of metropolitan life. He makes a clear distinction between primitive societies and modern civilisations: "Primitive man was forced to improve his environmental image by adapting his perception to the given landscape. He could effect minor changes in his environment with cairns, beacons, or tree blazes, but substantial modifications for visual clarity or visual interconnection were confined to house sites or religious enclosures. Only powerful civilisations can begin to act on the total environment at a significant scale. The conscious remolding of the large-scale physical environment has been possible only recently, and so the problem of the environmental imageability is a new one" (Lynch 2000: 12-13). Russia's technological advancement in the 1900s-1910s could not, of course, prefigure the cognitive mapping of metropolitan landscapes that arose in Europe and America in the 1920s-1930s. Nevertheless, Annenskii's poem displays the same utopian desire inscribed in Pushkin's lyric "Monument" — to be associated with the monument of an important cultural figure. Both poems suggest that the poet's immortality is secured by future generations of readers, not by static images representing the living experiences of poets that are not fully recoverable.

Annenskii's poem featuring the poet reading a book at the Pushkin statue in Tsarskoe Selo had a powerful effect on its readers; so great that we could say his desire to be associated with Pushkin through intellectual montage (to use Eisenstein's words) was fulfilled. The allusion to Annenskii's association with the Pushkin monument and his active engagement with Pushkin's poetry appears in Gumilev's 1912 poem "In Memory of Annenskii" («Памяти Анненского»), which instils in readers' minds the numerous encounters between poets and muses that took place at the famous summer residence of the Russian Imperial family. As Michael Basker convincingly argues, "the implied connection of Annenskii with Pushkin is perhaps the more persuasive in that Gumilev's narrative has now switched from personal recollection («ia pomniu») to the more remote realm of hearsay («mne skazali»), 'shadow imagery' (or image-*in-absentia*) and imagination — the natural stuff of legend" (Basker in Loseff and Scherr 1993: 225). Thus Annenskii's personal mythology became a legend, entering urban folklore. Both Annenskii and Gumilev contributed successfully to the creation of the perceptual image of this Petersburg suburb, demonstrating that certain landmarks might be retained in modern times of massive change; they provide citizens with a sense of continuity, and an illusion of conserved temporality.

Pushkin's Petersburg as a living experience in new contexts

Blok's long narrative poem "Requital" («Возмездие»), written in the 1910s, also advocates the view that the twentieth century was a more mercilessly pragmatic version of modernity than nineteenth-century Russian authors had known. Blok's narrative reinforces Pushkin's description in "Monument" of modernity as a "cruel century" ("and during my cruel century I glorified liberty" — «что в мой жестокий век восславил я свободу»):

> Век девятнадцатый, железный,
> Воистину жестокий век!
> Тобою в мрак ночной беззвездный
> Беспечный брошен человек!
> В ночь умозрительных понятий,
> Матерьялистских малых дел,
> Бессильных жалоб и проклятий
> Бескровных душ и слабых тел!
> С тобой пришли чуме на смену
> Нейрастения, скука, сплин,
> Век расшибанья лбов о стену,
> Экономических доктрин,
> Конгрессов, банков, федераций,
> Застольных спичей, красных слов,
> Век акций, рент и облигаций
> И мало действенных умов [...].
> Двадцатый век... еще бездомней,
> Еще страшнее жизни мгла [...].
> И отвращение от жизни,
> И к ней безумная любовь,
> И страсть и ненависть к отчизне...
> И черная, земная кровь
> Сулит нам, раздувая вены,

Все разрушая рубежи,
Неслыханные перемены,
Невиданные мятежи.
(Blok 1955: 485-86)

Nineteenth century, you are iron, a
Truly cruel century!
You cast the carefree person
Into the dark of the starless night!
Into the night of abstract notions,
Of insignificant pragmatic enterprises;
Of powerless complaints and curses
Of bloodless souls and weak bodies!
Upon your arrival you brought
Neurasthaenia, boredom and spleen
In place of plague;
You are the century of wall-beating heads,
Of some economic theories;
Of congresses, banks, federations,
Formal speeches, empty words;
The century of shares, rents and vouchers,
And of passive brains […]
The twentieth century… is even more homeless;
Its darkness even more frightening […].
And disgust with life;
And mad love for it;
Both passion and hatred for the native land…
And the black earthy blood
Makes us promises, making our veins swell,
Destroying all the borders,
Some unbelievable changes,
Unforeseen revolts […].

Blok's portrayal of modernity uses the device of listing, employed in Pushkin's texts such as "The Bronze Horseman" and *Eugene Onegin*. Blok's kaleidoscope-like overview of the two centuries offered in "Requital" strongly resembles Pushkin's impressionistic descriptions of urban life. Like Pushkin, Blok resorts to de-familiarising the poem's language in order to create a clash between the old and new forms, between standard language and colloquial speech. According to Jakobson, Russian poetry always used the creative potential of colloquial speech to de-familiarise and renew poetic speech: "From Simeon Polotskii on, through Lomonosov, Derzhavin, Pushkin, Nekrasov, and Maiakovskii, Russian poetry has continuously adopted newer and newer elements of the living language" (Jakobson, quoted in Steiner 1984: 217-18). The above passage from Blok's "Requital" also gives the impression of being an encyclopaedia of styles, blending old poetisms and clichés with new colloquialisms and words from the vocabulary of politics and consumerism. It parodies the language of consumption and estranges itself from the view that poetry should be merely another form of commodity. Blok's poem emphasises the strong physicality of the commercial world by mention of the financial terms share, bank, rent, economic theories, federations. The modern subject in "Requital" is characterised by hysteria (the Freudian disease of modernity) and spleen. It is fashioned in the clothes of both Pushkin's Onegin and Baudelaire's flâneur. It signifies thereby the existence of the dislocated bodies of modernity surrounded by a dark starless night.

Blok's "Requital" displays cinematic qualities corresponding to Eisenstein's theory of montage. For example, Eisenstein asserts that artistic dynamism stems from irregularity of the part in relation to the laws of the system as a whole. Eisenstein talks of the cinematic still as a montage cell and he gives it a corporeal presence (Leyda 1949: 53). In Eisenstein's view both film and poetry portay a body in flux. As Susan McCabe argues, "Eisenstein consistently construes montage as embodied poesis, even as that body composes itself through the collision of fragments" (McCabe 2001: 431). Blok's allusions to hitherto unheard-of changes and unseen revolts create the impression of anxiety and remind us of Pushkin's protagonist Evgenii in "The Bronze Horseman": Evgenii is driven to madness and homelessness by catastrophic events related in his mind to the advancement of modernity advocated by Peter the Great. The theme of requital which permeates Blok's narrative evokes Evgenii's belief that his destiny was prefigured by Peter the Great's creation of a space which was doomed to vanish and to threaten the lives of ordinary dwellers.

Gippius's 1909 poem "Petersburg" («Петербург») also echoes Pushkin's vision of modern urban space as a diseased space. The poem alludes to the victims of the first Russian revolution of

1905-1907, asserting that the Neva's waters will not be able to wash away the blood of its casualties: "The river will not wash away the rusty stains/ From the shores of its colossuses" («Река не смоет рыжих пятен/ С береговых своих громад») (Gippius 1999: 143). Gippius subverted the structures of authority and totality prevalent in nineteenth-century European culture as embodied in Pushkin's "The Bronze Horseman". She disguises her subversion in the voice of Avdot´ia Lopukhina who predicted the demise of Petersburg.

Gippius's "Petersburg" exemplifies the polyphonic metatextual space that had engaged various discourses embedded in Pushkin's narratives. According to Karol Berger, "A polyphonic lyric is conceivable, though a monophonic one is far more usual. And the lyrical voice may belong either to a personage (whether implied or explicit), making no difference between his own 'now' and the 'now' of the world of which he speaks, or it may belong either to a narrator whose 'now' is not that of the world of which he speaks (as happens when he uses the preterite)" (Berger 1994: 413). Gippius's poem makes us view the world she portrays as diegetically constructed. As Berger points out, "the world presented diegetically must consist of at least two distinct and hierarchically related ontological levels, the world to which the narrator belongs and the different, subordinated, world which he presents" (Berger 1994: 414). Gippius presents the Petersburg space of "The Bronze Horseman" as a dwelling space requiring redefinition. Her poem's narrator uses stylistic masks and parodic devices to differentiate the cultural constructs and worldviews to which she responds. Thus the epigraph taken from the introductory part of "The Bronze Horseman" that goes "I love you, Peter's creation" («Люблю тебя, Петра творенье!») is contrasted to the rest of the poem describing Petersburg as a city in pain, an open and still bleeding wound. Gippius's poem also presents a disembodied body: her verbal rendering of the monument to Peter the Great is focussed on the image of the bronze snake juxtaposed to the final stanza's scene of a worm eating in the corpse of the city:

Как прежде, вьется змей твой медный,
Над змеем стынет медный конь...
И не сожрет тебя победный
Всеочищающий огонь, —

Нет! Ты утонешь в тине черной,
Проклятый город, Божий враг,
И червь болотный, червь упорный
Изъест твой каменный костяк.
(Gippius 1999: 143)

As before, your bronze snake coils;
Above the snake the bronze horse poses...
And the all-cleansing victorious fire
Will not destroy you, —

No! You will drown in the black ooze,
The cursed city, God's enemy,
And the bog's worm, the stubborn worm
Will eat up your stone structure.

It would not escape a reader's attention that Gippius's poem "Petersburg" engages in a polemic dialogue with Pushkin. For example it employs the four-foot iambic meter found in Pushkin's "The Bronze Horseman": the epigraph she takes from Pushkin's text «Люблю тебя, Петра творенье» contains a classical example of Pushkin's use of the four-foot iambic meter: ox|ox|ox|ox|o. The four-foot iambic meter came to Russia from European poetry, introduced to Russian poetry by Vassilii Trediakovskii. According to A. Kviatkovskii's dictionary of Russian poetry, the four-foot iamb is Russian poetry's most popular meter, used in some 85% of all Russian verse. Kviatkovskii thinks its popularity is due to its successful use in the poetry of the great Russian nineteenth-century poets, including Gavriil Derzhavin, Baratynskii and Pushkin (Kviatkovskii 1966: 363).

The most interesting polemical contact of Gippius's "Petersburg" with Pushkin's text appears in the second stanza, especially because it reproduces the rhythmical and metrical pattern, and the rhymes, of the epigraph: "Your breathing is death and decay" («Твое дыханье — смерть и тленье») (Gippius 1999: 143). In a subversive manner, the inner rhyme which links the words 'death and decay' to the epigraph containing the phrase 'Peter's creation' implies that Peter's utopian project was faulty, ill-conceived from the outset. In montage-like manner, Gippius creates a new reading of Pushkin's phrase which erases the connotation of the odic tradition embedded in the introductory parts of "The Bronze Horseman" and suggests through the inner rhyme, concealed in her text, that Peter the Great's creation is full of decay («Петра творенье — тленье»). Viktor Zhirmunskii's 1968 article "On National Forms of Iambic Verse" points out "that Russian poetry beginning from Lomonosov developed, through the interaction of the metrical model of the disyllabic iambic (or trochaic) verse with the phonetic specificity of the Russian language material, a new national form of verse — the Russian iamb which, due to its variable rhythmical (accentual) content, permitted great poetic freedom that made this metre, particularly in Pushkin, a rich and varied instrument of artistic expression" (Zhirmunskii: 1985: 368-69).

Tomashevskii, another Russian scholar of versification of note, also advocates culture-specific tenets of metrical forms, suggesting that Russian verse is more capable of expressing certain specifics of Russian speech and culture. Tomashevskii writes: "The rhythmical law does not of course follow mechanically from the properties of a language: if that were so, everyone would speak and write in verse. But it is not something alien to language or added to language material… Each language has its own rhythmical material, and therefore each language works out its own metric system. International exchange of literary traditions may promote the bringing of these systems together, but it never obliterates the essential difference between them […]. Hence the consequence: rhythmicised material is in its very nature national. Painting and music are national only to the extent in which the artist's creative thought is formed under the influence of the historical cultural paths of the people to which he belongs. But the means of painting and music are international. Poetry, however, is national in its very material. In this respect, poetry, is much more national than prose" (Tomashevskii 1959: 29-32). Thus Gippius's gesture of reproducing the metrical pattern of Pushkin's line "I love you, Peter's creation!" («Люблю тебя, Петра творенье!») and replacing it with the phrase which semantically erases the creation of Peter the Great («Твое дыханье — смерть и тленье») undermines in a parodic manner the odic tradition employed in the introductory part of Pushkin's "The Bronze Horseman".

Gippius's poem introduces the notion of semantic authority, discussed in the works of Bakhtin and Gary Saul Morson. Morson comments on Bakhtin's concept of a parodic utterance thus: "A parodic utterance is one of open disagreement. The second utterance represents the first in order to discredit it, and so introduces a 'semantic direction' which subverts that of the original. In this way the parodied utterance 'becomes the arena of conflict between two voices ... the voices here are not only detached and distanced, they are hostilely counterposed' [*PDP,* 160] — counterposed, moreover, with the second voice clearly representing a higher 'semantic authority' than the first. The audience of the conflict knows for sure with whom it is expected to agree" (Morson 1989: 66-67). In his discussion of parody and history, Morson makes a useful observation on the role of parody in many of Pushkin's works, including the long poem "Ruslan and Ludmila" («Руслан и Людмила»), noting that it questions the kind of time in which the action unfolds, and he identifies its correspondence to Bakhtin's term *adventure-time*. Morson says: "In *Ruslan and Liudmila*, and in his numerous other generic parodies (e.g., *Gabrieliad, Tsar Nikita, Count Nulin,* and that encyclopaedia of parodies, *Eugene Onegin*), Pushkin also resembles his favourite models, Cervantes, Voltaire, and Sterne, in taking the stylized *language* of his target genres as emblem of their distance from biographical time and historical flux. Juxtaposing their language of 'remote allusions and obscure opinions' [...] — to a language that is clearly marked as characteristical of a particular group at a particular time. These parodies answer implicit claims to permanence and historical transcendence with the passing speech of a passing world" (Morson 1989: 80).

In Pushkinian manner, Gippius targets in "Petersburg" the stylised language of Pushkin's introductory passages in "The Bronze Horseman" that resemble the genre of Russian eighteenth-century odes. In "Petersburg" Gippius attacks the whole odic tradition that glorified the significance of Peter the Great to Russia. Rosenshield explains: "The glorification of Peter, his mission, and his vision for Russia was standard practice in the laudatory ode in Russian literature of the eighteenth century, even when the more immediate object of praise was later tsars or tsarinas. The ode to Peter at the beginning of *The Bronze Horseman* may be considered to be the last great ode in this tradition. [...] *The Bronze Horseman*'s introductory ode portrays a mission realised. In one hundred years Russia has been transformed into a mighty and feared power, and this transformation is most brilliantly reflected in the city Peter founded and planned. [...] The narrator often and forthrightly proclaims his love for Peter's creation: its beauty and grandeur, its social and military life, its royalty and imperial mission" (Rosenshield 2003: 91-2). Rosenshield valuably adds that the deific assessment of Peter's modernity is not the only view expressed in "The Bronze Horseman" but importantly "it is the one that sets up the parameters in which madness operates" (ibid.: 93).

Rosenshield's observation is easily extended to Gippius's poem to argue that Gippius uses allusions to the introductory parts of "The Bronze Horseman" in order to set the parameters in which madness and prophecy operate. As Rosenshield compellingly argues, Peter's creation of Petersburg described in "The Bronze Horseman" lends itself to comparison with the reference to the God in the gospel of St John (ibid.). In Gippius's mind, the parameters indicating where the modern is displaced and the mad subject operate include not only the city as an artefact created by Peter the Great, but also the entire space of Russian literature. The tradition of subversive laughter is employed in Gippius's poem with a clear understanding that laughter is not permissible; within the parameters of Russian culture governed by Russian orthodox belief in the association between the Devil and laughter, it is sinful. Avril Pyman sees similarities between Lev Shestov's apotheosis of groundlessness and venture into the absurd, and Gippius's nihilism, a fatal emptiness which Blok ascribed to the whole generation of decadents with whom he had strong personal ties (Pyman 1994: 148-49).

Unsurprisingly, Gippius found it difficult to publish "Petersburg" in 1909. It was declined by the Petersburg newspaper *Speech* (*Речь*), but eventually published in the eleventh issue of the Symbolists' journal *Scales* (*Весы*). On 22 April 1909 Gippius noted: "I was annoyed with *Speech*. By mistake I sent its editors my poem *Peter's creation* [...]. They accepted it, printed it and sent me its proofs, but still they are afraid to publish it, even though I tried to make it more palatable with the help of Viacheslav Ivanov! And, besides, the 1905 revolution is not really its main subject at all!" («Разозлила меня *Речь*. Я случайно дала туда стихи *Петра творенье*. [...] *Речь* их набрала, прислала корректуру... и до сих пор боится пустить, как я их ни смягчала с помощью Вячеслава! И притом вовсе не в революции дело там!») (Gippius 1999: 481).

The last stanza of Gippius's "Petersburg" predicts the demise of the city of Peter's creation in the manner predicted by Avdot′ia Lopukhina. Lopukhina, according to an eighteenth-century legend, foretold that Petersburg would vanish (Gippius 1999: 482). Gippius shared the vision of Merezhkovskii, her husband. Merezhkovskii followed in the footsteps of the Russian Old Believers and portrayed Peter the Great as the Anti-Christ in his 1905 novel *Antichrist. Peter and Alexis (Антихрист. Петр и Алексей)*. Gippius was seen as a more interesting thinker and poet than her famous husband, whose historical novels enjoyed enormous popularity in Russia and abroad. For example, Sergei Kablukov's diary entry of 5 June 1909 refers to Ivanov's view of Gippius as an important author of philosophical poetry: "In accordance with the opinion of Viacheslav Ivanovich, Zinaida Nikolaevna is more talented than Merezhkovskii as poet and author of fiction. She belongs to the guild of classical poets [...] which includes such figures as Catullus and Prospertius in Rome, Baratynskii in Russia, and others. She was the founder of the Religious-Philosophical Society; many ideas developed by Merezhkovskii originated in Zinaida Nikolaevna's head. Dmitrii Sergeevich only developed and explained them [...]. She also has much more mystical experience than Merezhkovskii" («По мнению Вячеслава Ивановича, З.Н. гораздо талантливее Мережковского как поэтесса и автор художественной прозы. Она принадлежит к классическим поэтам, [...] как, например, Катулл и Проперций в Риме, Баратынский у нас и другие. Она была творцом Религиозно-Философского общества; многие ее идеи, характерные для Мережковского, зародились в уме Зинаиды Николаевны. Д.С. принадлежит только их развитие и разъяснение. [...] мистического опыта в ней также несравненно более, чем у ее мужа» (Gippius 1999: 9). Nevertheless, it should be noted that Merezhkovskii's novel *Antichrist. Peter and Alexis* "not only reopened the Petrine era to imaginative literature [...], but succeeded in delving beneath the surface of history and exposing to his contemporaries the roots of the cultural divide. He also recalled to the modern mind the parallel myths of Petersburg and Kitezh which were to play an elusive but quintessential part in the prose and poetry of the next decades" (Pyman 1994: 129). Indeed, Pushkin's description of the 1824 flood in "The Bronze Horseman" also evokes the Kitezh legend, and this fact did not escape the attention of Gippius, who contrasted the immortal flow of poetic speech to the flow of historical time and architectural masterpieces. Her "Petersburg" demonstrates the vitality of the iambic meter, as the meter linked to the natural traits of Russian prosody, at its best.

Gippius belonged to the generation of Russian Symbolists who emerged in the 1880s-1890s whose art was closely linked to the period's philosophical and metaphysical discourses. In her insightful study of the influence of French Symbolist writing on Russian modernist poets, Donchin characterises Gippius and her contemporaries as infused with deep pessimism: "The generations of the 1880s and 1890s were deeply aware of the fact that they lived in a transient, chaotic period, that they belonged to a dying world, but stood at the same time on the threshold of a new one. Dissatisfaction and deep pessimism, fear of both the present and the future, and in some cases a faint hope, itself tinged with a disquiet, pervaded all the poets of the turn of the century. They seemed to have suddenly lost the ground from under their feet, and were terrified by the sudden appearance of a vacuum. They were prepared to fill it with anything, almost at any price" (Donchin 1958: 78).

But as a driving force at the Religious-Philosophical Society, Gippius wanted to replace Petersburg's glamorous façades that hid the spiritless existence of urban dwelling, and bring about a new organisation of life in tune with the living roots and creative spirit of the Russian nation. Thus Gippius levelled her attacks on Peter's vision of modernity in Dostoevskean fashion, blaming him for creating a Godless and ethically wanting modern world. Olga Matich refutes the idea that Gippius was a decadent poet: "If one must classify Gippius the poet, one should consider her with the second generation Symbolists, who in contrast with the decadents associate their art with religion rather than pure aestheticism. In attempting to overcome the loneliness and total self-centeredness of the decadents, the second generation poets wish to find meaning outside themselves by reaching out to God in their poetry. [...] Gippius's poetic visions are more akin to the younger generation's in that she hopes and attempts to escape the spiritual loneliness of her existence by finding her own path to God" (Matich 1972: 10). It is important to remember that at heart

Gippius was not an Old Believer, but that like Avdot´ia Lopukhina (to whose voice Gippius alludes in "Petersburg") Gippius aspired to create a new civilised society, and this competed with Peter the Great and Pushkin in her vision of modernity. She created a whole gallery of 'new people' whose spiritual bond would lead to a more organicist type of modernity.

Gippius's recipe for healing the wounds inflicted by Peter the Great's modernisation is especially clear in *New People* (*Новые люди*), her 1896 book of short stories and verse. Trina Mamoon outlines the main tenets of Gippius's philosophy in her analysis of Gippius writings: "The New People are a special breed of people who came into being as a result of the *Zeitgeist* which reflected two contradictory trends — an apocalyptic vision and an inhumane socio-political reality. In their reaction to the negative attributes of the *fin de siècle* mentality, Gippius's New People renounced all manifestations associated with the Antichrist and whole-heartedly embraced the principles associated with the Third Coming of Christ — spirituality, compassion, mercy, and love. The consciousness of the New People was shaped by their desire to overcome the handicaps of the past generation: inaction, apathy, and selfishness, and reach a high moral and spiritual state of being which was expressed through their faith and support of like-minded others. Even though the New People rejected the way of life of their 'fathers' they were forgiving of them and tried to assimilate them in their way of thinking. The New People wanted to teach their parents, and indeed, the whole world that the essence of being a new person lay in outgrowing past shortcomings through love and mercy. The New People believed that by following the teachings of Christ, they would be able to usher in a new era" (Mamoon 1998: 214).

Gippius might be labelled an archaicising modernist, in the style of Tynianov, particularly because she wanted to redefine and renew Russian culture's traditions and myths. As a friend of Henri Bergson and an advocate of his theory of creative revolution, Gippius in "Petersburg" was concerned to re-evaluate Peter the Great's vision of a new Russia and a new people. According to Boris Uspenskii and Lotman, "The image of *the new Russia* and *the new people* became a special kind of myth which had already come into existence at the beginning of the eighteenth century and was passed on into the later cultural consciousness. The idea that eighteenth-century culture forms a new stage, entirely separate from preceding development, has become so deeply rooted that it has in fact never been seriously questioned. There may be disputes as to whether the break with the old ways occurred at the end or in the middle of the seventeenth century, whether the break was instantaneous or gradual, and finally whether, in light of subsequent Russian history, to regard it positively as ensuring cultural progress or negatively as entailing the loss of national character" (Lotman, Uspenskii 1984: 18-9).

Gippius's "Petersburg" does not define the concept of Russian national character. But it does challenge Pushkin's overtly optimistic view of Peter the Great's reforms as instantaneous. It partly rewrites Pushkin's story of the origins of Petersburg, highlighting the negative aspect of the metropolis as a city always evolving and producing artefacts. Gippius concluded her poem with an apocalyptic prediction of a great flood to make Petersburg vanish. She thereby sympathises with the truth and rebellion arising from the mad visions of Evgenii in "The Bronze Horseman" as one of Russia's most submissive citizens. Gippius's Petersburg stands close to Dostoevskii's demythologised and desacralised representation of Petersburg as Peter the Great's city of dead souls. Pushkin in "The Bronze Horseman" links all types of rebellion with madness, and Gippius poem responds to this. She inscribes the prophetic voice denouncing any kind of violence: this authoritative voice of moral consciousness seems placed both outside Pushkin's text and outside the contemporary world to which she alludes. Gippius's "Petersburg" thus evokes the holy foolishness and madness found in the works both of Pushkin and Dostoevskii. It touches upon the issue of the living roots of Russian culture; challenges the art which is built on the assumption that a modern subject is superior to its predecessors; and promotes the Romantic figure of the male genius. "Petersburg" is an extension of her polemic with Merezhkovskii in particular and with the male canon in general. Thus in her 1951 book *Dmitrii Merezhkovskii* Gippius recalls that in the first draft of the novel *Antichrist. Peter and Alexis* Merezhkovskii's dislike of Peter the Great was so strong that she persuaded her husband to create a more balanced image. In the course of writing and conversing with Gippius, Merezhkovskii decided to reject all the romantic masks, including Peter the Great,

Mephistopheles and Lucifer, which to his mind embodied the archetypal image of the eternal impostor of God (Pyman 1994: 130).

Gippius's position vis-á-vis Peter the Great's reforms and the nature of her philosophical and artistic engagement with the Petersburg Pushkin constructed in "The Bronze Horseman" foreshadows the interpretation of Pushkin's responses to Russian modernity encapsulated in Semen Frank's phrase 'a lucent sorrow'. In Frank's view, Pushkin's tragic perception of life as manifested in his writings conveys his reconciled grief, not rebellion or a feeling of embitterment against life, because the poet's heart "cannot help burning and loving" (Richards and Cockrell 1976: 224). Frank's reading of Pushkin is enriched by his own philosophical and theological beliefs. He was a famous Russian modernist philosopher and theologian. His view of Pushkin as a forerunner of modern writing was entwined with his own search for ways to overcome modernist identity crises and the ills and illusions of individualism; this topic was the subject of lengthy critical analysis in the writings of Shopenhauer and Nietzsche.

Psychology and sociology at the turn of the century also discussed the autonomy and isolation of the individual, and his identity crisis, as the most ambivalent manifestation of modernity. Many writers explored the possibility of rebuilding identity through radical forms of individualism such as the mystic, the genius and Narcissus. According to Jacques Le Rider's analysis of the modernist movement in Vienna, "these types (the mystic, the genius and Narcissus) turn out in fact to be under particular threat, always bound to fleeting moments of supreme happiness or the fast-fading intoxication of omnipotence. Their inevitable collapse pitches the subject back into an even more painful feeling of discontinuity, of loss of identity. Utopian mysticism, genius and narcissism, as ways of being, share the same aspiration to transcend the limits laid down by life: they gloss over the male-female divide and incline towards an ideal of androgyny; they aspire to the self-destruction of an ego pained by its inability to accept the gifts of chance [...], and to the refashioning of an ego more perfect" (Le Rider 1993: 2). The attacks of sublime madmen, to use Le Rider's term (ibid.), on contemporary decadence, and plans to revamp the modern world performed in the manner of the protagonist in Pushkin's "The Bronze Horseman", can be also found in the poetry of Blok, Tsvetaeva and Pasternak.

The theme of the individual's inner spiritual life, which stands close to utopian mysticism, is strongly articulated in Pasternak's poetry. In the same manner that Benjamin talks of Baudelaire's depiction of mass psychology, Pasternak finds early manifestation of the modern consciousness in Pushkin's poetry. Pasternak reproduces the sensation not only of observing situations described in Pushkin's urban poetry but also the sensation of reading Pushkin's text. In his comments on the physicality of Pasternak's poetic language, Maurice Bowra notes: "He seizes on some significant trait in what he sees and relates it to something wider by his choice of a significant image. When, for instance, he writes 'But people in watch-chains are loftily grumbling / and sting you politely like snakes in the oats', the primary effect is visual, but the scene, so clearly portrayed, suggests the character and habits of a class of persons who are coldly polite and use good manners to inflict the wounds" (Bowra 1967: 136). Pasternak's image of passers-by evokes both the image of the indifferent crowd found in "The Bronze Horseman" and the bronze snake in Peter the Great's monument. Frank's passage, which encapsulates the modern approach to reading Pushkin's "The Bronze Horseman", illuminates the mind of a modernist poet relating to the narrator of Pushkin's text. It is clear from an extract from Pasternak's "Petersburg", to be quoted next, that he and Frank converge in their reading of Pushkin's urban writing. Frank explains: "In the same passage from *The Bronze Horseman* the insensibility of the forces of nature overlaps with the 'cold indifference' of the ordinary people walking along streets who have just experienced the flood's tragic onslaught. Pushkin's scorn and revulsion for 'the crowd', 'the rabble', 'the human herd' are such feelings that are well known [...]. His entire life and work are based on this acute awareness of the deep gulf dividing the inner spiritual life of man from the human community *en masse* and its society" (Richards and Cockrell 1976: 214). The theme of the deep gulf separating society from the individual's inner spiritual life underpins the many observations of Petersburg and Moscow urban life in Pasternak's poetry.

Pushkin's vision of a mad city of violence and death is reproduced more vigorously in Pasternak's cycle of poems

"Petersburg" («Петербург»), found in his collection of poetry *Above Barriers* (*Поверх барьеров*), written in 1914-1916. Pasternak's poems have a striking Baudelairian quality, explained in Benjamin's works in terms of the jerky movement and the parry of the shock experienced by the city. In Pushkinian vein, Pasternak depicts Peter the Great as a new God and poet, convulsed with the excitement of building the city of his dream:

> Как в пулю сажают вторую пулю
> Иль бьют на пари по свечке.
> Так этот раскат берегов и улиц
> Петром разряжен без осечки.
> О, как он велик был! Как сеткой конвульсий
> Покрылись железные щеки,
> Когда на Петровы глаза навернулись,
> Слезя их заливы в осоке!
> И к горлу балтийские волны, как комья
> Тоски, подкатили; когда им
> Забвенье владело; когда он знакомил
> С империей царство, край с краем.
> (Pasternak 1977: 90-91)

> Like the first bullet hit by the next shot
> Or the flame shot from a candle in a dare,
> This flat of shores and streets
> Was grasped by his immaculate precision.
> Oh, how great he was! How his bronze cheeks
> Criss-crossed with a grid of convulsions,
> When gulfs of sharp grass,
> Filled Peter's eyes, causing tears!
> And the waves of the Baltic sea stuck,
> In his throat like lumps of melancholy; when
> He was possessed by oblivious inspiration;
> when he introduced
> his empire to his kingdom, one land to the other.

Pasternak's rewrite of the introductory part of Pushkin's "The Bronze Horseman" is striking and elaborate. In Pasternak's poem, the Peter the Great figure merges with the image of the monument to Peter the Great. He is both creator and creation; actor and spectator; abuser and abused. It appears that Pasternak's poem instils into readers' minds a Peter the Great image moulded into a Futurist poet and visionary. Pasternak's inversion of the historical drama of Pushkin's text creates an atmosphere of the immediate present. Pasternak reproduces the convulsions of Evgenii's laughter preceding his madness in "The Bronze Horseman" in a novel way: it is Peter the Great who is possessed by the vision of his utopian dwelling and by the void caused by the destruction of the previous way of life. Pasternak's poem departs from the metrical pattern of Pushkin's texts. It uses the accentual type of verse usually known as dol′nik: most lines have three stresses. It would not be an exaggeration to say that Pasternak's poem "Like the first bullet hit by the next shot..." highlights the process of creation and clashes between fragmented images needing assembly into a coherent whole.

Pasternak's Peter the Great stands very close to the images of craftsmen found in the writings of Briusov and Mandelshtam. In the period of modernist aesthetic experimentation and Formalist theories, Mandelshtam equated architecture and literature. He showed a strong interest in the art of building. For example, in his seminal article "The Morning of Acmeism" («Утро акмеизма») he inferred a bond between acmeist constructions and gothic cathedrals, Mandelshtam lovingly created the portrait of a carpenter who complimented Maximilian Voloshin for his highly developed visual perception of landscape; the preferred location for his grave would be atop a Crimean hill. In Mandelshtam's view, Voloshin's exilic poetry and space-construction through poetry derived from Dante: "He developed the pioneering work of Dante that merged poetry and landscape, and he was rewarded for this work by the praise of a carpenter" («Он вел ударную дантовскую работу по слиянию с ландшафтом и был премирован отзывом плотника») (Mandelshtam 1987: 166). At the core of Pasternak's vision of Peter the Great is the issue of creative vision and ability to materialise creative projects. The issue was suggested tentatively by Pushkin's ode-like appraisal of Peter the Great's achievements in "The Bronze Horseman".

Another Pasternak cycle of poems to feature strong Pushkinian subtexts is "Theme With Variations" («Тема с вариациями», 1916-22). The whole cycle's core subject matter is the issue of creative psychology. Maurice Bowra, one of the first serious interpreters of Pasternak's poetry, noted that "This poetry is difficult just because it reflects the poet's sensations so exactly [...]. Pasternak has a remarkable gift for giving shape and colour to these inchoate states of the mind in its moments of excited sensibility [...]" (Bowra 1967: 137). The sphynx-like Peter the Great of Pasternak's cycle strongly resembles Pushkin himself, whose depiction appears in one of the poems in "Theme With Variations". Images of night, candles, light and facial gestures representing nervous tension are strongly pronounced in the poem "Stars raced...":

> Мчались звезды. В море мылись мысы.
> Слепла соль. И слезы высыхали.
> Были темны спальни. Мчались мысли,
> И прислушивался сфинкс к Сахаре.
>
> Плыли свечи. И, казалось, стынет
> Кровь колоса. Заплывали губы
> Голубой улыбкою пустыни.
> В час отлива ночь пошла на убыль.
>
> Море тронул ветерок с Марокко.
> Шел в снегах Архангельск.
> Плыли свечи. Черновик «Пророка»
> Просыхал, и брезжил день на Ганге.
> (Pasternak 1977: 194)

> Stars raced headlong. Seaward headlands lathered.
> Salt spray blinded. Eyes dried up their tears.
> Darkness filled the bedrooms. Thoughts raced headlong.
> To Sahara Sphinx turned patient ears.
>
> Candles guttered. Blood, it seemed, was frozen
> In the huge Colossus. Lips at play
> Swelled into the blue smile of the desert.
> In that hour of ebb night sank away.
>
> Seas were stirred by breezes from Morocco.
> Simoon blew. Archangel snored in snows.
> Candles guttered. First draft of *The Prophet*
> Dried, and on the Ganges dawn arose.

(translated by C.M. Bowra, in: Bowra 1967: 137)

According to Bowra, the subject matter of Pasternak's poem is the composition of Pushkin's poem "Prophet" (Bowra 1967: 137). I examine the observations on Pasternak's poem located by Bowra since he infers the above poem as an example of what I am calling imaginary creation of space and writing as dwelling. The images of the African landscape intensify the displacement of the poet in a modern urban environment. The images add a sense of estrangement and novelty to the poet's exotic existence outside the boundaries of modernity, outside the rationalised spaces determined by the legacy of the enlightenment.

Bowra's translation presents Pasternak as a poet who demystifies Pushkin's creative mystery and engages himself with the creative flow of life passed down to him through Pushkin's poetry. Bowra writes of the boundless imagination described in Pasternak's poem: "In the first place we hear of the circumstances in which the poem is written. It is begun at night, and finished at dawn. The dark bedrooms, the guttering candles, the racing stars, are the accompaniment of composition. The geographical setting, from Africa to Archangel, from the Ganges to Morocco, places the poem in its wider, cosmic relations and sets its birth on the stage of the world. But each of the details serves its purpose. They are symbols for the act of composition as it takes place in the poet. The storm at sea is his tumultuous energy, the freezing Colossus his state when the work begins, the listening Sphinx his expectant consciousness on the verge of starting, the swelling lips his joy that expands into creation, the snoring city of Archangel his indifference to all around him, and the dawn his final achievement. But though we may treat the poem at two levels, literal and symbolical, they are fused into a single result. [...] The composition of *The Prophet* is a display of creative energy in which the workings of the poet's inspiration have the power of natural forces and closely resemble them" (Bowra 1967: 138).

We should also stress that Pasternak's preoccupation with Pushkin's works revolve around the principle of writing as dwelling and imaginary landscapes. This is explained by the modernist concern with space that came to replace the linear vision of historical development and personal biography. As Foucault explains: "The present age may be the age of space instead. We are in an era of the simultaneous, of juxtaposition, of the near and far, of the side-by-side, of the scattered" (Foucault 2000: 175). Pasternak's poetry anticipated Foucault's concerns because of its clear manifestation of the modern concepts of simultaneity and space. And, as was pointed out earlier, in her 1932 essay "Epic and Lyric of Contemporary Russia" («Эпос и лирика современной России»), Tsvetaeva describes Pasternak in conspicuously Baudelairian manner as an invitation to travel: "Pasternak is solely an *invitation au voyage* of self-discovery and world-discovery, solely a point of departure; a place from which" (Tsvetaeva 1992: 119). The implied comparison between Baudelaire and Pasternak evokes the unmistakeable bond between modern poetry and urban experience. While the vision of modernity as part of urban experience constitutes a hallmark of Baudelaire's poetry, his 1859 poem "Le Voyage" instigates a search for a new dwelling and creates a metaphor for modern lyric poetry that sets readers' minds in perpetual motion of self-renewal.

Perhaps, the most interesting example of Pasternak's Bergsonian portrayal of walking and becoming is his 1914 poem "Opportunity" («Возможность»). Here the myth of Pushkin is employed as part of the poem's playful space to celebrate the moment of evolving artistic creation and to allow the participation of the reader. It has a double framing, presenting the lyric persona as a reader of both Pushkin's text and of the city landscape of Moscow's Tverskaia Street with its monument to Pushkin. The monument was unveiled in June 1880 coinciding with a three-day celebration of Pushkin. In their Pushkin studies both Marcus Levitt and Stephanie Sandler link this event to the emergence of the Russian national identity (Levitt 1980: 4; Sandler 2004: 88). Levitt's characterised the commemoration as "a brief and intoxicating moment when it seemed as if the long and painful conflict between state and nation would be happily and peacefully resolved, the moment when modern Russian national identity consolidated around its literature, with Pushkin as its focus" (Levitt 1980: 4). This observation is supported by the essay "The Opening of the Monument in Moscow" («Открытие памятника в Москве») by Dmitii Liubimov, a Russian émigré critic. Liubimov wrote that Dostoevskii's speech delivered at the ceremony to mark the unveiling of the Pushkin monument made people faint. Liubimov remembers Ivan Aksakov concluding the ceremony by stating: "Dostoevskii's speech is an event. Everything is explained, everything is clear. There are no more Slavophiles, no more Westernisers" (Liubimov 1937). In Liubimov's account, Dostoevskii's suggestion that Pushkin death at the height of his creative capacity prevented his full explanation of the mysterious message concealed in his writings had an overpowering impact on the audience. The audience was keen to respond to Dostoevskii's call to participate in the search for an explanation of the poet's mystery.

Translated into aesthetic categories, Dostoevskii's vision of Pushkin's life as unravelling mystery and a theological spectacle stands close to the modernist understanding of the poet's life in aesthetic terms. The effect of aesthetisation of life on the individual's consciousness is especially evident in Pasternak's early poetry. In "Safe Conduct" («Охраная грамота») Pasternak defined this period of his creative career as having a Romantic mode of writing and worldview, linked to an understanding of the poet's life as artistic creation-in-making, which he inherited from the German Romantics and Russian Symbolists. Pasternak felt that the drama of the poet's life, when understood as public spectacle, should have its own plot and legends to highlight the poet's qualities as a martyr. Pasternak refers to this mode of artistic becoming a visual understanding of biography as spectacle "because the poet is not just a living person obsessed by ethical learning but he is also a visual-biographic emblem that relies on its own background which makes it more distinct" (Pasternak: 227).

Pasternak's "Opportunity" provides us with an example of visual spectacle which, however, evokes association with Pushkin's poem "Monument" and draws playful analogies between young modernist poets and Pushkin. In Pasternak's poem the Pushkin monument comes alive. Pasternak uses the image of the Pushkin monument as a symbol of Russian national identity and presents it in a novel way, in comical Bergsonian manner. Pasternak's dissatisfaction with the canonical form of writing is also seen in his 1917 statements that play down Pushkin's metrics in favour of the strophic and metrical innovations of Maiakovskii, Rimbaud and Pierre Laforgue. One of Pasternak's rhetorical questions was: "How can one admire Pushkin who is so unlike Laforgue and Rimbaud?" (Barnes, vol.1, 2003: 188). Barnes informs us that Laforgue and Maiakovskii were of interest to Pasternak in 1914-1915, especially because of his experimental and innovative mode of writing as conveyed in a subsequently destroyed book of verse. As Barnes puts it, Laforgue and Maiakovskii "shared a common avoidance of regular strophic and metrical patterns, a rejection of traditional notions of harmony and balance, an interest in contemporaneity, and a tendency to use self-defensive irony and comedy" (ibid.).

The Pushkin monument is an outstanding landmark in Pasternak's personal mythology: Pasternak's meetings with Maiakovskii, Loks and Khodasevich took place in 1914 near the Pushkin monument in Moscow in a Greek coffee house, not far from Strastnoi Boulevard. Pasternak describes the Pushkin monument in great detail in "Safe Conduct" and also mentions it in "Opportunity". For Pasternak, this part of Moscow formed an important literary landscape that juxtaposed modernist poetry with canonical writing. The landscape acts as a distinctive background for Maiakovskii's recital of his narrative poem-tragedy *Vladimir Maiakovskii*. The imaginary space of Maiakovskii's poem, the sounds of his poem and the visual and aural perception of summer street life in Moscow merge in Pasternak's description into a vibrant surreal dwelling with strongly pronounced metatextual overtones. Pasternak thus describes his simultaneously perceived impressions of Moscow and of Maiakovskii's performance of his poem: "I listened to it and was completely absorbed by it. My heart was aching and my breathing went quiet. I never heard anything like it. It included everything: the boulevard, dogs, poplars and butterflies. It also included hairdresses, breadmakers, tailors and steam-engines. [...] In the distance steam-engines roared like sturgeon. Deep down in the throat of his creativity there was the same bottomless depth that existed on the earth. It had the depthless spirituality which is essential for any originality together with the infinite vastness visible from any point of life and stretchable in any direction; without which poetry is impossible" («Я слушал, не помня себя, всем перехваченным сердцем, затая дыханье. Ничего подобного я никогда не слыхал. Здесь было все. Бульвар, собаки, тополя и бабочки. Парикмахеры, булочники, портные и паровозы. [...] Вдали белугой ревели локомотивы. В горловом краю его творчества была та же безусловная даль, что на земле. Тут была та бездомная одухотворенность, без которой не бывает оригинальности, та бесконечность, открывающаяся с любой точки жизни, в любом направленьи, без которой поэзия – одно недоразуменье, временно не разъясненное») (Pasternak 1983: 264). In the above quote Pasternak again talks of the poet's dwelling in terms suggested by Holderlin, Heidegger and Bergson. To Pasternak's mind, Maiakovskii constructed his own "elastic" dwelling from his inner world and the Moscow summer cityscapes of 1914.

By the same token we can approach Pasternak's "Opportunity" as his own poetic dwelling combining surreal overtones with vivid descriptions of the Tverskaia Street and Strastnoi Boulevard. The reference in the opening line of the poem to Strastnoi Boulevard — "At nine o'clock, to the left, as soon as you leave Strastnoi Boulevard" («в девять, по левой, как выйти со Страстного») (Pasternak 1977: 65) is important to the semantic unity of the poem. Strastnoi Boulevard is used both as a point of departure for the lyric persona starting his evening stroll in Moscow, and is employed as paronamasia because the street's name alludes to "passion" («страсть»). The introduction of the theme of passion at the beginning of the poem is double-edged: it alludes both to Pushkin's jealous and passionate personality and to his death in a duel, which was preserved in the Russian cultural memory in Christian terminology as a martyr's death. Yet Pasternak's poem does offer a playful reading of Pushkin's fate, subverting any static and emblematic representations of his life personified by the Pushkin monument. The lyric hero of Pasternak's poem assumes the conversational tone of storytelling. The tone parodies a series of poses and a multiplicity of voices in a varying yet ever-present tension. It evolves as a dynamic process of role-playing. To read Pasternak's poem as a narrative of experience would be futile because the vibrant energy of its language presents the described interaction between a passer-by and the Pushkin monument as just one possible imaginary adventure on a Moscow street, and permits an infinity of ways to destroy Pushkin as a monument and thus animate the story of his life.

Pasternak in "Opportunity" is staging a theatrical spectacle in the centre of Moscow. The lyric persona is once again presented as a flâneur who acts like a moving camera, making an impressionistic assessment of the space where the drama of the poet's life is about to unfold. Thus, on his walk to the Pushkin monument, the lyric hero observes the damp façades of important companies with their signage missing («на сырых фасадах ни единой вывески»). Pasternak's flâneur registers in his mind that all the plaques might have been taken down for the night in anticipation of wind and snowstorm. He also notices a textile fabric resembling a mask, in the style of Nikolai Gogol's overcoat: it attempts to hide its identity and looks almost dead. In sum, Pasternak's flâneur sees the city as a sleepy space that bores him to death. This impression is reinforced in the line suggesting that Tverskaia Street sleeps like a dead one («спит, как убитая, Тверская»). The usage of the colloquial expression 'the sleep of the dead' in this context adds a humorous overtone to the poem that prefigures, farcically, a theme of violent death. By juxtaposing the dead street with the dead Pushkin, now a monument, Pasternak's poem reverses the roles of his characters and presents Pushkin as more alive than all Moscow's citizens. In this respect, Pasternak's text, featuring an imaginary encounter with Pushkin, is akin to Annenskii's poem "Bronze Poet" discussed above, in which the sleepy environment of Tsarskoe Selo becomes animated when the Pushkin monument comes alive.

Pasternak's monument to Pushkin is empowered with ability to remember the beginning of his immortal life. As with the bronze Peter the Great in "The Bronze Horseman", the historical figure of Pushkin merges in Pasternak's imagination with the Pushkin monument. It is difficult to separate the two, but Pasternak's image of the monument corresponds to Potebnia's concept of the outer form and inner image of the word: the monument represents the frozen, static image of Pushkin, but still evokes the idea of Pushkin the universal creative principle, to use Gasparov's expression mentioned earlier. Thus, the phrase "He remembers how his immortality began" («он помнит, как началось бессмертие») exemplifies a form of aesthetic deconstruction which points to the fictional basis of its own representational practices and unfolds the discursive fictions associated with the ideologically charged signifying practices of wider society. Pasternak playfully identifies the point in Pushkin's life when he turned into a national poet as a finalised moment: the lyric persona explains that Pushkin's immortality began at the moment of his return home from his duel («тотчас по возвращении с дуэли, дома»). Thus, the interior space is shown here as a vessel that contains Pushkin's body as if made of fluid. In a symbolic way, the fluidity of Pushkin's authentic voice is identified with infinity understood as immortality, not static, but dynamic and unfolding. Such an interpretation echoes Dostoevskii's approach and mocks the attempts of Russian ideologists to create from Pushkin's life the myth of a national poet and to turn his writings into museum artefacts. This is especially felt in the fourth stanza of the poem where Pushkin the monument is portrayed as a living person who kisses the hand of Tverskaia Street.

Erotic overtones are inscribed into the city landscape, and create an analogy with Pushkin the poet and his wife Goncharova. It is suggested that Pushkin the monument is just as jealous of Tverskaia Street as Pushkin the poet was jealous of his wife. This jealous rage has potential to finish in a duel and thereby destabilise the sleepy existence of Moscow in winter. As Pasternak teasingly explains, as if witnessing a theatrical peformance: "And this incident could turn into a duel/ When one of the newcomers blows Tverskaia a kiss/ having waved to it lightheartedly" («И дело начинает пахнуть дуэлью,/ Когда какой-то из новых воздушный/ Поцелуй ей шлет, легко взмахнув метелью»). An implied infatuation between poet and street brings to the fore the intimate bond between flâneur and city space. The poetic which Pushkin the poet constructs from his internal world and Moscow's landscape is threatened in Pushkin's eyes by newly-emerging modernist poet-flâneurs. The identities of Pushkin the poet and Pushkin the monument thus merge at this point, because both are presented as idols zealously guarding their own space. The male narrator of Pasternak's poem lives entirely within a surrealistic dreamworld of his own making, just like the above mentioned modern figure of the mystic. Through his dreams Pasternak's city dweller escapes the fragmentation and facelessness threatened by the city outside or even within the security of his own apartment. His dream world relies on simultaneous experience of the past and the present, as well as on simultaneous perception of Petersburg and Moscow landscapes. The poem locates the emergence of Pushkin the immortal genius in Moscow, not Petersburg where Pushkin was killed in a duel. Pasternak's "Opportunity" is a powerful gesture that rebuffs both historical truth and all legends and myths surrounding Pushkin's life and personality.

"Opportunity" also reflects on Russia's everlasting fascination with violence and duels. In her painstaking study of ritualised violence in Russia, Reyfman claims that "Russian cultural memory has preserved a glamorous image of the Russian duelist: a gentleman, he is always true to his honor; he elegantly challenges his offender for some equally elegant indiscretion, behaves courageously and magnanimously at the duelling site, and shows fortitude in the face of possible punishment afterward — if he survives" (Reyfman 1999: 1). According to Reyfman, Russians' persistent fascination with duellists continues to result in the erection of new monuments to famous duellists, including contemporaries of Pushkin. Thus Pasternak's "Opportunity" exemplifies Russia's fascination with poets who died in duels. It highlights the theme of contemporary rivalry between modernist poets, not just the rivalry between newcomers and canonical figures.

Pasternak addresses the duelling theme as a means of discussing his own physical and moral integrity. This helps him examine several important metaliterary issues related to his poetic identity. In Reyfman's view, the tradition of duelling as a subject of literary study, handed down by Dostoevskii to Russian modernist authors, had almost disappeared by the 1920s, but in the 1930s the duelling discourse still had not evaporated completely. As Reyfman convincingly argues, in various modernist texts "an idealist guarding his honor and dignity against all odds became a figure to admire, whereas a rationalist unconcerned with his personal space began to look suspicious and even ominous" (Reyfman 1999: 275). Indeed, Pasternak's poem expresses a desire to protect the poet's identity and his own space in the face of criticism that his strangeness and originality did not conform to the expectations of Russian modernists of the 1910s. Pasternak's image of the contemporary poet combines the figure of a little man (as constructed in Pushkin's "The Bronze Horseman") with the figure of the genius whose radicalised form of individualism is at odds with society's mediocre system of values. Lazar Fleishman, for example, in a major study of Pasternak's life and writings, says Pasternak's city poems differed from the urban poetry of Briusov because "they were demonstratively timeless in character" and "out of tune equally with the passéist and with the modernist line in Russian poetry" (Fleishman 1990: 42).

Fleishman makes the observation that some critics ascribe the strange traits of Pasternak's lyric poetry to his Jewish origin (ibid.) To the extent that this does shed light on the reception of Pasternak's poetry in the 1910s, it reveals that Pasternak in "Opportunity" wishes to fashion himself in the clothes of Pushkin, the famous duellist and gentleman, who needs to defend his honour and cultural space in Russia at the beginning of his career. He challenges his hostile critics and mocks their values which revolve around Russian national identity and established stereotypes. Pasternak employs Pushkin's "The Bronze Horseman" and "Monument" to build his own poetics of space and writing, as a document for a phenomenology of being. Pasternak presents Pushkin's monument as an illustration of the permanence of being in the face of changing and dislocated images of a life in flux. Pasternak's urban walks and observations on modern city life go hand in hand with his cognising the creative process and origins of creative life. Pasternak's poetry exemplifies Blanchard's thesis on modern poetry and imagination: "With poetry, the imagination takes its place on the margin, exactly where the function of unreality comes to charm or to disturb — always to awaken — the sleeping being lost in its automatisms. The most insidious of this automatisms, the automatism of language, ceases to function when we enter into the domain of pure sublimation" (Blanchard 1994: xxxv).

A striking feature of Pasternak's engagement with Pushkin's text is his presentation of images seen in dream, equating the language of poetry and film in Eisensteinian manner. In the poem "Stars raced..." discussed above in Bowra's translation, the draft of Pushkin's poem "Prophet" is the only static image around which all life revolves as a set of visual frames: stars raced headlong — seaward headlands lathered — thoughts raced headlong — candles guttered — lips swelled — seas were stirred by breezes — Simoon blew — candles guttered — the Ganges dawn arose. Pushkin's preoccupation with the poetics of movement is transformed by Pasternak into an exploration of the relationship between diverse figures and dislocated images that are subordinated to somatic disjointed rhythm. There is the impression of camera movement across the imaginary desert used as the setting of Pushkin's poem. Pasternak demystifies the mystery of writing so that in his artistic imagination Peter the Great the carpenter and architect stands close to Pushkin, the poet, who assembles objects and events of everyday life in montage fragments. As Schreurs aptly sums up, "the technique of montage creates a double-layered structure: on the one hand a very erratic surface structure, forming a sequence of thematically and stylistically conflicting parts; on the other hand a semantic superstructure (or deeper level) where those parts are integrated into associative patterns" (Schreurs 1989: 171). Pasternak's poem lends itself to be interpreted as a polyphonic lyric, a mini-ballad, since it contains a well developed plot, a story within a story. As Schreurs notes, "essential to a montage construction is that *what is not told*, but must be revealed by the interpretative activity of the spectator or reader" (Schreurs 1989: 172). The purpose of Pasternak's "Opportunity" is to shock the reader into thinking through the juxtaposition of the Petersburg and Moscow landscapes and private histories voicing individual suffering. It forces the reader to reflect upon the evaluation of the duel as a means to secure a better future, and sense of dignity, through violence and destruction.

The theme of clash between cultural space and the elements, between civilisation and chaos, is developed in Benedikt Lifshits's collection of poetry *Medusa of the Marshes* (*Болотная медуза,* 1914-1915). The Petrograd (renamed from Petersburg in 1914) of World War I was acutely reflected in Lifshits's apocalyptic vision of contemporary Petersburg that suggested the decay of Europe and the withering away of Peter the Great's vision for a Europeanised Russia. Throughout the book we see pessimistic overtones and an acute awareness of forthcoming crisis. For example, the glorious image of the Admiralty building, admired by the narrator of "The Bronze Horseman", is mocked in Lifshits's poem "Admiralty" («Адмиралтейство», 1915) as a geometrical monster that lends itself to deconstruction and re-assembly in the style of a Cubist painting. Peter the Great is equated to a circus performer. Lifshits addresses Petersburg in highly ironical manner: "It would have been impossible for your architect/ Not to become a juggler; so he he turned into a juggler and magician» («Не мог не быть и стать жонглером/ И фокусником зодчий твой») (Otradin 1988: 309). The rationalised Petersburg space is introduced as a circus space, filled with abstract and dislocated images. These images bring to mind the mechanically organised and impersonal space of commedia dell'arte: "and two equally beautiful spheres/ Compete with the cube" («И два равнопрекрасных шара/ Слепой оспаривают куб» (Otradin 1988: 309).

Lifshits's flâneur, observing urban life in Petrograd in terms of the puppet-like figures and geometric stage sets, seems to be influenced by the contemporary performances in which mechanical figures appeared. He promotes the ideals of speed and mechanisation, as conveyed in the paintings of the Rayonists and Futurists. Lifshits was closely associated with the Russian Futurists. Kasimir Malevich's design of the scenery and costumes for Aleksei Kruchenykh's 1913 opera *Victory Over the Sun* (*Победа над солнцем*) had considerable impact on Lifshits's artistic imagination. Lifshits merged various allusions to Pushkin's "The Bronze Horseman" with his own abstractions inspired by Petrograd architectural landmarks. Tomashevskii recollects that the opera *Victory over the Sun* had a very abstract setting: "The painted scenery was Cubist and non-objective: on the backdrops were painted conical and spiral forms similar to those painted on the curtain [...]. The costumes were made of cardboard and resembled armour painted in Cubist style" (Goldberg 1993: 36). Thus the post-flood void described in Pushkin's "The Bronze Horseman" is reinterpreted in Lifshits's poetry as an aesthetic concept. In the age of Malevich's geometrical abstractions, labelled by some critics as neo-Idealist icons (Marks 2003: 235), Pushkin's presentation of nothingness and of Evgenii's laughter as the only meaningful response to the void left by the destructive flood of 1824 would have appealed to Lifshits's aesthetic sensibilities as the prototype for Malevich's abstract art. As Marks puts it, Malevich's square "stood for the pure, Ideal universe of which the Silver Age dreamed — hence his choice of the term Suprematism [...] *White Square on White* (1918) depicted absolute nothingness, the ultimate reality farthest removed from earth" (Marks 200: 235-36).

Mikhail Gasparov thinks that Lifshits's portrayal of Petersburg contains some interesting ideological connotations that incorporate the Pushkinian tradition. M. Gasparov writes: "But the energy of *Medusa of the Marshes* is not only related to intonation: Lifshits's poetry embraces once again the theme of clash between elements and culture. Petersburg became an object of his poetry invoking two well-known *Petersburg myths.* The first one involves the idea of the battle between culture and elements; granite against the river Neva and marshes — this is the Pushkinian tradition. The second myth includes opposition between West and East, rationalised order and chaos: this myth is part of the post-Pushkin tradition, which stems from the teachings of Slavophiles and westernisers. In Lifshits's poetry their merger creates an artistic universe in which the revolt of the river Neva's elements becomes indistinguishable from the revolt of the Russian Asiatic self. Such a revolt is mighty but fruitless because it excludes the rationalised space of the West (even if it forms part of the binary opposition): *it is impossible to become the East, having lost the West*" («Но энергия *Болотной медузы* не только интонационная: в поэзию Лифщица возвращается тема противоборства стихии и культуры. Петербург, став героем его стихов, приносит с собой два хорошо известных *петербургских мифа*. Во-первых, это культура против стихии, гранит против Невы и болота, — пушкинская традиция; во-вторых, Запад против Востока, рациональный порядок против экологического хаоса, — послепушкинская традиция, идущая от западников и славянофилов. Налагаясь, это давало картину: бунт невской стихии и бунт русской Азии — одно и тоже, он могуч, но бесплоден без одухотоворяющей — хотя бы через отталкивание — рациональности запада: *невозможно быть востоком, навеки запад потеряв*») (Gasparov 1995: 323-24). M. Gasparov differentiates two versions of the Petersburg myth, which he defines as the Pushkinian and post-Pushkinian traditions.

We can see a similar clash in Larissa Reisner's 1916 poem "To the Bronze Horseman" («Медному всаднику») which portrays Petrograd as a space lacking creative impulse, impregnated with revolutionary forces voicing the anarchistic identity of Russian Asia. The concluding stanza of Reisner's poem states:

> Петровские граниты
> Едва прикрыли торф
> И правит Бенкендорф,
> Где правили хариты.
> (Otradin 1988: 316)

> Peter's granites
> Barely covered the moss
> And Benckendorff rules in the place,
> Formerly run by the Charites!

The sense of estrangement from the city and from herself that Reisner expressed in her poem stems from the decadent culture of the 1880s-1910s. The period was imbued with a premonition of the last days of humanity and a morbid attraction to decline and decay. Reisner's poem calls for a strong anti-conformist, individual existence. It seeks ways to rebuild a better life free of the conventions of the established culture. The mention of moss alludes to the possibility of some organic evolution of humaneness, and suggests that the universal ideal's man of reason had become something of a censor and policeman, something of a Benkendorff. Aleksei Benkendorff was Russia's chief of police who had spied on Pushkin and other liberally minded authors, and had personally censored several Pushkin's manuscripts. In Reisner's poem he is a symbol of modern bureaucracy that displaces critical thinking and creativity. The collision between the organic way of life and the artificial man-made world, between the somatic and the semantic, is also clear in the 1916 poem of well known Soviet poet Vsevolod Rozhdestvenskii, "Beyond moist clouds..." («За мокрыми облаками...»), in which the lyric persona wishes the wooden Petersburg to come alive: "Come alive, come alive, wooden Petersburg!" («Воскресни же, воскресни,/ Деревянный Петербург!») (Otradin 1988: 317). This incantation evokes Evgenii from Pushkin's "The Bronze Horseman" who witnessed the tragic disappearance of much of Petersburg's wooden infrastructure. The lyric persona of Rozhdestvenskii's poem is fashioned in the clothes of Pushkin's Evgenii and points to his estrangement from the dehumanised environment of the modern metropolis: "Oh, my heart does not know you,/ Petrograd, city of stone!" («Ах, сердце тебя не знает, каменный Петроград!») (Otradin 1988: 317). Both Reisner and Rozhdestvenskii alluded to Pushkin's "The Bronze Horseman" at a time when World War I had triggered the apocalyptic imagination of writers and artists in Europe and in Russia.

Resiner's poem is indicative of the emergence in the 1900s-1910s of a new image for the modern subject. This subject was unstable, changeable, in search of new ways of life. There is a shift from a mainly pessimistic worldview to one with utopian aspirations. This shift is captured well in Hermann Bahr's 1899 pronouncement that "modernity is everything that follows on the bankruptcy of individualism: everything which is no longer there, but in the course of becoming" (Le Rider 1998: 298). As in a montage, Reisner's poem juxtaposes the Charites and Benckendorff, creating a strong contrast between the modern organisation of life and the shrinking space of contemplation and the sublime. Reisner's poem offers a playful interaction of various subtexts: the image of a granite embankment contrasting with marshes and moss is borrowed from the introductory part of Pushkin's "The Bronze Horseman" written in the style of a Russian eighteenth-century ode. Yet Reisner's view also oscillates towards the elegiac sublime and reflects on the mass hysteria, universal fear and public panic prevalent in Russia around 1916.

In his monumental study of the Russian revolution *A People's Tragedy: The Russian Revolution: 1891-1924* Orlando Figes's account of the effects of World War I on Russian social and political life encapsulates the reason for the widespread hysteria: "Patriotic nobles like Brusilov and Lvov had hoped that a successful war campaign would bring the government and government together and thus forestall the need for radical reforms. They now realised that the opposite was true: radical reforms were a necessary precondition for military success. The growing shortage of food, fuel and basic household goods, the rapid inflation of prices, the breakdown of transport, the widespread corruption of government and its military suppliers, and the steep increase in crime and social order — all these combined with the endless slaughter of the war to create a growing sense of public panic and hysteria" (Figes 1997: 283). Figes refers to Alexander Guchkov's August 1916 letter to General Alekseev. In this letter Guchkov calls the Russian government pitiful, wretched and flabby; it "is preparing to face the cataclysm by taking measures only good enough to protect oneself from a shower. It puts on galoshes and open an umbrella!" (Figes 1997: 283).

In the context of this atmosphere of crisis in which the government was becoming alienated from its citizens, Reisner's powerful gesture to juxtapose Pushkin's post-1825 Russia with the Russia of 1916 allegorically introduces into the public discourse Pushkin's concerns for dignity and integrity. Reisner's poem echoes Vassilii Zhukovskii's attempts, in his elegy written on Pushkin's death and in his letter to Benkendorff, to identify himself with the dead poet. According to Sandler's penetrating analysis of Zhukovskii's responses to Pushkin's death, Zhukovskii "seems to ponder what it would be like to *be* Pushkin, and we sense his strong connection to him in his letter to Benkendorff. There, instead of reporting on the required inventory of Pushkin's papers, he defends Pushkin's integrity, as if feeling new kinship with a writer harassed by government surveillance" (Sandler 2004: 36). Reisner goes further than Zhukovskii and creates a sense of sharing an imaginary space constructed in Pushkin's poetry, and thus participating in the imaginary community of fellow writers.

Reisner's allusion to the Charites adds a new dimension to her poem on 1916 Petrograd: it resonates well with Benedict Anderson's formulation that "communities are to be distinguished [...] by the style in which they imagined" (Anderson 1991: 6). According to Pierre Grimal's dictionary of classical mythology, the Charites were Greek goddesses of beauty and joy, who lived on Olympus and together with the Muses spread "the joy of Nature in human hearts" (Grimal 1986: 99). By alluding to the city of Pushkin's days as a city governed by the Charites, Reisner establishes her direct kinship with the young Pushkin who in 1818 presented his friend Nikolai Krivtsov with a copy of Voltaire's narrative poem "The Maid of Orleans" ("Le Pucelle d'Orléans") featuring Jeanne d'Arc, a poem full of anti-religious mockery and erotic overtones. Pushkin wanted his friend to remember him as a poet of playfulness, liberty and love who had modelled himself on Voltaire (Shchegolev 1987: 295). In his poem "When will you squeeze this hand again..." («Когда сожмешь ты снова руку...»), written in 1818 on Kritsov's departure for England, Pushkin defines Voltaire's poem as the sacred bible of the Charites:

> Когда сожмешь ты снова руку,
> Которая тебе дарит
> На скучный путь и на разлуку
> Святую библию харит?
> (Pushkin 1956, vol.1: 333)

> When will you squeeze again
> This hand that gives you
> This sacred bible of the Charites
> As a gift to make your journey and our separation easier?

Reisner's vision of Pushkin's Petersburg, governed by the spirit of liberty and hedonism, lends itself to interpretation along the lines suggested in Anderson's study of imaginary communities. Anderson reveals anthropological roots for the mechanisms of creation of such an imaginary bond with people from the past or from afar. Anderson illustrates this mechanism by referring to communities in Java:

"Javanese villagers have always known that they are connected to people they have never seen, but these ties were once imagined particularistically — as indefinitely stretchable nets of kinship and clientship. Until quite recently, the Javanese language had no word meaning the abstraction 'society' [...] the nation is always conceived as a deep, horizontal comradeship. Ultimately it is this fraternity that makes it possible, over the past two centuries, for so many millions of people, not so much to kill, as willingly to die for such limited imaginings" (Anderson 1991: 6-7). By pronouncing her kinship with the Pushkin of the Lycée period, Reisner, a young poet and writer who edited the liberal journal *Rudin* (*Рудин*) (the same title as Ivan Turgenev's novel), also enlists herself into the community of Acmeist poets who mourned the death of Annenskii and promoted his cult as father of contemporary lyricism. As Gumilev stressed on many occasions, Annenskii's poetry is firmly rooted in the classical Tsarskoe Selo tradition of Pushkin and Zhukovskii.

In 1916 Reisner had an affair with Gumilev. In many ways she saw Gumilev as her mentor. Reisner's poem "To the Bronze Horseman" can be seen as an interesting attempt to use the Peter the Great's monument as her interlocutor who guides the city and to whom she reports on the state of contemporary affairs. The poem also reflects on the belief, propagated both by Annenskii and Gumilev, in the importance of neo-hellenism for contemporary aesthetic sensibilities. Reisner's images of the Charites might be also viewed alongside Annenskii's concept of Apollonism which Gumilev promoted. As Basker has noted, Annenskii's concept of Apollonism indicates "a way to the future through the reworking of the past" (Basker in Losef and Scherr 1993: 231). Gumilev saw himself as heir to Annenskii; in Gumilev's, view Annenskii was one of the major European poets to have merged new developments in contemporary French poetry (as exemplified by Leconte de Lisle's writings) with the Russian neoclassical poetic tradition as manifested in the works of Pushkin and Zhukovskii. Annenskii's vision of neo-Hellenism as a poetry of elegant restraint (Basker, ibid.: 231) is echoed in Reisner's nostalgic remembering of the neo-classical poetic tradition of Pushkin's times.

Urban spectacles and Eisenstein's montage of attractions

Vladimir Maiakovskii's poem "Last Petersburg Fairy Tale" («Последняя петербургская сказка» 1916) contains a radical gesture that reduces Pushkin's "The Bronze Horseman" to the format of a semi-humorous fairy tale. This format allows it to focus solely on the plot of Pushkin's Petersburg story. Through his formalist-like reading of Pushkin's "The Bronze Horseman" Maiakovskii, like the morphological Formalists, reduced the literary work to a formal construction and theme. The semantic richness of Pushkin's narrative is lost in Maiakovskii's rendering. The story set in 1916 tells of a statue of a horseman come to life. The statue stops by a fashionable Petrograd hotel to drink in celebration of his creation of the city. The poem reflects on the spirit of hedonism brought about by the apocalyptic mood and general feeling in 1916 that Russia was on the brink of disastrous catastrophe. This feeling was associated with fear of a social explosion in which the government would be unable to defend its citizens. Figes explains this wave of what he calls "hysterical hedonism" as an escape from reality deepened by the sense of powerlessness of ordinary individuals: "Sensing the coming disaster, the rich and the high-born lost themselves in a last desperate binge of personal pleasure. They drank their stocks of champagne, spent huge sums of money on black-market caviar, sturgeon and other peacetime delicacies, threw lavish parties, deceived their wives and husbands and gambled away fortunes in casinos. Foreigners were shocked by their luxurious lifestyles and, even more so, by the indiscretion with which they flaunted their enjoyment" (Figes 1996: 283). Maiakovskii's desire to couch his descriptions of modern life within the fantastic narrative reflects his alienation from the society that chose to forget the victims of World War I and all the shortcomings of a government responsible for many unnecessary sacrifices. As Tsvetan Todorov sums up, the nineteenth century expressed itself in "the metaphysics of the real and imaginary, and the literature of the fantastic is nothing but the bad conscience of this positivist era. But today we can no longer believe in an immutable, external reality, nor in a literature which is merely a transcription of such a reality. [...] Now, it would not be too presumptuous to assert that the literature of the twentieth century is, in certain sense, more purely 'literature' than any other" (Todorov 1973: 166). Todorov's study indicates, however, that the fantastic forms of expression are used by authors when some things cannot be discussed in the open either because of the taboo subject matter or censorship. Thus Maiakovskii's poem, disguised as a fairy tale, might be seen as a veiled comment on the amnesia of contemporary society and its inability to mourn the dead. The theme of mourning brings Maiakovskii's satirical poem very close to both the *Eugene Onegin* and the "The Bronze Horseman" of Pushkin because of the similar concerns they expressed.

Commenting on the cultural codes and language of mourning found in European literature of the period, Jay Winter identifies three modes of expression of the human catastrophe manifested in European culture of 1914-1918: first, the visual representation of images of the dead and of their return and an associated "set of metaphors which frequently shifted into meditations on apocalyptic themes"; second, a strong tendency conveyed in poetry and prose "to 'see' the dead among the living"; third, a form of cultural encoding defined as social since it was expressed through social action (Winter 1995: 225). Winter draws on the study by Kristeva that helps to understand various articulations of the language of mourning and suffering within traditional structures of thought. Kristeva's vision of the modern subject's "battle with the symbolic collapse" (Winter 1995: 225) is successfully applied to Winter's analysis of various responses by British poets to the meaning of loss of life in World War I. Winter states: "Following Kristeva, we can see how it was not only individuals, therefore, but also the symbols of meaning which were 'resurrected' during and after war. Through the elaboration, expression and revival, these images and icons were shared by millions in mourning" (Winter 195: 226-27). Winter's study makes the valuable point that Europe's cultural history of World War I has some common modes of expression, including the abandonment of clear distinction between high and low culture, the cultivated and the uncultivated, the elevated and the vulgar. Thus Maiakovskii's poem about the last Petersburg fairy tale can be seen as an extension of a trend current in European poetry of this period.

Given that Maiakovskii expressed his anti-war feelings on many occasions, his poem "Last Petersburg Fairy Tale" parries the shock of the modern condition of crisis. It combines the emotional effects and connotations of diverging and colliding semantic units, in a way comparable to the disjointed stills in film montage that produce an ideological synthesis in spectators' minds. The use of the fairy tale genre accentuates the importance of the narrative plot. If we view montage as an elaborate system of semantic arrangement, then Maiakovskii's poem is constructed in similar manner to Eisenstein's notion of the montage of attractions. Vladimir Propp's notion of the function of an acting character is fully applicable to analysis of Maiakovskii's fairy-tale in verse. Peter Steiner commented on Propp's theoretical positions that "on the most abstract level, he conceived of the fairy tale as a narrative about actions performed by certain characters. And it is the actions, and not the interchangeable characters, that count. Characters, as carriers of these actions, are functionally indispensable" and "their action", says Propp, is "defined from the point of view of its relevance for the course of action" (Steiner 1984: 84). We can see that in a parodic manner Maiakovskii's humorous portrayal of Peter the Great's monument is opposing Pushkin's embodiment of impersonal natural and historical forces in "The Bronze Horseman". Maiakovskii's Peter the Great does function as the city's guardian and as a prototype builder-worker overseeing the city's construction work. But at the same time he resembles a Petrograd street entertainer and cabaret performer from the 1910s:

    Стоит император Петр Великий,
    Думает:
    «Запирую на просторе я!» –
    а рядом
    под пьяные клики строится гостиница «Астория».
    Сияет гостиница,
    За обедом обед она
    дает.
    Завистью с гранита снят,
    слез император.
    Трое медных слазят тихо,
    Чтоб не спугнуть Сенат.
    (Otradin 1988: 323-24)

    Peter the Great, the emperor,
    Stands and thinks:
    "I should have a feast in front of this vast space!"

Nearby, drunken noises accompany
The construction of the hotel *Astoria*.
The hotel shines,
It serves dinner after dinner.
Jealousy drives the emperor from the monument.
The three bronze figures descend from the rock,
Quietly so as not to frighten the Senate.

Maiakovskii's poem presents the act of reading of Puskin's "The Bronze Horseman" from the viewpoint of the Futurist poet, the radical modernist. Given Iser's comment that "the reader often feels involved in events which, at the time of reading, seem real to him, even though in fact they are very far from his own reality" (Iser in Lodge 1988: 215), we can see how Maiakovskii's text engages its readers in a reading game that simultaneously brings into play the Petrograd of the 1910s, the imaginary space of Pushkin's "The Bronze Horseman" and the Petersburg from the time of Peter the Great that was renowned for numerous feasts and public gatherings.

Maiakovskii's approach to Falconet's statue constitutes a deconstructive analysis. Maiakovskii presents the sculpture as disjointed imagery: the horse, the snake and Peter the Great come to a party at the lavishly decorated hotel *Astoria* as three different guests. The poem also illustrates Maiakovskii's concern to study the inter-relationship between art and life as an expression of his desire to merge life with art. In his 1913 essay "Theatre, Cinema and Futurism" Maiakovskii states that Futurists are involved in the radical redefinition of the sublime: "In the name of art of the future, Futurists' art, we have started the grand destruction of all areas of beauty" (Maiakovskii in Proffer 1980:181).

Maiakovskii demystifies the concept of genius inscribed in Pushkin's "The Bronze Horseman". While Pushkin's protagonist Evgenii admires the Falconet-moulded image and how it captures Peter the Great's creative and analytical powers, Maiakovskii's poem concerns itself with socially engaged mass entertainment. By using the plot described in Pushkin's "The Bronze Horseman" in his own performance-oriented poem, Maiakovskii asserts that contemporary art must be spectacular and aimed at a new kind of performance to engage viewers and readers in creative dialogues. Maiakovskii's essay "Theatre, Cinema and Futurism" implies that poetry can also play a role in contemporary performance because of its phonetic and rhythmical properties. Maiakovskii says in the essay: "Those who have discovered that the word, the outline and its phonic aspect determine the flourishing of poetry, have the right to exist" (Proffer 1980:181). Maiakovskii envisages that his ideal readers and audience would immerse themselves in listening to his recitals so they could attempt to assemble various meanings from disjointed parts and devices.

Maiakovskii's poem "Last Petersburg Fairy Tale" is a good illustration of the concept of art as device developed in Viktor Shklovskii's article "Art as Technique" («Искусство как прием») published in 1917. Shklovskii proposed that images change little and that "they flow on without changing" "from century to century, from nation to nation, from poet to poet" (Shklovsky in Lodge 1988:17). Maiakovskii takes images from Pushkin's poem and uses them almost unchanged. Shklovskii's thesis about the importance of using such images in a creative way resonates well with Maiakovskii's treatment of Pushkin's canonical text. Shklovskii explains: "The works of poets are classified or grouped according to new techniques that poets discover and share, and according to their arrangement and development of the resources of language; poets are much more concerned with arranging images than with creating them. Images are given to poets; the ability to remember them is far more important that the ability to create them" (Shklovsky in Lodge 1988: 17).

Maiakovskii's poetry of the 1910s is not about just arranging images in an interesting way: it concerns itself with refashioning a set of ideas and images derived from a range of older traditions infused with new kind of romantic impulses. In overarching manner, it is possible to say that many artistic innovations found in Maiakovskii's poetry contributed to the creation of a new romantic figure: the soldier-poet, upholder of moral values, unafraid to speak the truth. As an interlocutor between the living and the dead, communities in mourning, young and old, the new type of romantic hero appearing in his poems of the 1910s-1920s is largely preoccupied with maximum expressivity, with creating language of direct contemporaneity, and with challenging traditional forms of communication. As early as 1913 Veliimir Khlebnikov and Kruchenykh identified two types of Futurist art, "one written and viewed in a moment, 'a sweeping away of cumbersome constructions' as in the art of Khlebnikov, Kruchenykh and Rozanova; the other written and read 'tautly' (tugo), with lots of tough spots, like the art of Maiakovskii and Malevich" (Stapanian 1985: 19). Stapanian observes that despite differences between the various Russian avant-garde movements in the 1910s-1920s, "a major feature of the Russian 'art of the future' centres upon a strong proclivity towards the primitive" (Stapanian 1985: 20). Stapanian labels this trend "neo-primitivism".

Maiakovskii's "Last Petersburg Fairy Tale" might be seen as neo-primitivist in its attempt to construct a verbal *lubok* (a kind of Russian popular print). While Stapanian does not explain in detail the Futurist concept of the poet as an artist-creator of speech, she gives an excellent outline of the major tenets of the worldview and artistic concerns shared by the Russian Futurist poets and artists. These tenets can be summarised thus: (1) "In the turn toward nonobjectivity, transformations of conventional language along with the breakup and reordering of old semantic 'objectives' yielded a new realism, whereby the word of communicative unit could project its self-value, based in the syntax of its own physical form"; (2) "building upon Futurist emphasis on dynamism and Cubist attention to distortion, dissymmetry, texture *(faktura)* and shift *(sdvig)*, Kruchenykh now declared *zaum'* an aesthetics of complete shift. It is this notion of shift — a movement from a previous or expected position or form — that provides a source of abstraction"; (3) "neo-primitivism, which cut away the elegant but lifeless surface of civilised culture, allowed artists-*rechetvortsy* to touch the living roots of art and pierce beyond the world of familiar forms into a realm of inherent logic of primal intuition" (Stapanian 1985: 20). Maiakovskii's "Last Petersburg Fairy Tale" has in mind the image of the badaud, the primitive urban spectator of Pushkin's *Eugene Onegin* discussed in the previous chapter. Like Pushkin, Maiakovskii holds in very low esteem any urban crowd that engages in mass spectacle without mental effort or emotional response. Maiakovskii describes Peter the Great's dinner in the hotel *Astoria*'s fashionable restaurant in a highly ironic manner:

Император,
Лошадь и змей
Неловко
По карточке

Спросили гренадин.
Шума язык не смолк, немея.
Из пивших и евших не обернулся ни один.
И только
Когда над пачкой соломинок
В коне заговорила привычка древняя,
Толпа сорвалась, криком сломана:
Жует!
Не знает, зачем они.
Деревня.
(Otradin 1988: 324)

The Emperor,
The horse and the snake
Awkwardly
Looked at the menu and
Asked for grenadine.
The crowd's jabber did not fall silent.
None of the drinkers and eaters paid them attention.
And only
When above a packet of cocktail straws
Pre-historic instinct
Gained its voice within the horse,
The crowd splintered, split with the cry:
The horse chews!
He knows not what they are for.
Simpleton!

In Maiakovskii's description of the imaginary adventure of the Peter the Great monument, the horse steals the show by breaking the code of behaviour in a fashionable restaurant. The performance is in the style of a touring troupe of clowns, and becomes an extraordinary urban spectacle. Contrary to usual expectations, the star of this show turns out not to be Peter the Great, the bronze horseman, but his horse. This adds a twist of estrangement to the routine and automaton behaviour of urban dwellers.

Maiakovskii's poem is one of the striking examples of Russian accentual poetry. It also contains several innovative rhymes based on a partial similarity of sounds (approximate rhymes), as well as compound rhymes such as «на просторе я — Астория», «обед она — медных», «гренадин — ни один», «соломинок — сломана», «древняя — деревня», «морде — городе», «без скипетра — Петра». We will return to the rhyme below.

Maiakovskii's aim may be not just to bring Pushkin's text to life, but also to change the mode of perception of Petersburg artefacts in order to merge high and low culture, and to present Pushkin's long poem as part of mass entertainment text. In the light of the urban theory of a 'soft' city, as developed in Jonathan Raban's book *Soft City,* it does not come as a surprise that Maiakovskii emphasises the special art of the actor "where the intonation of a word which does not have a specific meaning, and where movements of the human body which are invented but free in their rhythm, express the greatest inner feelings" (Proffer 1980: 182). Maiakovskii's art of creative engagement with the city and deconstruction of its text prefigures Raban's thesis on the theatrical nature of metropolises. Raban argues it is not simply that urban life has become more superficial and oriented towards consumption and seduction through images in the context of late capitalism; the city in itself has become an imaginary space: "Cities, unlike villages and towns, are plastic by nature. We mould them in our images: they in turn, shape us by the resistance they offer when we try to impose a personal form on them. In this sense, it seems to me that living in a city is an art, and we need the vocabulary of art, of style, to describe the particular relation between man and material that exists in the continual creative play of urban living. The city as we might imagine it, the soft city of illusion, myth, aspiration, nightmare, is as real, maybe more real, than the hard city one can locate in maps and statistics, in monographs on urban sociology and demography and architecture" (Raban 1974: 10). Raban explains that the basic dynamic of urban life derives from our living in close proximity with strangers. Interactions with strangers, and unexpected encounters with them in public places and on transport, make us see city life as theatricality. The experience of cities becomes a process of acting and perceiving ourselves as actors.

Maiakovskii's "Last Petersburg Fairy Tale" suggests that in the artificial environment of the city all natural instinct is oppressed, and a display of natural behaviour becomes a spectacle in its own right. The collision between nature and culture was already strongly pronounced in Pushkin's urban writing, but Maiakovskii's poem gives it a new twist. Maiakovskii's portrayal of the restaurant crowd disturbed by a bronze horse eating cocktail straws resonates well with the main thesis of the comic theory developed in Bergson's seminal work *Laughter: An Essay on the Meaning of the Comic* (published in France in 1900). Bergson defines the comic as a very special inversion of common sense. More importantly he sees in it a creative potential which breaks the automatic and conformist behaviour of modern subjects. "The comic character," Bergson indicates, "always errs through obstinacy of mind or of disposition, through absentmindedness, in short, through automatism. At the root of the comic there is a sort of rigidity which compels its victims to keep strictly to one path, to follow it straight along, to shut their ears and to refuse to listen" (Bergson 1999: 165). So, the bronze horse depicted in Maiakovskii's fairy tale in verse becomes ashamed of its uncivilised behaviour and quickly returns to its place in the city, to continue life as part of Falconet's monument:

> Стыдом овихрены шаги коня.
> Выбелена грива от уличного газа.
> Обратно
> По Набережной
> Гонит гиканье
> Последнюю из петербургских сказок.
> И вновь император
> Стоит без скипетра.
> Змей.
> Унынье у лошади на морде.
> И никто не поймет тоски Петра —
> Узника,
> Закованного в собственном городе.
> (Otradin 1988: 324)

> The horse's legs are whirlwinded with shame.
> Its mane is whitened from the street gaslight.
> A series of cries
> Chases the last of the Petersburg tales
> Along the embankment
> Back to its place.
> And again the emperor

Stands without its sceptre.
Snake.
The horse looks sad.
And nobody could understand
The longing of Peter —
A captive
Chained within his own city.

Despite the plot's simplicity, Maiakovskii's poem entwines Pushkin's text with Futurist performance in a remarkable and sophisticated way. It employs paronamasia to create an unexpected rhyme which brings together Peter and the sceptre. The poem's final stanza ridicules the imperial sublime manifested in the odic tradition of Russian eighteenth-century poetry inspired by Peter the Great's reforms, to which we referred above. The juxtaposition of the words 'emperor', 'Peter's longing' and '[without] sceptre' («император», «тоски Петра», and «скипетра») creates a pun that associates Peter with the emblem of imperial power. Furthermore, by creating a rhyme from the phrases «без скипетра» and «тоски Петра» Maiakovskii draws our attention to the performative potential of these lines. They can be seen as a rendering of Pushkin's iambic meter: to pronounce «без скипетра» in order to create an exact rhyme with Peter's name in the genitive case would require an artificial effort to recite the poem in a manner articulating the possibility of reproducing some examples of iambic meter embedded in the text. Such an exercise would give the impression of jerky camera movement; or present the tale's narrator as a walking person recording his urban impressions in verse.

As a narrator of a surreal incident, Maiakovskii seems to sympathise with the horse mocked by the wealthy Petrograd philistine restauranteurs, the consumers of culture and canonisers of bourgeois art works whose taste was often the target of Maiakovskii's criticism. The absurd situation described in Maiakovskii's "Last Petersburg Fairy Tale" is designed to subvert the 'common sense' of contemporary consumers' attacks on experimental modes of expression. In a short essay "The Relationship of Today's Theatre and Cinema to Art", Maiakovskii talks of the enemies of avant-garde art in these terms: "The people who are opposing us, as indeed they oppose any radical innovators, are armed with the only weapon possessed by every philistine — 'common sense'" (Maiakovskii 1977: 89).

Maiakovskii is clear that his aesthetic concern is not just for the novelty of artistic experiments and devices, but also for the spectators and readers who appreciate his visual and verbal artefacts. Maiakovskii's article painstakingly explains the essence of a new performance-oriented form of expression which could resurrect primeval logic and child-like creative imagination: "In taking some fact from the sphere of aesthetics, the history of the arts is interested not in the technical means of its enactment, but in the social currents which make its appearance inevitable and in the revolution which the fact in question causes in the psychology of the masses" (Maiakovskii 1977: 90).

By compressing Pushkin's "The Bronze Horseman" into a tale of absurdity, with some mythologised fairy-tale touches, Maiakovskii created a cultural artefact in its own right: a verbal *lubok* version of Pushkin's text ready for mass consumption. Such a gesture peeled away the lifeless surface of the elegantly constructed image of Pushkin's Petersburg that had been passed down from previous generations of readers and poets; and brought his creation closer to the roots of living art. The living art of poetry as an expression of the Russian language's creative potential appeared superior, to Maiakovskii's mind, to the architectural marvels created by Peter the Great and the sculptors of Russian and foreign origin. In this respect Maiakovskii's poem, seen as fairy tale in verse, functions similarly to Pushkin's *Eugene Onegin*, the novel in verse: it tells us more about poetry and its creative potential than it does about fairy tales. It is clear that Maiakovskii chooses to downplay Peter the Great's achievements, and favours the living art of verbal communication which incorporates national traits of prosody and cultural history. In fact, by being sensitive to the creative impulses of urban folk speech and contemporary colloquial expressions, Maiakovskii stands close to Pushkin's assessment of Peter the Great in his 1835 outline of the history of Russian literature. There we find this passage: "Peter the Great created the army, sciences, laws, but he could not create literature which emerges by itself, deriving from its own roots" («Петр создал войско, флот, науки, законы, но не мог создать словесности, которая рождается сама собою, от своих собственных начал») (Pushkin, volume 7: 533). It seems that Maiakovskii, just like Pushkin, wanted to use the image of Peter the Great as a symbol of Russian modernity and appropriate the image for his own poetic experiences conducted in the style of circus shows and Futurist aesthetics of hooliganism.

Michael Holquist points to the fact that, despite Maiakovskii's aspiration to become a leader of the revolutionary masses in the 1910s-1920s, he failed politically because he was a highly innovative poet of significant talent and his aesthetic goals outweighed his need for social engagement. Holquist supports his observations by references to observations made by Max Eastman, who visited Russia just after Maiakovskii's 1931 suicide. Eastman compares Maiakovskii's love for artificiality and performance to the circus, saying that he "came straight over to the Bolshevik revolution, bringing all his futuristic apparatus with him — the verbal circus work, the rhythmic and grammatic flying bars and coloured paper hoops. And his intemperate imagination somersaulting through them — sometimes very flimsy, sometimes very sublime" (Holquist 1967: 132). Holquist also refers to Leon Trotskii's criticism of Maiakovskii's eccentric individualism that was deemed unsuitable for Bolshevik education of masses, even though Trotskii saw Futurism as a necessary link to the art of the future that would accommodate the needs of the "toiling masses" (ibid.: 133). In the words of Trotskii, Maiakovskii's mode of expression stands close to the ancient Greek worldview. Trotskii writes: "Just as the ancient Greek was the anthropomorphist and naively thought of nature's forces as resembling himself, so our poet is a Maiakomorphist and fills the squares, streets and fields of the Revolution with his own personality [...] the poet is too much in evidence" (ibid.). Thus, Maiakovskii's eccentric personality might be seen as the real subject matter of the "Last Petersburg Fairy Tale" and the verbal artistry appears to be offered as a new kind of intellectual pursuit and spectacle.

Maiakovskii's most innovative addition to Pushkin's story in "Last Petersburg Tale" is seen, not in the description of events it narrates, but in the creation of new and unexpected rhymes which can be seen as a real challenge to Pushkin. Pushkin believed that the poetry of the future would be written without rhymes given the limited choice of rhyming words in the Russian language. In his seminal work "On the Composition of *Eugene Onegin*" («О композиции *Евгения Онегина*») Tynianov points to Pushkin's particular appreciation of the semantic unity of verse sustained by rhymes. Tynianov writes:

"Pushkin was conscious of the semantic role of rhymes in verse. The transition to *vers libre* meant to him a transition to a new semantics of verse. In his *Thoughts During the Journey* he writes, 'I think that in the future we will use *vers libre*. There are not that many rhyming words in the Russian language. One rhyming word necessarily evokes another. The word *fire* inevitably evokes the word *stone*'" («Пушкин сознательно относился к смысловой роли рифм. Переход к белому стиху был для него переходом к новой семантике стиха. В *мыслях на дороге* он пишет: 'Думаю, что со временем мы обратимся к белому стиху. Рифм в русском языке слишком мало. Одна вызывает другую. *Пламень* неминуемо тащит за собой *камень*' [...] ») (Tynianov 1977: 77). Tynianov makes the interesting observation that in a verse where we come across a rhyme that is quite common, then the first rhyming word is not perceived by itself but as a twin to the second rhyming word; and where we come across a rare rhyme, the second rhyming word would be perceived as less independent (ibid.) Following this observation, Maiakovskii's compound rhymes in the last stanza of his "Last Petersburg Fairy Tale" firmly places the image of Peter the Great alongside the image of the sceptre, creating thereby an interesting symbol of the imperial sublime as a result of his deconstructive reading of Pushkin's "The Bronze Horseman". The poet himself implicitly associates himself with Pushkin's mad Evgenii who distorts common logic through his subversive powers of laughter and surreal vision.

According to Kviatkovskii, Maiakovskii's discovery of new ways to rhyme words was based on a looser phonetical association and an orientation towards an oral performance of poetry (Kviatkovskii 1966: 249). In his famous article "How Are Verses Made?" («Как делать стихи?») Maiakovskii proudly states that his rhymes are original. More importantly, Maiakovskii thinks that rhymes function as a constructive device to enable poems to be perceived as semantically coherent units: "A poem will disintegrate without rhymes. Rhyme returns us to the previous line, forces us to remember it, enables all lines expressing the same thought to be bound together" («Без рифмы стих рассыплется. Рифма возвращает вас к предыдущей строке, заставляет вспомнить ее, заставляет все строки, оформляющие одну мысль, держаться вместе») (Maiakovskii 1955-61, volume 12: 105). Thus, Maiakovskii's vision of structural patterns of verse organisation presents a poem as a set of disjointed semantic units bound together by rhymes, as if these units are visualised as stills montaged together in a film. Maiakovskii perceived reality as a space in flux, a space becoming linked to his vision of modernity in terms of the creative flow of life.

Recent studies on Bergson have attempted to trace the impact of Bergson's ideas in works by Russian and Italian Futurists. For example, Neil Cox writes: "Whereas Bergson insisted that the homogenous and measurable time of the intellect was a false construct to be overcome by intuition, Futurist admiration for the dynamism or the speed of modern life recognised that rapid machine movements and technologies of communication could, by their very density and intensity, transform the utilitarian world of measurement and stasis into a new image of the underlying flux of reality discerned by intuition" (Cox 2000: 198). David Wedaman stretches this comparison further and suggests that the writings of Apollinaire and Maiakovskii add a new dimension to Bergson's writings on creative evolution and memory, enabling us to see these writings as part of the new methodological tool that he defines as 'Applied Bergsonism' (Wedaman 2003: 5-6). Wedaman sums up the core ideas of this approach to art as follows: "That particular sort of faith in indeterminacy; the idea that positive, cyclical change is necessary to evolution; the desire to shatter static systems with novelty; the refusal to accept intellectual constructions as given; the assumption that art can play a role in social evolution; the dogged attention to the preconceptual and pre-linguistic concrete; the belief that this concrete is fluid, real, and valuable; and the delight that comes from a view of the world as a creation in progress that permits, or even demands, the individual's participation" (Wedaman 2003: 205).

It is clear, from the above discussion of the Bergsonian tendency in the modernists' approach to Pushkin's Petersburg texts, that modernists did identify the creative potential of Pushkin's imaginary world of modernity, and that they used it for their own purposes. The modes of spectatorship developed in Pushkin's writing were successfully employed in Russian modernist poetry as a whole. Recent theoretical theses explain that readers engaged in reading a novel are not simulating a particular character, but rather contemplate the imaginary world in "a way that the world could be" (Meskin and

Weinberg 2003: 31). From this it is possible to suggest that the way Pushkin's text on modernity is read is determined largely by his texts. The poetic language of Pushkin's time, his metrical and stylistic peculiarities were often fused by later writers with their contemporary modes of artistic expression. What has been given less attention is Pushkin's concept of private space interwined with his understanding of the origins of modern creativity and contemplation, which we have analysed in Pushkin's Petersburg texts. Pushkin's architectural imagination and poetic vision were inspired not only by Petersburg artefacts of significance and scenes of sensational value, but also by some scenes of everyday life and humble pleasures of life in the city, such as walking, reading, writing, observing passers-by and contemplating the modest monuments and landmarks associated with cultural activities of his times. It is worth quoting here John Fennel's observations on the co-existance of the various selves of Pushkin in "The Bronze Horseman": "Having started the *poema* disguised as a courtly ode writer, aloof, but nonetheless communicating Peter's thoughts and omnisciently sweeping over the traditional 'hundred years' [...] between the foundation of the city and the present day, he emerges at last as the undisguised authoritorial *I*. [...] From the start of the great lyrical confession of love for the city [....] to the sombre beginning of the narrative proper in Part 1, Pushkin thrust himself upon the imagination. The evocations of the city are shown through his eyes and his eyes alone. After seven lines crammed with rich musical and rhetorical devices (chiasma, repetition, hypallage, oxymoron) Pushkin lowers the tone to the utmost simplicity of prosaic utterance — almost to understatement — to portay himself as the focal point of the whole poem, reading, writing, lampless in his room [...]. He has established himself in our minds as the poet capable of experiencing delight at the humble pleasures of the city [...] and rapture at its majestic aspects" (Fennel in Bloom 1987: 86).

Narrating the city: from modern object to postmodern sign

Khodasevich's collection of poetry *The Heavy Lyre* (*Тяжелая лира*), published in Moscow and Petrograd in 1922, revives the Pushkinian tradition which poeticises the humble pleasures of urban life and finds a sense of harmony in spite of shattering experiences. It appears that Khodasevich saw himself as a Pushkinian figure who, in a period deeply affected by World War I, the February/October 1917 revolutions and the Civil War, could remind readers about the significance of human life and the individual's right to control his own body and have a dignified death. In the year of the publication of *The Heavy Lyre* several discussions took place suggesting a fading away of the avant-garde search for novelty and the formalist wave of thought and expression. For example, in his 1922 survey of Russian literature "Letter to Peking" («Письмо в Пекин») Mikhail Kuzmin, whose philosophically charged poetry stands close to Khodasevich's writings, notes that art "was returning to its emotional, symbolic and metaphysical sources" (Malmstad 1999: 305). In his 1922 review of contemporary painting Kuzmin called upon artists and poets to "convey the emotional, personal, unique, unrepeatable perception" of reality, explore the forms of expression "brought about by emotional necessity" and abandon the fruitless search for novelty (ibid.). Kuzmin's attacks on "galloping contemporaneity" and "meaningless and harmful utopias" recall the dystopian tenets of Pushkin's Petersburg texts and resonate well with Khodasevich's move towards a Pushkinian orientation to the sacred present, to use Kuzmin's expression from his article "Declaration of Emotionalism" (ibid.).

The 'Pushkin Days', celebrating the 84th anniversary of Pushkin in January-February 1921, resulted in a series of exhibitions, concerts, readings and memorial meetings, and attracted many prominent critics and artists. On 13 February 1921 Blok, Kuzmin and Khodasevich took part in a literary evening to commemorate Pushkin, where Khodasevich gave his famous speech known as "The Shaken Tripod" («Колеблемый треножник») on the threatened eclipse of Pushkin and Russian culture. Prior to the 'Pushkin Days', the publication of two long narrative autobiographical poems — Blok's "Requital" (1910-1921) and Viacheslav Ivanov's "Childhood" («Младенчество», 1913-1918) — were seen as attempts to revive structural and thematic elements of Pushkin's *Eugene Onegin*. According to Carol Ueland's perceptive analysis of Ivanov's long poem "Childhood", despite Ivanov's use of the Onegin stanza, Ivanov's understanding of Pushkin is rather idiosyncratic and reveals "the basic incompatibility between the two poets" (Ueland in Gasparov et al 1992: 336). However, Ivanov claimed that Pushkin's *Eugene Onegin* had a strong realistic trait and revealed that Pushkin "was in the habit of unexpectedly becoming lost in admiration of the most prosaic reality" (ibid.: 342). Ivanov's statement helps us identify in the culture of the early 1920s a shift towards a new poetics of strict simplicity and elegance. It seems that the poems of Khodasevich included in *The Heavy Lyre* exemplify this neo-classical trend. Pushkin's more private visions of the city seen through the window of his study were depicted in the introductory chapters of "The Bronze Horseman" — captured in such lines, for example, as "When in my room/ I write or read without a lamp" («Когда я в комнате моей/ Пишу, читаю без лампады»). They are echoed in Khodasevich's 1921 poem "Out of the Window: 1" («Из окна: 1»):

> Нынче день такой забавный:
> От возниц, что было сил,
> Конь умчался своенравный;
> Мальчик змей свой упустил;
> Вор цыпленка утащил
> У безносой Николавны.
> Но настигнут вор нахальный,
> Змей упал в соседний сад.
> Мальчик ладит хвост мочальный,
> И коня ведут назад...
> Восстает мой тихий ад
> В стройности первоначальной.
> (Khodasevich 1922: 18)

> Today I'm having an amusing day:
> A horse, using all his strength,
> Detached himself from the carriage;
> A boy let his kite go flying way:
> A robber stole a chicken
> From noseless Nikolavna.
> But the impetuous robber was caught;
> The kite landed in the neighbour's garden;
> The boy is mending the kite tails;
> And the horse is being rehitched...
> My quiet hell is restored
> In its original elegance.

At first glance, Khodasevich's poem lends itself to comparison with Italian Renaissance's paintings. Svetlana Alpers demonstrates in her book on Dutch seventeenth-century art that the Italian Renaissance had developed a concept of the picture as a framed window through which a viewer looked at a world inhabited by human figures performing various actions. Alpers suggests a difference between the Dutch paintings that describe objects and the Renaissance paintings that narrate human actions (Alpers 1983). Khodasevich's "Out of the Window" also evokes the cinematographic mode of rendering incidents and objects encountered in everyday life, but not exactly in the manner expressed in *Eugene Onegin*. Khodasevich's camera-like vision of events is focussed just on one landscape observed through the window. It appears that in *The Heavy Lyre* Khodasevich consciously attempted to re-create Pushkin's realistic mode of expression, free from mannerism and over-dramatisation, in order to restore the aesthetics of contemplation and the sense of the elegiac sublime distorted by the barbaric experiences of the Civil War and the Red Terror. In his speech "The Shaken Tripod" Khodasevich defines the 1920s in Russia, the new post-Petrine and post-Petersburg period of Russian culture, as a period altering the aesthetic sensibilities of the Russian readership. Khodasevich writes thus about contemporary Russian readers: "They need to translate Pushkin's emotion into the language of their own sensations, barbarised by the extreme melodramas of cinema" («Чувство Пушкина приходится им переводить на язык своих ощущений, притупленных раздирающими драмами кинематографа») (Gasparov et al 1992: 207). The lyric hero of Khodasevich's poem is alienated from the outer world by its lack of spontaneity and warmth. At the same time, the window mentioned in the poem marks a clear boundary between the external world of everyday life, perceived by the lyric hero as abstraction, and his intimate world of the imaginary confined to a basic 1921 Petrograd dwelling offering an illusionary and transient escape from the Soviet utopia's hostile and barbaric environment. The image of the window also invokes Pushkin's metaphor used in "The Bronze Horseman", which presents Petersburg as a window upon Europe. Khodasevich's window functions as a means of observing everyday life in a Petrograd disrupted by war and revolutionary experiences.

Khodasevich's "Out of the Window" is subtly ironic in its reproduction of a stylised version of realism's cult of the typical and impersonalised gaze that favoured rational abstraction. Michel de Certeau points out that European culture as early as the sixteenth century placed Everyman at the centre of its obsession with abstract norms and general laws. Such a worldview held that the representative man in his ideal manifestation easily can dissolve into pure abstraction and nothingness (Certeau 1984). Furthermore, as Blanchot remarks, the question of the opening up of the everyday in history becomes especially accute for revolutionary periods, when private life appears insignificant to observers of history and "existence is public through and through" (Blanchot 1987: 12). Khodasevich's poem defends the precarious boundaries of the private space to which the poet is withdrawn to, where he could contemplate private thoughts possibly seen as counter-revolutionary by the State. Blanchot's interpretation of Hegel's comments on the relationship between the State and individual in the French revolution could be a blueprint for other revolutionary periods. Blanchot asserts that "Hegel showed that each time the universal is affirmed in its brutal abstract exigency, every particular will, every separate thought falls under suspicion. It is no longer enough to act well. Every individual carries in himself a set of reflections, of intentions, that is to say reticences, that commit him to an oblique existence. To be suspect is more serious than to be guilty [...]. The suspect is that fleeting presence that does not allow recognition, and, through the part always held back that he figures forth, tends not only to interfere with, but to bring into accusation, the workings of the State" (ibid.). The sense of wonder in Khodasevich's poem comes from a realisation that the everyday escapes and allows no hold upon itself. As Blanchot elaborates, "It belongs to insignificance, and the insignificant is without truth, without reality, without secret, but perhaps also the site of all possible signification. The everyday escapes. This makes its strangeness — the familiar showing itself (but already dispersing) in the guise of the astonishing. It is the unperceived, first in the sense that one has always looked past it, nor can it be introduced into a whole or 'reviewed', that is to say, enclosed within panoramic vision, for, by another trait, the everyday is what we never see for a first time, but only see again, having always already seen it by an allusion that is, as it happens, constituitive of the everyday" (Blanchot 1987: 14). However, Khodasevich's description of his everyday life as a quiet hell, as portrayed in "Out of the Window", is also closely linked to his desire to be viewed by the badaud as a person transcending his own insignificance by performing what Dmitrii Likhachev defines as a "quintessentially Petersburg identity".

Likhachev's observation that the Petersburg space inscribes the notion of border poses a question about the staging of self in a city with such a rich cultural history. For the lyric hero described in Khodasevich's poem, the time flow is perceived as spatial experience: he is caught between the two different epochs and two different names of the city: Petersburg and Petrograd. Thus the window appears to be also functioning as a tangible border between the two worlds, pointing at the employment of a framing device. Likhachev's definition of Petersburg resonates well with the intermediate identity of a Russian poet, an archaising innovator. Likhachev states that Petersburg is "a capital on the border of the state" which "represents not only the culture appropriated from the West, but also the culture that is typically a borderline culture". Likhachev also talks about the stylistic peculiarities of this cultural space and stresses that "it manifests itself also in art as a culture that lies on the borderline between styles; on the side of styles; in a transitional space from one style to another" (Likhachev 1999: 539). To stage a quintessentially Petersburg identity would require the mastery of various styles; a heightened awareness of extremes; stretched elasticity of personality; and an ability to inscribe border aesthetics into everyday life. The diversity of styles found in Petersburg predisposes a theatrical type of behaviour and participation in world culture. The dweller in Petersburg feels estranged both from the city and from himself; his worldview is fragmentary and impressionistic. Khodasevich used the imperative in a short lyric to thus reflect on the fluid state of the Petrograd dweller:

   Перешагни, перескочи,
   Перелети, пере-что хочешь –
   Но вырвись: камнем из пращи,
   Звездой, сорвавшейся в ночи…
   Сам потерял — теперь ищи…
   Бог знает, что себе бормочешь,
   Ища пенсне или ключи.
(Khodasevich 1922: 27)

> Step over, leap over,
> Fly over, over — whatever you wish to do —
> But move out of here, like a pellet from the shotgun,
> Like a star fallen from the night sky...
> You yourself lost it, so then you should find it ...
> God knows what one mumbles to oneself,
> Looking for spectacles or keys.

The lyric hero in the above poem resembles Pushkin's Evgenii from "The Bronze Horseman" who goes mad and homeless, and whose mumbling makes him the popular target of verbal and physical attacks by urchins. Khodasevich also addresses the question of spectatorship and monotony, which brings to mind Pushkin's allusion in "The Bronze Horseman" to the monotonous glamour of parades and symmetrically organised spaces. Lotman links the emergence of modernity in Russia with the rapid growth of theatricality in everyday life. He specifically makes the point that the early nineteenth century was marked by the incursion of art, especially theatre, into Russian life, to the effect that much of the nobility viewed their lives as part of a performance; if everyday life lacked performativity, they dismissed it as eventless and immobile. Lotman explains: "Viewing real life as a performance not only offered a person the possibility of choosing his type of individual behaviour, but also filled it with the expectation that things were going to happen. Eventfulness, that is, the possibility that unexpected phenomena and turns of events would happen, became the norm. It was precisely the awareness that any political turn of event was possible that shaped the sense of life that young people had in the early nineteenth century" (Lotman, Uspensky 1984: 160).

In Khodasevich's poem above, the concept of private space, a room of one's own, in the style, perhaps, of Tatiana's boudoir, is linked directly to creativity. His 1921-1922 poems were written in years of severe hardship, when poetry not written as propaganda would have been seen by many proletarian writers as a whimsical, idiosyncratic and superfluous activity. Blanchot remarks on the creative potential of the everyday offer a wonderful insight into Khodasevich's artistic psychology of the 1920s. Blanchot writes: "To live in the way of the quotidian is to hold oneself at a level of life that excludes the possibility of a beginning, an access. Everyday experience radically questions the initial exigency. The idea of creation is inadmissible, when it is a matter of accounting for existence as it is borne by the everyday" (Blanchot 1987: 20). In light of these observations, Khodasevich's belief in the forthcoming eclipse of Pushkin appears to be echoed in his poem "Step over...". It calls upon his readers not to abandon their subjectivity in favour of the universalising modernity and communist transformation which is symbolically represented as 'the metallisation of the revolutionary body' (Hellebust 2003: 29). As Rolf Hellebust points out, 'the transfigured revolutionary body' differs significantly from the transgressive grotesque body of Bakhtin's carnival because of its artificiality (Hellebust 2003: 153).

Khodasevich's "Out of the Window" advocates the concept of variety of space and time, articulating the poet's outsideness (to use Bakhtin's term) from the framework shaped by contemporary revolutionary discourses. As Morson and Emerson put forward, "outsideness creates the possibility of dialogue, and dialogue helps us understand culture in a profound way" (Morson and Emerson 1990: 55). Talking of the creative potential of the act of stepping out from one's space and time, Bakhtin writes: "In order to understand, it is immensely important for the person who understands to be *located outside* the object of his or her creative understanding — in time, in space, in culture. For one cannot even really see one's own exterior and comprehend it as a whole, and no mirrors or photographs can help; our real exterior can be seen and understood only by other people, because they are located outside us in space and because they are *others*" (Bakhtin, quoted in Morson and Emerson 1990: 55). The image of the silent hell mentioned at the end of "Out of the Window" might be understood then as an allusion to the fact that the gaze is not returned to spectator and the creative dialogue does not take place. The lyric hero of the poem situates himself in a different temporality that clashes with the presence he painstakingly observes. At the same time, the poem is not a typical lyric poem since it does not reveal any emotional or intellectual responses to the actions of the human figures observed from the window. It presents a description of action that is narratively configured. Ricoeur notes that "time becomes human to the extent that it is articulated through a narrative mode, and narrative attains its full meaning when it becomes a condition of temporal existence" (Ricoeur 1984-88, vol.1: 52).

Ricoeur's statement that "human lives need and merit being narrated" (ibid.: 74-75) explains the creative impulse behind Khodasevich's "Out of the Window". The thrust of this poem lies in the realisation that, in a context of Soviet modernity that relies on technology and media, the simple act of storytelling is vanishing rapidly, hampered by advancing propaganda and censorship. The pain expressed in the poem's concluding lines refers to the lack of a community of readers and listeners who could share their experiences of mourning the dead and telling the truth about contemporary suffering. This condition is aptly summarised in Benjamin's essay on Nikolai Leskov, written much later: "Less and less frequently do we encounter people with the ability to tell a tale properly. More and more often there is embarrassment all around when the wish to hear a story is expressed. It is as if something that seemed inalienable to us, the securest among our possessions were taken from us: the ability to exchange experiences" (Benjamin 1999: 83).

We can interpret Khodasevich's image of the runaway horse as a veiled allusion to Pushkin's image of the galloping horseman; thus the poem unfolds the lyric hero's sense of paranoia shared with Pushkin's protagonist Evgenii, who feels that Tsar Peter stole away his Parasha, depriving him of humble pleasures and happiness. In his illuminating article on "The Bronze Horseman" that provides a psychoanalytical reading of Pushkin's text, Daniel Rancour-Laferrière develops Belyi's view that the Neva is the real steed "of the Bronze Horseman chasing after the madman" (Belyi 1929: 186) and suggests: "The Neva, then, like Peter's horse, is his equivalent and/or his instrument. She seems to do his will. She is not merely contiguous to the Bronze Horseman but is tied to the Horseman in some essential way. The two *belong* together" (Rancour-Laferriere in Bethea 1993: 78). Khodasevich borrows the theme of thieving («вор нахальный») from Pushkin's "The Bronze Horseman" in order to implicate Peter the Great, as creator of Petersburg and Russian modernity, in various crimes against his own people; and that his city, devoid of true creative impulse, keeps reproducing the symbolic emptiness of a sign that has lost its reference.

In his profound analysis of Gogol's Petersburg tales, Nabokov provides an insight that adds a modernist twist to his reading of nineteenth-century narratives: "Passing as it were through Gogol's temperament, St Petersburg acquired a reputation of strangeness which it kept for almost a century, losing it when it ceased to be the capital of an empire. The chief town in Russia had been built by a tyrant of genius upon a swamp, and upon the bones of slaves rotting in that swamp; this was the root of that strangeness — and the initial flaw" (Nabokov 1961: 11). Just as Akakii Akakievich is involved in his own disrobing, and gradually reverses to "the stark nakedness of his own ghost" (Nabokov 1961: 146), so the lyric hero of Khodasevich's "Out of the Window" demystifies the myth of creation put in the minds of readers of Pushkin's "The Bronze Horseman" and presents it, in its all nakedness, as a story of theft. The semantic unit of the myth is faithfully reconstructed in Khodasevich's narration: we come across the key-words of Pushkin's "The Bronze Horseman" such as thief, snake, horse (вор, змей, конь). Yet by replacing the image of the snake with the image of the kite (usually called by Russians a paper snake — бумажный змей) Khodasevich creates an emotionally effective narrative structure, adding dramatic overtones to his narrative, with a sense of mystery and suspense.

Thus in an attempt to compete with the melodramatic adaptions of Pushkin, Khodasevich restores Pushkin's emotion by employing his own overtonal visual montage that incorporated his specific sensation of the flow of life in 1922 Petrograd. While Eisenstein in his 1942 essay "Dickens, Griffiths and Me" («Диккенс, Грифит и мы») says that some major montage devices (for example the pace of cutting; the emotional potential of the correlation of the single shot to the whole narrative; the cross-cutting between parallel actions) have similarities with numerous fragments found in Charles Dickens's novels, Khodasevich identified in Pushkin's works some narrative devices corresponding to the cinematic equivalents of long shot, cross-cutting, flashback and close-up. Pushkin's "The Bronze Horseman" gives the impression that a curious incident discussed in the poem is the bringer of a new angle and forces the viewer to develop a new perception, equivalent to montage in cinematic comprehension. Yet, if we bear in mind Pushkin's attempt in the concluding parts of *Eugene Onegin* to develop the poetics of sincerity that had been initiated in the 1830s by Baratynskii, then Khodasevich's poem might be viewed as an expression of desire to reveal the essentially human in the actor, a Petersburg dweller, by stripping away masks.

Yet, as Meyerhold suggested, the vulnerable state of the modern subject, involved in theatre for oneself, is just the inner mask. Like Khodasevich, Meyerhold used Pushkin as a source of his inspiration for the creation of a Soviet theatre which could fuse Russian and Italian tradition, developed in the seventeenth and eighteenth centuries, with contemporary improvisation. According to Robert Leach, "Meyerhold took his stand with Pushkin, who more and more in the last twenty years of his life seemed to offer Meyerhold inspiration or wisdom" (Leach 1989: 17). Leach lists the main tenets of Pushkin's drama theory as: "drama originated in a public square and constituted a popular entertainment"; "the common people, like children, require amusement, action"; "the drama confronts them with a strange incident"; "laughter, pity and terror are the three chords of our imagination" that contribute to dramatic enchantment (ibid.). However, Khodasevich's poem testifies to the necessity of shifting away from the symbolist aesthetisation of everyday life. His position is closer to Brecht's attempt to overthrow the spectator's identification both with the corporeal and the representational being of the actor. Brecht believed that the spectator could separate himself from the social identity imposed on him by the society. Brecht maintained that the critical distance between actor and spectator is achieved through the terror of recognition: "Spectator and actor ought not to approach one another but to move apart. Each ought to move away from himself. Otherwise the element of terror necessary to recognition is lacking" (Brecht 1964: 26). In a conspicuously similar manner, Khodasevich talks about the shock of recognition and metaphorically uses the image of the window to mark the boundary of the space from which the objective observation of the object should take place to preserve the loss of his own identity.

Thus Khodasevich challenges Peter the Great's desire to turn the city into his own image and advocates the uniqueness of emotional, unrepeatable and personal perception of reality. Khodasevich thereby responded to Kuzmin's call for a return to the emotional and metaphysical sources of art. Khodasevich's "Out of the Window" exemplifies the overtonal visual montage. Bearing in mind that Eisenstein's theory of montage highlighted the function of stylistic and thematic collision, the full message of "Out of the Window" can be only grasped by its readers if seen as a sequence of differentiated shots: the title creates an image of an observer who sees three different incidents (the horse ran away, somebody's chicken was stolen and the youngster's kite flew off). The implied image of wind bringing chaos into people's lives is a concealed allusion to Blok's narrative poem "The Twelve". In this poem the wind signifies external historical and natural forces that make individuals vulnerable and powerless. In Khodasevich's poem the wind image is juxtaposed with the image of the Bronze Horseman associated with the Petersburg myth. The allusion to harmony and silent hell presents the suffering of the artist-poet, whose artistic sensibilities clash with contemporary demands for revolutionary art and propaganda. Thus Khodasevich's text induces readers to reconstruct and experience the situation described in the poem, in order to achieve a synthesis between intellectual and emotional cognition of the conflicting images and allusions embedded in the narrative.

Akhmatova's lyric poetry also conveys a concentrated attack on Soviet-style modernity entwined with conformity and propaganda. In the late 1920s-1930s the Soviet version of modernity relied heavily on a resurrection of Peter the Great's ideas of forced labour and authoritarian rule. Akhmatova's poems invoke several Petersburg texts penned by Pushkin. Her poem "Everyone left and no one returned…" («Все ушли и никто не вернулся…») was written after a 1946 Central Committee resolution denounced the most talented who had survived the modernist period (including Shostakovich and Akhmatova herself). The poem reflects on Akhmatova's displacement and isolation from the mainstream of Soviet literature. Akhmatova's lyric persona, fashioned in the clothes of Pushkin's mad protagonist from "The Bronze Horseman", defines herself as an urban madwoman:

И до самого края доведши,
Почему-то оставили там —
Буду я городской сумасшедшей
По притихшим бродить площадям.
(Akhmatova, vol. 3, 1983: 72-73)

And after leading me right to the edge,
They left me there for some reason —
I shall wander the subdued squares
As an urban madwoman.

Pushkin's poetry had conceived in embryo form the image of a vagabond, of madmen pushed to the margins of existence. In Akhmatova's poetry the image attained a new function: it represents the voice of dissident culture opposed to any form of totalitarian governance. David Wells views Akhmatova's "Everyone left and no one returned..." as a catalogue of the misfortunes "which have befallen her over twenty years". He suggests that Akhmatova "has been allowed a licence to speak similar to that of the 'holy fools' of the Russian middle ages" (Wells 1996: 131). In the style of Pushkin's poem about his would-be monument "I erected a monument to myself...", Akhmatova crafts a dystopian image of immortality in her 1946 poem "And the sly half-moon saw..." («И увидел месяц лукавый...»):

> И увидел месяц лукавый,
> Притаившийся у ворот,
> Как свою посмертную славу
> Я меняла на вечер тот.
> Теперь меня позабудут,
> И книги сгниют в шкафу.
> Ахматовской звать не будут
> Ни улицу, ни строфу.
> (Akhmatova 1976: 497)

> And the sly half-moon,
> Lurking behind the gate,
> Saw me exchanging my immortal fame
> For this evening.
> Now I will be forgotten,
> And my books will rot in the bookcase.
> No street or stanza
> Will be named after me.

Akhmatova's poem alludes to Pushkin's so-called Onegin stanza, and to the streets named after Maiakovskii and Pushkin. She feels displaced from the male canon, and from contemporary history.

It is not coincidental that Susan Amert's book on Akhmatova's late poetry pinpoints the concept of homelessness as one of the prevalent themes in Akhmatova's late writings. As Amert puts it, "For Akhmatova, displacement and homelessness are the universal conditions of life in the Real Twentieth Century. In the harsh century poetry represents the sole refuge, the only source of comfort" (Amert 1992: 195). I would take this point further and suggest that many displaced authors substituted Russian poetry for home; Russian poetry functioned also as a repository of memories and joyful moments of transient modern life that destabilised a sense of identity and belonging to any particular space. Amert notes that many former dwellings cherished by Akhmatova in early years of her life were gone in post-war times: "The impossibility of returning to the cherished past home is a recurrent theme in her later autobiographical prose" (Amert 1992: 191). Amert provides a quote that finely encapsulated Akhmatova's mood: "A sad return does not threaten the people of my generation: there is nowhere for us to return" («Людям моего поколения не грозит печальное возвращение: нам возвращаться некуда») (ibid.). Amert's explanation notwithstanding, it is useful to point out here that a favourite Akhmatova poetic device was negation, often used as a rhetorical device. Akhmatova specially liked to use a kind of negation named 'counter-negation'. It has such constructions as "no/ none/ no one… but", equivalent to only. This form denies every subject except the one asserted. Such a form confers upon the asserted subject an exclusive status which stands opposite to everything that is negated (Dupriez 1991: 303). Thus, in the context of Akhmatova's late writing which is metatextual and autobiographical, it is clear that the question of immortality and posthumous fame was entwined in her mind with the fate of Pushkin.

The Pushkinian twist in Akhmatova's life and writings has been noted by many critics. For example Roman Timenchik suggests that in her poetry Akhmatova richly infuses the mythical, cyclical time chronotope with allusions to Pushkin: "Very often the motif of cyclical time is introduced into Akhmatova's texts by means of hidden quotations from Pushkin: if the situation described in the poem had a precedent in the past (Pushkin), then it should repeat itself in the future. Particularly common and important are references to Pushkin's 'Lycée anniversary' poems, where the theme of 'eternal returns' is especially developed" (Timenchik in Loseff, Scherr 1993: 366). In her insightful reading of Akhmatova's 1947 essay on Pushkin's "Stone Guest" Amert points out that while exploring the issue of Pushkin's relationship with his readers "Akhmatova is at the same time writing obliquely about herself — about the profound change in her poetry and the concomitant change in her relations with her readers" (Amert 1992: 2). It is well known that Akhmatova's situation in the post-war period was partly worsened by the Communist Party resolution of 14 August 1946 which attacked Akhmatova along with Mikhail Zoshchenko and Shostakovich. Akhmatova's poetry was labelled ideologically harmful and anachronistic (Amert 1992: 3). However Akhmatova's anxiety about displacement and lack of readership might be also viewed as a problem rooted in the aesthetic reasons linked to change in popular taste, and the fact that her private space had become more withdrawn from the mainstream of Soviet literary developments in the 1940s-1950s.

Akhmatova's anxiety about her posthumous fame and readership might be easily compared to Maiakovskii's reaction to the process of Pushkin's canonisation in the Soviet Union. Krystina Pomorska juxtaposes an analysis of Maiakovskii's lyrics "Jubilee" («Юбилейное», 1924) and "To Sergei Esenin" («Сергею Есенину», 1926) with Maiakovskii's 1924 essay "Do Not Trade in Lenin" («Не торгуйте Лениным») and Maiakovskii's last unfinished poem "At the Top of My Voice" («Во весь голос»): Pomorska detects in all of them a strongly manifested animosity to monuments and to readers who are keen to change poetic energy into 'death matter' («мертвечина») (Pomorska 1992: 178-79). Like Maiakovskii before her, Akhmatova deems reading as an important contribution to what Jürgen Habermas calls the "hermenetics of everyday communication" (Habermas 1983: 9). By abandoning the idea of turning into a monument, announced in her early cycle of poems "In Tsarskoe Selo" («В Царском селе», 1911) — which boasts such lines as "I will also become a marble statue" («Я тоже мраморную стану») — Akhmatova in her later works came to understand the concept of immortality and memory in terms outlined in Pushkin's poem "Monument".

Akhmatova followed in the steps of the avant-garde artists who reintegrated art and life: she redefined her on-going dialogue with Pushkin as a creation of an intimate interactive space. Given her total scepticism regarding the organisation of discursive meaning in society, this space was to be protected from attack by irrational authority. By creating a new phrase such as the 'Akhmatova stanza' in the poem "And the sly half-moon saw...", Akhmatova cleverly employs the device of estrangement (defamiliarisation), which was advocated by the Russian formalists as an important tool contributing to creative evolution. By suggesting that she could be remembered in the future for her creation of a new stanza, Akhmatova instils in her readers' minds the idea that her poetic achievements are comparable to some of Pushkin's innovative constructs. Indeed, Akhmatova envisaged her masterpiece narrrative poem "Poem Without a Hero" («Поэма без героя») as a polemical piece challenging Pushkin's *Eugene Onegin*. Written in 1943-1962, it exhibits the most innovative spirit of all of Akhmatova's poetry and resulted in the creation of the 'Akhmatova stanza', her own signature on a par with Pushkin's invention. In his detailed study of Pushkin's influence on Akhmatova, Wells observes that "Poem Without a Hero" reflected Pushkin's *Eugene Onegin* in many ways. Wells summarises Akhmatova's achievements thus: "She moulds the three-stress dol'nik into a new type of strophe. This has much in common with the step format used by Maiakovskii and other Futurists. [...] This 'Akhmatova stanza' is an open form, capable of indefinite extension. Because of the simple rhyme scheme — each strophe has two or more rhymed lines, and the strophes are linked by rhyming end lines — each forms a unit in which an idea can be treated at whatever length it requires, and new ideas added at any point without disturbing the verse structure. The technique of rhyming the last lines of the strophes gives the verse a forward movement which is increased by the step format. The system brings with it a considerable flexibility, being used with some strictness in 'Reverse' [...]. In '1913', on the other hand, the strophic structure is frequently interrupted or broken and the strophe length varies from three to six lines in conformity with the prevailing spirit of Carnival" (Wells 1996: 127). Thus, if we view Akhmatova's late poetry as a selection of counter-discursive texts, then we must bear in mind that her "Poem Without a Hero" discloses a reality obscured by the dominant Soviet ideology and the social discourses it produced: namely, the modernist project.

However, if we view Akhmatova's project as a Silver Age version of Pushkin's *Eugene Onegin*, then its stylistic richness and polyphonic quality bring to mind the generic peculiarities of the form aptly defined by Pushkin as novel in verse. As Wells pertinently suggests, Akhmatova's "Poem Without a Hero" stands conspicuously close to Alain Robbe-Grillet's film *Last Year at Marienbad* (*L'Année dernière à Marienbad*) which received the Golden Lion at the 1961 Venice Film Festival. According to Wells, Akhmatova herself noted some striking similarities between her long poem and Robbe-Grillet's film, in which he wanted to replace conventional film narrative with narrative based on mental time, which could inscribe the tempo of human emotions and human life (Wells 1996: 100). Such an approach suggests that Akhmatova did not just reproduce some of the structural forms and imagery of *Eugene Onegin* but also detected the novelty of such a poetic experiment that wanted to use cinematographic-like techniques in order to render some shocking and disjointed experiences of modern urban life. Akhmatova was, indeed, sensitive to the jolting experiences of life in a modern metropolis, and this shattering experience was reflected in her verse. Thus Timenchik points out that Akhmatova's usage of the anapaestic dimeter in her "Tsarskoe Ode" («Царскосельская ода», 1961) represents the stuttering rhythm of a speaker "who can never complete his utterance and thus is given to repetition" (Timenchik in Loseff and Scherr 1993: 366).

While Akhmatova felt the necessity to create a long narrative poem inspired by Pushkin's *Eugene Onegin*, her poem escapes from its structural constraints. In various interviews with Russian scholars and critics, Akhmatova made some far-reaching observations on the legacy of *Eugene Onegin* in Russian twentieth-century poetry. For example, Akhmatova pointed out that "*Eugene Onegin* appeared and brought down a boom-gate after it. Anyone who tried to make use of Pushkin's 'discovery' met with failure". And she said that her "Poem Without a Hero" was an "anti-Onegin piece, and herein lies its advantage [...] for *Onegin* spoilt both Lermontov's long poem and Blok's *Retribution*" (Wells 1996: 125).

Amert observed that Akhmatova in her late poetry created an image of poetry as a protective haven from suffering. Amert traces the comparison between the narrative poem and a house, as conveyed in "Poem Without a Hero", to the description of Lenskii's dead body presented in chapter six as an empty house with curtains shut: "Now, as in a deserted house,/ All is both still and dark inside" («Теперь, как в доме опустелом,/ Все в нем и тихо и темно») (Amert 1992: 192-94). Amert suggests that Akhmatova's words describing her poem as a house protecting her from the sultry heat («В ней прохладно,/ Как в доме, где душистый мрак/ И окна заперты от зноя») "is ascribed with all the connotations of felicity" which Bachelard links to dwellings (Amert 1992: 194). Akhmatova's allusion to heat in "Poem Without a Hero" invokes the references to heat found in Mikhail Bulgakov's novel *Master and Margarita* (*Мастер и Маргарита*), which Akhmatova had read before its publication because she and Bulgakov were good friends. In both works the image of heat stands out as euphemism for totalitarian discourse, merciless and unbearable. It seems that Akhmatova felt scared into her own self, hidden deep down in her subconsciousness that she defined as "The cellar of memory" («подвал памяти») in a 1940 poem of the same title. In this poem the image of a traditional home is equated with sanity: "But where is my house and where is my reason?" («Но где мой дом и где рассудок мой?» (Akhmatova 1976: 487).

In her poem "Requiem" («Реквием») Akhmatova requests her readers to entertain the idea one day of erecting a monument to Akhmatova next to the prison where she spent several hours queing for information about her imprisoned son. It echoes Pushkin's "Monument" in its juxtaposition of the state and the victimised poet. In her survey of the history of duels in Russia, Reyfman makes the point that in 1946 Soviet dissident poets were even worse off than had been Pushkin and his contemporaries, because the right to safeguard one's private place was forever gone. Reyfman quotes a humorous poem penned by Alexander Khazin "The Return of Onegin" («Возвращение Онегина», 1946). The poem was severely criticised as slanderous by Andrei Zhdanov, in his report on subversive texts published in the Leningrad literary journal *Star* (*Zvezda*). Reyfman quotes:

> Fate watched over Onegin in his plight:
> They just stepped on his toes […].
> He decided to end the confrontation by a duel
> And reached into his pocket… But long ago
> Somebody has swiped his gloves.
> For want of those,
> He held his tongue and kept still.
> (Reyfman 1999: 283)

In the absence of any proper code of behaviour and in an atmosphere of terror and human rights abuse, Akhmatova's request for a monument seems a gesture to inscribe pain into the landscape of Petersburg that could remind future generations about the failures of Stalin's modernisation project. The imaginary, therefore, must be revealed as construction. In the words of Murphy, if "ideology functions by concealing the real conditions and relations of existence beneath a system of discourses, images and representations, and if imaginary relationship of individuals to their real conditions of existence acts as a substitute for the real, then it is the imaginary which must be revealed as a construction, and thus opened by alternative perspectives" (Murphy 1998: 293). Murphy points out that obscured reality, suppressed by dominant ideology, could be restored to life through defamiliarisation. Thus the return of Onegin, described in the poem above, matches pefectly Akhmatova's observation on the impossibility of returning to the home to which her contemporaries had to adjust in the 1940s-1950s.

At the same time, Akhmatova's suggestion that her most elaborate narrative poem "Poem Without a Hero" is anti-Onegin in its essence might be viewed as a rhetorical device, one that was employed in Pushkin's *Eugene Onegin* with great vigour and which Akhmatova lavishly appropriated in her own poetry. William Harkins identifies this rhetorical device as *anentantiosis*. Harkins defines it "as a positive statement made in a negative form" and traces it to the Hellenistic rhetorical tradition. He also calls such statement "litotes" and explains: "Litotes seems generally to be used to denote assertion either by understatement or by negation: its burden is rather the irony of understatement of positive qualities. An example of litotes, using negation and chosen from *Eugene Onegin*, is: [...] 'And he remembered, if not without error,/ Some two lines of the *Aeneid*" (Harkins in Bethea 1993: 86). In Akhmatova's "Requiem" we come across one of the most striking examples of litotes, expanding on the poet's wish to have a monument in the Soviet Union. In the example cited below it appears that Akhmatova's real wish was for sites commemorating her life and works to be placed beyond the main landscapes of Petersburg:

> А если когда-нибудь в этой стране
> Воздвигнуть задумают памятник мне,
> Согласье на это даю торжество,
> Но только с условьем не ставить его

Ни около моря, где я родилась:
Последняя с морем разорвана связь,
Ни в царском саду у заветного пня,
Где тень безутешная ищет меня,
А здесь, где стояла я триста часов
И где для меня не открыли засов.
(Akhmatova 1989: 312)

And if one day in this country someone will think
To build a monument to me,
I give my permission for it,
But on one condition: to erect it
Neither by the sea where I was born since
The last bond with the sea is destroyed;
Nor in Tsarskoe Selo garden by the sacred stump,
Where one tormented shadow looks for me,
But erect it here, where I stood for three hundred hours
And where the gate was not opened for me.

Akhmatova's appeal to her readers to erect a monument to her is constructed in a form of elaborate montage that also employs Pushkin's device of litotes. The passage induces readers to engage in deciphering Akhmatova's 'hieroglyphic' montage, which has striking similarities with the use of intellectual montage in Eisenstein's film *October* (*Октябрь*, 1927-1928). According to Schreurs, "Eisenstein's objective was not to recount history, but to 'explain' the significance and ideological background of what happened. The basic historical linearity of the film is constantly interrupted, complicated by intellectual attractions" (Schreurs 1989: 15).

Thus one can detect in Akhmatova's "Requiem" a strong desire either to be commemorated in Tsarskoe Selo, together with her favourite poets Pushkin and Annenskii, or to be remembered as a true native of Odessa. The lines about the broken bond with the seaside in Odessa instils in readers' minds Akhmatova's strong bond with Pushkin's exilic poetry written in Odessa, especially with his "To the Sea" discussed earlier. The Pushkinian subtext suggests thereby the disruption of the liberal tradition in the Soviet Union and the prevalence of tyranny and the Enlightenment as the cornerstone elements constituting Stalin's vision of modernity. Akhmatova's

"Requiem" invokes the exilic discourse shaped by Pushkin's poetry as an important discursive framework that allows her to comment on the barbaric cultural condition of Stalin's Russia of the 1930s-1940s.

In his study of twentieth-century Russian architecture, Vladimir Papernyi offers a useful tool that helps approach Stalin's Russia in terms of style of thought. Thus Papernyi describes many cultural developments of the 1920s as a type he calls Culture One, and labels the trends of the 1930s-1950s as Culture Two. Papernyi states that the main characteristic of Culture One is a horizontal quality that reflects on the fact that "the values of the periphery become more important that those of the centre"; architects were left to themselves and enjoyed a sense of great freedom to generate ideas "that are almost never realised" (Papernyi 2002: xxiv). Papernyi says that Culture Two represents the transfer of values to the centre that results in society becoming ossified: "The authorities start showing an interest in architecture both as practical means for securing the population and as spatial expression of a new centre-based system of values" (ibid.).

Papernyi's model can be easily extended to the Soviet literary scene of the 1930s-1940s that displaced such creative and independent modernist spirits as Akhmatova and Tsvetaeva. Thus in contrast to the ossified image of Stalin's culture, Akhmatova wanted to be immortalised as a person who has a living bond with European liberal tradition, exemplified in her mind by Pushkin, Byron and Dante. Since Pushkin's poetic landscape of Odessa, as manifested in his "To the Sea", encapsulated this tradition well, Akhmatova used the opportunity in "Requiem" to introduce the concept of environmental imageability, to use Lynch's term. Akhmatova's "Requiem" is thus an attempt to consciously remould the physical environment so that it could incorporate the Russian liberal poetic tradition, and make it visible.

In his comments on Akhmatova's late poetry, Ivanov talks about the closeness of Akhmatova's metonymic descriptions of Russian life and history to twentieth-century fiction. Ivanov pointed to the fact that Akhmatova's "Poem Without a Hero" used as a model Russian nineteenth-century tales and novels with elements of the fantastic, and Byron's narrative poems (Ivanov in Dediulin and Superfin 1989: 134-35). It might be argued, though, that Akhmatova's late poetry lends itself to comparison with Eisenstein's film because of her reliance on intellectual montage that was modelled upon ninteenth-century novels and novelised works of poetry. Morson and Emerson, in their study of Bakhtin's writings, highlight the fact that "In Bakhtin's view, novelisation is a key process in literary history" (Morson and Emerson 1990: 304). According to this study, Bakhtin urged scholars to look beyond the concept of genres and recognise the novelisation of various literary works in what Bakhtin called a novelistic epoch: "Bakhtin offers a number of examples of 'novelised' works and genres: Byron novelised the epic when he wrote *Don Juan* and *Childe Harold*, Ibsen novelised the drama, and Heine prosified the lyric poem. Ultimately, Bakhtin suggests, some degree of novelisation is unavoidable in a novelistic epoch" (Morson and Emerson 1990: 304-305).

Mandelshtam in a 1922 article indicated that the 1920s signified the end of the traditional classical novel, because individuals lost the linear sense of time and personal biography. In this article Mandelshtam predicted that "The further development of novel will amount to the history of dispersal of biography as form of individual's existence; furthermore, it will amount to the catastrophic death of biography" («Дальнейшая судьба романа будет не чем иным, как историей распыления биографии, как формы личного существования, даже больше, чем распыления — катастрофической гибели биографии» (Mandelshtam 1987: 74). In the context of Mandelshtam's observations, we can view Russian twentieth-century poetic narrations of Pushkin's biography as a manifestation of the novelisation of poetry and the loss of the lyric conscience. The intertextual and metapoetic devices uncovered in this chapter engaged Pushkin's texts in a variety of ways, and most importantly they provided poets with the abstract concept of meta-biography that made them part of Russian literary evolution.

Echoing Akhmatova's belief in the immortality of the poetic word which represents the living monument, Ida Nappel'baum's 1991 poem transformed Pushkin's project of creating a monument into a collective enterprise, all embracing and all inclusive:

От арапа — до еврея
Длинный перечень творцов,
Восхитительна аллея

Стихотворцев, мудрецов,
Разных предков, разных наций.
Все в один вступили храм.
И проклятий, и оваций
Всем досталось пополам.
Русской речи чудо-слово –
Стихотворный инструмент
Ярче слитка золотого
Под его святым покровом
Всех сроднило, всех сковало
В нерушимый монумент.
(Nappel´baum 2004: 219)

There is a long list of creators,
Including Blackamoors and Jews;
It forms a delightful alley
Of verse-makers and wise men,
Of different ancestry, different ethnic backgrounds.
They all entered the same temple.
They had equal share of
Attacks and applause.
The miracle-word of the Russian speech,
The device for crafting verse,
Shinier than a bar of gold
Under the dome of the holy temple
Brought them together, welded them
In one undestructable monument.

Nappel´baum's poem is written in the form of a highly eccentric and idiosyncratic sonnet which features an irregular dol´nik meter. It contains two four-line stanzas and two three-line stanzas which have one unrhymed word: 'welded' ('сковало'). It creates an expanded metaphor suggesting that Russian poets' monuments to themselves can be viewed as one unbreakable monument in the temple of art. Nappel´baum sees all Russian poets as manifestations of one creative principle united by the usage of the Russian poetic speech which she identifies, in line with the teaching of Russian formalists and Bakhtin, as the highest manifestation of the language. She refers to its miraculous properties ('miracle-word'). Her poem presents a coherent picture of the sacred space that Russian poetry occupies, despite its origination more often or not on the margins of Russian culture.

Roman Jakobson's article "Two Aspects of Language Disturbance and Two Types of Aphasia" suggests that while prose has a flexible structure that is subjugated to various kinds of metonymic displacement, poetry favours development through relations based on similarity because of the need for coherence (Jakobson 1956). Jakobson stresses that in poetry there are various motives which determine the choice between metaphoric and metonymic constructions: "The primacy of the metaphoric process in the literary schools of romanticism and symbolism has been repeatedly acknowledged, but it is still insufficiently realized that it is the predominance of metonymy which underlies and actually predetermines the so called 'realistic' trend, which belongs to an intermediary stage between the decline of romanticism and the rise of symbolism and is opposed to both" (Jakobson in Lodge in 1988: 59). Clearly, Nappel'baum's monument lends itself to be interpreted in terms of avant-garde poetics, known for its focus on monumental and abstract forms of expression, conveying what Stephen Hutchings defines as "modernism's apotheosis of the iconic impulse" (Hutchings 1997: 231).

Talking about Russian Silver age narrative, Hutchings says that its defining achievement "is not to be thought in an overthrow of the stylistic canons of its predecessors, nor in the discovery of exotic new contents. It is rather to be looked for in the apotheosis of a deep-rooted structural phenomenon which had gathered course throughout the course of Russian realism, namely an assault on the spatio-temporal frame defining past-tense narration" (Hutchings 1997: 231). Hutchings compellingly argues that during the work of the revolutionary avant-garde a truly trans-aesthetic discourse of everyday life emerged and expanded beyond the boundaries of fiction, leading to the explosion of aesthetically marginal forms of art such as photography, architecture and poster art, and true convergence of creation and living (Hutchings 1997: 231). Nappel'baum's portrayal of the achievements of Russian modernist poetry enable us to view it as a collective creative enterprise. It evokes a statement made by Vladimir Tatlin that Russian everyday life is built upon natural principles which cannot be fully expressed by objects borrowed from the West. Dissatisfied with objects from the West, Tatlin proclaimed: "It is for this reason that I show such interest in organic form as a point of departure for the creating of the new object... Such as our principle tasks in working on the organizations of new object in the new collective way of life" (Hutchings 1997: 232-33). Thus, Nappel´baum's poem continues the avant-garde notion that art must work towards the transformation of reality and bring monuments alive.

So in Bergsonian vein Nappel´baum brings to the fore the living creative impulse, the miraculous living word, saturated with religious overtones, which moulds artists into iconic images. Hence her understanding of Pushkin's monument built not with hands but with words. Given that the production of meaning in Russian culture has been influenced by an epistimology that derives from Russian Orthodox tradition which treats images differently from the other versions of Christian eschatology, I would say that all the forms of urban spectatorship developed in Russian twentieth-century poetry were informed by Pushkin's self-representation of himself in terms of an iconic figure. Thus Bergsonian tradition converged with Russian tradition, resulting in an emphasis on the dynamic concept of vision and its merger with life.

Hutching's study outlines the main tenets of the interpretation of 'image' found in the teachings of four established Russian theologians, including Pavel Florenskii, Vladimir Losskii, Leonid Ouspenskii and John Meyendorf. Hutchings writes about their treatment of 'image' thus: "The system they embrace retains at its centre the notion (originally common to both eastern and western Christology, but progressively deemphasised in the latter) of Christ as *icon* of God. The features of this system [...] are: (i) its antipathy to mediation, dualism and the logic of identity; (ii) its emphasis on participation and embodiment; (iii) the 'mutual predication' of its constitutive elements; (iv) its integration of particular (self) and universal (other) in a relationship preserving the irreducibility and freedom of the former; (v) its dynamic concept of 'vision'; (vi) its gravitation towards merger with 'life' rather than abstract 'sign' (the outer limit of the 'image')" (Hutchings 1997: 28-9). Nappel´baum's vision, of the collective monument of Russian modernist poets who allied themselves with Pushkin, reasserted Florenskii's principle that the process of recognition and seeing is inseparable from action and becoming. By presenting the modernist project as one that is imbued with a miraculous living word, Nappel'baum implied her hope that the modernist image will be perceived in terms of likeness between Christ and the poet as outlined in Pushkin's monument.

In his seminal study *Column and the Assertion of Truth* (*Столп и утверждение истины*), published in 1914, Florenskii merged recognition and becoming into one when he said "Only in God the Son man does recognise the Father as Father, and for that reason, himself becomes a son" («Верующий [...] только в сыне Божьем узнает Отца, как Отца, и оттого сам делается сыном») (Florenskii 1989: 95). While accepting Bergson's philosophical notions of time and memory in general terms, Florenskii detected hellenistic traits in the Russian mentality that sought to bring together truth and static image as manifestation of eternal memory (Florenskii 1989: 18-19). But at the same time Florenskii proposed a notion with Bergsonian overtones, suggesting that from an ontological point of view memory is 'an activity of the soul' ('творчество души') amounting to intellectual creativity: "Memory constitutes an intellectual activity of cognition; to be precise, it is a creative reconstruction from images of something that is revealed through mystical experience in eternity, or, to put it differently, it is creation of eternal symbols at a present moment" («Память есть деятельность мыслительного усвоения, то есть творческое воссоздание из представлений, — того, что открывается мистическим опытом в Вечности, или иначе говоря, создание во времени символов вечности») (Florenskii 1989: 210). Bakhtin's concept of eventness stands close to Florenskii's notion of unfolding memory, experienced as present. As Morson and Emerson point out, Bakhtin was very interested in Goethe's chronotopic visualisation, Goethe's ability to see time (Morson and Emerson 1990: 416). Morson and Emerson observe that Bakhtin differentiated between the epic time of epic poems and novels: "The novelist and his readers exist in a 'zone of familiar' contact with heroes", but the epic time is understood as "absolute past" (Morson and Emerson 1990: 420). Bakhtin talked of the stylistic limit of poetry and pointed out that a poet tries to speak "directly and without the meditation" and that "there must be no distance between the poet and his word" (Bakhtin 1981: 297).

The visualisation of time that exists in Russian poetry, and derives from Pushkin's texts, gives us the possibility to talk of the 'novelisation' of twentieth-century poetry because it gravitates towards hybrid constructions, estrangement and polyphony. The texts discussed here evoke strangeness which can be understood both as a resource of realist details and as a device for opposing hierarchy and authoritarianism.

David Bethea in his insightful study *Realising Metaphors: Alexander Pushkin and the Life of the Poet* refers to Sergei Davydov's observation that Pushkin's "Monument" could be read as part of the *Stone Island* cycle of poems which is structured around the Easter week calendar (Bethea 1998: 220). Viewed in this light, Pushkin's "Monument" points toward the day of Resurrection and "retraces Pushkin's own final thoughts about the simultaneity (but not necessarily equality) of Christian resurrection and secular fame (Bethea 1998: 221). Bethea reads Pushkin's poem as a story about "lived biography" and links it to Pushkin's poem "Recollections at Tsarskoe Selo" ("Воспоминания в Царском селе»). Bethea makes the very valuable comment that "'I have erected...' is a return to origins, above all to Tsarskoe Selo, but from the position of 1836 and from the now poetically *constructed* life implicated in this return. It forms, to a significant degree, the capstone of that 'bio-aesthetic' cycle as well" (Bethea 1998: 221). Bethea's position can be expanded and extended to the position expressed in Nappel'baum's poem. Thus in his study of the modern object in theatre, art and poetry John Erickson states: "In modernism one can observe a cross-pollination that can be described as the 'artifactualisation of language' and the 'literalisation of art'. Literature becomes artifactual through the self reflective concentration placed upon how language operates, how it is perceived, received and preconceived" (Erickson 1995: 25).

Thus Nappel'baum's poem featuring a collective monument to all Russian poets might be interpreted as an attempt not only to canonise Russian modernists but also as a manifestation of the shift from the labour-intensive nature of writing poetry (best understood in terms of building, construction and dwelling as expressed in the essays and poems of Russian Futurists and Acmeists) to another level of demystification of art. If in modernist narrative we can say that narrative logic was displaced by the effect of simultaneity, synchronic technique of collage or intellectual montage, then in postmodernist mode of expression we come across "a vision of a plurality of coexisting life forms and partial, local stories that make sense of these life forms" (Berger 2000: 7). Yet, as Berger aptly reminds us, we have to be cautious in separating the modernist and postmodernist discourses, since the boundaries between them are blurred. Berger argues that "what is postmodern is not the world, but the pluralist acceptance that there is more than one true story to be told about it" (ibid.). Berger suggests that engaging competing life forms in a rational dialogue is an important step forward: "Without accepting any all-embracing universal meta-narratives, one must be prepared to exchange one's own story, as well as the story told by one's interlocutor, for a slightly less local and parochial, but still far from universal, story one will be able to tell together with one's interlocutor as a result of the dialogue" (Berger 2000: 7-8). It seems that Nappel'baum's monument is an allegorical representation of such a dialogue, signifying the revival of polyphonic narratives.

FOUR

MODERNITY AS WRITING: PUSHKIN READERS & THE PUSHKIN MYTH

Preamble

In his seminal study *The Practice of Everyday Life* de Certeau sees writing as a manifestation of modernity and modernisation. He gives a summary of a few major changes in everyday practices brought about by writing: "'Modernisation, modernity itself, is writing', says François Furet. The generalisation of writing has in fact brought about the replacement of custom by abstract law, the substitution of the state for traditional authorities, and the disintegration of the group to the advantage of the individual. The transformation took place under the sign of a 'cross-breeding' of two distinct elements, the written and the oral" (de Certeau in Bennett 1995: 153-54). The abilities to read and to write, attests de Certeau, were for a long time separated, resulting in the fact that many adults in post-World War II Europe still continued to dissociate reading and writing. De Certeau convincingly argues that the models of reading advocated by religious groups led to the assimilation of reading in passivity and identifies the act of creative readings with various manifestations of modernity. Yet he compares modern institutions to the Church of the Middle Ages in their role to manipulate readers' ability to read certain texts. De Certeau tells of attempts to resist ready-made recipes for reading literature that schools, press or television imposed upon modern subjects; but "behind the theatrical décor of this new orthodoxy is hidden (as in earlier ages) the silent, transgressive, ironic or poetic activities of readers (or television viewers) who maintain their reserve in private and without the knowledge of the *masters*" (de Certeau in Bennett 1995: 157). Talking about authority figures in culture and politics who try to manipulate readers's reception of literature, and about readers who disseminate literary texts "in the networks of private life", de Certeau suggests that the two groups "collaborate in making reading into an unknown out of which emerge, on the one hand, only the experience of the *literate* readers (theatricalised and dominating), and on the other, rare and partial, like bubbles rising from the depths of the water, the indices of a *common* poetics" (de Certeau in Bennett 1995: 158).

This complex dynamics of the relationship between readers and writers is illustrated well in Pushkin's unfinished tale "Egyptian Nights" («Египетские ночи»), written in 1833-1835, and featuring a Russian poet and an Italian improvisor who could write any poem on the spot and perform it for an audience. Leslie O'Bell in her book *Pushkin's "Egyptian Nights": The Biography of a Work* suggests reading the story of the artist embedded in "Egyptian Nights" as a two-fold narrative: "as the triumph of the independence of art and the fellowship of the poets" and as "the instructive tragedy of the poet as man who is threatened by his dependence on society" (O'Bell 1984: 110-11). For David Herman "Egyptian Nights" expresses Pushkin's anxiety about the future of poetry, and of poets who might emerge from society's lower classes due to the advancement of technology and the spread of culture. Herman explains: "The improviser challenges the authority of social exclusions and violates the defenses of Charskii's home with the same ease as his artistic self–reinventions make a mockery of the borders of identity. Superior poetry turns out to be merely the flip-side of dissolving hierarchies and social disruption" (Herman 1996: 665). Herman observes that the Italian's livelihood depends on creation on demand, and is symbolically dialogised since it begins always with somebody else's word (Herman 1996: 668). The vibrancy of the Pushkin myth in Russian cultural history in the twentieth century conforms to Pushkin's vision of modernity that could undermine the autonomy of the reader and impede the creative process emerging from a constructive dialogue with the poets of the past.

Sandler's study of various institutions in Russia that wanted to control the image of Pushkin, so to speak, provides us with numerous examples of Russian cultural totalitarianism. According to Sandler, "Two hundred years after his birth, Alexander Pushkin is more than just a monument: the example of his life and work gives meaning to Russia's identity and to the culture of its people" (Sandler 2004: 1). Sandler sees the story of Pushkin's life in terms of the Pushkin myth since it lends itself to interpretation as "a narrative in which modern Russia sees signs of its own beginnings" (Sandler 2004: 5). Sandler's statement that Pushkin is "taken as the first modern writer because he worked in a European and not purely native context, or because he was a professional writer trying to earn his livelihood through his work" (ibid.) is particularly relevant for the discussion of the Pushkin myth and Pushkin readers whose poetic works were shaped by their attempts to read Pushkin's poetry creatively.

Sandler's observations on the educational popularisation of Pushkin's works in Russia might be viewed in a broader context that can be directly linked to the legacy of the Enlightenment's ideology, to an understanding of the public's consumption of cultural products. De Certeau asserts that belief in the educational powers of books was firmly rooted in the eighteenth-century ideology: "In the eighteenth century, the ideology of the Enlightenment claimed that the book was capable of reforming society, that educational popularisation could transform manners and customs, that an elite's products could, if they were sufficiently widespread, remodel a whole nation" (de Certeau in Bennett in 1995: 152). It appears that Russia's long-standing fascination with Pushkin's works and life is inseparable from what de Certeau identifies as the myth of Education that inscribes a theory of consumption within the frameworks and structures regulating cultural politics (ibid.). De Certeau makes the valuable comment that these structures degraded in post-war Europe "to the point of abandoning as useless or destroying the professional 'body' that perfected them over the span of two centuries". De Certeau thinks that today "they make up the apparatus which, by realising the ancient dream of enclosing *all* citizens and *each one* in particular, gradually destroys the goal, the convictions, and the educational institutions of the Enlightenment" (ibid.). Paradoxically, the reception of Pushkin's writings and his ideas in Russia co-existed alongside with the Education myth rooted in the ideology of the Enlightenment that Pushkin detested in his 1824 poem "To the Sea", as discussed earlier.

Playful gestures to undermine the Pushkin myth in the post-war period are manifested in the works of Bitov, Bulat Okudzhava, Brodsky, Kushner and Siniavskii, to name just a few important authors of the 1960-70s. These gestures reflect a logic of economic and technical development derived from the Enlightenment's utopian aspirations to reform society, which introduced a system to diffuse the ideology's dominant ideas. As de Certeau puts it, "the media is replacing the message" (ibid.). By the same token, we could say that, according to Sandler's discussion of the Soviet institutions that promoted Pushkin's poetry, these institutions developed to the point when they began to replace Pushkin with their own cultural product, depriving thereby readers of a historical role in shaping various interpretative strategies of the texts passed on to them for consumption. The process of institutionalisation of Pushkin in the Soviet era further removed readers of Pushkin's poetry from Pushkin the historical figure, who, to a large degree, as Belinskii convincingly argued, was a product of his times.

De Certeau muses that the idea of producing a society by a scriptural system continues to propagate the conviction that the public is moulded by verbal or iconic writing, "that it becomes similar to what it receives, and that it is *imprinted* by and like the text which is imposed on it" (ibid.). De Certeau's remarks that this text "was formerly found at school", yet today "the text is society itself" because it takes "urbanistic, industrial, commercial, or televised forms"; such a deduction corresponds to Tatiana's Tolstaya's description of post-Soviet members of Russian society as Pushkin's children. In this sense, Tolstaya's 1992 essay "Pushkin's children" («Дети Пушкина») exemplifies not only that in the twentieth century all Russian poets of significance resembled the texts Pushkin's imprinted upon them, but also that readers and writers became alike, moulded in Pushkin's image.

I would emphasise that such an overarching view of Pushkin's influence on Russian literature constitutes a one-sided approach to Pushkin's legacy to twentieth-century poetry. I am convinced that, by focussing on the more subtle dynamics of the binomial reading-writing set of relations, we might resolve some specific mechanisms embedded in Pushkin's texts that co-opt the reader to participate in the experience of reading the canon in a more balanced way, one that credits equally the contributions of both text and reader. One of the most striking examples of such a creative act of reading was achieved in Soviet-era fiction by Mikhail Bulgakov. According to Peter Kenez, this most un-Soviet of all Soviet novels by Bulgakov is an important contribution to the debates about artistic autonomy and the social commissions of Soviet educators, politicians and LEF artists in the late 1920s-early 1930s. In discussing the Pushkinian overtones in Bulgakov's novel, Kenez convincingly demonstrates that "the complex narrative structure and intertextual affiliations of *The Master and Margarita* steer us away from the danger of subscribing to simplistic ideas that would not do justice to the tragedy of either character or author" (Kenez in Kelly and Shepherd 1998: 54-55). Kenez identifies in Bulgakov's novel what he calls "the Pushkinian opposition of inspiration which is not for sale and a manuscript which requires a careful consideration of the nature and limits of autonomy" (ibid.: 55). Kenez explains that these forms of autonomy can be understood in two ways: as "freedom from direction from above, from political tutelage and censorship" and as freedom "from ties to one's times, as well as from the marketplace in which all cultural products, high or low, must circulate" (ibid.). Kenez's model, however, lacks provision for the dynamics of writing and readership that might exist within the boundaries of the political framework outlined in his study. Yet, as Tomashevskii argued, intersubjective factors will always be important in ensuring the immortality of any poetic voice that heavily depends on the development of language containing culturally-specific meanings and connotations.

As discussed earlier, the method of polar reading advocated by Kennard permits the participation of any reader in the text, and offers a wide range of literary experience including the affirmation of the reader's value through the polarising aspect of one's real self. Below I will discuss a few examples of a playful acting-out of new imaginary behaviour — one that does not necessarily constitute real behaviour — through the act of reading Pushkin's texts or engaging creatively with them. De Certeau talks of the mutation that caused "the transition from educational archaeology to the technocracy of the media" with the result that "the massive installation of standardised teaching has made the intersubjective relationships of traditional apprenticeship impossible" (de Certeau in Bennett 1995: 152). De Certeau itemises the consequences of this trend: "the 'informing' technicians have thus been changed, through the systematisation of enterprises, into bureaucrats cooped up in their specialties and increasingly ignorant of users"; "productivist logic itself, by isolating producers, has led them to suppose that there is no creativity among consumers"; "a reciprocal blindness, generated by this system, has ended up making both technicians and producers believe that initiative takes place only in technical laboratories" (de Certeau in Bennett 1995: 152-53). These observations of de Certeau are particularly relevant to the explosion of technological discourse in Russia in the 1960s (the Thaw period) and in the 1990s (the post-Perestroika period).

The Soviet Union's period of cultural liberalisation, commonly known as the Thaw period, coincided with rapid technological advancement. A debate revolved around the importance of technological values, as opposed to pure aesthetic concerns, and was well encapsulated in Andrei Voznesenskii's 1964 narrative poem "Oza" and in the lyrics of Leonid Martynov and Boris Slutskii. In her lively discussion of the Russian poetic landscape of the 1960s, Vera Dunham cites a passage from Slutskii's poem that articulates the tension between lyricists and physicists:

> Что-то физики в почете.
> Что-то лирики в загоне.
> Значит, что-то не раскрыли
> Мы, что следовало нам бы!
> Значит — слабенькие крылья —
> Наши слабенькие ямбы...
> (Slutskii in Dunham 1965: 57)

> It seems the honours go to physicists
> And the backstage is for lyricists.
> This means we have not probed
> Some things we should have.
> This means our sacharine iambics
> Have but feeble wings...
> (Translated by Dunham: Dunham 1965: 57).

Dunham detects change in the aesthetic sensibilities in 1960s Soviet poetry, highlighting the re-discovery in the Thaw period of private space: "However, the return to things one can call one's own — hi-fi equipment and antiques, silver and perfume bottles, boxes and icons — speaks clearly enough of the main need of Soviet man, the right to privacy" (Dunham 1965: 60). Duhham also detects a trend among liberal poets, such as Akhmadulina, Voznesenskii and Evgenii Vinokurov, to name just a few, to seek security in the past and to transpose their conversations with the past into internalised monologues. More importantly, however, Dunham underlines the preoccupation of 1960s liberal poets with the discourse about discourse that "hovers between poetry and programming" (Dunham 1965: 69).

Dunham concludes her analysis of the major innovative features of 1960s Soviet poetry with the gloomy statement that the precondition for free poetry did not exist in Russia in the Thaw period. She makes a far-reaching observation that the fascination of liberal poets with spokesmanship, which is both trying and seductive, distracted them from the Pushkinian tradition. Dunham writes about the self-reflexive nature of 1960s Soviet liberal poetry with some scepticism, especially because she sees a substantial gap between morality and art. Her characterisation of the Soviet liberal poets of the Thaw period contains sharp criticism: "The flow of poetry about poetry is not subsiding. One of the many reasons is surely the urge of liberal poets to assume active leadership of young intelligensia. Thus, in a way, they doom themselves to become primarily spokesmen. This, in turn, introduces problems of the stage, the declamatory vicissitudes of a performing profession. It is not easy to be a member of the exacting brotherhood of innovators, to lead, and to declaim all at the same time. That poets are unaware of Pushkin's view on the compromise implicit in spokesmanship from the stage is inconceivable. Nor is it possible that the validation of that view through Maiakovskii's tragedy, for example, or Pasternak's and Akhmatova's triumph, is overlooked. Why is the warning not heeded?" (Dunham 1965: 73). Dunham sees Soviet liberal poets' neo-avant-garde aspirations to shape reality in accordance with their artistic vision as a sophisticated temptress. Her portrait of the 1960s Soviet poets resembles strongly the image of Soviet avant-garde poets, especially Maiakovskii. She defines a typical liberal Soviet poet thus: "Leading the liberal intelligentsia in its struggle against servitude to the state, the poet carries the all-purpose banner of truth, integrity, sincerity. Through the honesty of his individual commitment, he helps the general cause of civil rights. As of old, this has precious little to do with aesthetics" (ibid.).

Yet Dunham overlooks the strongly pronounced Maiakovskian creative impulse in the liberal poetry of the 1960s —

the impulse to use the defamiliarisation device as a weapon to help subvert bureaucratic impersonalism and the automation in everyday Soviet life. One of the most important achievements of Maiakovskii was that he made a dichotomy from art and everyday life, as a struggle between two authentic forces of life. Maiakovskii thus departed from the Romantic model that articulated the difference between the authenticity of the poetic self and the banal, unauthentic worldview of the crowd. The increased sense of triviality, detected by Dunham in 1960s Soviet liberal poetry, came at a time when the new grand slogans of Soviet ideology attempted to revolutionise the concrete realia in the style of the 1920s, when new projects to rebuild life were advanced, including the industralisation of virgin lands, space exploration and the birth of chemical engineering. Dunham's observations notwithstanding, I would suggest that the emergence of debate beween the physicists and lyricists in 1960s Russian poetry and critical studies might indicate the attempt to re-compose and redefine the three spheres of cultural modernity that Max Weber identified as science, morality, and art. Jürgen Habermas's article "Modernity versus Postmodernity" explains Weber's idea of cultural modernity in terms associated with Enlightenment ideology: "He characterised cultural modernity as the separation of the substantive reason expressed in religion and metaphysics into three autonomous areas. They are: science, morality and art. These came to be differentiated because the unified world conceptions of religion and metaphysics fell apart. Since the 18th century, the problems inherited from these older worldviews could be rearranged so as to fall under specific aspects of validity: truth, normative rightness, authenticity and beauty [...]. Enlightenment thinkers [...] still had the extravagant expectations that the arts and the sciences would promote not only the control of natural forces, but would also further understanding of the world and of the self, would promote moral progress, would promote the justice of the institutions [...] and even the happiness of human beings. The twentieth century shattered this optimism" (Habermas 1981: 8-9). It appears from Dunham's survey of the poetry of the Thaw period that some liberal poets felt capable of addressing this question formulated by Habermas: "Should we try to hold on to the *intentions* of the Enlightenment, feeble as they may be, or should we declare the entire project of modernity a lost cause?" (Habermas 1981: 9). For

Voznesenskii, the type of Soviet modernity that resulted in uncritical thinking of readers and in mass conformity was certainly a lost cause.

In his provocative 1959 poem "In the Shop" ("В магазине") Voznesenskii labels his fate 'mute'. He attempts to externalise the internal pain triggered by the oppressive culture to which he belongs. An everyday incident in a Soviet shop, where a cashier discovered a forged note lacking the image of Lenin printed on all Soviet notes, is used in Voznesenskii's poem as a pretext to describe the powerless and deceived crowd of ordinary Soviet consumers, victimised by the totalitarian regime. The graphic images produced by Voznesenskii in this poem heavily rely on visualisation of the pain and protest gestures resembling a pantomime in the style of Brecht's theatre:

> Немых обсчитали.
> Немые вопили.
> Медяшек медали
> Влипали в опилки.
> И гневным протестом,
> что все это сказки,
> Кассирша, как тесто,
> Вздымалась от кассы.
> И сразу по залам,
> Сыркам, патиссонам,
> Пахнуло слезами,
> Как будто озоном.
> О, слез этих запах
> В мычащей ораве.
> Два были без шапок,
> Их руки орали.
> А третий с беконом
> Подобием мата
> Ревел, как Бетховен,
> Земно и лохмато!
> В стекло барабаня,
> Ладони ломая,
> Орала судьба
> Глухонемая!
> Кассирша, осклабясь,
> Косилась на солнце

И ленинский абрис
Искала в полсотне.
Но не было Ленина.
Она была фальшью...
Была бакалея.
В ней люди и фарши.
(Voznesenskii 1975: 551-52)

The mute ones weren't given the right change.
They screamed.
The medals of coins
Were dropping into sawdust on the floor.
And in a form of angry protest,
Dismissing this as a figment of the imagination,
The cashier, like dough,
Grew out of her till.
And immediately across the halls,
Across tubs of cheeses, tins of pâtés,
The smell of tears spread out,
Like ozone.
Oh, the smell of these tears
In the grunting crowd.
Two men weren't wearing hats
And their hands were screaming.
The third one, who was holding a cut of bacon,
Was roaring something like obscenities,
Just like Beethoven: earthy and haphazard!
Tapping on the glass,
Breaking my palms,
My fate, deaf and dumb,
Was also screaming!
The cashier, looking grumpy,
Was looking sideways at the sun
Trying to find Lenin's image on a 50-rouble note.
But there was no Lenin.
The note was forged.
There was only the grocery
Containing people and mincemeat.

Voznesenskii's poem displays strong Maiakovskian overtones, in its subject matter, its approximate rhyming patterns and its graphic description of pain. At the same it is difficult to define it as completely un-Pushkinian in spirit, in that its main thrust is an attempt to verbalise pain. Pushkin's poetry contains numerous examples of such attempts to verbalise pain and trauma by using the language of gesture and allusion to laughter. In addition to the several examples from Pushkin's poetry discussed earlier, I would point to the image of the mute nation/audience in Pushkin's drama "Boris Godunov", to the image of the speechless chairman Walsingham in the tragedy "Feast at the Time of the Plague" and to the implied image of a speechless audience in "Egyptian Nights" treated to the recital of a poem featuring Cleopatra and a suicidal young man prepared to die in exchange for one night with her.

Voznesenskii's "In the Shop" in fact articulates the main tenets of Brecht's non-Aristotelian theatre. Benjamin illuminates the innovative aspects of Brecht's theatre, explaining that Brecht wanted to replace appeal to the spectators' empathy with the art of epic theatre that could astonish the audience at the circumstances in which characters function. Benjamin pays special attention to the employment of gestures in Brecht's plays that interrupt the action and the plot. As Benjamin puts it, "the discovery (alienation) of conditions takes place through the interruption of happenings" (Benjamin 1999: 147). Given Benjamin's characterisation of the epic theatre (as exemplified in Brecht's productions) as gesture-oriented theatre, and his observation that "for the more frequently we interrupt someone in the act of acting, the more gestures result" (Benjamin 1999: 148), it is possible to infer in Voznesenskii's "In the Shop" a call for a more direct confrontation with the government, made possible after Stalin's death despite all the liberal trends that manifested themselves in the Soviet culture of this period. In an all-inclusive and open-ended didactic form of expression, Voznesenskii redefines the modernist notion of Evreinov's 'theatre for oneself' into a form of avant-garde social drama; this drama is free of the effects produced by empathy, and is orientated towards spectators' mental participation in the actions they observe. The chronotopic qualities of Voznesenskii's "In the Shop" resembles the avant-garde spirit. As Habermas illuminates, "the time consciousness articulated in avant-garde art is not simply ahistorical; it is directed against what might be called a false normativity of history. The modern, avant-garde spirit has sought, instead, to use the past in a different way; it disposes over those pasts which have been made available by the objectifying scholarship of historicism, but it opposes at the same time a neutralised history, which is locked up in the museum of historicism" (Habermas 1981: 5).

Habermas's description of "modernity that lives on the experience of rebelling against all that is normative" (ibid.) resonates well with Voznesenskii's poem with a poet and a crowd of urban spectators and mute actors astonished to discover that no revolutionary conscience is alive in their country. The image of the cashier also brings to mind Daniil Kharms's short story "Sonnet" («Сонет») featuring Leningrad citizens in the early 1930s struck by amnesia: they have forgotten if 7 comes before or after 8. Their desperate attempt to establish the truth from a grocery store's cashier is futile; the whole search for truth goes awry, resulting in a child falling off the bench and breaking his jaw. In fact, Voznesenskii's poem has several intertextual links, and in a playful manner also alludes to Soviet historiography's presentation of Lenin as a great lover of Beethoven's music, especially of his "Sonata. Opus 54. Appassionata" (1804), as was reported in Maxim Gorkii's essay "Lenin". The image of mute person resembling Beethoven, and attempting to assault the authorities with sounds strongly resembling obscenities, was an intentionally politically charged gesture by the young Voznesenskii to subvert the socialist mode of expression in every radical way possible, and to engage his readers in a new way of thinking about poetry.

Works of prominent Soviet Thaw period poets, including Martynov, Voznesenskii, Akhmadulina and Evtushenko, continued the utopian aspirations of Russian avant-garde cultural figures. Their works exemplified concerns about audience and active author-reader dialogue, concerns that resonate well with de Certeau's meditation on the politicisation of reading discussed above. De Certeau argues that reading is just one aspect of consumption that cannot satisfy the will to re-write history on the basis of scriptual writing; therefore the existing division between reading and writing must be recognised. More importantly, Dunham's acknowledgement of the existence of pastiche and parody in 1960s Soviet poetry, together with the liberal poets' widely shared sense of a 'vision of interconnectedness' and recognition of reality of the past more as discursive reality than objective fact (Hutcheon 1988: 24), testify to the partial emergence of postmodernist aesthetics in the Soviet Union in the Thaw period.

In assessing the role of parody in 1960s Soviet poetry, we could also bear in mind Tynianov's theoretical pronouncements on parody as manifested in his 1927 essay "On Literary Evolution" («О литературной эволюции»). In this work Tynianov points to the importance of parody as a spur to the evolution of forms of representation. He sees parody as a response of new schools to the worn-out forms of expression and clichés of previous movements. In the case of 1960s Russian liberal poets, their attempts to use parody reflect a move to break the stifling mould of Socialist Realism which ceased its ability authentically to represent reality. Socialist Realism's revolutionary mode of expression gradually transformed into a false, insincere language that, by the end of the 1950s, had become totally automatised.

Dunham's survey of the 1960s poetic landscape corresponds well to Silvio Gaggi's observation on the postmodern re-writing of what was perceived by writers as an already written world: "Art after the sixties often reasserted representationality, but what was represented were things that were already images [...] and stories and novels began to be concerned with the processes and problems of writing" (Gaggi 1989: 20). The latter comments can be easily extended to Russian poetry of the period after World War II, produced by poets living in the Soviet Union and by those in exile. For these poets, reading Pushkin's poetry became an act of re-writing of the poems that already became perceived as partially mutated through the interference of the educators, institutions and media that were propagating the Pushkin myth. Soviet poets desire to perform their poems on the stage stems from their feeling threatened by the inability of their poetic works to impose their own rhythms on the subject, in the way of pre-Soviet times. 1960s Russian poetry displays a strong tendency towards visualisation and graphic decription of ideas. Thus Voznesenskii, a leading poet of his generation, was also an architect and an artist. De Certeau argues that at the most elemental level, reading has become, over the past three centuries a visual poem: "To read without uttering the words aloud or at least mumbling them is a 'modern' experience, unknown for millennia. Today, the text no longer imposes its own rhythm on the subject, it no longer manifests itself through the reader's voice. This withdrawal of the body, which is the condition of its autonomy, is a distancing of the text" (de Certeau in Bennett 1995: 160-61). This is due to the fact that the media extends their power over the imagination of the reader, despite the reader's increased autonomy.

Also in relation to the creative responses to Pushkin in the post-war Russian poetry, we can observe that the Pushkin myth became associated with attempts by Soviet institutions and the media to impede the initiatory modes of reading. These attempts were resisted by many poets wanting to defend the intimacy of reading and the concept of inter-subjectivity. The existence of the Pushkin myth presupposes the existence of a reader who weaves his own story into the story of the life of the national poet. Yet, if we move away from this reductionist model that identifies the reader with a stable subject or with the act of reading with the production of a single meaning, then we are faced with the another extreme view which is encapsualted in Blanchot's writings. Namely, this extreme position suggests that reading does not necessarily result in the affirmation of identity, but brings about a dissolution of the reader's sense of self. Blanchot's provocative statement that "the reading of poem is the poem itself" (Blanchot in Bennett 1995: 188) reveals the other end of the spectrum of reader response to the text being read. Blanchot's understanding of reading as a creative but anonymous act supports my previously discussed notion of writing as dwelling inasmuch as it emphasises the singularity and uniqueness of the reading experience understood in spatialised terms.

In his book *The Gaze of Orpheus and Other Literary Essays* (1981) Blanchot writes: "In some sense the book needs the reader in order to become a statue, it needs the reader in order to assert itself as a thing without an author and also without a reader" (ibid.: 191). In Blanchot's view, reading makes the book and transforms it into a work with its own existence beyond the author, beyond his experiences expressed in the book and the various traditions that informed it.

What follows below is a discussion of some readers of Pushkin's poetry whose acts of reading include both creative responses to the Pushkin myth and attempts to articulate the freedom of reading and its singularity. Iser's notion of the two poles — the artistic and the aesthetic — between which the literary work is situated assists in a closer examination of the impact of the Pushkin myth on poetic imagination. Iser identifies the artistic pole with the author's text and the aesthetic pole with the actualisation of the text accomplished by its reader. According to Iser, the reader sets the work in motion as he "passes through the various perspectives offered by the text" (Iser in Bennett 1995: 21). Viewed in this light, the Pushkin myth might be also seen as a brand name for the various modes of readership of Pushkin's texts that stand in stark contrast to the cultural totalitarianism with its focus on commemorating Pushkin, not reading him.

Russian émigré poets as readers of Pushkin's texts

Georgii Adamovich, a leading Russian émigré critic, in his 1962 speech "Pushkin" commemorating the 125th anniversary of Pushkin's death, identified Pushkin as a lonely figure in the history of Russian literature because of his strong bond with Renaissance culture. Adamovich writes: "Berdiaev defined Pushkin as a Renaissance man [...]. Despite all its deep Russianness, which sometimes displays a stylised version of Russian folklore, in our literature Pushkin was the great (and most importantly — the only) representative of the foundations that shaped the mentality of European humankind during the Renaissance and that nourished so many generations with creative energy, inspiration and joy. In short, this feeling amounts to the realisation that one can live on this earth and it is worth living [...] " ("Бердяев назвал Пушкина *ренессанским* человеком [...]. При своей глубочайшей *русскости*, порой даже не лишенной какой-то нарочитой фольклорности, Пушкин был великим — а главное, в нашей литературе единственным великим — представителем тех начал, которые в эпоху Возрождения возобладали в сознании европейского человечества и вдохнули в несколько поколений столько творческой энергии, вдохновения и радости. В двух словах начала эти сводятся к чувству, что на земле можно жить и стоит жить» (Adamovich in Nepomniashchii and Filin 1999: 305).

Adamovich notes that Pushkin's works reveal Pushkin's humane qualities and spontaneous character, which he defines as alive and complex: "He is dear to us because of his humane character, his living and complex spontaneity that does not always accommodate an even and academically dispassionate attitude towards reality" («он дорог нам именно своей человечностью, своей живой и сложной непосредственностью, не допускающей всегда одинакового, академически бесстрастного отношения») (Adamovich in Nepomniashchii and Filin 1999: 304). Adamovich unfolds in Pushkin's artistic psychology a tension between the somatic and semantic that is also evident in many acts of writing and performance prevalent in the modernist period. He suggests that Pushkin could bring to life many of the formal and conceptual ideas on which the making of his art was based.

Adamovich chooses to talk about Pushkin in terms that favour a man of action over the man of letters. As Harold Segel's illuminating 1998 study *Body Ascendant: Modernism and the Physical Imperative* convincingly demonstrates, modernist anti-intellectualism favoured action over contemplation. As Segel puts it, "Sensing a certain insufficiency in being a man of letters, the writer now strove to become a man of action as well. Experience was what mattered most; that was how the world was to be learned, not through intellectualisation and language" (Segel 1998: 6). Talking about modernist theatre, Segel also detects a shift towards gesture and pantomime, instigated by the growing belief in the primacy of the body over art and intellect. Taking into account the wider context of cultural developments in Europe, Segel writes about the object of his study: "Since the retreat from speech [...] was taking place in the theatre more or less at the same time serious artists began experimenting with pantomime, I follow the more striking developments in pantomime (beginning with Max Reinhardt's great spectacle, *The Miracle*) with examples of the enhanced semantic weighting of gesture and silence at the expense of dialogue in plays by a few leading dramatists of the modernist period" (Segel 1998: 9).

The primacy of spontaneity and intuition that forms an important aspect of modernist physicality was also manifested in the anti-traditionalist works of such philosophers as Friedrich Nietzsche, Bergson, Fritz Mauthner, and Ludwig Wittgenstein that express the epistemological value of language and the direct experience of the phenomenalist world through contact with the living roots of life and physical sensation. Mauthner's proposition that language is not well suited for knowledge, because "words are memories and no two people have the same memories" (Mauthner, in Segel 1998: 179), is particularly useful for understanding Russian émigré poets' fascination with the female images Pushkin expressed in some of his poetic works. They are often taken for symbols of Russian national identity: these images include Pushkin's nanny Arina Rodionovna and Tatiana Larina, the protagonist of *Eugene Onegin*.

While the importance of these images to the formation of Russian identity has been well documented (Tyrkova-Williams; Hasty; Sandler), I will examine the question of their reception in Russian émigré poetry in the context of the anti-intellectual trend outlined above. I note that Adamovich's emphasis on the importance of Pushkin's own experiences for his artistic psychology (as conveyed in Adamovich's 1962 speech "Pushkin") reflects the numerous debates on the relation between life and culture that took place in the modernist period both in Europe and in Russia.

Before assessing the appropriation of the images of Pushkin's nanny and Tatiana Larina by Russian émigré poets, I note that Bakhtin's accounts of aesthetic activity help to shed light, too, on the specifics of Russian modernist thought and cultural values. According to Craig Brandist, German phenomenologist Max Scheler, who introduced the notion of value essences that "can be intuited in the process of interaction between subjects", was an important influence on Bakhtin and on members of the Bakhtin Circle (Brandist 2002: 21). Scheler's ideas can be summarised as follows: dismissed is the concept of empathy which implies that the self should merge with the other to experience what the other experiences, in favour of the notion of a phenomenological distance; subjects are urged to resist being absorbed by the flow of life, since this resistance could lead to the attainment of the realm of spirit through an understanding of one's uniqueness and through personal development (Brandist 2002: 21). According to Adamovich, all Russian writers can be seen as Pushkin's disciples insofar as formal techniques are concerned (Adamovich in Nepomniashchii and Filin 1999: 304). At the same time, Adamovich presents Pushkin as a lonely figure whose mindset is rooted in Russian and European cultural traditions that celebrate human life and humanist values. Adamovich sees post-Pushkinian Russian culture as breeding artificiality and straddling the borders between the great and the grotesque. Although Adamovich does not quote Scheler, he seems to be aware of the concept of the phenomenological distance outlined in Scheler's theoretical works.

Scheler's concept of phenomenological distance helps illuminate Adamovich's belief that perhaps Pushkin's epoch in Russia will truly manifest itself in the future. Adamovich poses an interesting question about Pushkin's relevance to future generations of readers: "Perhaps, the true kingdom of Pushkin is ahead of us and the true Pushkinian day will arrive in the future. This is a big issue and it is of great importance to the whole Russian culture" («Может быть, настоящее царство Пушкина еще впереди, может быть, истинный пушкинский день еще придет. Это очень большой вопрос и для всей русской культуры очень важный») (ibid.). Adamovich illustrates Pushkin's phenomenological distance from the objects of his admiration, including books, by referring to the fact that Pushkin, who was free of any mannerisms, looked in the last minutes of his life at his bookshelves and said to the books "Goodbye, friends!" («Прощайте, друзья!») (ibid.: 305). Adamovich wryly suggests that no other writer after Pushkin could have bid a farewell to books in such a natural way. Adamovich's comment points to Pushkin's purpose and very broad understanding of creativity and its role in everyday life, including the creativity of reading. To Adamovich's mind, the most representative examples of Pushkin's creativity are those poetic works in which Pushkin talks about life in the most prosaic way and points to the novelisation of life.

A lengthy quote from Adamovich's assessment of Pushkin's poetic achievements will highlight Adamovich's aesthetic sensibilities rooted in Petersburg modernist culture but developed in France. In some ways, Adamovich might have felt close to Pushkin's Russian European identity, having witnessed modernist cultural developments manifested both in Russian émigré literature and in French literature and cinema. Adamovich writes: "The most remarkable poems written by Pushkin and the most Pushkinian of all his poems are the works in which he does not force his voice and raises his tone of voice, as he does in his lyric "Prophet"; my list of the most Pushkinian poems exclude also the Chairman's Song from his tragedy "Feast at the Time of the Plague" [...]; it includes those poems in which Pushkin in a completely casual manner, using an absolutely natural tone of voice, without any mannerism, speaks about being which in its smallest manifestation in everyday life is as mysterious as it is in the expressions of significant world affairs. He also talks with sadness, rather than with a sense of mourning, that not so many people's lives work out the way they want them to; as well as that everyone has only so much time to do everything he or she wishes to do" («Самые удивительные пушкинские стихи и, во всяком случае, наиболее пушкинские среди пушкинских стихов не те, где он напрягает голос и повышает тон, не «Пророк» и даже не песнь Председателя из «Пира во время чумы» [...], а те, по-моему, где он с совершенной непринужденностью, с полнейшей естественностью интонации, не форсируя стиля, говорит о жизни, которая и в каждой повседневной мелочи так же таинственна, как и в огромных мировых событиях. И скорее с грустью, чем со скорбью говорит еще о том, что мало у кого жизнь складывается так, как надо бы, и что для каждого из нас срок ее ограничен» (Adamovich in Nepomniashchii and Filin 1999: 309-10). To Adamovich's mind the essence of Pushkin's poetics and philosophy was manifested in Tatiana's monologue at the end of *Eugene Onegin*, where she remembers her youth and in which she proclaims her boredom with the theatricality of everyday life in Petersburg, defining it as "a tinsel of this anaemic life" («постылой жизни мишура») (ibid.). Arguably, Adamovich sees Pushkin's Tatiana as a person who is capable of maintaining a phenomenological distance from the objects she worships, including the novels and poems she reads.

In other words, Adamovich perceives Tatiana's evolution as a creative individual in similar terms to the subjective interaction described in Scheler's book *The Nature of Sympathy* (1954). Scheler's model of personal development comparable to children's development is similar to the child's imaginary space discussed earlier, in which the child's identity is forged in relation to the identity of the m/other. Tatiana's example fits this model. Scheler describes the achievement of moral consciousness and individual responsibility through personal development in a way analogous to the child's attainment of his own identity. Scheler articulates the gradual process of child's develoment thus: "Only very slowly does he raise his mental head, as it were, above the stream flooding over it, and finds himself as a being who also, at times, has feelings, ideas and tendencies of his own. And this, moreover, only occurs to the extent that the child *objectifies* the experiences of his own environment in which he lives [...], and thereby gains *detachment* from them» (Scheler 1954: 247).

To Adamovich, both Pushkin and his protagonist from *Eugene Onegin* — Tatiana Larina — exemplify the ability described above to objectify the experiences of everyday life in an aesthetic manner. Adamovich's own poetry developed a strong orientation towards the novel and it is not coincidental that he highly praised Akhmatova's poetry throughout his life, seeing in it the same tendency towards novelisation, as Bakhtin puts it. Morson and Emerson remind us that "in ages when novels predominate, they 'novelise' or 'prosify' other genres". Morson and Emerson explain: "Moreover, the social forces that lead to the novel's preeminence — say, a sceptical sense of the world — also act directly on other genres; at such times novelisation happens both directly and indirectly" (Morson and Emerson 1990: 304). The Formalists argued that the Russian language expresses itself in the most creative way in poetic speech; but Bakhtin suggested shifting away from the view that prose is just a form of incomplete poetry and urges an examination of prose on its own terms. Bakhtin maintained that such a shift in the perception of poetry and prose will help us to see all verbal art in a new way (Morson and Emerson 1990: 304). Morson and Emerson point out that Bakhtin's theoretical framework for analysing novelistic discourse was not extended to lyric poetry but, nevertheless, Bakhtin believed that his prosaic approach will help to "discern features of lyric poetry previously overlooked, and that even those features that have been analysed will be understood quite differently" (ibid.).

Reading Pushkin's *Eugene Onegin*, and reading modernist period novels saturated with theoretical approaches to reading, linguistics and narratology, changed Russian poets' perception not only of Pushkin but also of their own writings. Such reading alerted them to the required phenomenological distance to realise the creative potential arising from a dialogue with their predecesors or their contemporaries. In her pioneering examination of Tsvetaeva's reading of Pushkin, Hasty claims that "Tsvetaeva insists on the creativity inherent in the act of reading and foregrounds the role of the reader on whom a poet ultimately depends" (Hasty 1999: 228). Hasty stresses the importance of *Eugene Onegin*, in particular to Tsvetaeva's poetic self, and rightly notes that "for Tsvetaeva, Tatiana's strength lies in the fact that she can only love, but not be loved", because she admires Pushkin's heroine's determination to remain "in the enchanted circle of her own loneliness in love" (Hasty 1999: 230). Hasty convincingly argues that Pushkin's verse novel provided Tsvetaeva with a productive model of cross-fertilisation between life and literature to the extent that "on the strength of such cross-fertilization" Tsvetaeva "styles herself as Tatiana's grandchild" (Hasty 1999: 234). I will further extend this line of investigation and unfold another layer behind Tsvetaeva's highly positive view of Pushkin's Tatiana.

It is worth noting that Tsvetaeva in her 1937 essay "My Pushkin" advocates the view that Pushkin's Tatiana surpasses all the female protagonists of world literature because of her will power to remain true to herself, vigorously defending her private space as a creative female reader. Similar to Adamovich's comparison of Pushkin to Tolstoy in his speech "Pushkin", Tsvetaeva juxtaposes Pushkin's Tatiana as a creative reader to Tolstoy's Anna Karenina who, after her affair with Vronsky, becomes a writer of fiction for children. Tsvetaeva appears to be highly appreciative of Tatiana's phenomenological distancing from the texts she reads. Tsvetaeva sees this state of loneliness in love, as she puts it, as an indeterminate space, full of opportunity. By contrast, Tsvetaeva dismisses Karenina's way of reading novels that leads her to suicide. Karenina's experience as reader and writer fully corresponds to the popular theories of empathy propagated in the early modern period, in which the self dissolves itself in the other through the act of full merger in order to experience what the other experiences. Tsvetaeva suggests that any unconditional merging with the other is counterproductive and potentially destructive. That is why Tsvetaeva writes about Tatiana's experience in terms of the communicative situation, presenting it as a model of resistance to the other and to the flow of life: "Yes, yes, girls, do declare your love to your beloved ones first and listen to didactic reproaching speeches afterwards; and do not lower yourselves to the level of such speeches; and then marry wounded noble men; and then listen to declarations of love and do not lower yourselves to their level — and you will be a thousand times happier than another female protagonist, who had no choice but to die under the train in fulfillment of all her wishes" («Да, да, девушки, признавайтесь — первые, и потом слушайте отповеди, и потом выходите замуж за почетных раненых, и потом слушайте признания и не сходите до них — и вы будете в тысячу раз счастливее нашей другой героини, той, у которой от исполнения всех желаний ничего другого не осталось, как лечь на рельсы» (Tsvetaeva 1984, volume 2: 318). Tsvetaeva's allusion to Tolstoy is not out of place in a text offering a modernist discursive framework for reading literature, since Tsveteava appears to reject Tolstoy's anti-aesthetic stance. As Hutchings's book 1997 *Russian Modernism: The Transfiguration of the Everyday* convincingly demonstrates, in Tolstoy "the equation of reality and anti-aesthetic, representation and participation, forces the fragmentation of daily existence into (i) the deathly automatism of anonymous codes, and (ii) pure, unmediated life" (Hutchings 1997: 45).

The metaphorical representation in Tsvetaeva's "My Pushkin" of two types of female readers of novels carries special significance for the construction of Tsvetaeva's identity in such an autobiographical story reflecting on her own experiences of reading Pushkin. Bearing in mind that the story starts with the depiction of Naumov's painting featuring the wounded body of Pushkin being returned home from the duel, Tsvetaeva suggests that to her the poet's wounded body became an allegorical symbol of the poet's fate. She stops short from saying that this is an allegorical depiction of poetic experiences in modern times. More importantly, however, is that Tsvetaeva considers the underlying theme of "My Pushkin" — empathy and its implications for creativity — for its ethical value and aesthetic significance. The issue of lived experience, which has a trace of any meaningful fact with creative potential that becomes aesthetically consolidated, was discussed at a more theoretical level in the works of literary theoretists, including Bakhtin and Scheler; but it is noteworthy that Tsvetaeva remains the only Russian of great significance who addressed the issue of reading and modernity at such a length.

Brandist reminds us that "Bakhtin adopts Scheler's argument that the percepient must not only empathise, that is, feel and perceive what the other feels and perceives, but must subsequently return to his or her own position outside the other and give shape and wholeness to the one perceived" (Brandist 2002: 46). In his relationship analysis in "Author and Hero in Aesthetic Activity" («Автор и герой в эстетической деятельности») Bakhtin introduces the important concept of the 'surplus of vision' as a precondition for creativity (Bakhtin 1979: 24-25). We can see Bakhtin's study treating various types of outsidedness through which the author bequeaths completion on the hero, allowing at the same the hero to maintain autonomy; so we can see Tsvetaeva in "My Pushkin" appropriating the image of Tatiana in order to exemplify the modes of perception described in Bakhtin's work. Tsvetaeva's Tatiana is presented as the author in command of her own text and life, as if she displays awareness that aesthetic completion is possible only from the author's viewpoint. Tsvetaeva's Onegin is deprived of such a perspective; he stands out as a Bakhtinian hero who does not experience his life as a whole, but who functions as a free unit within the open event of being: his life exists for other heroes and for the author. In sum, Tsvetaeva's "My Pushkin" offers a model of reading understood in ethical terms as a contribution to the on-going co-creation of the experienced world.

Bakhtin identified this creative dialogue with aesthetic and everyday objects as an important basis for creativity: "In general, any serious attitude towards anything and anyone is creative and productive in its essence. The object we call a certain object in life, in our act of learning experience, in our deed, gains its certainty its unique character only through our attitude towards it" («Вообще всякое принципиальное отношение носит творческий, продуктивный характер. То, что мы в жизни, в познании и в поступке называем определенным предметом, обретает свою определенность, свой лик лишь в нашем отношении к нему») (Bakhtin 1979: 8).

In terms similar to Bakhtin's language, Tsvetaeva stresses her own unique reading experience related to Pushkin's *Eugene Onegin*. She affirms Tatiana's creative and ethical ability to be a creative reader of novels she chooses to read. Thus Tsvetaeva's perspective on human self-education and the formation of the self — which derive from the German tradition of *Bildung* — reveals her concern not with the final product but with the creative energy itself that remains self-contained within the dimension of the pure image, not in its actuality. Tsvetaeva's reading of Pushkin stands conspicuously close to

Bakhtin's reading of Goethe, whom Tsvetaeva also admired throughout her life. In the words of Brandist, "Goethe shows the formative principles behind the rise of the modern worldview, the rise of a new type of person in a new world liberated from the shackles of mythical thinking. Realism thus signifies an elaboration not of knowledge about an empirical world that lies beyond human consciousness, but the process of creating the image world that is culture. The rise of the modern subject and the formation of the modern world here become a unity precisely because of Goethe's rejection of the duality of subject and object" (Brandist 2002: 153-54). Brandist explains Bakhtin's comment on Goethe: "Like Dostoevskii [...] Goethe is presented as a sort of spontaneous neo-Kantian thinker" (ibid.). Tsvetaeva claimed in "My Pushkin" that since birth and early childhood she knew everything she needed to cognise in nature, fashioning herself in the image of a microcosm; this claim stems from the same philosophical position Brandist describes as spontaneous and neo-Kanthian. More important is Tsvetaeva's Goethean trait not to separate subject and object but to be "located in a mutually innate part of what is perceived" («является соприродной частью познаваемого») (Bakhtin 1979: 396). This is evident in her discussion of Pushkin's works and their impact on her artistic psychology: she defines it as liberating. Tsvetaeva's thinking in "My Pushkin" is focussed on co-creativity, revealing her understanding of Pushkin as "a new type of person in a new world liberated from the shackles of mythical thinking", to borrow Brandist's characterisation of Bakhtin's Goethe (Brandist 2002: 153-54).

The creative possibilities in the position of independence offered by reading *Eugene Onegin* in the age of modernity triggered a variety of responses from Russian émigré readers. An extreme example is the narrative poem by Russian émigré poet Mikhail Eisenshtadt published under the pseudonym 'Argus'. His narrative poem "Eugene Onegin in New York" («Евгений Онегин в Нью-Йорке») employs the Onegin stanza and presents Tatiana as a modern Russian girl, born to émigré parents, who fashioned herself in the clothes of a modern American girl fond of tennis and jazz. Eisenshtadt light-heartedly suggests that his Tatiana lacked the traditional upbringing reliant on the old-fashioned Russian support and education usually provided by a nanny who would have instilled distinctly Russian values in her charge:

Для вящей полноты романа
С прискорбьем должен я сказать,
Что воспитанием Татьяны
Не занималась даже мать.
Она росла, как цвет, привольна,
Своей семьею недовольна,
Всегда одна и без подруг.
Ее семья, закончив круг
Нелепых беженских скитаний
Нашла в Америке приют.
Нельзя же требовать, чтоб тут
Вдруг к ней свалилась с неба няня...
Притом, как знает целый свет,
В Нью-Йорке русских нянек нет.
(Argus in Filin 1994: 221)

For the sake of more objectivity for my novel
I must say with some disappointment
That even Tatiana's mother
Did not contribute to her education.
She grew by herself, like a flower;
She was unhappy with her family.
She felt lonely, growing with no girlfriends.
Her family, having ended the circle
Of exilic wandering, found
Its home in America.
One cannot expect, of course,
To have a nanny land upon them as God's gift.
Besides, as everyone knows,
New York has no Russian nannies.

Eisenshtadt's allusion to the nanny of Pushkin's *Eugene Onegin* suggests that Pushkin's inclusion of the nanny in the repository of cultural values and stories of Russian life signifies to modern readers the dying out in modern culture of the storytelling critical to the development of imagination.

Benjamin reminds us that the source from which all storytellers have drawn is "experience which is passed on from mouth to mouth" (Benjamin 1999: 84). Benjamin's essay "The Storyteller", which reflects on the works of Leskov, was published in 1936. It offers a view of a grim modern reality dependent on the media rather than on living experience which, as Benjamin acknowledges, has fallen in value. Benjamin writes: "More and more often there is an embarassment all around when the wish to hear a story is expressed. It is as if that seemed inalienable to us, the securest among our possessions, were taken from us: the ability to exchange experiences. One reason for this phenomenon is obvious: experience has fallen in value. And it looks as if it is continuing to fall into a bottomless abyss. Every glance at a newspaper demonstrates a new low has been reached, that our picture, not only of the external world but of the moral world as well, has undergone changes overnight that were never thought possible" (Benjamin 1999: 83). Tsvetaeva's 1935 poem "Readers of Newspapers" («Читатели газет») reveals a similar concern for a Paris — where she lived as an émigré poet —dressed in newspaper from top to bottom. Commenting on the numerous newspaper readers eager to read sensationalist stories, Tsvetaeva identifies the artificiality of the virtual reality they belong to as depriving people of the imagination and creativity that requires constant interaction with the living roots of culture. In other words, Tsvetaeva suggested that many of her contemporaries valued the sensationalist reading of newspapers higher than the living experience of storytelling and reading aloud. Both traditions had been observed in her own family life, as Ariadna Efron's memoirs remind us. Tsvetaeva writes of those whose mentality is shaped by the media:

>   Что для таких господ –
>   Закат или рассвет?
>   Глотатели пустот,
>   Читатели газет!
>   (Tsvetaeva 1984, volume 1: 330)

>   What sort of meaning these citizens
>   Extract when they look at sunset or sunrise?
>   Readers of newspapers
>   Are swallowers of empty words.

As has been discussed in chapter two, Tatiana at the end of Pushkin's *Eugene Onegin* appears to be fully aware of the sensationalist newspaper stories and conveys her belief in the importance of everyday life experiences for creativity.

It appears that Eisenshtadt's Tatiana lacks a creative view on life and happily embraces the identity created by glossy magazines and newspapers for the modern girl. Her Russian identity is also mutated as a result of not being exposed to Russian culture's living oral tradition: Eisenshtadt playfully remarks that his modern Tatiana Larina uses the English expression "Oh, boy!" instead of the Russian "My God!", and acquired also a strong English accent:

> И изъяснялась кое-как
> По-русски с англицким акцентом,
> И заменяла «Боже мой»
> Англо-саксонским «бой, о, бой».
> (ibid.)

> She spoke Russian poorely,
> Talking with the strong English accent,
> Replacing the phrase «My God»
> With the Anglo-Saxone phrase «Boy, oh, boy!».

More importantly, Eisenshtadt not only laments the disappearance of spiritual and cultural values from young Russians in New York in the 1930-40s, but also ponders the issue of identity shaped by modern values. He reveals a strong orientation towards the physicality of modern culture that propagates jazz, dance and sport, thereby undermining the value of the verbal arts. His Tatiana has a list of habits and hobbies that strike the narrator as too modern. The list includes listening to jazz and dancing:

> Готова жизни не щадить,
> Татьяна проявляла прыть,
> Когда касалось танцев дело;
> Умела ночи напролет
> Шагать вперед, назад, вперед,
> И в пламенном восторге млела,
> Когда неистовый трубач
> По залу будто несся вскачь.
> (ibid.: 222)

She was prepared to sacrifice her life
For dispaying her enthusiasm
For vigorous dancing;
She was able to march for the whole night
Forward, backwards, and forward;
And she was over the moon from happinees,
When she saw a zealous trumpet player
Jumping around the hall like a horse.

Through the act of re-writing of Pushkin's text, Eisenshtadt voices his concerns over the cult of the body and the celebration of the pagan and the primitive that often arose in the 1920s-1930s at the expense of the Judaeo-Christian moral tradition. As twentieth-century history demonstrates, such concerns were well grounded in reality. Segel reflects on anti-intellectualism in twentieth-century Germany: "The road traveled from the ascendancy of pantomime in the late nineteenth and early twentieth centuries to the extremist cultivation of the body as a symbol of racial superiority was frighteningly short" (Segel 1991: 251).

It is not exactly clear from Eisenshtadt's text if his own novel in verse should be read as a collection of stylistic masks, or not. It strongly gravitates towards a didactic narrative about the loss of Russian identity in emigration. The narrator of Eisenshtadt's "Eugene Onegin in New York" displays his Russian European identity with great enthusiasm: for example he prefers to listen to Bach and classical tragic symphonies than to contemporary music. He admits, however, that classical music has a mentally therapeutic effect, distracting him from his busy American everyday life, misfortunes and news about the war («люблю забыть о свете бурном, о неприятностях, войне») (ibid.). Although Eisenshtadt replaces Pushkin's masterpiece with his own stylistically succesful imitation, his attempt reduces *Eugene Onegin* to the format of a 'novel of becoming' in the style of the classical *Bildungsroman*. In his assessment of the chronotopic peculiarities of this type of novel of emergence, Bakhtin unravels not the cycle of becoming of age, but "the path from idealism to scepticism and resignation", as Morson and Emerson put it (Morson and Emerson 1990: 410). Bakhtin notes that in such novels life is seen as an experience that encourages people to become more sober and accepting. In this respect, Eisenshtadt's idea of writing a modern parody on Pushkin's masterpiece seems a fitting expression of the exilic experiences of Russian émigrés in America. The cinematic and impressionistic qualities of Pushkin's text proved suitable for depicting a Russian émigre's observations on bustling New York life in the 1930s-1940s. Convinced that modern society is heading towards self-induced destruction, the narrator of Eisenshtadt's "Eugene Onegin in New York" constructs his own mythopoetic city that validates the palimpsest-like nature of history and human experience through the merger of Bach, classical symphonies and Pushkin.

The issue of the importance of maintaining a tradition of Russian storyteller and interlocutor, with whom the poet shares memories and emotionally painful experiences, is well articulated in Nabokov's poem "Exile" («Изгнанье»), written in 1925 under his pen name V. Sirin. In this poem Nabokov muses on the possibility of seeing Pushkin among his friends in exile:

> Я занят странными мечтами
> В часы рассветной полутьмы:
> Что если б Пушкин был меж нами —
> Простой изгнанник, как и мы?
> (Nabokov in Filin 1994: 59)
>
> Strange dreams occupy me
> In the twilight hours:
> I'm thinking what would happen
> If Pushkin, an ordinary émigré, could be among us?

Nabokov's poem displays the quality of montage: his poem is addressed to his fellow émigré authors whom the lyric hero engages in the mental assembly of meaning from fragments. Bearing in mind Peter Bürger's assertion that "montage presupposes the fragmentation of reality and describes the phase of the constitution of the work" (Bürger 1984: 73), we could view Nabokov's poem as a flow of mnemonic images that slowly unfold the whole space of imaginary dwelling in the past. It focuses on his childhood which is entwined with Nabokov's thoughts on the role of a Russian poet in emigration. The poem's seven four-line stanzas employ the four-foot iambic meter that imparts authenticity to a poem evoking Pushkin's name. He wonders if Pushkin would be struck by nostalgia and melancholy —

"he might be truly doomed to sigh about sad Russia" («он вправду был бы обречен *вздыхать о сумрачной России*, как пожелал однажды он»); or would use his exilic experiences for creative purposes, enabling his talent to develop and reach greater heights as a poet of world significance — "he would have spread around the world/ a new motif of unheard quality" («еще неслыханным напевом/ он мир бы ныне огласил»); or would stay silent for fear of spoiling the beautiful moment of longing for the past. This last thought for the solemn beauty of the Romantic poet's solitude is encapsulated in two stanzas:

> А может быть и то: в изгнанье
> Свершая страннический путь,
> На жарком сердце плащ молчанья
> Он предпочел бы запахнуть, –
>
> Боясь унизить даже песней,
> Высокой песнею своей,
> Тоску, которой нет чудесней,
> Тоску невозвратимых дней...
> (Nabokov in Filin 1994: 59)

> Or perhaps another option is possible:
> In exile, having embarked on the path of exilic person,
> He would have preferred to cover tightly
> His ardent heart with the cloak of silence, —
>
> Out of fear to undermine even with his
> High-spirited song
> The longing, more miraculous than anything else,
> The longing for the past which will not return.

Nabokov's poem illustrates the cognition process of adaptation to an exilic condition. Nabokov's reversed logic is associated with reconfiguring his spatial and temporal thinking: the new country, once the product of imagination, becomes familiar territory, while the native land becomes an imaginary destination. The poem's description of Nabokov's imaginary encounter with Pushkin questions the ability of a Russian poet of significance to develop in another country and to transgress linguistic and cultural boundaries.

Nabokov emphasises the alluring and seductive nature of lingering through repeating the word 'longing' («тоска»). The stanza, however, has a mirror structure: in the first two lines Nabokov repeats 'song' («песня») in the Instrumental case and in the second two lines he repeats the word 'longing'. Yet he rhymes 'song' with 'miraculous', ascribing it a special meaning of miracle-making and wonder. Brodsky also defines the past, in his essay "The Condition We Call Exile", as safe territory because it was already experienced. Brodsky talks of a heightened sense of retrospection in the life of an exiled author: "Retrospection plays an excessive role — compared with other people's lives — in his existence, overshadowing his reality and dimming the future into something thicker than its usual pea soup. Like the false prophets of Dante's *Inferno*, his head is forever turned backward and his tears, or saliva, run down between his shoulder blades" (Brodsky 1994: 3).

Nabokov finishes his poem in Pushkinian manner by putting a human touch to the image of the past evoked in the previous stanzas: the final stanzas draw a portrait of Pushkin's nanny and appropriate Pushkin's own words without quotation marks. Thus Nabokov mentions the image of the old and fragile little dove («голубка дряхлая») borrowed from Pushkin's poem "To My Nanny" («К няне»). The final two stanzas suggest that Pushkin was certain that his nanny awaited his return. The description of this imaginary meeting is emotionally charged, and is presented animatedly, focussing on the lively noises of the house in Mikhailovskoe. The old lady's act of knitting by the window is depicted in the present tense, contrasting with the abundance use of the future tense:

> Но знал бы он: в усадьбе дальней
> Одна душа ему верна,
> Одна лампада тлеет в спальне,
> Старуха вяжет у окна.
>
> Голубка дряхлая дождется!
> Ворота настежь... Шум живой...
> Вбежит он, глянет, к ней прижмется,
> И все расскажет — ей одной...
> (Nabokov in Filin 1994: 60)

But he would have known that in the faraway estate
One soul remained loyal to him,
One lantern glows in the bedroom,
An old lady knits by the window.

The old dove will be rewarded for her patience!
The gates are wide open... Lively noises...
He will run in, look around, and give her a big hug,
And tell her, only her, everything...

The final scene depicts Pushkin's nanny bringing alive an image from Pushkin's "To My Nanny". The theme of a creative spirit (understood here with Bergsonian rooting in specific language) awakening ossified objects is entwined with the theme of a sympathetic interlocutor who makes you feel at home anywhere in the world. The image of Russian literature as home is implied here through visualisation of the scenes from Pushkin's lyrics. Consonance based on the repetition of consonant sounds in a short sequence of words was well explored by the Russian Futurists and is found in Nabokov's poem, too. It employs the repetition of the sound 'zh' ascribed with the semantic meaning signifying the living word and living memory: 'knitting' («вяжет»), 'will wait long enough' («дождется»), 'wide open' («настежь»), 'living' («живой»), 'run into' («вбежит»), 'will warmly hug' («прижмется»), 'will tell' («расскажет»). All these words seem connected on the semantic and phonetic levels to the word 'life' («жизнь»). In sum, Nabokov's poem employs the device of montage in order to weave in the poem both exact quotes from Pushkin's works and Nabokov's own renderings of some of Pushkin's images. The mental reconfiguration of all the fragments into a unified whole achieves the juxtaposition of Nabokov's personal exilic experiences with Pushkin's life in exile.

Nabokov's "Exile", with its intertextual links to Pushkin's texts, expects readers to be actively engaged in the simultaneous process of deconstruction and construction of its meaning. The image of an old nanny taken from Pushkin's "To My Nanny" is incorporated into the stanza with the image of open gates that evokes the scene from Pushkin's "The Bronze Horseman" (where Evgenii notices the absence of the gate and realises the tragic consequences of the flood). In the poem's second stanza Nabokov precisely quotes, in quotation marks, from the first chapter of Pushkin's *Eugene Onegin*. The line 'to sigh about sad Russia' appears in stanza 50 in chapter one. This quote from Pushkin contains a meditation on the poet's fate and a possibility of freedom, understood in terms of escape from life's misfortunes and impersonal forces of historical destiny. Here Pushkin also talks about his African roots, thereby suggesting Pushkin's estrangement from his immediate surroundings and from a world driven by the Eurocentric ideals of the Enlightenment:

> Пора покинуть скучный брег
> Мне неприязненной стихии
> И средь полуденных зыбей,
> Под небом Африки моей,
> Вздыхать о сумрачной России,
> Где я страдал, где я любил,
> Где сердце я похоронил.
> (Pushkin, 1957, volume 5: 31)

> It is time to leave this dull shore
> Of the elements I dislike;
> And amidst the afternoon ripples of waves,
> Beneath the sky of my Africa
> To sigh about sad Russia,
> Where I suffered, where I loved,
> Where I buried my heart.

From Nabokov's own explanation of this stanza in his commentary to his translation of *Eugene Onegin*, we can interpret Nabokov's "Exile" as being politically charged. Nabokov writes about the image of bad weather in the above passage from *Eugene Onegin*: "One cannot afford to overlook the well-known fact that here, as in other poems, Pushkin makes an allusion to his political plight in meteorological terms" (Nabokov in Pushkin 1981, volume 2: 188). Through allusion to Pushkin's texts, Nabokov weaves into the narrative of exile his own story of a young Russian émigré in Berlin. Nabokov's father, a prominent Russian politician and editor of the Russian émigré newspaper *Руль*, was killed by right-wing assassins; Nabokov's mother settled in Prague after the loss of her husband. In order to avoid any political implication associated with the death of his father, Nabokov began to publish short stories and poems under his pseudonym V. Sirin. Pushkin had been particularly proud of Abram Petrovich Ganibal (Annibal), his African great-grandfather, Peter the Great's godson, whose promotion to the rank of general made his family part of Russia's hereditary nobility (Shaw in Bethea 1993: 121). Nabokov's quote from Pushkin's *Eugene Onegin* used in "Exile" serves to remind readers of Nabokov's own bond with the Russian nobility that ended as a class with the 1917 Bolshevik revolution.

Thomas Shaw, a distinguished Pushkin scholar, identifies stanza 50 in chapter one of *Eugene Onegin*, which Nabokov's "Exile" quotes, as Pushkin's most important publication on the subject of his heritage (Shaw in Bethea 1993: 124). Pushkin wrote it in 1823 in Kishinev where he spent some time in exile before moving to Odessa. Shaw reminds us, that at time of its publication, Pushkin was in open exile in Mikhailovskoe; under the censorship of Pushkin's times, no direct mention of exile was allowed in print — that is why Pushkin veils his comments on his exilic condition in the discourse of poetic flight of imagination. Shaw points to the paradoxical nature of Pushkin's stanza "Will the time of my freedom come?" and ponders: "The point of view expressed here is paradoxically and typically Pushkinian: he will take a 'free flight' from the Russian shore where the sea 'is hostile to me', to the friendly southern billows under the skies of 'my Africa'. However, once there, he will sigh for Russia. The important themes include 'poetic flight' (for one whose actual fleeing would have constituted a crime), travel to the south, memory of Russia from afar (from south to north, and my Africa") (Shaw in Bethea 1993: 125). Shaw convincingly argues that Pushkin's explanatory note for this stanza — published twice in 1825 and in 1829 — raises the question of his great-grandfather's return without permission from Siberian exile to Petersburg (during the reign of Anna he had been sent to Siberia under an implausible pretext) (Shaw in Bethea 1993: 126). Shaw considers Pushkin's stanza not only as a homage to his exiled grandfather, but also as an expression of desire to return to Petersburg without the Tsar's permission (ibid.). It is plausible, of course, that Nabokov could have shared Pushkin's desire to flee to Petersburg illegally. However it seems to me that Nabokov was concerned with the state of memory and historical knowledge in Russia. Pushkin's commentary to the stanza "Will the time of my freedom come?" raises the important question of memory and amnesia in relation to Russian history. Pushkin felt that his works could inscribe the story of the lives of the Russian nobility whose names became erased from historical accounts. Pushkin writes: "In Russia, where the memory of noteworthy people soon disappears for reason of lack of historical memoirs, the strange life of Annibal is known only from family traditions" (quoted in Shaw in Bethea 1993: 125). Shaw's contextual evidence suggesting the existence of important autobiographical overtones in stanza 50 in chapter one of *Eugene Onegin* helps to broaden our understanding of the significance of this passage to Nabokov, who saw himself upholding Russian aristocratic tradition.

Nabokov's personal circumstances also shed light on the themes of memory and poetic flight found in "Exile". It seems that the young poet not only pined for the traditional house that had disappeared in modern times, but also expressed a desire to transgress the captivity of his own epoch. Pushkin's dream of being united with his nanny might be perceived as an allegory for a future re-unification of the two Russian literatures that became divided after 1917: the Bolshevik revolution forced over two million prominent Russians to emigrate to Europe and America. According to Gleb Struve's painstaking survey of Russian émigré literature, Nabokov in 1925 was widely recognised as the most interesting young Russian poet to emerge in Berlin's Russian community. By the time Nabokov wrote "Exile" he had already published in Berlin two books of poetry in Russian: *Path Through the Mountains* (*Горний путь*, 1922) and *The Bunch* (*Гроздь*, 1923). Struve points out that many Russian émigré critics highly praised the artistry and inventiveness of Nabokov's poetry, detecting strong similarities between his verse and the poetry of Ivan Bunin, Maiakovsky, Pasternak and Khodasevich (Struve 1984: 165-167). Struve particularly notes Nabokov's ability to combine eleborate sound structure and alliteration with the strongly expressed physicality of his visual imagery (ibid.: 167). Struve claims that some of Nabokov's poems are exquisitely and brilliantly written, but they all give an impression that they were written by a fiction writer in that they lack a natural musical flow (ibid.: 170-71).

Nabokov's reading of Pushkin's poetry as autobiographical resonates well with Khodasevich's interpretation of Pushkin's life as expressed in his 1924 book *Pushkin's Poetic Economy* (*Поэтическое хозяйство Пушкина*) and his 1924 poem "He Left his Carriage at the Gate" («Оставил дрожки у заставы»), analysed in detail in Sandler's study on the Pushkin commemorations (Sandler 2004: 105-107). Sandler points out that several of Khodasevich's poems, articles and speeches on Pushkin indicate that Khodasevich held the strong belief that "Pushkin's poetry was autobiographical, and that all poetry shares this autobiographical project" (Sandler 2004: 106-107). Nabokov considered Khodasevich to be the most important poet of Russian emigration. Their poetry displays similar features that include the use of irony, strong intertextual links and neo-Classical overtones. In his introduction to the English edition of his novel *The Gift* (*Дар*), Nabokov writes: "The tremendous outflow of intellectuals that formed such a prominent part of the general exodus from Soviet Russia in the first years of the Bolshevist Revolution seems today like the wanderings of some mythical tribe whose bird-signs and moon-signs I now retrieve from the desert dust. We remained unknown to American intellectuals [...]. That world is now gone. Gone are Bunin, Aldanov, Remizov. Gone is Vladislav Khodasevich, the greatest Russian poet that the twentieth century has yet produced. The old intellectuals are now dying out and have not found successors in the so-called Displaced Persons of the last two decades" (Nabokov 1963: 8). Those words illuminate the concerns Nabokov expressed in "Exile" for the continuity of tradition, concerns possibly triggered by his father's death.

Perhaps, due to the strongly expressed interest in such matters as everyday life, aesthetic freedom and historical memory, but above all in the preservation of living memories of the past, Nabokov's poetry gives the impression of being an extension of his fiction. It displays a form of thinking that stands close to the genre of the novel and focuses on the interaction between poetry and novel. Bakhtin explains this thinking in terms of polyphonic vision: "What is realised in the novel is the process of coming to know one's own language as it is perceived in someone else's language, coming to know one's own conceptual horizon in someone else's horizon" (Bakhtin 1981: 365). Struve observes a strong tendency in Nabokov's poetry towards novelisation, suggesting that his verse lacks intrinsic music; he defines the surrealist grotesque entwined with parody as the trademark of Nabokov's poetry and fiction (Struve 1984: 171). In addition to Struve's observations, I would link the surrealist trait of Nabokov's poetry to the device of estrangement that adds a sense of novelty to the objects he chooses to describe: thus, the poem about exile might be seen as a deeply personal and traumatic story about visionary experiences evoking Pushkin and his works. For Nabokov, exilic discourse became associated with the condition of modernity. His "Exile" addresses the question of the discontinuity of modern experience and recognises its transitory and arbitary nature. "Exile" seeks to complete the fragment by redeeming it aesthetically and politically and by turning the readers' attention to the actual modes of experiencing modernity in everyday life. As David Frisby emphasises in his study of theories of modernity, "viewed historically, modernity could be investigated as eternal present, as a contradictory (and transitory) actuality and as prehistory" (Frisby 1986: 271).

Talking about the various events and publications in the Soviet Union in 1937 commemorating Pushkin and related to the 100th anniversary of his death, Sandler suggests that "the new slogan of realism was stretched to fit the emerging canon of Pushkin's writings" (Sandler 2004: 107). This resulted in a tight control of all the publications of Pushkin and Pushkin's scholarship. Sandler sums up this trend: "Censors and party officials kept a tight watch on quotations from the political writings, ensuring that they could not be misread as anti-revolutionary and that inferences about Pushkin's changing political views could not be easily drawn. More easily available and readily cited in academic journals and the popular press were his historical writings and lyrics with social content, such as 'My ruddy faced critic', with its understated description of life in poverty" (Sandler 2004: 107). Sandler rightly links the Pushkin celebrations to the performances of happiness and socialist achievements aimed at sidelining any manifestation of the historical experience of collective trauma associated with Stalin's terror and gulags that affected the everyday life of Soviet citizens. Sheila Fitzpatrick's painstaking study *Everyday Stalinism. Ordinary Life in Extraordinary Times: Soviet Russia in the 1930s* identifies 1937 as a peak year for Stalin's purges. The book lists the localised waves of terror that had been steadily increasing since the death in 1934 of Sergei Kirov, a popular Leningrad party leader; the trial of Zinov´ev and Kamenev in August 1936; and the mass arrests of the communist elite and hysterical witch-hunting in the first months of 1937 (including the January show trial of Iurii Piatakov and other former Communist leaders for sabotage and counter-revolutionary activities; and the removal of Nikolai Ezhov as head of the NKVD) (Fitzpatrick 1999: 194).

The Pushkin celebrations coincided with the period of the Great Retreat, which "was inaugarated at the beginning of 1935, when the lifting of bread rationing was the occasion of a propaganda campaign celebrating the end of privation and the coming of plenty" (Fitzpatrick 1999: 90). Fitzpatrick stresses that Joseph Stalin's 1935 pronouncement "Life has become better, comrades, life has become more cheerful [...] was one of the favourite slogans of the 1930s" (ibid). Fitzpatrick also remarks that "the lip-smacking public celebration of commodities in the mid 1930s was virtually a consumer-goods pornography" (ibid.). It was a shift from the anti-consumerist approach of previous years to a new appreciation of commodities — surprising for a society advocating marxist values. Nevertheless, Fitzpatrick indicates a certain kind of cultural indulgence and a rapid increase in activities associated with carnivals, concerts, jazz, dancing, parks of culture and leisure, and masquerades. Many of Pushkin's life-asserting, optimistic-sounding and hedonistic poems celebrating life's humble pleasures were published in the Soviet Union with great enthusiasm. Sandler notes that Pushkin's poem "Bacchic Song" («Вахкическая песня») that celebrates the light of the day "resonated well with the public discourse of the mid-1930s" (Sandler 2004: 108). Fitzpatrick describes at great length the emergence of a pseudo-carnivalesque atmosphere in the Soviet Union during this period. In addition to the politicised image of Pushkin produced by the Soviet establishment and the media, the trend towards the carnivalisation of Pushkin is worth mentioning. Fitzpatrick's discussion of the first carnival in Moscow in 1935 gives insight into consumers' perception of Pushkin as a romantic poet whose poetry allows the expression of intimate emotions and ideas of transitory happiness. The image of Pushkin became associated with a new wave of theatricalisation of life and the culture of parodic laughter. Fitzpatrick writes about the first Soviet carnival in Moscow: "For the first nighttime carnival, held in Gorky Park in July 1935 to celebrate Constitution Day, costumes and masks were obligatory, with a carnival parade and cash prizes for the best. Newspaper reports did not neglect the romantic possibilities of the mask, while also describing the variety of costumes worn: Pushkin's Onegin and Tatiana, Charlie Chaplin, Gorky's Mother, eighteenth-century marquesses, toreadors, Mark Anthony, and so on. Laughter was emphasised: as *Krokodil* reported, carnival slogans proposed by individual enthusiasts included 'He who does not laugh, does not eat', and 'make fun of those who fall behind!'" (Fitzpatrick 1999: 95).

Russian émigré cultural activists and authors were actively involved in the unprecedented wave of events and publications celebrating Pushkin as the living creative impulse of Russian culture. The process of commemorating Pushkin was all-inclusive: it brought together disparate groups of Russian émigrés in Prague, Belgrade, Paris, London, China and America. Among the most monumental works and interesting achievements of the Pushkinian trend in Russian émigré literature are Ariadna Tyrkova-Williams's two-volume biography of Pushkin (written in 1923-29); Raisa Lomonosoff's unpublished play "Pushkin" and Lidiya Nelidova-Fiveiskaia's narrative poem "Captive of Noble Deed" («Невольник чести»). "Captive of Noble Deed" was written in 1936 in New York as a poetic narrative of Pushkin's life; it boasts strong Lermontovean overtones not free of mannerism and melodramatic excess. The most lively depiction of the Pushkin Days in Paris in 1937 appears in Don Aminado's poem "It was raining. It was slushy. There was black ice..." («Дождь был. Слякоть. Гололедица...»). Don Aminado is the pseudonym of Arnold Petrovich Shpolianskii (1888-1957), poet and author of satirical sketches. His humorous accounts of the cultural and political life of Russians in Paris was well recorded in the form of satirical and semi-humorous poems published on the regular basis in the leading émigré newspaper *Last News* (*Последние новости*). Rendered in lively four-foot trochaic meter stanzas, his "It was raining..." contains highlights from the Pushkin Days that transformed Paris into Russian territory:

На углу ажаны кутались
В ихний плащ непромокаемый.
Под ногами дети путались
Вереницей нескончаемой.

А за ними все ценители,
Все любители словесности,
Шли их взрослые родители,
Затоплявшие окрестности.

И от площади Согласия
До предместия парижского
Шла такая катавасия,
Песни, пляски Даргомыжского.
(Don Aminado in Filin 1994: 173)

On the corner the agents hid
In their mackintoshes.
Children were getting in the way,
Walking in a long line.

And all the devotees
Of culture, lovers of literature,
Walked behind them, as well as the adult parents,
Overwhelming the surroundings.

And from the Place de la Concorde
To the Paris suburbs
There were such chaotic festival carryings-on,
Including Dargomyzhskii's songs and dances.

Don Aminado's poem alludes to Aleksandr Dargomyzhskii's opera *Mermaid* (*Rusalka*, 1948-1955) based on a Pushkin poem about the Don Juan legend and orchestrated, after his death, by Rimskii-Korsakov. It presents the Russian community of Russian literature and music lovers as carnival goers (at least for the time of the duration of the Pushkin days activities) who were seen by French police agents as a subversive force.

In light of this mass spectacle pivoting around the anniversary of Pushkin's death, Tsvetaeva's 1931-1935 cycle "Poems to Pushkin" («Стихи к Пушкину») might be seen as a powerful attack on the contemporary Russian-speaking readership and media, both within the Soviet Union and in emigration. The cycle parries the shock from mass culture's assault, not only on Pushkin but on any contemporary poet, in truly Baudelairean manner. There already exist three complementary readings of this cycle (Smith 1994; Zubova 1999; Sandler 2004), so I will only focus on the cycle's theme of violence. Sandler identifies violence as an important subject matter of

Tsvetaeva's cycle and pays special attention to the unusual recurrence of words associated with beating (through the device of paronomasia), including battle, whipping, glass breaking, and so on. More importantly, Sandler observes that Tsvetaeva's language also appears to be traumatised: "She uses the root meaning meaning *to beat* in two other ways, one in a reference to broken glass («bokal/Bityi»), the other one in commenting on a battle («bitva»). Tsvetaeva does something similar with other words and phonetic groupings in the poem, often related to themes of violence, struggle, and unexpected action" (Sandler 2004: 254). According to Liudmila Zubova's insightful observations, Tsvetaeva's cycle "Poems to Pushkin" stands out in Tsvetaeva's oeuvre as a link between her body of poetry and her prose works, including autobiographical fiction and essays: "On the one hand, this cycle is densely packed with all Tsvetaeva's favourite devices that she had developed in her previous works. On the other hand this cycle, while changing the romantic tone of her poems about Pushkin written in 1913, 1916 and 1920 into a polemical mode of expression, contains the emotional, conceptual and logical foundations of her future essays such as 'Art in the Light of Conscience' (1932), 'My Pushkin' (1936), and 'Pushkin and Pugachev' (1937)" («С одной стороны, в стихах этого цикла сконцентрированы практически все излюбленные цветаевские приемы, выработанные ею в течение всего предшествующего опыта. С другой стороны, этот цикл, меняя романтический тон стихов о Пушкине 1913, 1916 и 1920гг. на полемический, содержит в себе эмоциональные, концептуальные и логические основы будущих прозаических произведений «Искусство при свете совести» (1932), «Мой Пушкин» (1936), «Пушкин и Пугачев» (1937)) (Zubova 1999: 119).

Zubova rightly observes that Tsvetaeva highly valued Pushkin's poetry for its non-conformism, wanting to use Pushkin's name as a means to attack the conservative taste of her fellow émigré readers and workers who were antagonistic to experimental modes of expression, including the innovative language and aesthetic sensibilities of Russian avant-garde artists and poets (ibid.). Zubova sees the abundant use of the military vocabulary in "Poems to Pushkin" as a very expressive feature that focuses on the image of Pushkin as a weapon (a canon) that kills the nightingales of words. The examples of alliteration and paronomasia used in the cycle are very elaborate but Zubova considers the whole cycle as being subjugated to one phrase that equates Pushkin to the weapon that functions in the hands of so-called lovers and canonisers of Pushkin's poetry against the living creative impulse embedded in the Russian language:

> То-то к пушкинским избушкам
> Лепитесь, что сами — хлам!
> Как из душа! Как из пушки –
> Пушкиным – по соловьям
> Слова, соколам полета!
> Пушкин – в роли пулемета!
> (Tsvetaeva 1984, volume 1: 292)
>
> You are attaching yourselves to Pushkin's huts
> Because you are made up of rubble!
> You are firing, just like shower,
> From the canon-Pushkin
> The nightingales of words,
> The eagles of flights.
> You use Pushkin as a machine gun!

Zubova legitimately identifies various allusions in "Poems to Pushkin" to the poetry of Pushkin, Zhukovskii and Pasternak. I would add the significance of Tsvetaeva's cycle being written in Paris, the city that was the subject of Baudelaire's poetry. I have talked elsewhere about Tsvetaeva and Baudelaire (Smith 2004), so here I only stress that for Tsvetaeva the image of Pushkin as a precursor of modernity is entwined with the image of Baudelaire. Baudelaire remained a favourite poet of Tsvetaeva throughout her life, and her own copy of Baudelaire's *Les Fleurs du Mal* (*Flowers of Evil*), covered with numerous comments by her, is located in the National Library in Paris.

A striking feature of "Poems to Pushkin" is its excessive use of irony subjugated to the subversive interruption of speech. Tsvetaeva's irony has similar origin in *Les Fleurs du Mal*: it articulates the shock defence and counter-violence of consciousness, in response to the urban crowd's attacks on the sublime. The image of readers of Pushkin is portrayed in "Poems to Pushkin" as a homogeneous urban crowd enjoying the mass spectacle created out of

Pushkin's life and writings. Benjamin wrote that "the mass was agitated veil; through it Baudelaire saw Paris" (Benjamin 1999: 164). In his poem "To the Reader" («Au Lecteur»), for example, Baudelaire mentions the modern crowd as marionettes manipulated by the Devil — "It is the Devil who pulls the strings that move us!" («C'est le Diable qui tient les fils qui nous remuent!») (Baudelaire 1964: 18). Baudelaire's poem considers the important question of the poet's fate that is often weaved into sensationalist stories of violence reported by the media. Undoubtedly, the automatic and repetitive behaviour of readers and critics of Pushkin eager to take control of his life's story merged in Tsvetaeva's imagination with the story of Maiakovskii's life and death. In 1930 Tsvetaeva published a cycle of poems "To Maiakovskii" («Маяковскому») in which she commemorated him, at the same time vehemently attacking the special issue of *The Literary Newspaper* (*Литературная газета*) dedicated to Maiakovskii's suicide:

> *Литературная* – не в ней
> Суть, а вот кровь пролейте!
> *Выходит каждые семь дней.*
> Ушедший – раз в столетье
> Приходит. Сбит передовой
> Боец. Каких, столица,
> Еще тебе вестей, какой
> Еще передовицы?
> (Tsvetaeva 1990: 405)

> *The Literary Newspaper* – there is no point in it;
> Try instead to bleed yourself!
> *It appears every seven days.*
> But the deceased one like this
> Appears in our world once a century.
> This front-line soldier
> Is shot dead. What other news,
> Capital of ours, do you need
> For your front page?

The concerns over technologically produced, reproduced and modified artistic images and works of literature, voiced in Tsvetaeva's "To Maiakovskii" and "To Pushkin" anticipate similar anxieties expressed in Benjamin's seminal 1936 article "The Work of Art in the Age of Mechanical Reproduction". In her cycle of poems "To Pushkin" Tsvetaeva talks about reproduced images of Pushkin and his works and compares the process of appropriation of Pushkin to a machine gun. This image highlights the accelerated process of printing newspapers and books. In the manner of Eisenstein's montage of attractions, Tsvetaeva in "To Pushkin" creates a collision between various images of Pushkin and his works. The tension and struggle between the authentic story of Pushkin's life and artificially created legends are brought to the fore in the most dynamic way possible, paving the way to the intensified physicality of the scenes in her cycle. Her mode of expression, oriented towards verbalisation of physical sensation of pain and muscle tension, resembles Baudelaire's technique. As Wallace Fowlie asserts, "Modern poetry presupposes a system of metaphysics. It affirms, first with the example of Baudelaire and later with the philosophy of Bergson, that the poet should place himself in the very centre of what is real and merge his consciousness and his sensibility with the universe" (Fowlie in Baudelaire 1964: 3).

The highly stylised speech employed in "Poems to Pushkin" weaves numerous allusions to the images of Pushkin created by Russian poets, scholars and film-makers. Tsvetaeva sees Paris, so to speak, in manner akin to that of Baudelaire: through the agitated veil of the crowd of Russian critics, authors, readers and other representatives of the Russian diaspora in Paris. Thus one of the cycle's poems, "Poet and Tsar" («Поэт и царь»), evokes two of the first films dedicated to Pushkin's death: Vassilii Goncharov's "The Life and Death of Pushkin" («Жизнь и смерть Пушкина» 1910) and Vladimir Gardin's "Poet and Tsar" («Поэт и царь» 1927) which narrate the last days of Pushkin's life. Both films reflect on the popular opinion existing in the 1910s-1920s that Pushkin initiated his own death and provoked Georges d'Anthès to duel. Tsvetaeva's "To Pushkin" produces novelistic images of speech modes that she hears around herself: a range of voices, from those who see Pushkin as subversive and rebellious, to those who wish to portray him as a liberally minded conservative thinker. Her cycle therefore presents the concept of the Pushkin myth in polyphonic manner, underpinning numerous appropriations of Pushkin by contemporary readers.

Bearing in mind that "Poems to Pushkin" was written in exile, it is important to see it as a poetic narrative recreation of exile. Exiled authors define themselves in relation to what is absent, their homeland, which they simultaneously accept and deny, so their representation of homeland is infused with irony. "Poems to Pushkin" allegorically demonstrates memory as a revisionary act, presenting history as an exercise in narrating memory. Tsvetaeva laughs at the imaginary Pushkin, a cultural construct who became interchangeable with the absent homeland, suggesting that any act of memory is fluid and fragmentary.

Tsvetaeva views memory as a narrative of homecoming and at the same time rebuffs the utopian dream of the possibility of return. She skillfully demonstrates in "Poems to Pushkin" that origin is recoverable only through mnemonic traces that blend into delusion. A search for one Pushkin as an imaginary dwelling is doomed to failure, because the images of home possessed by exiles keep changing. In "Poems to Pushkin" Tsvetaeva presents these images as shattered and scattered, through the articulation of the theme of violence and through repeated use of dashes that prevent a smooth reading of the texts of Pushkin to which she alludes in the cycle. The novelistic images that Tsvetaeva creates in the cycle advertise the problematic nature of return: they encourage Pushkin's readers' desire to return to the homeland that they shared with Pushkin, but at the same time estrange them from the images they hold onto, demonstrating that products of memory amount to fiction.

Tsvetaeva turns the narrative engagement into a dialectical relationship between desire and loss. For example, through several repetitions of Pushkin's name three times at the end of the poem, she demonstrates the process of alienation from the object that any mechanical reproduction of art brings about. Tsvetaeva is highlighting that any mechanical repetition and automation of life destroys the living creative impulse and the very possibility of creativity through the lack of phenomenological distance from the text with which readers empathise:

> Пушкин, Пушкин, Пушкин — имя
> Благородное — как брань
> Площадную — попугаи.
> Пушкин? Очень испугали!

(Tsvetaeva 1984, volume 1: 293)

Pushkin, Pushkin, Pushkin — the noble
Name — that you use as the marketplace's
Swearing word — repeating it like parrots.
Pushkin? You make me so frightened!

In her insightful analysis of this poem, Zubova detects the presence of dialogised speech. On the one hand, Zubova identifies Pushkin's own voice constructed through the usage of words and connotations relating to military vocabulary, suggesting a semantic association between the surname Pushkin and the word «canon» (пушка). Such a reading of Pushkin's art adds an avant-garde stance to Tsvetaeva's understanding of modernity that inevitably relied on such devices as defamiliarisation and parody in order to secure literary evolution. On the other hand, in oxymoronic manner, by bringing together the notion of the noble name that become as devalued as the marketplace swear word, Zubova suggests Tsvetaeva's own appreciation of the sublime nature and uniqueness of Pushkin's talent. The avant-garde theory of the non-organic work of art, as Bürger convincingly argues, could be well explained in terms of Benjamin's concept of allegory, developed in his analysis of the literature of the Baroque.

Bürger's schema extracted from the analysis of Benjamin's concept of allegory, can be successfully applied to the analysis of Tsvetaeva's treatment of the Pushkin myth in "Poems to Pushkin". Bürger suggests three components: 1: "The allegorist pulls one element out of the totality of the life context, isolating it, depriving it of its function. Allegory is therefore essentially fragment and thus the opposite of the organic symbol"; 2: "The allegorist joins the isolated reality fragments and thereby creates meaning. This is posited meaning; it does not derive from the original context of the fragments"; 3: "Benjamin interprets the activities of the allegorist as the expression of melancholy [...]. Allegory, whose essence is fragment, represents history as decline [...] in allegory, the observer is confronted with the [...] deathmask of history as a petrified primordial landscape" (Bürger 1984: 69). Thus, in Tsvetaeva's cycle we come across various manifestations of the Pushkin myth and parodic renderings of numerous jubilee speeches commemorating the poet —

the final meaning posited in the text is based on the dialectical and dialogised relationship between the two competing tendencies: to forget and to remember. The construction of the meaning of Tsvetaeva's cycle depends upon readers' ability to embrace the principle of open-endedness. Tsvetaeva accentuates the decline of history through her references to Pushkin in the cycle as the last poet and as the last gift of Peter the Great to Russia, in contrast to her definition of Nicholas I as the first murderer of poets («певцоубийца царь Николай Первый»).

Tsvetaeva also questions the ethics of reading: it is clear from her cycle that she is vehemently opposed to what Nabokov identified as "smooth reading" of poetry, a reading with no intellectual engagement in the text being read. Tsvetaeva's concerns for the imagination of the semi-educated, with a reductivist reading of Pushkin, anticipates Nabokov's conscious attempts to resist production of a *Eugene Onegin* translation tailored to the average reader's needs. In his foreword to *Eugene Onegin* Nabokov distinguishes himself from the translators who produce what he defines as readable translations, palatable for consumption by a semi-educated readership: "I have been always amused by the stereotyped compliment that a reviewer pays the author of a 'new translation'. He says: 'It reads smoothly.' In other words, the hack who has never read the original, and does not know its language, praises an imitation readable because easy platitudes have replaced in it the intricacies of which he is unaware" (Nabokov in Pushkin 1964: ix). Tsvetaeva's cycle also questions the ethics of reading that devalues the creative potential of poetic texts. Her autobiographical essay "My Pushkin" strongly articulates the connection between modes of reading and ethics, by demonstrating her act of reading Pushkin creatively as the process with the most significant impact on her formation as a poet.

In attacking the uncreative use of Pushkin's language in modern context by numerous authors, readers and critics, Tsvetaeva is referring not only to Pushkin's death per se, but also to the destruction of the Russian language both in the Soviet Union and among the Russian diaspora in Paris. Unlike Khodasevich, Tsvetaeva refused to read Pushkin's writings as largely autobiographical, implying the disappearance of Pushkin into the realms of the language itself. In his discussion of Mallarmé's poetry, Blanchot explains the same vision of the poet's death as exemplified in Tsvetaeva's "Poems to Pushkin" and "My Pushkin": "It is not enough to say that things dissipate and the poet is effaced; you still have to say that both of them, while not experiencing any actual destruction, assert themselves in this disappearance itself and in the development of this disappearance — one vibratory, the other elocutory. Nature is transposed by language into the rhythmic movement that makes it disappear, endlessly and indefinitely; and the poet, by the fact that he speaks poetically, disappears into the language and becomes the very disappearance that is accomplished in language, the only initiator and principle: the source. 'Poetry, ritual.' The 'omission of self', 'death of the individual', which is linked to the poetic rite, thus makes poetry into an actual sacrifice, but not in view of vague magic exaltations — for an almost technical reason: because the one who speaks poetically exposes himself to the kind of death necessarily at work in actual speech" (Blanchot 2003: 229).

Blanchot's insightful comment on poetic evolution helps explain Tsvetaeva's preoccupation with images of death and violence in "Poems to Pushkin", since she speaks of the theme of death in a double-voiced manner: laying the death of poet at the door of readers and of modern bureaucrats, and through natural disappearance into the language. In "Art in the Light of Conscience" («Искусство при свете совести»), published in 1931-32, Tsvetaeva demonstrates a reading of Pushkin's "Hymn to the Plague" from his tragedy in verse "Feast at the Time of the Plague" («Пир во время Чумы») and suggests that the poet's immortality is located not in the vicinity of God but is guaranteed by the immortality of nature itself and of readers who also are part of nature. In this essay Tsvetaeva suggests not to read smoothly Pushkin's line praising the plague, but to develop a moral judgement. She proposes breaking the spell of an automatic reading of the lines praising destruction, and instead awaking conscience from its deep sleep.

Tsvetaeva's profound interest in Bergson's comic theory is evident in her various games with readers, including the numerous examples of self-mockery in «Poems to Pushkin» and "Art in the Light of Conscience" that demonstrate how to achieve a novel experience in reading a familiar text through defamiliarisation. Any Russian reader of Tsvetaeva's cycle might also easily recognise that

Tsvetaeva fashions herself in the clothes of the author-fool when she even mocks herself as an author and reader of Pushkin. Likhachev and Alexander Panchenko, in their seminal study of laughter in medieval Russia, argue that authors mocking themselves and undermining their own narrative discourse enables the authors who pretend to be holy fools to reveal the absurd nature of the world and society in which they live: "Authors pretend to be fools, 'play the fool', create nonsense and feign incomprehension. In actual fact they believe themselves to be clever, and only portray themselves as fools in order to be free in their laughter. Their 'authorial image' is necessary for their 'comic work', which consists in both 'making nonsense' [durit´] and 'nonsensifying' ['vozdurit´'] the whole world" (Likhachev and Panchenko, quoted in Roberts 1997: 37-38).

Tsvetaeva's appropriation of the primordial worldview in her demonstration of misreading of Pushkin's works is rooted in Tsvetaeva's long-standing interest in Russian folklore, especially manifest in her long narrative poems that use folkore stories and imagery, such as "Side-Streets" («Переулочки»), "The Swain" («Молодец») and "Tsar-Maiden" («Царь-Девица»). In his review of Tsvetaeva's narrative poem "The Swain", Dmitrii Mirskii points to the existence in Tsvetaeva's poetry of the Bergsonian simultaneity that blends folkloric tradition, the living grassroots of art and contemporary rhythms: "Word for Tsvetaeva is more ontological than object; it bypasses the object and connects itself with the essentials of life; it is absolute, self-contained, untranslatable. Her poems are inseparable from the Russian language, they are the most inseparable from the Russian tradition in all contemporary poetry. And while for Pasternak rhythm represents an abstract scheme [...], for Tsvetaeva it signifies the essence of the poem, the poem itself, its soul, its nourishing living impulse. Pasternak's rhythm conveys Kantian time, and Tsvetaeva's rhythm expresses the Bergsonian flow of time" («Слово для нее 'онтологичнее' вещи, — прямо, мимо вещи связано с сущностями, абсолютно, самоценно, независимо и непереводимо. Стихи ее неотрывно русские, самые неотрывно-русские во всей современной поэзии. И ритм, который для Пастернака только данная схема [...] для Марины Цветаевой — сущность стиха, сам стих, его душа, его живящее начало. Пастернаковский ритм — кантовское, Цветаевский — Бергсоновское время») (Mirskii, quoted in Shevelenko 2002: 317).

Thus the disjunctive and jolting rhythmical patterns found in "Poems to Pushkin" might be also seen as an expression of the modern poetic consciousness that needs to parry the shock of everyday life in the metropolis.

Although Mirskii does not extrapolate the value of Bergsonian time to Tsvetaeva's poetics, we can infer that by this definition of Tsvetaeva's rhythm Mirskii implies that her rhythmical patterns are based on the collision of traditional and new rhythms reflecting the accelerated pace of cognition in modern times. She narrates Pushkin's life and works cinematographically at such a fast pace that the poem's rhythmical patterns amount to a polyphonic rendering of writing with camera-like lenses in mind, in the style of marching, running and walking. The subject presented in her cycle becomes dynamically mutiplied and pluralised in many viewpoints, which at the same time approach the object of her discussion. Thus the Pushkin myth as an object of the cycle becomes deconstructed by the pluralised subject, paving the way to a state of fragmentation and multi-perspectivism in which the interaction between subject and object is kept alive.

Pushkinian readings of the city in pain & dynamics of subjectivity in Russian contemporary poetry

In his preface to the book *Russia's Alternative Prose*, Robert Porter reflects on those works that have emerged in the West since the early 1960s calling for a new classification for dissonant voices in post-war Soviet literature. As Porter points out, many recent studies referred to the alternative type of Soviet writing which did not conform to the West's stereotyped perception of 'Soviet Literature'. Attempts to lump together various subcultural and unconventional works that subverted the stifling canon of Socialist Realist literature have led to a perception that the post-Stalin revival of the modernist tradition gave way to the birth of alternative forms of expression based on subjectivity, critical evaluation of reality and scornful attitudes towards the dominant culture. Porter's list of subversive literary texts includes dissident literature, literature published only outside the Soviet Union or in samizdat, and works "which had squeezed through all the procedures which then, in Soviet times, were operative and had achieved official publication, only to be vilified by conservative critics" (Porter 1994: 1).

Porter also surveys the 1990s discussions in the Russian media that investigated the postmodernist tenets of post-1985 Russian literature that critics juxtaposed with cultural developments of the Thaw period. In the rapidly growing scholarship on Russian postmodernism of the 1990s, the role of post-Stalin culture in the formation of the Russian postmodernist worldview and aesthetics is increasingly acknowledged. As Mark Lipovetsky observes, "despite the fact that the aesthetics of the 'sixties generation' was oriented primarily toward the traditions of Russian realism, this generation played a crucial role in the history of Russian postmodernism" (Lipovetsky 1999: 316). While this is true, it is also important to bear in mind that not all authors working in the Soviet Union in the 1950s-1960s can be treated as representatives of the Thaw generation of authors known for their utopian aspirations and commitment to social change. Lipovetsky asserts: "Joseph Brodsky or Sergei Dovlatov, who are the same age as Yevgeny Yevtushenko and Andrei Voznesensky, do not belong to the generation of the Thaw, because they never had any illusions about the possibility of 'improving' socialism on the basis of humanist values and because they never shared the almost religious belief in the ideals of the revolution that was typical of the Thaw culture on the whole" (ibid.).

Lipovetsky's remarks imply that the 1960s generation of Soviet authors was divided into various subcultural groups with a distinctive worldview that was manifested in their experiments and new modes of expression. Yet, despite that today many scholars see Brodsky and Bitov as the forerunners of Russian postmodernism of the 1990s, their links with the Leningrad 'underground' culture of the post-Stalin period is often overlooked. In the light of recent studies on Soviet 'underground' culture and Russian literature of the post-Soviet period, it is timely to investigate the roots of Brodsky's postmodernist outlook and to assess the literary output of his fellow-authors who might have been influencing him. Below I discuss the group of Leningrad authors of the 1950s-1960s in the light of the picaro myth that marks their works and ascribes them with distinctly dissonant qualities.

Firstly, Alexander Kushner — whose poetic oeuvre awaits rediscovery — should be viewed as a poet of great importance to the young Brodsky. His experimental poetry has not caught the critics' eye until relatively recently. American scholar Vitaly Chernetsky, for example, approaches Kushner as something of both the outsider and participant in cultural developments of the Thaw Period. Chernetsky labels Kushner as "the semi-dissident St Petersburg poet" but points out that Vladimir Druk's playful statement that "Pushkin is Kushner" reads like an oxymoron (Chernetsky 2000: 156). Following several decades of non-recognition by Soviet critics, Kushner was finally awarded the Pushkin prize for his literary achievements in July 2001. In John Elsworth's view, Kushner in the 1960s was "overshadowed at the time by poets who gained a mass following from the topicality of their themes" and in his later career his writings of an "uncommitted and non-ideological nature" were officially condemned on many occasions (Elsworth 1998: 479). Kushner's recently published memoirs and interviews testify that, together with Bitov and Brodsky, Kushner has established himself as an important representative of the Leningrad subcultural authors who, at the beginning of their careers, opposed the Soviet literary mainstream. In the 1950s-1960s they were closely associated with surviving advocates of the modernist tradition, such as Lidiia Ginzburg and Akhmatova, with whom they shared similar values relating to historical self-consciousness and cultural renaissance. In a nutshell, the formation of their selves lay outside both the dominant cultural paradigm of socialist realism and of the Thaw writing that was more prominent in Moscow.

In her 1980 essay "We are one with law and order..." ("И заодно с правопорядком...") Ginzburg comments on this period with a sense of nostalgia: "Beginning in the mid-1950s some of us became active in the thaw. We assumed the rights of the older generation, the keepers of the flame, around whom the youthful renaissance could develop. A major sign of renewal was the stormy outpouring of verse in which everyone suddenly — also for a short time — placed their faith. This period brought historical self-consciousness both to the older generation and to the youth, although it was an extremely precarious consciousness. The renaissance did not gather strength and thus dried up; youth did not mature, and somehow we lost interest in each other" (Ginzburg 1988: 230). While the impact of Akhmatova on the formation of the worldview of Kushner,

Brodsky and Anatolii Naiman is well documented (Naiman 1991; Kralin 1990), the influence of Ginzburg on young Leningrad authors of the 1950-1960s seems to be unjustly forgotten.

Alongside Akhmatova, Ginzburg as the upholder of the Formalist tradition in criticism and having been a victim of Stalin's anti-Semitic campaign against cosmopolitanism was a cult figure among young authors who were anxious to develop the modernist tradition suppressed by the 1930s-1940s Soviet cultural establishment. Jane Harris, Ginzburg's friend for many decades, said after Ginzburg's death on July 15 1990 she would be remembered not only as an established literary theorist and critic but also "as a splendid conversationalist, as a beloved mentor and constant support for young writers, poets and literary scholars, as a reliable spokesperson for her generation, and above all, as the author of remarkable prose narratives, essays, and 'notebooks'" (Harris 1994: 145). In her 1986 interview "Field of Tension" ("Поле напряжения") Ginzburg said that she had almost no disciples. Nevertheless, she also suggested that some young writers did learn something from her, especially Bitov, who became a genuine prose writer, and Kushner, who became a genuine poet (Ginzburg 1986: 7).

Ginzburg's concept of special language related to a cultural space shared by a particular generation (Ginzburg 1989: 382-83) is fully applicable to Kushner, Bitov and Brodsky, especially because in their essays and interviews they all point to the existence of a common bond, highlighting the importance of their generation to the emergence of a distinctive creative outlook that might be defined as alternative. Thus Brodsky in his Nobel Prize acceptance speech stressed his dependence on the Leningrad circle of authors of the 1950s-1960s who maintained a link between modern and postmodern cultures: "My generation contributed to the development of modernist ideas in Russia. And I'm proud that I am part of this generation" (Brodsky 1992: 14). Brodsky goes on to assert that his bond with the Leningrad generation of the 1950s-1960s made his Nobel award possible.

The interconnectedness between many important Leningrad authors of the 1950s-1960s extended beyond personal friendship, although it might be worth noting that a special role in this process can be ascribed to both Kushner and Ginsburg. Kushner, a close friend of Bitov and Brodsky, was well-known in Leningrad subculture as a guru of the movement definable as the alternative to the Thaw generation. In the words of Bitov, although all representatives of this alternative writing, including Ginsburg and Berkovsky, learned much from the contemporaries of the Russian modernists, to a great extent the young authors also learned from each other. For Bitov it is noteworthy that Ginzburg stands out not just a scholar and disciple of the established Russian Formalist scholar Iurii Tynianov, but also as a founder of the experimental literary criticism that brings together creative writing and scholarship (Bitov 1994: 244). In a recently published interview, Kushner comments that in 1956 he and his friends discovered the works of Russian modernists such as Tsvetaeva, Khodasevich, Kuzmin, Mandelshtam, Akhmatova and Pasternak: "When there arose the opportunity to read all of these through, it became a remarkable event in our lives. Everybody read poetry together" (Kushner in McFayden 2000: 21). Yet in his essay "Here on Earth" («Здесь на земле» 1996) Kushner insists that Leningrad post-Stalin poetry was not as loud as the Moscow version, because it was more intimate, voicing the loneliness and existential outlook that was part of the landscape. "If Brodsky were to have been born in Moscow," muses Kushner, "a lot of things would have turned out differently for him. He would have never met those people, whom he met when he was nineteen or twenty years old. Most importantly, however, he would have been left without the company of 'sunless, gloomy gardens and the voice of the softly spoken Muse' " (Kushner 1998: 236). In other words, Kushner suggests that in the formative years of his generation's authors, the city itself was used as important subject matter for the new writing, acting perhaps as an interlocutor.

David MacFayden, in his assessment of Brodsky's evolution as a poet, states: "The arrogant materialist, who shapes the world, becomes the Christian existentialist who chooses to shape the world, in imitation of a divine precursor. The existentialist climbs in order to reach that before which he must fall." (McFayden 2000: 8). By examining Brodsky's pre-American writing, in conjunction with the texts written by other representatives of the Leningrad generation of authors who came to prominence in the 1950s-1960s (notably Bitov and Kushner), it is possible to identify the roots of Brodsky's existential worldview that was characteristic of innovative Leningrad writing of this period as a whole. In Brodsky's view, his generation managed to create a new language of representation that is not only post-Holocaust, but also post-Stalin. "My generation," asserts Brodsky, "was destined to come to this world, it seems, in order to continue things that were meant to disappear in the Nazi gas chambers and in Stalin's nameless gulags" (Brodsky 1992: 14).

Another tragic event contributing to the formation of the existential worldview during the Thaw period was the Leningrad blockade of 1942-1943 in which two million people died. Bitov in his 1990 interview with Evgenii Shklovskii points out that post-war Leningrad was a city of huge ethical potential. As Bitov reminds us, the city survived the "horrendous blockade, which, as it is known now, was not that inevitable, for it was the result of some military strategy, or something worse." (Bitov 1991: 10). Bitov's outspoken criticism of the Soviet authorities, who in 1946 launched their merciless campaign against Zoshchenko and Akhmatova, suggests that this campaign targeted the whole city renowned for a liberal atmosphere that was deemed threatening to the Soviet regime. As Bitov puts it, "Nevertheless, Leningrad formed a huge ethical potential from this tragedy, expressed in tiredness, resurrection and dignity. Therefore the 1946 campaign was not only against Zoshchenko and Akhmatova, but also against Leningrad, against its intelligentsia, who started to raise its head" (Bitov 1991: 10-11).

The context I have outlined for the purpose of reading Leningrad's post-Stalin texts provides a useful insight into the world of the Shakespearean masquerade, in which authors have to mask their inner selves and explore artistically the precarious relation of modern man to the devalued society he lives in. In this light, it comes as no surprise that the Leningrad texts of the 1950s-1960s (to be examined below) seem to create a new paradigm of representation of the city: the image of the idle flâneur prevalent at the onset of Russian modernism is replaced with the image of the picaro, or half-outsider. Given that the picaro lives at the diminishing point where life and death, truth and falsehood, good and evil appear as tragically convertible, the Leningrad of the post-Stalin period fits the setting for 'cosmic homelessness', to use Camus's expression (Camus in Blackburn 1979: 16). In other words, the political context of the marginal world of Leningrad in Soviet times, as defined in Bitov's essay "Family Relations" («Связан фамильно»), gave way to the emergence of marginal men who were compelled to live in two worlds, adopting the role of cosmopolitan and stranger.

Alexander Blackburn's redefinition of the picaresque tradition in terms of the picaresque myth provides us with a concept more applicable to twentieth-century narratives than any other framework based on pure generic criteria. As Blackburn convincingly argues, "Now Western civilisation as a whole could be described as 'picaresque': the picaro is modern man without faith." (Blackburn 1979: 25). Reflecting on recent studies on the picaresque mode of writing, Blackburn continues by explaining his understanding of the picaresque myth thus: "The critical focus is no longer narrowed to the subject matter or episodic autobiographies of Spanish fiction. Rather, the presence is recognised of something universal, the trickster hero of folklore recreated as the lonely individual cut off from, though yearning for, community and love" (ibid.). Therefore it becomes possible to use the modal approach as a legitimate starting point for a generic inquiry into the picaresque, although such an approach is open to criticism by the advocates of the historical study of generic traditions. This problem is addressed in Ulrich Wicks's study *Picaresque Narratives, Picaresque Fictions: A Theory and Research Guide* which lays the foundations for further investigations into the picaresque and provides us with extensive analysis of the picaresque mode of writing as manifested in modern and postmodern European and American fiction. As Wicks states, "The problems that exist at the modal level will persist — and multiply manyfold — as we move into the thick of the phenomena, the texts themselves. Only they can provide the building blocks for constructing our hypothetical fiction P. The picaresque mode, as conceived by Scholes, Jolles, and Guillén, has provided the foundation" (Ulrich 1989: 51).

As I will demonstrate, some of the 1950s-1960s texts of Leningrad authors convey the myth of the picaro, rather than call for revolutionary transformations of society, as the most prominent Moscow poets of the Thaw period urged literature to do. By contrast, the early writings of Bitov, Kushner and Brodsky express the picaresque point of view, for "the myth of the picaro emerges as the negative journey of the soul toward order, meaning, and that full humanity implied by the word love" (Wicks 1989: 51). Furthermore, according to Wicks's summary of the main features usually ascribed to the picaro, he stands out as "a protean figure who cannot only serve many masters but play different roles, and his essential character is his inconstancy (of life roles, of self-identity), his own personality flux in the face of an inconstant world" (Wicks 1989: 60). Various manifestations of the picaro myth are embedded in the early poetry of Kushner and Brodsky that also use Petersburg locations as a chaotic landscape. It helps them present the picaro's personality flux which mimics the inconstant world itself. Given that Bitov and Kushner were close friends in the 1950s-1960s, it does not come as a surprise that in his poem "Two Boys" («Два мальчика», 1962), which is dedicated to Bitov, Kushner establishes his kinship with Bitov by presenting the two delinquent boys. The poet affectionately calls these two friends 'two charming rogues' («два обормотика»), portraying them going up and down on the same swing in the imaginary playground where there is "no sadness, no love, no mean scoundrels" ("ни горя, ни любви, ни мелкой сволочи") (Kushner 1962). Kushner chooses to mould his own self in the image of the picaro whose life is fragmented and shattered. At the end of the poem Kushner, an adult author, asserts that he might be one of the boys who are used as the object of this poem. In other words, the link between the author and the object of his narration is severely disrupted. To this end, the alienation from the narrator's own self takes place in this discursive narrative in the most puzzling way, since the confessional statement "I think I am one of these boys" («Я думаю, что я один из этих мальчиков») implies the existence of the well-hidden delinquent self that Kushner so skillfully masks.

Kushner's poem "A Photograph" («Фотография», 1966) also portrays the Leningrad picaro of the 1960s, who is symbolically expressive of the nihilism, unreality and disintegration of one's identity that blurs with the unreal landscape of the city. The narrator of the poem contemplates a photograph in which he appears next to the Neva as an idle walker with two noses and a surreal-looking cheek: "Under the clear sky/ Above the transparent river Neva/ I am walking: I have two noses/ and a squashed cheek" («Под сквозными небесами,/ Над пустой Невой — рекой/ Я иду с двумя носами/ И расплывчатой щекой») (Kushner 1962). The narrator's comment on the photograph defines the image as that of an ordinary city dweller («городской обычный житель»). The narrator, the subject of the photograph, congratulates the photographer for producing the best yet image of him: "I look like a typical city dweller./ This is your success, my photographer./ Your amateur photograph/ is the best picture of me so far" («Городской обычный житель./ То, фотограф, твой успех./ Ты заснял меня, любитель,/ Безусловно лучше всех»). In picaresque vein, the narrator of Kushner's "A Photograph" observes the disintegration of his image into a dual self: "My life within a second was stretched into two moments" («Растянулась на два мига/ Жизнь мгновенная моя»). Needless to say, the humorous allusion to two noses in Kushner's poem might be seen as a playful appropriation of Gogol's image of the wandering nose detached from the body of its master in the picaresque story "The Nose" («Нос»). Yet the narrator perceives his double self as something ordinary, in common with other inhabitants of Petersburg, exposing their sinister double identities. The embankment of the Neva is immortalised in Pushkin's *Eugene Onegin* and in Pushkin's self-portrait that depicts Pushkin and Onegin leaning against a balustrade. Arguably Kushner turns the static image of Pushkin's alter ego (double self) into the animated presentation of self-conscious theatricality: "Leaning against the balustrade/ I am running somewhere in such a manner/ That I am almost not present/ On the deserted side of the river" («Прижимаясь к парапету,/ Я куда-то так бегу,/ Что меня почти — что нету/ На пустынном берегу»).

The narrator's journey and symbolic flight into chaos clearly puts him in conflict with the society not understanding that he masks his loneliness and does not belong to the world of order and meaning. In the final stanza the narrator couches his interaction with society in the overtones of tragicomedy: "At home my family will say:/ 'This is charming, /For some reason you have three arms...'/ I'll reply to them, 'This is how it really happened!/ Don't worry about this trifle'" («Дома скажут: 'Очень мило!/ Почему-то три руки...'/ Я отвечу: 'Так и было!/ Это, право, пустяки'»). Pushkin's landscape presented in the first chapter of *Eugene Onegin* that boasts a harmonious and rationalised space becomes severely distorted in Kushner's poem. However, this distortion enables the poet to establish new modes of representation that would correspond to the fragmented self shaped by the post-Stalin worldview. What Kushner's poem seems to affirm is that it is not ethical for a poet of the post-Stalin era to write a city landscape using Pushkin's language and happy imagery. Kushner violently breaks the representations of the city presented in Pushkin's canonical texts on Petersburg writen in the style of odic tradition (such as the introductory parts of "The Bronze Horseman" and *Eugene Onegin*, as discussed earlier), to the effect that his poetic persona stands out as nothing but an ugly monster with two noses and three arms. This image seems to be a particularly powerful symbol of the irrationality and marginality in the city created by Peter the Great, who in his battle to establish reason and order had institutionalised all deviations from bodily perfection in his museum of monsters, known as the Kunstkamera.

In fact, Kushner's "A Photograph" lends itself to interpretation as a distorted reproduction of Pushkin's self-portrait. The disturbing walk, captured in the photograph described in Kushner's poem, takes place on the bank opposite Peter the Great's Kuntskamera, near the Admiralty and the beginning of Nevskii Prospekt. In other words, Kushner's lyric pesona is pushed to the margins of organised space and feels displaced. To some extent, the lyric persona's self-representation seem to symbolise the animal world and pre-civilised existence. Kushner's text reveals an impulse of negation and reduction to an individual consciousness, one that existed before the creation of the city that was supposed to celebrate the Enlightenment's vision of a civilised world. Kushner reiterates the state of mind of the 'invisible' man and strip his social masks to expose his profound solitude. In the words of Blackburn, "Picaresque myth may be an ultimate kind of humanism whereby we are led to a tower or abyss from which to contemplate and accept life as it is with all its folly" (Blackburn 1979: 202).

Blackburn's definition of the picaro as "essentially a con artist" and "potentially a poet-maker of new social identities and new cultures" who "presents a masquerade of episodic adventures that are inevitably 'to be continued' as long as experience remains open and mankind sane and human" (ibid.) is fully applicable to Brodsky's poetic persona of the 1950s-1960s. In his 1961 short cycle of poems "Three Chapters" («Три главы») Brodsky simulates the existence of a Petersburg novel that was used by him for the formation of his self. The images of the Liteinyi Prospekt portrayed by Brodsky are autobiographical, since the poet used to live on this street before his emigration to America. It is worth bearing in mind that autobiographical is the most appropriate form for expressing the picaresque myth, with its semantic overtones related to a literature of loneliness. In the style of picaresque novels, Brodsky's fragments from the novel of his own life bring to the fore the moral passion and honesty of an authentic experience.

The images of the Liteinyi Prospekt, as conveyed in Brodsky's cycle, evoke tragic memories of past experiences that relate both to the poet and to the city as the whole. Disturbing references to walking shoes, World War II, an empty street and empty staircases create an atmosphere of grief and alienation: "In my noisy Baltic motherland/ in the middle of the sick half-spring/ the semi-shoes will move loudly/ along the staircase of half-war" («[...] на шумной родине балтийской/ среди худой полувесны/ протарахтят полуботинки./ По лестнице полувойны...») (Brodsky 1992, volume 1: 50) The narrator urges his memory to witness the empty surface of the Liteinyi Prospekt: "Oh, memory,/ Have a look at the way this street looks empty/ with the only surface under the heels,/ with the bend of Liteinyi Bridge" («О, память,/ смотри, как улица пуста,/ один асфальт под каблуками/ наклон Литейного моста») (ibid.). The city looks terrifying and unreal in its cruel indifference to the fate of its dwellers. As the poet asserts, "they will not catch you here; they will not kill you; they will not go mad; they will take you to a poet; warmth, treachery, orphanage" (ibid.). Furthermore, the poet disguises himself as picaro who understands the tricks of the city played on its inhabitants, because he is a trickster himself who concerns himself with artefacts. His solitude elevates him to a position from which he could fully comprehend his life that rises above "the half truth of existence" («над полуправдой бытия»). The poet negates the possibility of a spiritual transformation of the world and accepts the world of theatricality, since he is a person with many selves who can adapt to any social environment: "well, we will change everything, move elsewhere,/ we will survive, half-breathing" («что ж, переменим, переедем,/ переживем, полудыша») (Brodsky 1992: 53).

Brodsky's narrative poem "Petersburg Novel" («Петербургский роман», 1961), which to some extent might be defined as a picaresque novel in verse, inscribes into the text the KGB headquarters located on the Liteinyi Prospekt and the security services as contemporary embodiments of the ideology of order and reason:

"The Liteinyi Prospekt, the greyish fortress, entry number four of KGB headquarters" («Литейный, бежевая крепость,/ подъезд четвертый кгб»); "I praise you, security services,/ and I denounce human reason" («хвала тебе, госбезопасность,/ людскому разуму хула») (Brodsky 1992, volume 1: 68-9). The picaro's identity is constructed in juxtaposition with the city presented as the real hero of the narrative: "I should not be here any longer, since my protagonist is my city, not me" («нельзя мне более. В романе/ не я, а город мой герой»). The narrator becomes gradually detached from himself and compares himself to a person looking at mirrors, or attending a theatre show where he feels completely lonely: "and he goes to a little theatre, where he will feel lonely once again" («и едет в маленький театр, где будет сызнова один») (ibid.: 69). This narrative poem is dedicated to Anatolii Naiman, and undoubtedly it strongly echoes Akhmatova's "Poem Without a Hero", which also features mirrors, theatrical imagery and the semi-veiled images of landscapes that are associated with Soviet law and institutions. The space of Petersburg is presented in Brodsky's narrative as a stage of a cosmic tragedy that is also comic, in the style of Pushkin's comic apocalypse discussed earlier in chapter two. In his lonely walks along the city's streets the narrator becomes both amused and amazed at the banality of urban theatricality, which he presents as if he is drunk and confused. Thus, in Chekhovian manner he exclaims to himself, while leaning against the wall and trying to find his way home from Tavrisheskii Park: "Oh, my God! I am lost." He longs for death as a more orderly home for himself: "Taxi, cathedral. I can't understand./ The Officers' Place; the May Ball;/ Order a funeral service for yourself;/ How did I end up here, my God." («Такси, собор. Не понимаю. Дом офицеров, майский бал?/ Отпой себя в начале мая,/ куда я, Господи, попал.») (Brodsky 1992, volume 1: 76).

Perhaps, one of the most important urban writings of this period is Brodsky's poem-mystery "Procession" («Шествие» 1961), which represents a spiritual journey both in space and in time. It mixes various modes of behaviour as represented by many literary protagonists, including such picaresque characters as Don Quixote and Prince Myshkin, who personify, in Brodsky's view, the banality of life. As Brodsky explains in his brief introduction to the poem — which should be performed as a play — the main idea of the work is to personify various worldviews, so in this respect the poem should be viewed as a hymn to travesty (Brodsky 1992, volume 1: 95). In addition to the above observations, I would emphasise the importance of the inclusion of numerous ballad-style parts in the narrative. In the Russian language, ballad is traditionally called "романс" and has references to love affairs. This name points to the hidden link between this poetic form and the genre of the novel, and especially the romance novel. This is noteworthy from the point of view that Brodsky appears aware that the first Spanish picaresque novels reacted against pastoral novels and novels of chivalry. They were seen as an alternative, a truthful literature, in response to the demands imposed by the Counter-Reformation. In this respect Brodsky's narrative paves the way for the distinctive heroism and hedonism of the picaresque anti-heroic attitude, mocking the realist tradition of self-creation. It is a tragicomedy of self-creation based on the picaresque notions of role-playing and disintegration.

Brodsky's poem is a complex narrative that moulds the image of the narrator as modern artist in the clothes of a picaro rather than a revolutionary. This especially felt in the strong metatextual atmosphere that points to Petersburg itself as a place for an imaginary picaresque voyage into an unnatural man-made world. However Brodsky's procession along the streets of Petersburg might be seen as a journey towards the affirmation of life, associated with a celebration of freedom and positive ongoing creation. In this sense Petersburg is viewed by Brodsky as a cradle of eternal revolution, to be understood in aesthetic, not ideological terms. In other words, in his search for new modes of expression in "Procession", Brodsky discovers that everything including society, selfhood, love and landscapes are made, and that the pure manifestation of goodness, beauty and truth are destroyed for ever. The city appears to be a wasteland of worn-out absolutes, which might be used for the development of new potentialities of human freedom.

Passion for self-creation is asserted in the works of Brodsky and Kushner as the essence of the Petersburg tradition firmly located in the image of the city that personifies survival and ongoing creative revolution. Yet the young Leningrad authors of the 1960s approached the modernist tradition in picaresque terms, displaying their precarious historical existence and a profound sense of psychological insecurity that affects the man-society relationship. As Blackburn points out, the picaresque myth continues to exist in contemporary literature, because "for what it comes down to is not just the way of life of vagabonds and juvenile delinquents but any way of life that seems to lead away and down from meaning and full humanity" (Blackburn 1979: 205). In his provocative article "Living in the New Middle Ages", Umberto Eco compares modern times with the Middle Ages that were marked by the collapse of universal truths and powers: "Our own Middle Ages, it has been said, will be an age of 'permanent transition' for which new methods of adjustment will have to be employed" (Eco 1995: 84). Eco asserts that the culture of constant readjustment inspired by various utopian aspirations is coming into existence with the return of the Middle Ages; and suggests the postmodern artistic project of retranslation of traditional forms of expression lends itself to analogy with the Middle Ages. Eco states: "The Middle Ages preserved in its way the heritage of the past but not through hibernation, rather than through a constant retranslation and reuse; it was an immense work of bricolage, balanced among nostalgia, hope, and despair" (ibid.) It seems that in the post-Stalin period marked by anxieties and insecurities about the future of Russian culture, exemplified in the Petersburg tradition, young Leningrad authors produced their own variation of the Petersburg myth as conveyed in the works of Pushkin. In the words of Maija Könönen, the essence of the Petersburg myth is "the theme of the road to purification through the experience of the evil" (Könönen 2003: 20). In a recent study of Leningrad unofficial literature of the 1960s-1980s, Stanislav Savitskii highlights the marginal role of this experimental writing in the context of socialist cultural development in the Soviet Union, arguing that "it developed the project of modernism and avant-garde in the situation of crisis of utopia" (Savitskii 2002: 172).

In their study of Bakhtin's theoretical works, Morson and Emerson talk of Bakhtin's concept of intervalic chronotope "that interrupts and casts light upon the chronotope of the main narrative" and "tends to be one of theatricality, of a kind of play separated from but related to the life in which it is an interval" (Morson and Emerson 1990: 404). The poems by Kushner and Brodsky described above do lend themselves to be seen as manifestations of this intervalic chronotopic conscience, especially because it is associated with the poets' view of the city in terms of novelistic hybridisation. As Morson and Emerson note, "the intervalic chronotope is also well suited to exploring this potential of dialogically interacting chronotopes" (ibid.). It is worth looking at three more examples that reveal the presence of Pushkinian overtones in poems that broadly can be identified with postmodernist attempts to employ the intertextual parody of historiographic metafiction.

Probably the most important achievement of Russian post-Perestroika poetry is exemplified in Parshchikov's narrative poem "I Lived on the Battlefield of Poltava" («Я жил на поле Полтавской битвы»). It appeared for the first time in the third issue of *Mitin zhurnal* in 1985 and was awarded the Andrei Belyi prize in the same year. In 1989 it was included in Parshchikov's collection of poetry *Figures of Intuition* (*Figury intuitsii*). "I Lived on the Battlefield of Poltava" reveals Parshchikov's neoclassical techniques and his strong interest in historical themes containing a powerful message that history is written by those who have a creative talent to bring it alive. Parshchikov considers the Battle of Poltava as an important event in Russian and European history. The work includes autobiographical overtones: Parshchikov lived in a house located between Poltava and Dikan´ka, which he inherited from his relatives. Parshchikov's poem incorporates archaic elements mixed with references to contemporary Russian life: thus, for example, it uses hexameters associated with Greek and Latin poetry. Parshchikov's reference to the Ukraine battle in 1708 also alludes to Pushkin's 1829 long narrative poem "Poltava" («Полтава»). Parshchikov's metapoetic invocation of his craft — "Run, my verse, my hound — fetch it! — and come back to my heel/ with the branch clasped in your jaws, again serve the arc" («Беги, моя строчка, мой пес, — лови!/ И возвращайся к ноге») — also presents a paraphrase of Pasternak's poem "My poems, run, run over there…" («Стихи мои, бегом, бегом...»). Here Parshchikov brings to life the whole poetic tradition of addressing the poet's tools, exemplified most vividly in Pushkin's "To My Inkpod" («Моей чернильнице»). It highlights the poet's preoccupation with language itself and with the poetic tradition to which he belongs, rather than with the truthful depiction of a historical event. Although Mikhail Epstein firmly situates Parshchikov's poems in the tradition of metarealist poetry that emerged in Moscow in the 1980s (Epstein 1999: 118), I think a less confusing approach is from the viewpoint of the poetics of historiographic metafiction discussed at great length in Linda Hutcheon's painstaking study 1988 *A Poetics of*

Postmodernism: History, Theory, Fiction. As Hutcheon reminds us, "what historiographic metafiction challenges is both any naive realist concept of representation but also any equally naive textualist or formalist assertions of the total sepration of art from the world. The postmodern self-consciously art 'within the archive' (Foucault 1977: 92), and that archive is both historical and literary" (Hutcheon 1988: 125). Given Foucault's formula in a nutshell of the postmodern mode of expression, I tend to agree with Andrew Wachtel's characterisation of contemporary poets, including Olga Sedakova and Parshchikov, as "the youngest archaists" (Wachtel in Sandler 1999: 270).

Parshchikov's "I lived on the Battlefield of Poltava" has a palimpsest quality and incorporates not only allusions to various episodes of Russian and Soviet history, bur also parodic renderings of Karl Marx, Pushkin, Pasternak and Voznesenskii. According to Wachtel, the battle described in the poem reaches its culmination "when, to the already existing planes of action (the battle and the present day), Parshchikov adds a third level: that of literary history" (Wachtel in Sandler 1999: 285). Parshchikov redefines Pushkin's Peter the Great, depicted in "Poltava" as a hero and benevolent ruler, as a comic-tragic figure who used the war as an opportunity to become famous and immortal. Parshchikov also has a high critical assessment of Peter the Great's concept of rationality. His image of Peter the Great has several parodic touches and playfully suggests that the Tsar's body was disproportionately larger than his head:

У царя голова была мала.
Тело ело царя.
Поскольку материя неуничтожима,
Главное в ней – выносливость.
Не с людьми сражаетесь, а со смертью.
А из бессмертия какую свободу ты вынес?
Если сражаешься ради резона,
Резоннее сдаться.
(Parshchikov 1985: 15)

The tsar had a small head.
The body ate the tsar.
Since the matter is not destructable,
The main feature of it is stamina.

You don't fight people, you fight death.
If you fight for a particular reason,
It's more reasonable to surrender.

Parshchikov's critical vision of the development of the Russian imperial sublime corresponds well to the general belief that, both in literature and the visual arts, postmodernist rethinking of the past never amounts to a nostalgic return offering a critical reworking of past experiences (Hutcheon 1988: 4). Parshchikov debuffs Peter the Great's myth about progress and rationalisation understood in terms of the Enlightenment project. He questions the necessity of expansion of the Russian empire through endless engagement in military action. His Peter the Great is the author of the grand narrative of Russian history driven by the imperial sublime. Parshchikov sees both literary narratives (including Pushkin's "Poltava") and historical narratives as human construct and historiographic metafiction. As Epstein aptly notes, the gaze found in Parshchikov's poetry is dehumanised and his poetics of presentism is oriented towards signs, resulting in the fact that even nature is described in his works as a repository of artefacts (Epstein 1999: 148). For example the narrator of Parshchikov's poem mentions the asylum standing near the battlefield and notes an ant crawling towards it. He ascribes the ant he sees with some historical significance that allegorically depicts Russian history in the last three hundred years: "You, ant, who started crawling across this field in Peter the Great's times, your journey amounts to crossing this battlefield" («Ты, начавший еще при Петре, муравей, через поле твое странствие длится!») (Parshchikov 1985: 7). Parshchikov's work gravitates strongly towards the elegiac sublime, oscillating between the two poles of reflexive satire and reflexive idyll (represented by the battlefield and the garden tended by the narrator: it appears that the garden is located close to the Poltava battlefield).

By mentioning some contemporary poems written by locals, Parshchikov presents the Poltava battle in a true postmodernist vein: neither as an event that can be remembered as a historical fact, nor as an event that can be forgotten. This idea is expressed in a metonymical way with the help of various subtexts interwoven into the narrative. For example he imagines the poppies and wormwood as images symbolising Russian soldiers who died in the battle, alluding to the images associated with death and bitter Russian historical experiences found in Tsvetaeva's poetry. Although Wachtel finds some neo-Classical tendencies in Parshchikov's poetry, I see Parshchikov as a romantic ironist who relies on the positive self in poetry, which pivots around the idea of creation and self-discovery (including self-criticism). His "I Lived on the Battlefield of Poltava" contains strong autobiographical overtones and addresses the issue of identity: since Parshchikov spent most of his life in Ukraine, not Russia, his identity as a Moscow poet becomes destabilised when he finds himself settled in Poltava for a time. In very subtle manner Parshchikov establishes his links with Gogol who was born in Poltava on 1 April, 1809 — April Fool's Day. Like Gogol and Tsvetaeva, the narrator of Parshchikov's narrative poem fashions himself in the clothes of an author/holy fool. The self-fashioning into a fool's clothes occurs in Pushkin's poetry, too, but the image of a contemporary asylum located on the former Poltava battlefield brings to mind the theme of madness expressed in "The Bronze Horseman" very prominently. Although Parshchikov's self appears discursively constructed, we can sense in his narrative poem a trace of romantic irony which Ernst Behler appropriately characterised as a mode in which irony and masquerade serve as the devices "for this intellectual attitude which often cloaks a vulnerable personality plagued by melancholy, loneliness and profound suffering" (Behler 198: 43).

The issue of cultural memory and self-expression is also strongly pronounced in the poetry of Shvarts, the prominent contemporary Russian poet who emerged as a samizdat poet in the 1980s. As Sandler notes, "Shvarts balances historical injustice with personal injuries and in her most compelling poems [...] she shows us a culture in flight from itself and history in which ghosts return to the living because of their messages have not been heeded" (Sandler 1999: 256). In her brief summary of the main tenets of Shvart's poetry, Sandler stops short of comparing Shvarts's painful experiences and modes of expression that revolve around the manifestations of counter-violence to the position of Pushkin's protagonist in "The Bronze Horseman", Evgeny, who went mad after realising the loss of his fiancée and her house in the violent Neva flood of 1824. In her insightful analysis of Shvarts's poem "Kindergarten After Thirty Years" («Детский сад тридцать лет спустя», 1986), Sandler points to the fact that this poem is "about injury – to things, people, and poetry itself" (Sandler 1999: 257). In this poem Shvarts describes the metallic landscape where her kindergarten was located near the Baltiisky factory, bread-baking factories and a former Old Believer cemetery. Shvarts takes the opportunity to juxtapose the new and old ways of life. Her allusion to new people whose revolutionary conscience is determined by their factory work suggests that this landscape is pregnant with revolutionary spirit:

> Ржавые зубы растут из бугров,
> Изо ртов больших тракторов.
> Кажется – будет –
> Народятся на них новые люди,
> И пойдут на Исакий войной, волной....
> (Shvarts 1999: 187)

> Rusty crooked teeth grow from the mounds,
> From the mouths of huge tractors.
> It seems that one day —
> They will give birth to a new people
> Who will march on St Isaac's in war, in waves.
> (Sandler 1999: 257).

In addition to Sandler's careful analysis of the poem, I would like to point to the Pushkinian subtext in the passage cited above that alludes to the theme of madness in Pushkin's "The Bronze Horseman". As has been discussed earlier, the image of a mad river is equated to the image of the angry injured and insulted Petersburg dwellers whose protest against the Russian form of modernisation instigated by Peter the Great undermined the dominant social and political discourses. Shvarts alludes to the fact that Evgenii angers the Bronze Horseman when he threatens him: she refers to St Isaac's Cathedral located next to the Peter the Great monument. The lyric persona of Shvarts's poem fashions herself in the clothes of Pushkin's Evgenii, an innocent victim, who finds himself caught between the overwhelming forces of nature and Russian history. The allusion to Pushkin is entwined in Shvarts's poem with a semi-veiled reference to Gippius's image of the new people (discussed earlier) who could bring new forms of Christian thinking and will manage to heal the wounds of a divided and fragmented society through spiritual teaching.

In one of her very exquisite semi-humorous poems, "Ballad of an Occult Seance and Alexander Pushkin's Shadow" («Баллада о спиритическом сеансе и тени Александра Пушкина», 1967), Shvarts portays a seance involving three Tartu University students who wish to ask the spirit of Pushkin various questions about Russia's future and to find out more about the poet's personal habits. The end of Shvarts's poem evokes Nabokov's concept of the presence of the otherworld dimension in everyday life. The poem creates an image of the impersonal gaze of the poet who might be keeping an eye on life in Russia today:

> Электричество зажгли...
> Так неловко стало вдруг,
> Будто кто-то нас обидел,
> Будто кто из темноты
> Видит нас, а мы не видим.
> В муках блюдечко дрожит...
> (Shvarts 1999: 31).

> The electrical light was switched on...
> All of a sudden it became awkward,
> As if somebody insulted us,
> As if someone gazes at us from the darkness
> But we don't see this person.
> The saucer is trembling in torments...

Shvarts's poem presents writing as dwelling, pointing to the omnipresence of Pushkin's spirit in the realms of Russian poetry. The ballad employs a three-foot iambic meter which is very rarely used in Russian poetry. According to Kviatkovskii, it is occasionally found in Russian poetry of the 1810s-1830s (Kviatkovskii 1966: 364). In its subject matter it evokes both Vassilii Zhukovskii's ballad "Svetlana" and his short poem that depicts Pushkin's body straight after the moment of the poet's death. In the words of Sandler, Zhukovskii's poem "fixes on that moment of transition between life and death" and "its glance typifies the Romantic urge to peer into the experience of death" (Sandler 2004: 34). The importance of the glance, perceived as action understood in terms of the continuous present, should not be understated. It embodies the notion that language speaks for itself, but that one of its most important functions is communication involving interaction among subjects, and it relates to the referential sphere.

Shvarts employs the device of simultaneism elaborated by Russian avant-garde artists and poets. Through this notion it becomes possible to see the relationship between the linguistic sign and the signified object in terms of interaction that paves the way to an intersubjective space at work. The existence of the narrator of Shvarts's poem under the gaze of Pushkin's would-be spirit creates a double-edged message, since it is implied in the poem that the speaking spirit might have assumed the identity of the narrator. In other words, Shvarts's poem exemplifies a shift from mythical consciousness that, as Bakhtin suggests, is aligned with poetic genres and monologue towards a critical consciousness usually associated with novel and discursive plurality. The ending of Shvarts's poem might be also seen as an allegorical representation of the gaze of the alienated person, of the *flâneur*, since the city is the chief showplace of modernity. To Shvarts, Pushkin is clearly associated with 'the flâneur' whom Benjamin identified as an optical, as opposed to tactile, collector stressing that the nineteenth century was a period of the primacy of the optical sense (Benjamin quoted in Frisby 1986: 228). Talking about the cognition developed during this period, Benjamin claimed that "in the fields with which we are concerned, knowledge comes only in flashes. The text is the thunder rolling afterwards" (Benjamin in Frisby 1986: 266). The image of the tormenting and trembling saucer might be viewed as an allegorical representation of the text that the lyric heroine of Shvarts's "Séance" is writing.

Benjamin suggests that the concept of modernity might be viewed as a way of looking at old things anew: "No epoch has existed that did not feel itself, in the most eccentric sense, to be 'modern' and consider itself to be standing immediately before an abyss. The despairing, wide-awake consciousness, standing immersed in a decisive crisis, is chronic in humanity. Every period appears to be an unavoidably new. This 'modernity', however, is precisely that which is as diverse as the aspects of one and the same kaleidoscope" (Benjamin in Frisby 1986: 266). Bearing in mind Simmel's exploration of the metropolis as the social space that accommodates the experiences of modernity, it is not surprising that poetry in twentieth-century Russia became a suitable medium for expressing these experiences and conveying the jolting experiences of moving in the city. As Frisby suggests, the central focus for Benjamin was "the working out and exemplification of commodity fetishism within the fragments of modernity" because he was "fascinated by the fantasy world world which which such a process generated and reproduced" (Frisby 1986: 271). Russian twentieth-century poets appear to be equally interested not only in the discontinuity of modern experience and recognition of its ephemeral nature, but also in "the dialectic of the ever-new face of commodity and its ever-same circulation and exchange" (Frisby 1986: 271).

The cultural commodity of fetishism was exemplified by the expansion of the Pushkin myth in Russia and among the Russian diaspora abroad. All poets of significance explored various modes of reading Pushkin that were more often than not subordinated to the search for modes of expression of experiencing modernity in everyday life. However, this was a problematic process, as this chapter has attempted to uncover. As Frisby aptly summarises various attempts to cognise modernity in the twentieth century, "whereas Simmel could still conceive of the preservation of a quasi-autonomous sphere of creativity for the individual in the artistic and moral realms against the growing fragmenting power of objective culture, Kracauer maintained that the individual retreat from modernity was no longer possible [...]. The world of modernity, for Benjamin, was a world of fantasy and illusion generated, ultimately, by the domination of commodity production, circulation and exchange" (Frisby 1986: 275).

Evaluated in conjunction with the main theoretical approaches to modernity listed above, an awareness of the illusory nature of modernity seems to have steadily gained credibility since the 1960s. The culmination of the responses to the interaction between the public and private contributions to the so-called Pushkin myth is exemplified in the 1999 poem by a well-known Russian-American poet Vera Zubareva, who entered her short poem dedicated to Pushkin in a competition organised by Russian cultural figures resident in London and in Moscow (in conjunction with some literary institutions based in Moscow) for the best poem commemorating Pushkin. This eight-line poem draws a comparison between London and Moscow, playfully representing an old lady from Pushkin's fairy tale about a goldfish gazing at the fragments of modernity; utopian dreams are shattered;

with a truly postmodernist gesture she ponders whether Pushkin ever existed:

> В запое витязи. В тоске старуха:
> Опять всё то же – нищета, разруха...
> Глядит в разбитое корыто у избушки
> И думает: «А был ли Пушкин?»
> (Zubareva 1999)

> The knights are drinking heavily. The old lady is sad:
> The same poverty, the same disarray...
> She looks at her broken tub by the old hut
> And ponders: "Was there ever really a Pushkin?"

CONCLUSION

In his final remarks in a book treating different theoretical approaches to modernity, Frisby points to Benjamin's aspiration to break the cycle of reification of the modern world "by means of his dialectical images in order to awaken 'the dreaming collectivity' from its dream" (Frisby 1986: 272). For Russian twentieth-century poets, the opposition between individual lived experience and concrete experience — recorded in textbooks, historiographic materials and poetry written in the style of the eighteenth-century odic tradition that celebrated Peter the Great's vision of modernity — became of prime concern. These Russian poets, having discovered in Pushkin's poetry an optical view of modernity's fragmented world, and modes of oscillation between the odic and elegiac sublimes, were quick to explore Pushkin's experimentation with such devices as listing, montage, intervalic chronotope and defamiliarisation, in order to voice their cognition of fast-changing reality and everyday life experiences shattered by the events of war and three revolutions. Both Tynianov and Bakhtin, the most outstanding Russian modernist theoreticians of culture and literature, pointed to the incredibly artificial nature of Pushkin's novel in verse *Eugene Onegin* proposing to view it as a polyphonic narrative. Nabokov vehemently rejected Belinskii's treatment of *Eugene Onegin* as a mimetic narrative, an encyclopaedia of life in Russia in the first three decades of the ninetenth-century — an indication that Russian modernist practitioners and thinkers discovered some early manifestations of modernity in this novel in verse, manifestations that corresponded to their own experiences of modernity in everyday life, include such acts as readership, city strolls, participation in cultural associations and exposure to the media. The European avant-garde's aspiration to integrate art and life led to the emergence of a differentiated linking of modern culture with the praxis of everyday life, and to the active participation of Russian poets in the project of modernity. The examples in this book that pivot around a creative reading of Pushkin illustrate well that the Pushkin myth was an integral part of this process of closing the gap between life and literature.

As has been argued here, the rise of the Russian and European novel to a large extent changed the poets' ways of looking at themselves and at the poetic language. Although Bakhtin maintained that "any sense of the boundedness, the historicity, the social determination of one's own language is alien to poetic style" (Bakhtin 1981: 285), this book has demonstrated that a certain degree of novelisation of poetry is detectable in most serious works of poetry that were engaged in a creative dialogue with Pushkin, with the effect that even polyphonic lyric has become possible. This was achieved through the use of intertextuality, montage, apostrophic modes of expression, dialogised images and defamiliarisation. As Morson and Emerson demonstrate, Bakhtin believed that a rich intertextuality was possible in the early history of poetry when the poetic self was more impersonal. In such a situation, "the poet speaks out of language itself, he speaks as it were out of poetic tradition itself, taken as a whole" (Morson and Emerson 1990: 321). To this end, I think that the impression of both Sandler and Gerald Smith that "poetry after the Silver Age had been steadily in decline in Russia" (Sandler 1999: 287) is indicative of the crisis of the subject, associated with the end of belief in the Cartesian subject as the autonomous centre of knowledge and self-consciousness during the early modernist period. Subjectivity and inter-subjectivity appear to be large concerns of many twentieth-century artists, philosophers, writers and poets. Lyric poetry, usually perceived as monophonic, was affected by the subject's loss of its wholeness, its destabilisation and fragmentation. Willem Weststeijn's article "The Subject in Modern Russian Poetry" addresses the issue of the shift in perception linked to subjectivity in Russian modernist and postmodernist poetry and sums up: "The attempts to recapture the unity of the subject led to the existential quest and flight into ideology (nazism, communism). Postmodernism, the cultural movement of the second half of the twentieth century, did not consider the subject any longer as an important category. Attention was focused on the 'I' and the 'Other', on dialogism and polyphonism (Bakhtin). Ideology lost its appeal and so did the 'great' stories (Lyotard)" (Weststeijn 1999). Since the modernist tradition was largely suppressed in the Soviet Union during the communist period, some postmodernist trends in Russian poetry became visible only in post-Soviet times when previously unpublished (or samizdat- or émigré-journal published) poetry came into the open and became widely accessible. This includes, for example, the rediscovery of some important Russian dissident and émigré poets such as Gubanov, Irina Odoevtseva,

Nikolai Otsup, Shvarts. Future studies will undoubtedly take into account the influx of new texts into the mainstream of publications, in order to assess their value to understanding the formation of the modernist canon and the nature of the creative dialogue between modernist and postmodernist modes of poetic expression (including neo-modernist and neo-avant-garde poetic works).

My study has aimed at demonstrating the presence of ongoing dialogue with Pushkin in Russian modernist and postmodernist poetic narratives, paving the way to an assessment of the impact it had on the poetic conscience and artistic psychology. As has been shown, Russian twentieth-century poets of significance discovered new semantic values embedded in Pushkin's writings, especially in his narrative poem "The Bronze Horseman", in his novel in verse *Eugene Onegin*, in his lyric poems "To the Sea" and "Monument", to name just a few of the most influential of Pushkin's canonical works. As has been shown, Russian twentieth-century poets viewed cultures as open-ended entities in the manner of Bakhtin, who wrote: "In each culture of the past lie immense semantic possibilities that have remained undisclosed, unrecognised, unutilised through the entire historical life of a given culture" (Bakhtin quoted in Morson and Emerson: 290). I believe that a major discovery of the twentieth-century poets and film-makers was the optical consciousness of Pushkin, noticed briefly by only one contemporary critic of Pushkin: Nadezhdin. Yet during Soviet times most of Nadezhdin's articles on Pushkin that concerned themselves with aesthetic rather that with socio-political issues were resolutely dismissed by Soviet scholars; these included Blagoi who rejected attempts to explore any manifestaion of Pushkin's subversive laughter that might have undermined the carefully-moulded image, constructed by Soviet cultural institutions and educators of Pushkin the critic of the Russian monarchy. Pushkin's dialogised modes of thinking as manifested in some lyrics, as well as in larger works, were carefully studied by his followers who unfolded the mode of engaging in readership from the viewpoint of phenomenological distance rather than empathic reading. Thus, this study has also brought forward Tsvetaeva's attempts to develop a coherent ethical approach to reading creatively through her prose, essays and lyrics that dealt with Pushkin. Creative readings of Pushkin found in the twentieth-century Russian poetry stem from Pushkin's own creative dialogues with Byron and Dante. Theoretical aproaches to inter-subjectivity were employed in this book alongside the aesthetic theories of Bakhtin and Berger.

The book has developed and incorporated approaches found in Sandler's pioneering study of the acts of Russian readers and authors who wanted to commemorate Pushkin. I believe this book complements Sandler's monumental account of the various responses to Pushkin in Russian and Soviet cultures. Yet, it is beyond the scope of this book in all-encompassing manner to finalise or exhaust the topic of the reception of Pushkin's poetry in Russia in modern and postmodern times, for the reasons outlined above. More work is required to assess all the modes of forgetting and remembering that shaped some of the twentieth century's poetic development. I chose to focus on those responses that have an interesting angle on the creative process and display the visions of modernity that are inseparable from the image of Pushkin, whom I see as the Russian precursor of Baudelaire and a poet whose experiments with organisation of visual and verbal images in his narratives stand close to the usage of montage in Russian films of the avant-garde period. It is not coincidental, for example, that in his essay "Pushkin — Montage-Maker" («Пушкин-монтажер») Eisenstein draws readers' attention to the skillful usage of montage in Pushkin's narrative poems "Ruslan and Liudmila" («Руслан и Людмила») and "Poltava". Eisenstein especially praises Pushkin as a master of battle scenes found in "Poltava" (Eisenstein 2000: 273). This book has also located several examples of Pushkin's cinematographic cognition of reality, suggesting that such dynamic descriptions of Petersburg helped create a highly original animated image of the city as comic apocalypse. Eisenstein also finds in Pushkin some signs of the primordial and surreal thinking that can compress action and deliver various messages quickly to readers' minds. In this respect, Eisenstein's vision of Pushkin stands close to that of the avant-garde Russian poets who saw in Pushkin the creative impulse or even poetic principle per se, as understood in Bergsonian light. It is emphasised that Russian poets fought hard against the automation of modern life and the technological reproducibility of the images uncreatively appropriated from Pushkin's letters and writings. At the same time, poets whose works have been scrutinised in this analysis of Pushkinian motifs and imagery appear to have been fully aware of the formula advocated by

Benjamin that "the uniqueness of a work of art is inseparable from its being embedded in the fabric of tradition" (Benjamin 1999: 216).

BIBLIOGRAPHY

Alpers, S.
1983 *The Art of Describing: Dutch Art in the Seventeenth Century.* (The University of Chicago Press). Chicago.
Akhmadulina, B.
1997 *Sochineniia.* vol.1 (Pan. Korona-Print). Moscow.
Akhmatova, A
1965-83 *Sochineniia.* 3 volumes. [G. P. Struve and B. A. Filippov, editors.] (Inter-Language Literary Associates and YMCA-Press). Washington, D.C. and Paris.
1976 *Stikhi i proza.* (Lenizdat). Leningrad
Amert, S.
1992 *In a Shattered Mirror.* (Stanford University Press). Stanford, California.
Anderson. B.
1983 *Imagined Communities: Reflections on the Origins and Spread of Nationalism.* (Verso). London.
Andrew, J., Reed, R. (editors)
2003 *Two Hundred Years of Pushkin II: Myth and Monument.* (Rodopi). Amsterdam.
2003 *Two Hundred Years of Pushkin III: Pushkin's Legacy.* (Rodopi). Amsterdam.
Annenskii, I.
1988 *Izbrannye proizvedeniia.* (Khudozhestvennaia literatura). Leningrad.
Antal, F.
1962 *Hogarth and His Place in European Art.* (Routledge and Kegan Paul) London.
Averintsev, S.
1993 "Bakhtin and the Russian Attitude to Laughter", in: Shepherd, David, editor. *Bakhtin Carnival and Other Subjects: Selected Papers from the Fifth International Bakhtin Conference, University of Manchester, July 1991,* (Rodopi). Amsterdam-Atlanta, GA: 13-19.
Baak, J. van
1994 "Mif doma v russkoi literature. Programma literaturnogo u kul′turologicheskogo analiza". In Weststeijn, W. (editor). *Dutch Contributions To the Eleventh International Congress of Slavists, Bratislava, August-September 9, 1993.* (Rodopi). Amsterdam – Atlanta, GA: 21-44.
Bachelard, G.
1994 *The Poetics of Space: The Classic Look at How We Experience Intimate Places.* [Translated from the French by Maria Jolas]. (Beacon Press). Boston.

Bailey, J.
  1971 *Pushkin: A Comparative Commentary.* (Cambridge University Press). Cambridge.
Bakhtin, M.
  1979 *Estetika slovesnogo tvorchestva.* (Iskusstvo). Moscow.
  1981 *The Dialogic Imagination: Four Essays.* [Translated by Caryl Emerson and Michael Holquist]. (University of Texas Press). Austin.
Barthes, R.
  1977 *Image. Music. Text.* [translated by Stephen Heath]. (Hill and Wang). New York.
Baratynskii, E.
  1979 *Stikhotvoreniia i poemy.* ("Kareliia"). Petrozavodsk.
Bauman, Z.
  2000 *Liquid Modernity.* (Polity Press). Cambridge.
Belinskii, V.
  1988 *Vzgliad na russkuiu literatury.* (Sovremennik). Moscow.
Bely, A.
  1910 *Simvolism.* Moscow.
  1929 *Ritmika kak dialektika i "Mednyi vsadnik".* (Izdatel'stvo "Federatsiia"). Moscow.
  1979 *Petersburg.* [Translated, annotated and introduced by Robert A. Maguire and John E. Malmstad]. (Harvester Press). Hassocks, Sussex.
Benjamin, W.
  1973 *Charles Baudelaire : A Lyric poet in the Era of High Capitalism.* [Translated from the German by Harry Zohn]. (NLB). London.
  1983 *Charles Baudelaire. A Lyric Poet in the Era of High Capitalism.* [translated by Harry Zohn]. (Verso). London.
  1999 *Illuminations.* [translated by Harry Zohn]. (Pimlico). London.
Bennett, A. (editor)
  1995 *Readers and Reading.* (Longman). London and New York.
Berger, K.
  1994 "Diegesis and Mimesis: The Poetic Modes and the Matter of Artistic Presentation". *The Journal of Musicology.* Vol.12, No.4, Autumn 1994: 407-433.
  2000 *A Theory of Art.* (Oxford University Press). New York. Oxford.
Bergson, H.
  1999 *Laughter: An Essay on the Meaning of the Comic.* [Translated from the French by Clodesley Brereton and Fred Rothwell]. (Green Integer). Kobenhavn and Los Angeles.
  2002 *Key Writings.* [Edited by Keith Ansell Pearson and John Mullarkey]. (Continuum). New York, London.
Bethea, D.
  1980 "Sorrento Photographs: Khodasevich's Memory Speaks". *Slavic Review.* Volume 39, no.1 (March 1980): 59-69.
  1993 *Pushkin Today.* (Indiana University Press). Bloomington and Indianapolis.
  1994 *Joseph Brodsky and the Creation of Exile.* (Princeton University Press). Princeton, New Jersey.

1998   *Realising Metaphors: Alexander Pushkin and the Life of the Poet.* (University of Wisconsin Press). Madison.
Blackburn, A.
1979   *The Myth of Picaro: Continuity and Transformation of the Picaresque Novel, 1554-1954.* (The University of North Carolina Press). Chapel Hill.
Blagoi, D. (editor)
1941   *Pushkin rodonachal'nik novoi russkoi literatury.* (Izdatel'stvo akademii nauk SSSR). Moscow-Leningrad.
Blagoi, D.
1950   *Tvorcheskii put' Pushkina (1813-1826).* (Izdatel'stvo akademii nauk SSSR). Moscow.
Blanchot, M.
1987   "Everyday Speech". [translated by Susan Hanson]. *Yale French Studies.* (1987), No.73: 12-20.
2003   *The Book to Come.* [tranlsated by Charlotte Mandell]. (Stanford University Press). Stanford, California.
Blok, A.
1955   *Sochineniia v dvukh tomakh.* (Gosudarstvennoe izdatel'stvo ktohudozhestvennoi literatury). Moscow.
1976   "The Poet's Role", in Richards, D. and Cockrell, C.R., editors. *Russian Views of Pushkin.* (Willem A. Meeuws, Publisher), Oxford: 127-134.
1972   Sobranie sochinenii. 6 volumes. Moscow.
Bloom, H. (editor)
1987   *Alexander Pushkin.* (Chelsea House Publishers). New York.
Bloom, H.
1995   *The Western Canon: The Books and School of the Ages.* (Papermac). London.
Boele, O.
1996   *The North in Russian Romantic Literature.* (Rodopi). Amsterdam, Atlanta, GA.
Bollas, C.
2000   *Hysteria.* (Routledge). London and New York.
Bradbury, M., McFarlane, J.
1976   "The Name and Nature of Modernism". *Modernism: 1890-1930.* (Penguin Books). London.
Brand, D.
1991   The Spectator and the City in Nineteenth-Century America. (Cambridge University Press). Cambridge.
Brandist, C.
2002   *The Bakhtin Circle: Philosophy, Culture and Politics.* (Pluto Press). London, Stirling, Virginia.
Brecht, B.
1964   *Brecht on Theatre: The Development of an Aesthetic.* [edited by Willet, John]. Methuen, London.
Bréton, A.
1972   *Manifestoes of Surrealism.* [Translated by Richard Seaver and Helen R. Lane]. (The University of Michigan Press). Ann Arbor.

1999 *Nadja.* [translated from the French by Richard Howard]. (Penguin). London.
Briusov, V.
1987 *Sochineniia v dvukh tomakh.* (Khudozhestvennaia literatura). Moscow.
Brodsky, J.
1987 *Less Than One: Selected Essays.* (Penguin Books). Harmondsworth, Middlesex.
1991 *Stikhotvoreniia.* ("Eesti Raamat", "Aleksandra"). Tallinn.
Bowra, C.M.
1967 *The Creative Experiment.* (Macmillan). London. Melbourne. Toronto.
Bürger, P.
1984 *Theory of the Avant-Garde.* (Manchester University Press / University of Minnesota Press). Manchester.
Byron, G.
1987 *Poetical Works.* [edited by Frederick Page]. (Oxford University Press). Oxford. New York.
Certeau, M., de
1984 *The Practice of Everyday Life.* (University of California Press). Berkeley.
Cherednichenko, T.
2002 *Muzykal'nyi zapas: 70-e. Problemy. Portrety.* (Novole literaturnoe obozrenie: biblioteka zhurnala "Neprikosnovennyi zapas"). Moscow.
Chernetsky, V.
2000 "Iosif Vissarionovich Pushkin, or Sots-Art and the New Russian Poetry", in Balina, Marina et al, *Endquote: Sots-Art Literature and Soviet Grand Style,* Northwestern University Press, Evanston, Illinois, 2000: 146-166.
Ciepiela, C.
1996 "The Demanding Woman Poet: On Resisting Marina Tsvetaeva". *PMLA,* vol. 111, No.3, 9 May 1996): 421-434.
Cixous, H.
1997 *Rootprints: Memory and Life Writing.* (Routledge) London & New York.
Clayton, J. D.
1985 *Ice and Flame.* (University of Toronto Press). Toronto, Buffalo.
2000 *Wave and Stone.* (Slavic Research Group at the University of Ottawa). Ottawa.
Conrad, P.
1998 *Modern Times, Modern Places: Life and Art in the 20th Century* (Thames and Hudson). London.
Cornwell, N.
1999 *Vladimir Nabokov.* (Northcote House in association with the British Council). London.
Cox, N.
2000 *Cubism.* (Phaidon). London.
Culler, J.
1975 *Structuralist poetics : structuralism, linguistics and the study of literature.* (Routledge and Kegan Paul). London.
1982 *On Deconstruction: Theory and Criticism after Structuralism.* (Cornell University Press). Ithaca.

Dante, A.
1970-75 *The Divine Comedy.* [translated by Charles Singleton]. 3 volumes. (Princeton University Press). Princeton.
Davidson, P.
1989 *The Poetic Imagination of Vyacheslav Ivanov. A Russian Symbolist's Perception of Dante.* (Cambridge University Press). Cambridge.
Debreczeny, P.
1997 *Social Functions of Literature: Alexander Pushkin and Russian Culture.* (Stanford University Press). Stanford.
Dediulin and Superfin
1989 *Akhmatovskii sbornik.* (Institut slavianovedeniia). Paris.
Dixon, S.
1999 *The Modernisation of Russia: 1676-1825.* (Cambridge University Press). Cambridge.
Doherty, J.
1995 *The Acmeist Movement in Russian Poetry: Culture and the Word.* (Oxford University Press). Oxford.
Donchin, G.
1958 The Influence of French Symbolism on Russian Poetry. (Mouton & Co.). The Hague.
Dunham, V.
1965 "Poems about Poems: Notes on Recent Soviet Poetry". *Slavic Review.* Vol.24, No.1 (March 1965): 57-76.
Dupriez, B.
1991 *A Dictionary of Literary Devices.* [translated and adapted by Albert W. Halsall]. (Harvester Wheatsheaf]. New York, London, Toronto.
Eikhenbaum, B.
1969 "Literatura i kino", *Literatura: Teoriia, Kritika, Polemika.* (Russian Language Specialties, University of Chicago). Chicago, Illinois: 296-301.
1969 *O poezii.* (Sovetskii pisatel'). Leningrad.
Elsworth, J.
1998 "Aleksandr Semenovich Kushner", in: Cornwell, Neil. *Reference Guide to Russian Literature.* (Fitzroy Dearborn Publishers). London, Chicago: 478-479
Emerson, C.
1998 "Pushkin, Literary Criticism, and Creativity in Closed Places", *New Literary History*, 29/4: 653-672.
Epstein, M., Genis A., Vladiv–Glover, S., editors
1999 *Russian Postmodernism: New Perspectives on Post-Soviet Culture.* (Bergham Books). New York, Oxford.
Erickson, J.
1995 *The Fate of the Object: From Modern Object to Postmodern Sign in Performance, Art and Poetry* (University of Michigan Press). Ann Arbor.
Evreinov, N
1915-7 *Teatr dlia sebia.* 3 volumes. (Bukovskaia). Petrograd.
Eysteinsson, A.
1990 *The Concept of Modernism.* (Cornell University Press). Ithaca and London.

Felski, R.
1995　*The Gender of Modernity.* (Harvard University Press). Cambridge, Massachussetts; London, England.
Fetterley, J.
1978　*The Resisting Reader: A Feminist Approach to American Fiction.* (Indiana University Press). Bloomington.
Figes, O.
1996　*A People's Tragedy: The Russian Revolution: 1891-1924.* (Pimlico). London.
Fink, H.
1999　*Bergson and Russian Modernism: 1900-1930.* (Northwestern University Press). Evanston.
Fitzpatrick, S.
1999　*Everyday Stalinism: Ordinary Life in Extraordinary Times: Soviet Russia in the 1930s.* (Oxford University Press). Oxford.
Fleishman, L.
1990　*Boris Pasternak: The Poet and His Politics.* (Harvard University Press). Cambridge, Massachussetts, London.
Flynn, E., Schweickart, P.
1986　*Gender and Reading: Essays on Readers, Texts, and Contexts.* (The John Hopkins University Press). Baltimore and London.
Fomichev, S.
1986　*Poeziia Pushkina; Tvorcheskaia evoliutsiia.* (Nauka). Moscow.
Foucault, M.
1988　*Madness and Civilisation: A History of Insanity in the Age of Reason.* [translated from the French by Richard Howard]. (Vintage Books: A Division of Random House). New York.
1997　"Theatrum Philosophicum", in Timothy Murray (ed.) *Mimesis, Masochism, and Mime: The Politics of Theatricality in Contemporary French Thought.* (University of Michigan Press). Ann Arbor.
2000　"Different Spaces", *Aesthetics: Essential Works of Foucault: 1954-1984*, volume 2. (Edited by James D. Faubion, translated by Robert Hurley and others). (Penguin Books). London: 175-185.
Fowlie, W. (editor)
1964　*A Bantam Dual-Language Book: Flowers of Evil and Other Works by Charles Baudelaire.* [Edited by Wallace Fowlie, with translations, a critical introduction, and notes by the editor]. (Bantam Books). New York.
Frisby, D.
1985　*Fragments of Modernity: Theories of Modernity in the Work of Simmel, Kracauer and Benjamin.* (Polity Press). Cambridge.
Gasparov, B., Hughes, R., Paperno, I.
1992　*Cultural Mythologies of Russian Modernism: From the Golden Age to the Silver Age.* (University of California Press). Berkeley, Los Angeles, Oxford.
Gasparov, M.
1974　*Sovremennyi russkii stikh.* (Nauka). *Moscow.*
1995　*Izbrannye stat'i: o stikhe, o stikakh, o poetakh.* (Novoe literaturnoe obozrenie). Moscow.

Gippius, Z.
1999 *Stikhotvoreniia.* (Gumanitarnoe agenstvo "Akademicheskii proekt"). St Petersburg.

Goldberg, R.
1993 *Performance Art: From Futurism to the Present.* (Thames and Hudson). London.

Gordin, A., Gordin, M.
1999 *Pushkinskii vek.* ("Izdatel'stvo pushkinskogo fonda"). St Petersburg.

Greenleaf, M.
1992 "Tynianov, Pushkin and the Fragment: Through the Lens of Montage", in Gasparov, B. et al, editor. *Cultural Mythologies of Russian Modernism: From the Golden Age to the Silver Age.* (University of California Press). Berkeley, Los Angeles, Oxford: 264-292.
1995 *Pushkin and Romantic Fashion: Fragment, Elegy, Orient, Irony.* (Stanford University Press). Stanford, California.

Grimal, P.
1986 *The Dictionary of Classical Mythology.* [translated by A.R. Maxwell-Hyslop]. (Blackwell Reference). Oxford.

Gregson, I.
1996 *Contemporary Poetry and Postmodernism: Dialogue and Estrangement.* (St Martin's Press). New York.

Gunning, T.
1997 "From the Kaleidoscope to the X-Ray: Urban Spectatorship, Poe, Benjamin, and *Traffic in Souls* (1913), *Wide Angle,* 19. 4: 25-61.

Habermas, J.
1981 "Modernity versus Postmodernity", *New German Critique,* No.22. Special Issue on Modernism (Winter 1981): 3-14.
1983 "Modernity – An Incomplete Project", *The Anti-Aesthetic: Essays on Postmodern Culture.* [edited by Hal Foster]. (Bay Press). Port Townsend, Washington: 3-15.
1989 *The Structural Transformation of the Bourgeois Public Sphere.* [translated by Thomas Burger]. Cambridge, Massachussetts.

Hasty, O.
1996 *Tsvetaeva's Orphic Journeys in the Worlds of the Word.* (Northwestern University Press). Evanston, Ill.
1999 *Pushkin's Tatiana.* (The University of Wisconsin Press). Madison. Wisconsin.

Heidegger, M.
1971 *Poetry. Language. Thought.* Poetry, Language, Thought. (Harper and Row). New York.
2001 *Poetry, Language, Thought.* (Translated and with introduction by Albert Hofstader). (Perennial Classics). New York.

Hellebust, R.
2003 *Flesh to Metal: Soviet Literature and the Alchemy of Revolution.* (Cornell University). Ithaca and London.

Herman, D.
1996 "A Requiem for Aristocratic Art: Pushkin's 'Egyptian Nights'". *Russian Review.* vol. 55, No.4, October 1996 : 661-680.

Holquist, M., Liapunov, V., (editors)
1990 Bakhtin, Mikhail M.: *Art and Answerability: Early Philosophical Essays.* [Trans. Vadim Liapunov]. (University of Texas Press). Austin.

Hutcheon, L.
1988 *A Poetics of Postmodernism: History. Theory. Fiction.* (Routledge). New York and London.

Iser, W.
1978 *The Act of Reading: A Theory of Aesthetic Response.* (The John Hopkins University Press). Baltimore.
1989 *Prospecting: From Reader Response to Literary Anthropology.* (The John Hopkins University Press). Baltimore and London.
1993 *The Fictive and the Imaginary: Charting Literary Anthropology.* (The John Hopkins University Press). Baltimore.

Jakobson, R.
1967 "The Generation that Squandered Its Poets (Excerpts)". *Yale French Studies.*No.39: Literature and Revolution (1967): 119-115.
1975 *Pushkin and His Sculptural Myth.* (The Hague). Paris.
1987 *Language in Literature.* (Harvard University Press). Cambridge, Mass.

Karamzin, N.
1964 *Izbrannye sochineniia v dvukh tomakh.* (Khudozhestvennaia literatura). Leningrad.

Karlinsky, S.
1985 *Marina Tsvetaeva: The Woman, Her World and Her Poetry.* (Cambridge University Press). Cambridge.

Kelly, C. and Shepherd, D. (editors)
1998 *Constructing Russian Culture in the Age of Revolution: 1881-1940.* (Oxford University Press). Oxford.

Kennard, J.
1986 "Ourself Behind Ourself: A Theory for Lesbian Readers", in: Flynn, E. and Schweickart, P, editors. *Gender and Reading: Essays on Readers, Texts, and Contexts.* (The John Hopkins University Press). Baltimore and London: 63-82.

Khodasevich, V.
1922 *Tiazhelaia lira: chetvertaia kniga stikhov, 1920-22.* (Gosudarstvennoe izdatel´stvo). Moscow.
1999 *Pushkin i poety ego vremeni. 3 volumes* (edited by Hughes, R.). (Berkeley Slavic Specialties.) Oakland, California.

Kline, G.
1990 "Variations of the theme of Exile", in: Lev Loseff and Valentina Polukhina (eds.). *Brodsky's Poetics and Aesthetics.* (The Macmillan Press). London: 56-88.

Kodjak, A.
1976 *Alexander Pushkin: A Symposium on the 175th Anniversary of His Birth.* (New York University Press). New York.

Könönen, M.
2003 *Four Ways of Writing the City: St Petersburg-Leningrad as a Metaphor in the Poetry of Joseph Brodsky.* (Slavica Helsingiensia 23: University of Helsinki). Helsinki.

Kristeva, J.
1980 *Desire in Language: A Semiotic Approach to Literature and Art*. [translated by Thomas Gora]. (Basil Blackwell). Oxford.
1986 "A New Type of Intellectual: the Dissident", *The Kristeva Reader* [translated by Seán Hand; Toril Moi, editor]. (Columbia University Press). New York.
1989 *Language: The Unknown: An Initiation into Linguistics*. [Translated by Anne M. Menke]. (Harvester. Wheatsheaf). London. Sydney. Tokyo.
Kuhns, O.
1899 "Dante's Influence on English Poetry in the Nineteenth Century". *Modern Language Notes*. Vol.14, no.6 (June 1899): 176-186.
Kviatkovskii, A.
1966 *Poeticheskii slovar'*. (Sovetskaia entsiklopediia). Moscow.
Lachmann, R.
1997 *Memory and Literature: Intertextuality in Russian Modernism*. [translated by Roy Sellars and Antony Wall]. (University of Minnesota Press). Minneapolis, London.
Lawlor, L.
2003 *The Challenge of Bergsonism*. (Continuum). London-New York.
Leach, R.
1989 *Vsevolod Meyerhold*. (Cambridge University Press). Cambridge.
Lefebvre, H.
2003 "Preface to the Study of the Habitat of the Pavilion". *Key Writings*. (Edited by Stuart Elden, Elizabeth Lebas and Eleonore Kofman), (Continuum). New York, London: 2003: 121-135.
Lerner, N.
1909 "O Pushkine" and "Novonaidennye stat'i Puskina". *Novaia Rus'*. No.274 (6 October): 5.
1910 *Trudy i dni Pushkina*. St Petersburg.
Leyda, J. (editor)
1949 *Film Form*. (Harcourt, Brace and Company). New York.
Levitine, G.
1972 *The Sculpture of Falconet*. (New York Graphic Society Ltd.). Greenwich, Connecticut.
Levitt, M.
1989 *Russian Literary Politics and the Pushkin Celebration of 1880*. (Cornell University Press). Ithaca, N.Y.
Likhachev, D.S.
1999 *Razdum'ia o Rossii*. (Logos), St Petersburg. 1999.
Lilley, E.
1994 "The Name of the Boudoir", *The Journal of the Society of Architectural Historians,* vol.53, no.2, June 1994: 193-198.
Lipovetsky, M.
1999 *Russian Postmodernist Fiction: Dialogue with Chaos*. (M.E. Sharpe). Armonk, New York; London, England.
Liubimov, D.
1937 "Otkrytie pamiatnika v Moskve", *Illiustrirovannaia Rossiia: Pushkinskii nomer: 1837-1937,* No.7 (613), Paris, February 6.

Lodge, D. (editor)
1988　*Modern Criticism and Theory: A Reader.* (Longman). London and New York.
Losev. A.
1977　*Antichnaia filosofiia istorii.* (Nauka). Moscow.
Loseff, L., Scherr, B. et al. (editors)
1993　*A Sense of Place: Tsarskoe Selo and Its Poets: Papers from the 1989 Dartmouth Conference Dedicated to the Centennial of Anna Akhmatova.* (Slavica Publishers, Inc.). Ohio.
Lotman, Iu. (editor)
1984　Semiotika: trudy po znakovym sistemam XVIII, Uchenye zapiski Tartuskogo gosudarstvennogo universiteta.
Lotman, Iu.
1980　Roman A.S. Pushkina "Evgenii Onegin" : kommentarii : posobie dlia uchitelia. ("Prosveshchenie", Leningradskoe otd-nie), Leningrad.
1984　"Simvolika Peterburga i problemy semiotiki goroda". *Semiotika:Trudy po znakovym sistemam, XVIII.* (Edited by Iu. M. Lotman). (Uchenye zapiski Tartuskogo gosudarstvennogo universiteta, 664). Tartu: 30-45.
1992-3　*Izbrannye stat'i v trekh tomakh.* (Aleksandra). Tallinn.
1996　O poetakh i poezii: Analiz poeticheskogo teksta. Stat'i; Issledovaniia; Zametki. ("Isskusstvo– SPB"). Sankt-Peterburg.
2000　Uchebnik po russkoi literature dlia srednei shkoly. (Iazyki russkoi kul'tury). Moscow.
2000　*Ob iskusstve.* (Iskusstvo). St Petersburg.
2002　*Stat'i po semiotike kul'tury i iskusstva.* (Akademicheskii proekt). St Petersburg.
Lotman, Iu., Uspenskii, B.
1984　*The Semiotics of Russian Culture.* (Edited by Ann Shukman). (Michigan Slavic Contributions). Ann Arbor
Lynch, K.
2000　*The Image of the City.* (The MIT Press). Cambridge, Massachussetts.
Lyotard, J.-F.
1984　*The Postmodern Condition: A Report on Knowledge.* [translated by Geoff Bennington and Brian Massumi]. (University of Minnesota Press). Minneapolis.
MacFayden, D.
2000　*Joseph Brodsky and the Soviet Muse.* (McGill-Queen's University Press). Montreal and Kingston, London, Ithaca.
Malmstad, J., Bogomolov, N.
1999　*Mikhail Kuzmin: A Life in Art.* (Harvard University Press). Cambridge, Massachussetts.
Mamoon, T.
1998　*Evolution of the "New People" in the Prose of Zinaida Hippius.* Unpublished Ph.D.Thesis. (University of Illinois at Urbana-Champaign). Urbana-Champaign.
Mandelshtam, O.
1987　*Slovo i kul'tura.* (Sovetskii pisatel'). Moscow.

Marks, S.
2003　*How Russia Shaped the Modern World: From Art to Anti-Semitism, Ballet to Bolshevism.* (Princeton University Press). Princeton and Oxford.
Mashinskii, S., (editor)
1974　*V mire Pushkina.* ("Sovetskii pisatel'"). Moscow.
Matich, O.
1972　*Paradox in the Religious Poetry of Zinaida Gippius.* (Wilhelm Fink Verlag). München.
Mazzotta, G.
1984　"Dante and the Virtues of Exile", *Poetics Today,* vol.5, no.3, Medieval and Renaissance Representation: New Reflections, (1984): 645-667.
McCabe, S.
2001　"Delight in Dislocation": the Cinematic Modernism of Stein, Chaplin, and Man Ray", *Modernism/Modernity.* Volume 8, issue 3: 492-452.
Mederskii, L.
1949　"Arkhitekturnyi oblik pushkinskogo Peterburga". *Pushkinskii Peterburg.* (Edited by B.V. Tomashevskii). (Leningradskoe gazetno-zhurnal'noe knizhnoe izdatel'stvo). Leningrad: 285-352.
Meskin and Weinberg
2003　"Emotions, Fiction, and Cognitive Architecture", *The British Journal of Aesthetics,* volume 43(1):18-34
Mintz, Z, et al.
1984　"Peterburgskii tekst i russkii simvolizm". *Semiotika:Trudy po znakovym sistemam, XVIII.* (Edited by Iu. M. Lotman). (Uchenye zapiski Tartuskogo gosudarstvennogo universiteta, 664). Tartu: 78-92
Mitchell, S.
1988　*Relational Concepts in Psychoanalysis: An Integration.* (Harvard University Press). Cambridge, Massachussetts.
Morson, G. and Emerson, C. (editors)
1987　*Rethinking Bakhtin: Extensions and Challenges.* (Northwestern University Press). Evanston, Illinois.
1990　*Mikhail Bakhtin: Creation of a Prosaics.* (Stanford University Press). Stanford, California.
Murphy, R.
1998　*Theorizing the Avant-Garde: Modernism, Expressionism, and the Problem of Postmodernity.* (Cambridge University Press). Cambridge.
Nabokov, V.
1961　*Nikolai Gogol.* (New Directions Paperbook). New York.
1970　*Poems and Problems.* (Weidenfeld and Nicholson). London.
Nadezhdin, N.
2000　*Sochineniia v dvukh tomakh.* [edited by Z.A. Kamenskii]. (Izdatel'stvo russkogo khristianskogo instituta). St Petersburg.
Nappel'baum, I.
2004　*Ugol otrazheniia: Kratkie vstrechi dolgoi zhizni.* (Izdatel'skii dom "Retro"). St Petersburg.
Nepomniashchii, V., Filin, M. (editors)
1999　*Rechi o Pushkine: 1880-1960 gody.* (Tekst). Moscow.

O'Bell, L.
1984 *Pushkin's "Egyptian Nights": The Biography of a Work.* (Ann Arbor). Ardis.
Ospovat, A.L, Timenchik, R.D.
1987 *"Pechal'nu povest' sokhranit'...".* ("Kniga"). Moscow.
Otradin, M., (editor)
1988 *Peterburg v russkoi poezii; XVIII-nachalo XX veka. Poeticheskaia antologiia.* (Izdatel'stvo Leningradskogo universiteta). Leningrad.
Papernyi, V.
2002 *Architecture in the Age of Stalin: Culture Two.* [translated by John Hill and Roann Barris]. Cambridge University Press: Cambridge.
Parshchikov, A.
1985 "Ia zhil na pole Poltavskoi bitvy", *Mitin zhurnal,* No.3.
1989 *Figury intuitsii.* (Moskovskii rabochii). Moscow.
Parsons, D.
2000 *Streetwalking the Metropolis: Women, the City and Modernity.* (Oxford University Press). Oxford.
Pasternak, B.
1970 *Okhrannaia gramota.* (Aquario) Rome.
1977 *Stikhotvoreniia i poemy.* (Sovetskii pisatel'). Leningrad.
1983 *Vozdushnye puti.* (Sovetskii pisatel'). Moscow.
Pensonen, P., et al. (editors)
2000 *Perelomnye periody v russkoi literature i kul'ture.* (University of Helsinki). Helsinki.
Peshkovskii, A.
1938 *Russkii sintaksis v nauchnom osveschenii.* Moscow.
Pollak, N.
1993 "Annensky's 'Trefoil in the Park' (Witness to whiteness)". In: Lev Loseff and Barry Scherr, editors. *A Sense of Place: Tsarskoe Selo and Its Poets.* (Slavica Publishers, Inc.) Columbus, Ohio: 171-190.
Porter, R.
1994 *Russia's Alternative Prose.* (Berg). Oxford.
Potebnia, A.
1993 *Mysl' i iazyk.* (Sinto). Kiev.
Pushkin, A.S.
1957-8 *Polnoe sobranie sochinenii v desiati tomakh: Izdanie vtoroe.* (Izdatel'stvo Akademii Nauk SSSR). Moscow.
1981 *Eugene Onegin: A Novel in Verse* (Translated from the Russian, with a Commentary by Vladimir Nabokov). Paperback edition in two volumes. (Bollingen series LXXII, Princeton University Press). Princeton.
1991 *The Bronze Horseman.* [Edited with Introduction by T.E. Little]. (Bristol Classical Press). Bristol.
Pyman, A.
1979 *The Life of Aleksandr Blok.* (Oxford University Press). Oxford.
1994 *A History of Russian Symbolism.* (Cambridge University Press). Cambridge.

Raeff, M.
1984 *Understanding Imperial Russia: State and Society in the Old Regime.* (Columbia University Press). New York.
Raban J.
1974 *Soft City.* (Hamish Hamilton). London.
Ram, H.
2003 *The Imperial Sublime. A Russian Poetics of Empire.* (The University of Wisconsin Press). Madison, Wisconsin.
Ramazani, V.K.
1996 "Writing in Pain: Baudelaire, Benjamin, Haussmann". *Boundary 2*, vol.23, No. 2, summer: 199-224.
Reyfman, I.
1999 *Ritualised Violence Russian style: The Duel in Russian Culture and Literature.* (Stanford University Press). Stanford, California.
Richards, D., Cockrell, C. (editors)
1976 *Russian Views of Pushkin.* (Willem A. Meeuws - publisher). Oxford.
Ricoeur, P.
1984-88 *Time and Narrative.* 3 volumes. (The University of Chicago Press). Chicago.
Rider, J., Le
1993 *Modernity and Crisis of Identity: Culture and Society in Fin-de-Siècle Vienna.* [Translated by Rosemary Morris]. (The Continuum Publishing Company). New York.
Roberts, G.
1997 The Last Soviet Avant-Garde: OBERIU - Fact, Fiction, Metafiction. (Cambridge University Press). Cambridge.
Rose, G.
1978 "The Creativity in Everyday Life". *Between Reality and Fantasy: Transitional Objects and Phenomena.* [Edited by Grolnick, S. and Barkin, L.]. (Aronson). New York: 347-62.
1987 *Trauma and Mastery in Life and Art.* (Yale University Press). New Haven, CT.
2004 *Between Couch and Piano: Psychoanalysis, Music, Art and Neuroscience.* (Brunner-Routledge). Hove and New York:
Rosenshield, G.
2003 *Pushkin and the Genres of Madness: The Masterpieces of 1833.* (The University of Wisconsin Press). Madison, Wisconsin.
Rubins, M.
2003 *Plasticheskaia radost' krasoty: Akmeizm i Parnas.* (Akademicheskii proekt). St Petersburg.
Said, E.
2004 *Beginnings: Intention and Method.* (Columbia University Press). New York.
Sandler, S.
1989 *Distant Pleasures: Alexander Pushkin and the Writing of Exile.* (Stanford University Press). Stanford, California.

Sandler, S. (editor)
1999   *Rereading Russian Poetry.* (Yale University Press). New Haven and London.
Sandler, S.
2004   *Commemorating Pushkin: Russia's Myth of a National Poet.* (Stanford University Press). Stanford, California.
Savitskii, S.
2002   *Andeground: Istoriia i mify leningradskoi neofitsial'noi kul'tury.* (Novoe literaturnoe obozrenie). Moscow.
Shapiro, B.
1998   *Literature and the Relational Self.* (New York University Press). New York and London.
Schönle, A.
1998   "The Scare of the Self: Sentimentalism, Privacy, and Private Life in Russian Culture, 1780-1820". *Slavic Review*, vol.57, No. 4, winter: 723-746.
Schreurs, M.
1989   *Procedures of Montage in Isaak Babel's Red Cavalry.* (Rodopi). Amsterdam-Atlanta, GA.
Schwartz, V.
1998   *Spectacular Realities: Early Mass Culture in Fin-de-Siècle France.* (University of California Press). Berkeley.
Schwarzband. S.
1988   *Logika khudozhestvennogo poiska: ot "Ezerskogo" do "Pikovoi damy".* (The Magnus Press. The Hebrew University). Jerusalem.
Schweickart, P.
1986   "Reading Ourselves: Toward a Feminist Theory of Reading". *Gender and Reading: Essays on Readers, Texts, and Contexts.* [Edited by Elizabeth A. Flynn and Patrocinio P. Schewickart]. (The John Hopkins University Press). Baltimore and London: 31-62.
Segel, H.
1998   *Body Ascendant: Modernism and the Physical Imperative.* (The John Hopkins University Press). Baltimore and London.
Seiden, M.
1967   *Dickens's London: The City as Comic Apocalypsis.* Unpublished PhD thesis. Cornell University.
Shakespeare, W.
1982   *The Illustrated Stratford Shakespeare.* (Chancellor Press). London.
Shaya, G.
2004   "The *Flâneur,* the *Badaud,* and the Making of a Mass Public in France, circa 1860-1910". *American Historical Review.* February 2004: 41-77.
Shevelenko, I.
2002   *Literaturnyi put' Tsvetaevoi: Ideologiia – poetika – identichnost' avtora v kontekste epokhi.* (Novoe literaturnoe obozrenie). Moscow.
Shvarts, E.
1998   *Stikhotvoreniia i poemy.* (Inapress). St Petersburg.
Smirnova-Rosset, A.
1989   *Dnevnik: Vospominaniia.* ("Nauka"). Moscow.

Smith, A.
1994 *The Song of the Mockingbird*. (Peter Lang). Berne, Berlin, New York, Paris.
1998 "Conformist by Circumstance v. Formalist at Heart: Some Observations on Tynianov's Novel Pushkin" in: *Neo-Formalist Papers: Contributions to the Silver Jubilee Conference to Mark 25 Years of the Neo-Formalist Circle*. [Edited by Joe Andrew and Robert Reid]. (Rodopi). Amsterdam: 296-315.
2003 "Pushkin's Imperial Image of St Petersburg Revisited". In *Two Hundred Years of Pushkin, volume 2: Alexander Pushkin: Myth and Monument*. [Edited by Robert Reid and Joe Andrew]. (Rodopi). Amsterdam-New York.
2003 "Vladimir Nabokov as Translator of Russian Poetry". *Wiener Slawistischer Almanach, Band 51*. Wien: 133-166.
2004 "Toward the Poetics of Exile: Marina Tsvetaeva's Translation of Baudelaire's 'Le Voyage'", *Ars Interpres*, Stockholm-Moscow-New York, No.2, May 2004: 179-199. (web version at: http://ars-interpres-2.nm.ru/a_s_an_2.html).

Stallybrass, P., White, A.
1989 *Politics and Poetics of Transgression*. (Cornell University Press). Ithaca.

Steiner, P.
1984 *Russian Formalism: A Metapoetics*. (Cornell University Press). Ithaca. London.

Stelliferovskii, P.
1988 *Evgenii Abramovich Baratynskii*. ("Prosveshchenie"). Moscow.

Stolovich, V.
1992 *Sbornik statei k 70-letiiu prof. Iu. M.Lotmana*. (Tartuskii Universitet). Tartu.

Stern, D.
1985 *The Interpersonal World of the Infant*. (Basic). New York.

Struve, G.
1984 *Russkaia literatura v izgnanii*. (YMCA-Press). Paris.

Tambling, J.
1997 "Dante and the Modern Subject: Overcoming Anger in the *Purgatorio*", *New Literary History*, 28.2 (1997): 401-420.

Terts, A. (Siniavskii, A.)
1999 *Puteshestvie na Chernuiu rechku*. (Zakharov). Moscow.

Todd, W. M. III.
1986 *Fiction and Society in the Age of Pushkin*. (Harvard University Press). Cambridge, Massachussetts.
1999 "Evgenii Onegin: roman zhizni", in *Sovremennoe amerikanskoe pushkinovedenie: sbornik statei*. [Edited by I.F. Danilova]. ("Akademicheskii proekt"). St Petersburg: 153-188.

Todorov,T.
1973 *The Fantastic: A Structural Approach To A Literary Genre,* [Translated from the French by Richard Howard]. (The Press of Case Western Reserve University), Cleveland/London.

Tomashevskii, B.
   1949   "Peterburg v tvorchestve Pushkina". In *Pushkinskii Peterburg*. [Edited by B.V. Tomashevskii]. (Leningradskoe gazetno-zhurnal'noe knizhnoe izdatel'stvo). Leningrad: 3-40.
Tsiavlovskaia, T. G.
   1956   "Avtograf stikhotvoreniia 'K moriu'". *Pushkin. Issledovaniia i materialy*, vol.1. (Nauka). Leningrad: 187-207.
Tsvetaeva, M.
   1972   *Neizdannye pis'ma*. (YMCA-Press). Paris.
   1984   *Sochineniia v dvukh tomakh*. (Khudozhestvennaia literatura). Moscow.
   1988   *Sochineniia v dvukh tomakh*. (Khudozhestvennaia literatura). Moscow.
   1990   *Stikhotvoreniia i poemy*. (Sovetskii pisatel'). Leningrad.
   1992   *Art in the Light of Conscience*. (Translated with Introduction and Notes by Angela Livingstone). (Bristol Classical Press). London.
Tsvetaeva, M; Pasternak, B.
   2004   *Marina Tsvetaeva, Boris Pasternak: Dushi nachinaiut videt': Pis'ma 1922-1936 godov*. (Vagrius). Moscow.
Tynianov, Iu.
   1977   *Poetika. Istoriia literatury. Kino*. (Nauka). Moscow.
   1981   *The Problem of Verse Language*. [Translated and edited by M. Sosa and B. Harvey]. (Ardis). Ann Arbor.
Ueland, C.
   1992   "Viacheslav Ivanov's Pushkin: Thematic and Prosodic Echoes of *Evgenii Onegin* in *Mladenchestvo*". *Cultural Mythologies of Russian Modernism: From the Golden Age to the Silver Age*. [Gasparov, B. et al, editor]. (University of California Press). Berkeley, Los Angeles, Oxford: 337-356.
Viazemskii, P.
   1984   *Estetika i literaturnaia kritika*. (Iskusstvo). Moscow.
Vinogradov, V.
   1972   *Russkii iazyk. Grammaticheskoe uchenie o slove*. (Vysshaia shkola). Moscow.
Virolainen, M.
   1999   "'Mednyi vsadnik'; peterburgskaia povest'". *Zvezda, No.6*: 208-219.
Voznesenskii, V.
   1975   *Dubovyi list violonchel'nyi*. (Khudozhestvennaia literatura). Moscow.
Wachtel, M.
   1998   *The Development of Russian Verse: Meter and Its Meanings*. (Cambridge University Press). Cambridge.
   2004   *The Cambridge Introduction to Russian Poetry*. (Cambridge University Press). Cambridge.
Wedaman, D.
   2004   *Apollinaire and Maiakovsky: Applied Bergsonism*. (PhD thesis). Brandeis University.
Weitzman, A.
   1975   "Eighteenth-Century London: Urban Paradise or Fallen City?", *Journal of the History of Ideas*, vol.XXXVI, Number 3, July-September.
Wells, D.
   1996   *Akhmatova: Her Poetry*. (Berg Publishers). Oxford.

Weststeijn, W.
1999 "The Subject in Modern Russian Poetry", *Avant-Garde Critical Studies*, volume 12: 169-192.
Winnicott, D.
1971 *Playing and Reality*. (Tavistock). London.
Winter, J.
1995 *Sites of Memory. Sites of Mourning: The Great War in European Cultural History*. (Cambridge University Press). Cambridge.
Zhirmunskii, V.
1985 *Selected Writings*. [Translated from the Russian by Sergei Ess]. (Progress Publishers). Moscow.
Zinker, J.
1977 *Creative Process in Gestalt Therapy*. (Random House). New York.
Zubova, L.
1989 *Poeziia Mariny Tsvetaevoi: Lingvisticheskii aspect*. (Izdatel'stvo Leningradskogo universiteta). Leningrad.

ADDITIONAL READING

Balina, M., et al. (editors)
    2000   *Endquote: Sots-Art Literature and Soviet Grand Style*. (Northwestern University Press). Evanston, Illinois.
Bennet, Tony (editor)
    1990   *Popular Fiction. Technology. Ideology. Production*. (Routledge). London.
Bocharov, S.
    1978   *Poetika Pushkina. Ocherki*. (Nauka). Moscow.
Boym, S.
    1996   "Estrangement as a Lifestyle: Shklovsky and Brodsky", *Poetics Today*, vol.17, No.4, Creativity and Exile: European/American Perspectives II, (Winter 1996): 511-530.
Buck-Morss, S.
    1989   *The Dialectics of Seeing: Walter Benjamin and the Arcades Project*. (MIT). Cambridge, Massachussetts.
Huyssen, A.
    1986   *After the Great Divide: Modernism, Mass Culture and Postmodernism*. (Macmillan). London.
Klein, M.
    1990   *Envy and Gratitude and Other Works, 1946-1963*. (Dell). New York.
Mann, Iu.
    1995   *Dinamika russkogo romantizma*. (Aspekt). Moscow.
Rabinow, P. (editor)
    1984   *The Foucault Reader*. (Pantheon Books). New York.
Riasanovskii, N.
    1985   *The Image of Peter the Great in Russian History and Thought*. (Oxford University Press). Oxford, New York.
Shchegolev, P.
    1987   *Perventsy russkoi svobody*. (Sovremennik). Moscow.
Stapanian, J.
    1985   "Universal War and the Development of Zaum: Abstraction Toward a New Pictoral and Literary Realism". *Slavonic and East European Journal*. Vol.29, no.1 (1985): 18-38.
Urbaszewski, L.
    2002   "Canonising the 'Best, Most Talented' Soviet Poetry: Vladimir Maiakovsky and the Soviet Literary Celebration", *Modernism/Modernity*, November 2002, 9, 4: 635-665.

Vail', P. and Genis, A.
   1996   *60-e: Mir sovetskogo cheloveka.* (Novoe literaturnoe obozrenie). Moscow.
Vasil'ev, I.
   1999   *Russkii poeticheskii avangard XX veka.* (Izdatel'stvo Ekaterinburgskogo universiteta). Ekaterinburg.
Venclova, T.
   1997   *Sobesedniki na piru.* (Baltos Lankos). Vilnus.
White, A.
   1993   *Carnival. Hysteria and Writing.* (Clarendon Press). Oxford.
Woolf, J.
   1985   "The Invisible *Flâneuse*: Women and the Literature of Modernity", *Theory, Culture and Society*, 2/3, (1985); 37-46.
Zholkovsky. A., O'Toole, L.
   1978   "The Window in the Poetic World of Boris Pasternak", *New Literary History.* Vol.9, No.2. Soviet Semiotics and Criticism: An Anthology. (Winter 1978): 279-314.

INDEX

Adamovich, Georgii, 26, 34, 269–75
Akhmadulina, Bella, 13, 31, 260, 266
  "The Duel", 13
Akhmatova, Anna, 18, 25, 28, 31, 32, 34, 40, 98, 149, 154–55, 163–65, 167, 176, 238–48, 261, 274, 306–9, 315
  "1913", 242
  "A swarthy youth walked in these alleys..." (1911), 28
  "And the sly half-moon saw..." (1946), 239, 241
  "Everyone left and no one returned..." (1946), 238, 239
  "In Tsarskoe Selo" (1911), 241
  "Poem without a Hero", 32, 242, 243, 244, 245, 247, 315
  "Pushkin and the Baltic Coast" (1963), 154
  "Requiem", 18, 244, 245, 246, 247
  "Reverse", 242
  "The Cellar of Memory" (1940), 244
  "Tsarskoe Ode" (1961), 243
Aksakov, Ivan, 198
Aldanov, Mark, 290
Alekseev, General, 210
Alexander I, 42, 130, 132, 159
Alpers, Svetlana, 230
Amert, Susan, 239–41, 243, 244
Aminado, Don. Pen name of Shpolianskii, Arnold Petrovich
  "It was raining. It was slushy. There was black ice..." (1937), 293
Anderson, Benedict, 211–12
Annenskii, Innokentii, 167–79, 202, 212, 246
  "Bronze Poet" (1910), 167–69
  "Pushkin and Tsarskoe Selo" (1899), 174
  "Trefoil in the Park" (1910), 167, 176, 177
  The Cypress Chest (1910), 167
Antal, Frederick, 137
Anthès, Georges d', 298
Apollinaire, Guillaume, 48, 226
Apollon Apollonovich. *See* Belyi, Andrei *Petersburg*
Aragon, Louis, 87, 88, 92
  Le Paysan de Paris (1926), 87, 92
Averintsev, Sergei, 37
Baak, Joost van, 127–28, 164
  "Myth of House in Russian Literature", 127
Bach, Robert (R.R.), 168
Bachellard, Gastón, 81, 152, 153
Bahr, Hermann, 209
Bailey, John, 39, 112
Bakhtin, Mikhail, 74–76, 79–80, 101, 132, 141–46, 149, 155, 171, 186, 234, 248–49, 252, 271, 274–78, 282, 290, 317, 324, 327–30
Baratynskii, Evgenii, 146–51, 154, 156, 157, 161, 184, 188, 236
  "Skull", 147
  "The Ball", 146, 150–52, 154
  "The Mistress", 146
Barthes, Roland, 119
Basker, Michael, 179, 212
Baudelaire, Charles, 12, 13, 19, 105, 114–15, 124, 126, 128, 129, 135, 182, 193, 198, 296–98, 330
  "Au Lecteur", 297
  "Le Voyage" (1859), 198
  Le Fleurs du Mal, 296
  Le Spleen de Paris, 114
Bauman, Zygmunt, 127

Behler, Ernst, 321
Belinskii, Vissarion, 41–43, 48, 258, 327
Belyi, Andrei, 12, 40, 103–5, 235, 318
  "The Laurel Wreath" (1906), 103
  Petersburg, 12
Benckendorff, Aleksei, 208, 209
Benjamin, Walter, 15, 19, 115–16, 124, 128, 129, 135, 140, 193–94, 235, 265, 279, 280, 297–98, 300, 324–27, 331
  "On Some Motifs in Baudelaire", 115
  "The Storyteller" (1936), 279
  "The Work of Art in the Age of Mechanical Reproduction" (1936), 298
Benkendorff, Aleksei, 209, 210
Berdiaev, Nikolai, 269
Berger, Karol, 20, 28, 167, 183, 254, 330
Berggolts, Olga, 31
Bergson, Henri, 27, 51, 47–53, 70, 96, 101–2, 108, 109, 119, 139, 160, 168, 190, 198–201, 221, 226, 251–52, 270, 286, 298, 302–4, 330
  Laughter (1900), 139, 221
  Matter and Memory, 50
  The Two Sources of Morality and Religion, 50
Berman, Marshall, 105
Bethea, David, 253
Bitov, Andrei, 23, 257, 305–11
  "Family Relations", 309
Blackburn, Alexander, 309, 310, 313, 316, 317
Blagoi, Dmitrii, 23, 329
Blanchot, Maurice, 57–58, 60, 101, 157, 231, 233, 234, 268, 301–2
  "Death of the Last Writer", 57
Blok, Alexander, 15, 18, 23, 34, 40, 46–49, 96, 106–7, 126, 163, 180–82, 187, 193, 228, 243
  "Requital" (1910-21), 180–82, 228
  "Pushkin! We sang you a song of secret freedom", 15
  "The Poet's Role" (1921), 46

  "The Snow Mask", 107
  "The Twelve", 18, 238
  The Puppet Booth, 106
Bloom, Harold, 26, 27
Boccacio, 72
Boele, Otto, 40
Bollas, Christopher, 58
Bowra, Maurice, 193, 195–97, 205
Bradbury, Malcolm, 15, 16
Brand, Dana, 135
Brandist, Craig, 271, 276–78
Brecht, 237, 263, 265
Bréton, André, 70, 71, 87, 88
  "Manifesto of Surrealism", 70
  Nadya, 71
Briusov, Valerii, 14, 34, 103–6, 112, 113, 161, 195, 204
Brodsky, Joseph, 27, 40, 97–102, 149, 150, 257, 285, 305–11, 313, 314, 315, 316, 305–17
  "Petersburg Novel" (1961), 314
  "Procession" (1961), 315, 316
  "The Condition We Call Exile", 285
  "The Fifth Anniversary", 100
  "Three Chapters" (1961), 313
  "To Evgenii", 98, 99, 100
Bulgakov, Mikhail, 244, 258, 259
  Master and Margarita, 244, 259
Bunin, Ivan, 290
Bürger, Peter, 283, 300
Byron, Lord, 42, 56, 57, 58, 59–62, 65, 66, 71–74, 75, 76, 77, 88, 97, 98, 102, 149, 160, 247, 248, 329
  Childe Harold, 72, 97, 142, 144
Camus, Albert, 309
Certeau, Michel de, 231, 255–60, 266–68
Chenier, André, 51
Chernetsky, Vitaly, 306
Chernetsov, Grigorii, 11, 12, 19
  Parade on Tsaritsyn Field, 11
Chukovskii, Kornei, 48
Ciepiela, Catherine, 75, 88
Cixous, Hélène, 122
Clayton, J.Douglas, 22, 23
Cleopatra, 14, 265
Conrad, Peter, 88, 92, 93, 94

Index

Constant, Benjamin, 161
Cornwell, Neil, 25, 37
Cox, Neil, 226
Culler, Jonathan, 30, 31, 75
Dante, 40, 58, 68–74, 77, 99–100, 135–36, 160, 177, 195, 247, 285, 329
  Divine Comedy, 26, 40, 72, 73, 99, 135, 136
Dargomyzhskii, Aleksandr, 294
  Mermaid (1948-55), 294
Davydov, Sergei, 253
de Parny, Evariste, 28
Debussy, 166
Deleuze, Gilles, 48
Derzhavin, Gavriil, 182, 184
Dickens, Charles, 132, 236
Didérot, Denis, 131
Dixon, Simon, 41–43, 65–67
Döblin, Alfred, 95
Don Quixote, 315
Donatello, 130
Donchin, Georgette, 189
Dostoevskii, Fyodor, 32, 33, 104, 191, 198, 199, 203, 204, 278
Duncan, Isadora, 86, 87
Dunham, Vera, 260–62, 266–67
Dürer, Albrecht, 129
Eagle, Chris, 34
Eastman, Max, 224
Eco, Umberto, 317
Efron, Ariadna, 280
Eikhenbaum, Boris, 69, 134, 135
Eisenshtadt, Mikhail, 278–83
"Eugene Onegin in New York", 278, 282, 283
Eisenstein, Sergei, 36, 97, 119, 120, 165–66, 167, 174, 177–79, 182, 215, 236–37, 246–48, 298, 330
  "Dickens, Griffiths and Me" (1942), 236
  "Pushkin — Montage-Maker", 330
  October (1927-8), 246
  Qué Viva Mexico!, 97
Elsworth, John, 306
Éluard, Paul, 94
Emerson, Caryl, 109, 252. *See also* Morson, Gary

Eng, Jan van der, 167
Epstein, Mikhail, 318, 320
Erickson, John, 253
Esenin, Sergei, 18
  "Pugachev", 18
Evreinov, Nikolai, 21, 22, 86, 265
Eysteinsson, Astradur, 35
Ezhov, Nikolai, 292
Falconet, Étienne-Maurice, 13, 130, 131, 132, 216, 221
Felski, Rita, 15, 16, 21, 105
Fennel, John, 227
Fetterley, Judith, 31, 83
Figes, Orlando, 210, 213
Fink, Hilary, 49
Fitzpatrick, Sheila, 291, 292, 293
Fleishman, Lazar, 204
Florenskii, Pavel, 251, 252
Foucault, Michel, 27, 125, 129, 197, 198, 319
Fowlie, Wallace, 298
Frank, Semen, 192, 193
Franque, François, 155
Frisby, David, 291, 324, 325, 327
Gaggi, Silvio, 267
Gardin, Vladimir
  "Poet and Tsar" (1927), 298
Gasparov, Boris, 44, 45, 116, 202
Gasparov, Mikhail, 207, 208
Ginzburg, Lidiia, 306, 307, 308
Gippius, Zinaida, 48, 182–92, 322, 343
  "Petersburg" (1909), 182–91
  Dmitrii Merezhkovskii (1951), 191
  Living Persons (1925), 48
Girardon, François, 130
Goethe, 252, 278
Gogol, Nikolai, 202, 235, 312, 321
  "The Nose", 312
Goldberg, RoseLee, 53, 54
Golitsyn, Count A.N., 130
Goncharov, Vassilii
  "The Life and Death of Pushkin" (1910), 298
Goncharova, Natalia, 25, 203
Gordin, A.M. and M.A., 19, 20, 36
Gorkii, Maxim
  "Lenin", 266

Greenleaf, Monika, 34, 116
Grimal, Pierre, 211
Gubanov, Leonid, 18, 328
  "Ivan the Terrible", 18
  "Peter the Great", 18
  "Pugachev", 18
Guchkov, Alexander, 210
Guillén, Claudio, 310
Gumilev, Nikolai, 48, 167, 179–80, 212
  "In Memory of Annenskii" (1912), 179
Gunning, Tom, 140
Guro, Elena, 25
Habermas, Jürgen, 141, 241, 262, 265, 266
Harkins, William, 245
Harris, Jane, 307
Hasty, Olga, 144, 145, 149, 152, 271, 274, 275
Hegel, 231
Heidegger, Martin, 28–30, 79–81, 158
Hellebust, Rolf, 234
Herman, David, 256
Hobbes, Thomas, 174
Hogarth, William, 136, 137
Hölderlin, Friedrich, 28, 158
Holquist, Michael, 80, 224
Hutcheon, Linda, 267, 318, 319, 320
Hutchings, Stephen, 250–51, 276
Iakushkin, Evgenii, 61
Iser, Wolfgang, 30, 31, 33, 170, 171, 216, 269
Iudina, Maria, 13, 14, 119
Ivanov, Viacheslav, 187, 188, 228, 229, 247
  "Childhood" (1913-18), 228
Izmailov, Aleksandr, 132, 161
Jacques-Dalcroze, Emile, 48
Jakobson, Roman, 36, 39, 182, 250
Jolles, André, 310
Kablukov, Sergei, 188
Kamenev, Lev, 291
Karamzin, Nikolai, 22, 156
  My Confession, 22
Karlinsky, Simon, 74, 91, 92
Kenez, Peter, 258, 259
Kennard, Jean, 33, 259
Kharms, Daniil, 266
  "Sonnet", 266
Khazin, Alexander, 244
  "The Return of Onegin" (1946), 244
Khlebnikov, Velimir, 217, 218
Khodasevich, Vladislav, 34, 52, 53, 118, 128, 200, 227–38, 289, 290, 301, 308
  "He Left his Carriage at the Gate" (1924), 290
  "Out of the Window" (1921), 229, 230, 231, 232, 236, 237
  "The Shaken Tripod" (1921), 228, 230
  Pushkin's Poetic Economy (1924), 289
  The Heavy Lyre (1922), 227, 228, 229, 230
Kibirov, Timur, 23, 34
Kirov, Sergei, 291
Kiukhel´becker, Wil´gel´m, 61
Kline, George, 99
Kodjak, Andrei, 39
Komarovskii, Vassilii, 176
Könönen, Maija, 99, 100, 317
Kracauer, Siegfried, 325
Kristeva, Julia, 99, 119–22, 214
Krivtsov, Nikolai, 211
Krivulin, Viktor, 27
Kruchenykh, Aleksei, 25, 207, 217, 218
  Victory Over the Sun (1913), 207
Kuhns, Oscar, 71, 72
Kushner, Alexander, 16, 257, 306–13, 316–17
  "A Photograph" (1966), 311, 312, 313
  "Two Boys" (1962), 311
Kuzmin, Mikhail, 228, 237, 308
  "Letter to Peking" (1922), 228
Kviatkovskii, A., 184, 225, 323
Lachmann, Renate, 108–10, 156–60
Laforgue, Pierre, 199
Lamartine, Alphonse, 59
  "Adieu à la mer" (1822), 59
Larionov, Mikhail, 25

Lawlor, Leonard, 50
Leach, Robert, 237
Leconte de Lisle, Charles-Marie-René, 212
Lednitskii, Vaclav, 39
Lefebvre, Henri, 30, 79, 80, 81
Lermontov, 243
Lerner, Nikolai, 62
Leskov, Nikolai, 235, 280
Levitine, George, 130, 131, 132
Levitt, Marcus, 198
Lifshits, Benedikt, 26, 206, 207
  "Admiralty" (1915), 206
  Medusa of the Marshes (1914-15), 206, 207
Likhachev, Dmitrii, 232, 303
Lilley, Ed, 155
Lipovetsky, Mark, 305
Liubimov, Dmitrii, 198
Lomonosoff, Raisa, 293
  "Pushkin", 293
Lomonosov, Mikhail, 182, 185
Lopukhina, Avdot´ia, 183, 188, 190
Losev, Aleksei, 99
Losskii, Vladimir, 251
Lotman, Iurii, 36, 39, 63–70, 79, 80, 147, 190, 191, 233
Lozinskii, Mikhail, 48
Lynch, Kevin, 178, 179, 247
Lyotard, Jean-François, 136
MacFayden, David, 308
Maiakovskii, Vladimir, 18, 48, 49, 96, 182, 199–201, 213–26, 239, 241, 242, 261, 262, 297
  "At the Top of My Voice", 241
  "Do Not Trade in Lenin" (1924), 241
  "Jubilee" (1924), 241
  "Last Petersburg Fairy Tale" (1916), 213, 214, 217, 218, 220, 222, 224, 225
  "Lenin", 18
  "The Relationship of Today's Theatre and Cinema to Art", 222
  "Theatre, Cinema and Futurism", 216
  "To Sergei Esenin" (1926), 241

Malevich, Kasimir, 207, 218
Mallarmé, Stéphane, 101, 102, 301
Mamoon, Trina, 190
Mandelshtam, Osip, 40, 195, 248, 308
  "The Morning of Acmeism", 195
Marks, Steven, 18
Martynov, Leonid, 260
Marx, Karl, 105, 319
Massalskii, K.P., 132
Matich, Olga, 189
Mauthner, Fritz, 270, 271
Mazzotta, Giuseppe, 72, 73
McCabe, Susan, 182
Merezhkovskii, Dmitrii, 34, 188, 191
  Antichrist. Peter and Alexis, 188, 191
Meyendorf, John, 251
Meyerhold, Vsevolod, 106, 237
Mickiewicz, Adam, 112, 113
  "Oleshkevich", 112
  "The Monument of Peter the Great", 112
Mintz, Zara, 36, 39
Mirskii, Dmitrii, 303, 304
Mitchell, Stephen, 44, 45, 46
Morson, Gary, 186
Morson, Gary and Emerson, Caryl, 234, 248, 252, 274, 282, 317, 328
Mozart, 14, 68, 119
Murphy, Richard, 35, 95, 245
Myshkin, Prince, 315
Nabokov, Vladimir, 15, 21, 23–25, 34, 36, 37, 144, 164, 235, 236, 283–91, 301, 323, 327
  "On Translating *Eugene Onegin*" (1955), 24, 25
  Eugene Onegin, 15, 21, 301
  Path Through the Mountains (1922), 289
  The Bunch (1923), 289
  The Gift (1935-37), 37, 290
Nadezhdin, Nikolai, 136, 137, 329
Naiman, Anatolii, 307, 315
Napoleon, 62, 65, 71, 110
Nappel´baum, Ida, 248–52, 253–54
Nekrasov, Nikolai, 182
Nelidova-Fiveiskaia, Lidiya, 293

"Captive of Noble Deed" (1936), 293
Nezhinskii, Vassilii, 86
Nicholas I, 17, 42, 132, 301
Nietzsche, Friedrich, 49, 192, 270
O'Bell, Leslie, 256
Odoevskii, Vladimir, 61, 132
"The Joke of a Dead Man" (1833), 132
Odoevtseva, Irina, 34, 47, 328
Okudzhava, Bulat, 257
Ospovat, Alexander and Timenchik, Roman, 14, 26, 36, 119, 132, 133
Otsup, Nikolai, 48, 167, 329
Ouspenskii, Leonid, 251
Panchenko, Alexander, 303
Papernyi, Vladimir, 247
Parade on Tsaritsyn Field. *See* Chernetsov, Grigorii
Parshchikov, Alexei, 18, 29, 30, 34, 318–21
"I Lived on the Battlefield of Poltava" (1985), 18, 318–21
"Money", 29
Figures of Intuition (1989), 29, 318
Parsons, Deborah, 103
Pasternak, Boris, 13, 18, 26, 27, 28, 48, 74, 87, 88, 91, 92, 93–96, 101, 102, 126, 152, 153, 193–206, 261, 289, 296, 303, 308, 318, 319
"1905", 18, 91, 93
"Lieutenant Schmidt", 18
"Like the first bullet hit by the next shot..." (1914-16), 194–95
"My poems, run, run over there...", 318
"Opportunity" (1914), 198, 199, 200, 201, 203, 204, 205, 206
"Petersburg" (1914-16), 194
"Safe Conduct", 199
"Stars raced...", 196, 205
"Theme With Variations" (1916-22), 195, 196
"Variations" (1918), 94, 95, 96
Above Barriers (1914-16), 194
Pecherin, Vladimir, 132
"The Feast of Death" (1833), 132

Peshkovskii, Alexei, 64
Piatakov, Iurii, 291
Poe, Edgar Allen, 135, 139
"The Man of the Crowd", 135, 139
Pollak, Nancy, 167, 168, 177
Polotskii, Simeon, 182
Pomorska, Krystina, 241
Porter, Robert, 304, 305
Potebnia, Alexander, 168, 177, 202
Propp, Vladimir, 215
Pushkin, Alexander
"A Message to Del'vig" (1827), 147
"Bacchic Song", 292
"Boris Godunov", 265
"Devils", 29
"Drums signal sunrise..." 1829, 68, 69, 70, 71, 136, 177
"Egyptian Nights" (1835), 14, 44, 108, 256, 265
"England is a Homeland of Caricature and Parody", 23
"Feast at the Time of the Plague", 265, 273, 302
"Gypsies", 79
"I visited again..." (1835), 153
"Incantation", 29
"It's time, my friend, it's time!" 1834, 77, 78, 80, 100
"Journey from Moscow to Petersburg" (1833-4), 111
"Madonna" (1830), 172
"Monument" (1836), 20, 29, 39, 108, 133, 156–60, 179, 180, 199, 205, 241, 244, 253, 329
"Mozart and Salieri" 1833, 68
"Near the places, where a golden Venice rules..." (1827), 51
"On National Education" (1828), 17
"Poltava", 318, 319, 320, 330
"Prisoner of the Caucasus" (1822), 42
"Prophet", 29, 51, 197
"Recollections at Tsarskoe Selo", 253
"Ruslan and Liudmila", 186, 330
"The Bronze Horseman", 14, 26,

39, 105, 106, 108–33, 158, 161, 163, 168, 178, 181–95, 202, 204–7, 209–10, 213–16, 223, 225, 227, 229–30, 233, 235, 236, 238, 286, 313, 321, 322, 329
"The Countryside", 54
"The Little Town" (1815), 22
"The Queen of Spades", 109
"To My Inkpod", 318
"To My Nanny", 285, 286
"To Ovid", 54
"To the Poet" (1830), 172
"To the Sea" (1824), 40, 42, 46, 51, 54–77, 81–84, 85–88, 91, 93, 96–102, 118, 142, 149, 167, 246, 247, 257, 329
"To Viazemskii" 1826, 63, 64
"What a night! The crispy frost..." (1827), 112
"When will you squeeze this hand again..." (1818), 211
Eugene Onegin, 23, 26, 32, 39, 108, 109, 111, 133, 135–46, 149–52, 154, 155, 163, 177, 214, 218, 223, 228, 230, 236, 242–43, 245, 271, 273–75, 277–79, 287–89, 312, 313, 327, 329
Pyman, Avril, 187, 188, 192
Raban, Jonathan, 220
Raeff, Mark, 17
Ram, Harsha, 30, 42
Ramazani, Vaheed, 12–13, 114, 128–29
Rancour-Laferrière, Daniel, 235
Reinhardt, Max, 270
Reisner, Larissa, 210, 208–12
"To the Bronze Horseman" (1916), 208, 212
Remizov, Aleksei, 290
Reyfman, Irina, 17, 150, 203–4, 244
Richter, Jean-Paul, 137
Ricoeur, Paul, 234, 235
Rider, Jacques Le, 192, 209
Rilke, Rainer-Maria, 75
Rimbaud, 57, 58, 199
Rimskii-Korsakov, 294
Robbe-Grillet, Alain

Last Year at Marienbad, 242
Rose, Gilbert, 58, 59
Rosenshield, Gary, 113, 114, 123, 186, 187
Rousseau, Jean-Jacques, 79
Rozanova, Olga, 25, 218
Rozhdestvenskii, Vsevolod, 209
"Beyond moist clouds..." (1916), 209
Rubens, Peter-Paul, 64, 65
"The Union of Earth and Water" (1618), 64
Rubins, Maria, 174
Sade, Marquis de, 94
Said, Edward, 165
Sandler, Stephanie, 16, 54, 55, 59, 66, 153, 154, 165, 198, 210, 211, 256–58, 271, 291, 290–92, 294, 295, 319, 321, 322, 323, 328, 330
"Distant Pleasures - Alexander Pushkin and the Writing of Exile", 54
Savitskii, Stanislav, 35, 317
Scheler, Max, 271, 272–74, 276
Scholes, Robert, 310
Schönle, Andreas, 155, 156
Schreurs, Marc, 36, 165, 166, 167, 174, 205, 206, 246
Schwartz, Vanessa, 141
Schwarzband, Shmuel, 39, 112
Schweickart, Patrcinio, 30–32
Schweickart, Patrocinio, 83, 84
Scott, Sir Walter, 42
Sedakova, Olga, 27, 34, 40
Segel, Harold, 270, 271, 282
Seiden, Mark, 132
Shakespeare, 25, 27, 37, 122, 123
Hamlet, 122, 123, 147, 148, 149
Ophelia, 122
Shapiro, Barbara, 55, 60
Shaw, Thomas, 288
Shaya, Gregory, 139
Shestov, Lev, 187
Shklovskii, Viktor, 27, 217, 309
"Art as Technique" (1917), 217
Shopenhauer, 192
Shostakovich, Dmitrii, 13, 238, 241
Opus 143 (1973), 13

Shvarts, Elena, 31, 34, 321–24, 329
  "Ballad of an Occult Seance and
    Alexander Pushkin's Shadow"
    (1967), 323
  "Kindergarten After Thirty Years"
    (1986), 321
Simmel, Georg, 325
Siniavskii, Andrei, 16, 257
Sirin, V.
  (pen name of Nabokov).
  "Exile" (1925), 283, 286–91
Skriabin, 166
Slutskii, Boris, 260
Smith, Adam, 43
Smith, Alexandra, 158, 294, 296
Smith, Gerald, 102, 328
Solov´ev, Vladimir, 34
Soupault, Philippe, 87, 88
Stalin, Joseph, 14, 62, 245, 246, 247, 265, 291, 292, 304, 305, 307, 308, 309, 312, 317
Stallybrass, Peter, 19
Stapanian Apkarian, Juliette, 218
Steiner, Peter, 168, 182, 215
Struve, Gleb, 289, 290
Sumarokov, Aleksandr, 67
Swedenborg, Emanuel, 43
Tatlin, Vladimir, 250, 251
Timenchik, Roman, 240, 243. See also Ospovat, Alexander
Todd, William Todd III, 109
Todorov, Tsvetan, 213
Tolstaya, Countess Anna, 132, 133
Tolstaya, Tatiana, 258
  "Pushkin's children" (1992), 258
Tomashevskii, Boris, 39, 110, 185, 207, 259
Toporov, Vladimir, 176
Trediakovskii, Vassilii, 184
Tretiak, Jósef, 112
  Mickiewicz and Pushkin, 113
Trévoux, Dictionnaire de, 154
Trotskii, Leon, 224
Tsaritsyn Field, 11, 12
Tsarskoe Selo, 28, 167, 168, 174, 176, 177, 178, 179, 202, 212, 246, 253
Tsiavlovskaia, Tatiana, 61, 62, 63, 66

Tsvetaeva, Marina, 13, 18, 23, 25, 27, 28, 31, 32, 34, 37, 40, 48, 49, 74–77, 81–94, 95–102, 152, 158, 164, 193, 198, 247, 274–80, 294–304, 308, 321, 329
  "Living about the Living" (1931), 48
  "Art in the Light of Conscience" (1932), 295, 302
  "Epic and Lyric of Contemporary Russia" (1932), 27, 198
  "Essay of a Room", 74
  "From the Seaside" (1926), 74, 87–95, 98, 99
  "My Pushkin" (1937), 75–77, 81–85, 275–78, 295, 301, 302
  "Naiad", 85, 86, 87
  "New Year Greetings" (1927), 74, 75, 77
  "Poem of a Hill" (1926), 32
  "Poem of the Air", 74
  "Poem of the End" (1926), 32
  "Poems to Pushkin" (1931-35), 13, 49, 294, 295, 296, 298, 299, 300, 302, 304
  "Pushkin and Pugachev" (1937), 295
  "Readers of Newspapers" (1935), 280
  "Side-Streets", 303
  "The Poet and Time" (1832), 96, 98
  "The Swain", 303
  "The Swan Encampment", 18
  "To Maiakovskii" (1930), 297
  "To Pushkin", 297, 298
  "To you after a hundred years", 75
  "Tsar-Maiden", 303
  "You, so similar to me, are passing by…", 75
Turgenev, Alexander, 66
Turgenev, Ivan, 212
Turgenev, Nikolai, 63, 66
Tvardovskii, Alexander, 18, 34
  Vassily Terkin, 18
Tynianov, Iurii, 27, 34, 36, 68, 69, 101, 102, 116–19, 138, 139, 143, 144, 146, 157, 170, 174, 190, 224,

Index   361

225, 267, 308, 327
Tyrkova-Williams, Ariadna, 271, 293
Ueland, Carol, 228
Uspenskii, Boris, 190, 191
Verrocchio, 130
Viazemskii, Petr, 63, 66, 136, 161
Viazemskii,Petr
  "The Sea", 63
Vinogradov, Aleksandr, 64
Virolainen, M., 36, 112, 130, 132
Volokhova, Natal'ia, 107
Voloshin, Maximilian, 48, 195
Voltaire
  "The Maid of Orleans", 211
Voznesenskii, Andrei, 9, 260, 263,
  265, 266, 267, 319
  "In the Shop", 265
  "Oza" (1964), 260
Wachtel, Michael, 37, 319, 321
Weber, Max, 262
Wedaman, David, 48, 49, 226

Weitzman, Arthur, 110, 111
Wells, David, 239, 242, 243
Weststeijn, Willem, 328
White, Allon, 19. *See* Stallybrass,
  Peter
Wicks, Ulrich, 310, 311
Winnicott, Donald, 45, 46, 54, 55, 57,
  58, 74, 75, 96
Winter, Jay, 214
Wittgenstein, Ludwig, 270
Zhdanov, Andrei, 244
Zhirmunskii, Viktor, 185
Zhukovskii, Vassilii, 210, 211, 212,
  296, 323
  "Svetlana", 323
Zinker, Joseph, 33, 34
Zinov'ev, Grigorii, 291
Zubareva, Vera, 8, 325, 326
Zubova, Liudmila, 37, 64, 294, 295,
  296, 300